MW01063641

Dyslexia

Dyslexia
Revisiting Etiology, Diagnosis, Treatment, and Policy

edited by

Julie A. Washington, Ph.D.
Georgia State University
Atlanta, Georgia

Donald L. Compton, Ph.D.
Florida State University
Tallahassee, Florida

and

Peggy McCardle, Ph.D., M.P.H.
Peggy McCardle Consulting, LLC, Tarpon Springs, Florida
Haskins Laboratories, New Haven, Connecticut

with invited contributors

Baltimore • London • Sydney

Paul H. Brookes Publishing Co.
Post Office Box 10624
Baltimore, Maryland 21285-0624
USA

www.brookespublishing.com

Typeset by Absolute Service Inc., Towson, Maryland.
Manufactured in the United States of America by Sheridan Books, Inc., Chelsea, Michigan.

The following was written by a U.S. government employee within the scope of his
or her official duties and, as such, shall remain in the public domain: Chapter 2. The
opinions and assertions contained herein are the private opinions of the authors and
are not to be construed as official or reflecting the views of the U.S. government.

The Empower Reading Programs described in Chapter 17 are published and
trademarked by The Hospital for Sick Children, Toronto, Canada.

The views expressed in this book are those of the authors and do not necessarily
represent those of the National Institutes of Health, the *Eunice Kennedy Shriver*
National Institute of Child Health and Human Development, the U.S. Department of
Education, the Economic and Social Research Council of the United Kingdom, or the
Drs. Richard Charles and Esther Yewpick Lee Charitable Foundation.

Library of Congress Cataloging-in-Publication Data

Names: Washington, Julie A., editor. | Compton, Donald L., 1960- editor. |
    McCardle, Peggy, editor.
Title: Dyslexia : revisiting etiology, diagnosis, treatment, and policy /
    edited by Julie Washington, Donald L. Compton, and Peggy McCardle.
Description: Baltimore : Paul H. Brookes Publishing Co., [2020] | Series:
    Extraordinary brain series ; [volume 17] | Includes bibliographical
    references and index.
Identifiers: LCCN 2019015374 (print) | LCCN 2019980487 (ebook) | ISBN
    9781681253626 (epub) | ISBN 9781681253633 (pdf) | ISBN 9781681253619
    (hardcover)
Subjects: LCSH: Dyslexia.
Classification: LCC RC394.W6 (ebook) | LCC RC394.W6 D975 2020 (print) | DDC
    616.85/53--dc23
LC record available at https://lccn.loc.gov/2019015374

British Library Cataloguing in Publication data are available from the British Library.

2023   2022   2021   2020   2019

10   9   8   7   6   5   4   3   2   1

Contents

About the Editors

Julie A. Washington, Ph.D., Professor and Program Director in Communication Sciences and Disorders, Georgia State University, Atlanta

Dr. Washington is Co-Director of the Center for Research on the Challenges of Acquiring Language and Literacy and Chair of the Communication Sciences and Disorders department at Georgia State University. Her work focuses on understanding cultural dialect use in African American children, with a specific emphasis on the impact of dialect on language assessment, reading, and academic performance. Her work with preschoolers has focused on understanding and improving the emergent literacy skills necessary to support later reading proficiency in high-risk groups, with a special focus on the needs of children growing up in poverty in urban contexts. Dr. Washington is Principal Investigator of the Georgia Language Disabilities Research Innovation Hub, funded by the National Institutes of Health, *Eunice Kennedy Shriver* National Institute of Child Health and Human Development. This research hub is focused on improving identification of reading disabilities in elementary school-age African American children and includes a focus on children, their families, their teachers, and their communities.

Donald L. Compton, Ph.D., Professor of Psychology and Education at Florida State University and Director of the Florida Center for Reading Research (FCRR)

Dr. Compton was formerly Professor and Chair of Special Education and John F. Kennedy Center Investigator at Peabody College, Vanderbilt University. After earning a Ph.D. from Northwestern University's School of Communication Sciences and Disorders, he was a learning disabilities resource teacher in Skokie, Illinois. He was an assistant professor in the Department of Curriculum and Instruction at the University of Arkansas, then a National Institute of Child Health and Human Development (NICHD) postdoctoral research fellow at the Institute for Behavioral Genetics, University of Colorado-Boulder. From there he accepted a position at Vanderbilt University, and in 2015, he accepted his current position at FCRR. Dr. Compton is experienced in designing, managing, analyzing, and disseminating data from cross-sectional and longitudinal studies as well as randomized controlled trials (RCTs). His research involves modeling individual differences in the development of children's reading skills and the identification and treatment of children with reading disabilities. Compton has served as Principal Investigator and Co-Principal Investigator on multiple NICHD and Institute of Education Sciences (IES) studies using RCTs to evaluate academic interventions for children with learning difficulties. He has more than 80 peer-reviewed publications and is on the editorial boards of the *Journal of Educational Psychology, Journal of Learning Disabilities, Scientific Studies of Reading, Reading Research Quarterly,* and *Exceptional Children.* Dr. Compton is the past president of the Society for the Scientific Study of Reading and currently serves as Associate Editor of *Scientific Studies of Reading.*

Peggy McCardle, Ph.D., M.P.H., President/Consultant, Peggy McCardle Consulting, LLC, and an affiliated research scientist at Haskins Laboratories in New Haven, Connecticut

As former Branch Chief at the *Eunice Kennedy Shriver* National Institute of Child Health and Human Development (NICHD), U.S. National Institutes of Health, Dr. McCardle developed and directed the research program in language, bilingualism, and biliteracy and various literacy and child development initiatives. Dr. McCardle is a linguist, former speech-language pathologist, and former university faculty member, and she currently works as a private consultant, science writer, and editor (including volume and thematic journal issue design and implementation). Her publications address various aspects of public health, developmental psycholinguistics, and human development. She is currently involved in various projects related to literacy, English language learners, early childhood, education and learning difficulties, and human–animal interaction.

About the Contributors

Ruben P. Alvarez, Ed.D., Program Director of the Language, Bilingualism, and Biliteracy Program at the *Eunice Kennedy Shriver* National Institute of Child Health and Human Development (NICHD), Bethesda, Maryland

Dr. Alvarez completed his doctorate in human development and psychology (bilingual development and neuroscience) at the Harvard University Graduate School of Education. Prior to joining the NICHD, he held a postdoctoral fellowship at the National Institute for Mental Health and was an assistant professor at the Laureate Institute for Brain Research and the University of Tulsa. The program he directs at NICHD supports research on all aspects of normative language development, bilingualism, and second-language acquisition, from infancy through early adulthood. Of particular interest is research with dual language learners, and children and youth learning English as a second or additional language.

Emily Binks-Cantrell, Ph.D., Clinical Assistant Professor, Texas A&M University, College Station

Dr. Cantrell is Clinical Assistant Professor and Program Coordinator of Reading and Language Arts Education and the Reading Clinic at Texas A&M University. Her research interests are in identification of reading problems and teacher knowledge.

Jennae Bulat, Ph.D., Director of the Teaching and Learning Team, International Development Group (IDG) at RTI International, Raleigh-Durham, North Carolina

Dr. Bulat specializes in early-literacy development and educational technologies, has a strong commitment to facilitating learning across all populations, especially among at-risk populations, and manages a team providing technical support to educational programs for all ages, across the globe. She also serves as RTI International's international education disabilities inclusion expert and has authored important RTI International tools to promote inclusive education and guide the production of low-cost, high-impact teaching and learning tools: *Learning Disabilities Systems Guide for Low- and Middle-Income Countries; School and Classroom Disabilities Inclusion Guide for Low- and Middle-Income Countries; Disabilities Inclusive Education Systems and Policies Guide for Low- and Middle-Income Countries;* and *Teaching and Learning Materials Development Production Handbook.*

Philip Capin, doctoral student, The University of Texas at Austin

Mr. Capin is a doctoral student studying special education with a concentration in learning disabilities and behavioral disorders. As a researcher for Meadows Center for Preventing Educational Risk and experienced special education teacher and certified school administrator, he has played a primary role in the development and testing of reading intervention programs for elementary and secondary schools. He has authored research articles addressing reading outcomes for students at risk for or identified with learning disabilities. His research interests include interventions for persistent reading difficulties, the role of treatment fidelity in reading interventions, and approaches to content-area reading instruction that support content acquisition and reading comprehension.

Anne Castles, Ph.D., Distinguished Professor of Cognitive Science at Macquarie University, Sydney, Australia, and Scientific Director of the Macquarie University Centre for Reading

Dr. Castles' research focuses on variability within individuals with reading impairments and in the causes of different types of dyslexia, including genetic, perceptual, and language factors. She is a Fellow of the Academy of Social Sciences in Australia (FASSA) and serves on the editorial boards of several journals, including *Scientific Studies of Reading, Cognitive Neuropsychology,* and the *Journal of Experimental Child Psychology.* In 2017–2018, she served as President of *Learning Difficulties Australia.*

Carol McDonald Connor, Ph.D., CCC-SLP, Chancellor's Professor in Education at University of California, Irvine

Dr. Connor investigates individual differences and the links between children's language and literacy development to better understand difficulties of atypical and diverse learners, including children with dyslexia. Her recent research focuses on individualizing students' classroom learning opportunities—from preschool through fifth grade, developing technology and interventions to improve teacher efficacy and students' literacy, math, and science outcomes. Awarded the Presidential Early Career Award for Scientists and Engineers (PECASE) in 2008, she is also a fellow of the American Educational Research Association (AERA) and American Psychological Association (APA), and a principal investigator funded by the U.S. Department of Education and the National Institutes of Health, including the Early Learning Research Network and the Florida Center for Reading Research Learning Disabilities Research Center. She is past Editor of the *Journal for Research in Educational Effectiveness* and Associate Editor for *Child Development* and *AERA Open.*

Marie-France Côté, Ph.D., Professor, Department Didactique des Langues, Université du Québec à Montréal

Dr. Côté recently completed her Ph.D. with Dr. Robert Savage at McGill University. She has experience as a special education teacher and a reading specialist. Her research focus is on developing effective interventions for children at risk for or experiencing difficulties in learning reading and writing in elementary schools. To be specific, she has a strong interest in the cognitive mechanisms underlying transfer of learning and the development of effective interventions to support it in schools. Dr. Côté has also been involved in the training of elementary school teachers for more than 5 years in Montreal.

Peter F. de Jong, Ph.D., Professor of Psychology and Education in the Department of Child Development and Education, University of Amsterdam, The Netherlands

Dr. de Jong's research involves the acquisition of basic academic skills (reading, spelling and arithmetic) and the etiology, diagnosis, and treatment of learning disorders, in particular dyslexia.

Maria De Palma, M.A., Program Manager for the Learning Disabilities Research Program (LDRP), The Hospital for Sick Children, Toronto, Canada

During Ms. De Palma's 23 years with the LDRP, she has coordinated several systems-based research studies and is one of two program managers for Empower Reading. She has led the expansion of Empower Reading globally into low- and middle-income countries such as India and has trained and mentored teachers, onsite and remotely, to deliver Empower Reading in Indian resource centers and schools. Ms. De Palma is also a senior trainer and mentor for teachers in and across Canada and in the United States.

Eileen Dombrowski, Early Childhood Development Specialist, RTI International

Ms. Dombrowski focuses on ensuring that early childhood programming meaningfully includes children with disabilities, and she supports teachers to provide the differentiation of instruction these children need to be successful. Prior to joining RTI International, Ms. Dombrowski was a policy and programs specialist at Easter Seals, where she advocated for increasing funding for programs that affect children with disabilities and their families. She started her career as an early childhood special education teacher and has taught in public schools in Washington, DC, and Baltimore City.

Ms. Dombrowski was a Peace Corps volunteer in Romania (2006–2008) and a Peace Corps response volunteer in The Gambia (2010–2011).

Margaret (Peggy) M. Dubeck, M.Ed., Ph.D., Senior Literacy Researcher at RTI International, International Education Team, Washington, District of Columbia

Dr. Dubeck holds an M.Ed. at George Washington University as part of the Peace Corps Fellows program and a Ph.D. in reading education from the University of Virginia. She did postdoctoral work at the Harvard Graduate School of Education. Interested in literacy in readers with dyslexia learning in multilingual contexts, Dr. Dubeck has expertise in multidisciplinary randomized controlled trials, tracer studies, piloting, implementation, evaluation, analysis, and dissemination. She has created, modified, and established the technical adequacy of literacy, math, attention, and affective instruments in multiple languages. Her literacy interventions, designed for schools, community programs, and individualized settings, include teacher and student materials, trainings, supportive technology, and measures of fidelity.

Kristy Dunn, doctoral student in special education, University of Alberta, Canada

Ms. Dunn has 15 years of experience as an elementary teacher in mainstream and special education classrooms and is the Reading Research Project Manager in the Reading Research Laboratory. Her recent research interests include the early identification and remediation of reading difficulties in English language learners and the contribution of executive functioning to academic achievement. Her previous work has examined the cognitive profiles of gifted readers and the PASS (planning, attention, simultaneous, and successive) processes that predict superior reading and mathematics performance.

Hank Fien, Ph.D., Associate Professor in School Psychology, Department of Special Education and Clinical Sciences (SPECS), College of Education, and Director of the Center on Teaching and Learning (CTL), University of Oregon, Eugene

Dr. Fien is an expert on reading and mathematics development in young children and on instructional design. He is Director of the National Center on Improving Literacy and has been Principal Investigator and Co-Principal Investigator on 16 Institute of Education Sciences (IES) and National Science Foundation grants. Dr. Fien has 62 publications in refereed journals and is a standing member of the IES Reading, Writing, and Language review panel.

Barbara R. Foorman, Ph.D., Francis Eppes Professor of Education and Director of the Regional Educational Laboratory Southeast and Director Emeritus of the Florida Center for Reading Research, Florida State University, Tallahassee

Dr. Foorman's research focuses on language and reading development, instruction, and assessment.

Nadine Gaab, Ph.D., Associate Professor of Pediatrics at Boston Children's Hospital and Harvard Medical School and faculty at the Harvard Graduate School of Education, Harvard University, Cambridge, Massachusetts

Dr. Gaab received her Ph.D. from the University of Zurich, Switzerland, and conducted doctoral research at the Harvard Medical School and postdoctoral work at Stanford and the Massachusetts Institute of Technology. She primarily works on early identification of children at risk for language-based learning disabilities (e.g., developmental dyslexia), their environmental and genetic influences, and the neural correlates of reading development. She develops and implements screening practices for young children, working at the intersection of developmental cognitive neuroscience, clinical/educational practice, and public policy, focusing on early identification and implementation of real-world changes for struggling readers, in collaboration with numerous public and private schools. For more info, please see http://www.gaablab.com.

Brian Gearin, Co-Lead of Dissemination at the National Center on Improving Literacy and doctoral student, University of Oregon, Eugene

Mr. Gearin's research is broadly focused on the development of executive function and on reading and mathematics achievement. He is particularly interested in how educational policies support student development in these areas. His research has appeared in outlets such as *Journal of Education Policy, Educational Policy,* and *Trends in Neuroscience and Education.* Mr. Gearin is pursuing a Ph.D. in quantitative methods in educational research in the University of Oregon's Department of Education Methodology, Policy, and Leadership.

George Georgiou, Ph.D., Professor of Special Education at the University of Alberta, Canada, and Director of the Reading Research Laboratory

Dr. Georgiou has published extensively on the cognitive and environmental bases of reading development and disabilities. Research interests include early identification and remediation of reading difficulties across languages. He has trained both preservice and in-service teachers to teach and assess different aspects of reading with a particular focus on phonemic awareness, phonics, fluency, vocabulary, and reading comprehension. Over the last 8 years, he and another contributor to this volume, Dr. Parrila, have trained more than 500 primary and secondary teachers in Edmonton, and the schools that have participated in their professional development program have demonstrated measurable growth over time (in particular decreasing the number of poor readers requiring additional services).

Anne M. Hayes, Ed.M., Independent Consultant

Ms. Hayes has more than 20 years of technical expertise focusing on disability-inclusive development, inclusive education, gender equity, and human rights, working in more than 30 countries in Asia, Africa, Eastern Europe, Latin America, the Caribbean, and the Middle East. She is lead author for *Literacy for All: How to Use Universal Design for Learning to Promote Literacy Skills for Students with Disabilities,* supported by United States Agency for International Development (USAID). She was previously Senior Technical Advisor at Perkins School for the Blind; Director of Collaborative Initiatives, World Bank Global Partnership on Disability and Development; and Disability and Gender Specialist, USAID. Currently she is an independent consultant supporting disability-inclusive development and inclusive education programming for various non-governmental organizations, contractors, United Nations agencies, and organizations for individuals with disabilities.

R. Malatesha (Malt) Joshi, Ph.D., Professor, Texas A&M University, College Station

Dr. Joshi serves as Editor of *Reading and Writing: An Interdisciplinary Journal* and the monograph series "Literacy Studies: Perspectives from Cognitive Neurosciences, Linguistics, Psychology, and Education." From 1980 to 2002, Dr. Joshi directed six highly successful North Atlantic Treaty Organization Advanced Study Institutes in Europe on the topics of neuropsychology, cognition, and literacy, which helped to bring various fields together. Active internationally in education and literacy research he has served as a visiting research scholar in China, Germany, Taiwan, and New Zealand. Dr. Joshi has published numerous books and scientific papers and has received several awards. He is a Fellow of the American Educational Research Association (AERA). His research interests focus on teacher knowledge and literacy development among monolinguals and second language learners.

Devin M. Kearns, Ph.D., Assistant Professor of Special Education, Department of Educational Psychology, Neag School of Education, University of Connecticut, Mansfield

Dr. Kearns is a research scientist for Haskins Laboratory and the Center for Behavioral Education & Research (CBER). Dr. Kearns researches reading disability—including dyslexia—in elementary- and middle school-age children. He also teaches educators the most effective strategies for supporting students with serious reading problems. He is an investigator on multiple projects to prevent and remediate reading difficulties funded by the Institute for Education Sciences, the *Eunice Kennedy Shriver* National Institute of Child Health and Human Development, and other national and local organizations.

Young-Suk Grace Kim, Ed.D., Professor, University of California at Irvine, and Faculty Associate, Florida Center for Reading Research, Florida State University, Tallahassee

Dr. Kim holds an Ed.D. from Harvard University and is a former primary and secondary school classroom teacher. Her research interests include development and instruction of language, cognition, and literacy skills as well as dyslexia and dysgraphia across languages and writing systems. She has conducted several large-scale longitudinal studies and intervention work supported by the Institute of Education Science, the *Eunice Kennedy Shriver* National Institute of Child Health and Human Development, and the National Science Foundation, as well as the National Research Foundation of Korea. A recipient of the Presidential Early Career Award for Scientists and Engineers and research and teaching awards, Dr. Kim serves as Associate Editor for the *Journal of Educational Psychology* and as an editorial board member for several journals.

Saskia Kohnen, Ph.D., Clinical Director, Macquarie University Reading Clinic, and Senior Researcher, Department of Cognitive Science at Macquarie University, Sydney, Australia

Dr. Kohnen's research interests include typical and atypical reading and spelling development and the assessment and treatment of reading and spelling difficulties. Her clinical work focuses on translating research into practice.

Nicole Landi, Ph.D., Associate Professor of Psychological Sciences at University of Connecticut, Storrs, and the Director of EEG Research at Haskins Laboratories, New Haven, Connecticut

Dr. Landi's research seeks to better understand typical and atypical reading and language development through the use of multiple cognitive neuroscience methodologies (magnetic resonance imaging and electroencephalography) and genetic analyses. Through this work, her lab hopes to identify neurobiological and environmental mechanisms that contribute to individual differences in reading and language skill and to the complex etiology of disorders such as dyslexia, specific comprehension deficit, and developmental language disorder.

Ryan Lee-James, Ph.D., Assistant Professor, Communication Sciences and Disorders, Adelphi University, Garden City, New York

Ryan Lee-James is an assistant professor in the Department of Communication Sciences and Disorders at Adelphi University and a speech-language pathologist certified by the American Speech-Language-Hearing Association (ASHA). Her work contributes to the larger body of research that is focused on better understanding the impact of African American English dialect use on assessment and treatment of language disorders for children reared in poverty.

Maureen W. Lovett, Ph.D., C-Psych., Senior Scientist in the Neurosciences and Mental Health Program at The Hospital for Sick Children, Toronto, Canada, and Professor of Paediatrics and Medical Sciences, the University of Toronto

Dr. Lovett's research focuses on questions about the effective remediation of decoding, word identification, fluency, and reading comprehension deficits in struggling readers in elementary, middle, and high schools. As Co-Principal Investigator of the Institute of Education Sciences-funded Center for the Study of Adult Literacy, she is developing interventions for adult literacy learners as well. She and her team are also involved in knowledge translation initiatives: Their Empower Reading interventions are now used to teach struggling readers in school districts in four Canadian provinces.

Kristina Maiorino, B.A.

Ms. Maiorino holds a bachelor's degree in psychology from McGill University. After her graduation, she worked as coordinator of McGill's bilingual acquisition lab for a year, and then taught English abroad for 2 years. On her return to Montreal, she worked in many research labs focused primarily on language and literacy, collaborating on a variety of projects that studied language attrition through electroencephalography, bilingualism in adopted children through functional magnetic resonance imaging, and, most recently, coordinating a response-to-intervention study with struggling elementary school readers.

Matthew H. C. Mak, doctoral student, Department of Experimental Psychology, the University of Oxford, Oxford, England

Mr. Mak's research interest lies in the interface of language and memory. He is investigating the mechanisms that underlie long-term orthographic memory formation and how various factors, such as context and sleep, promote this process. He also has a long-standing interest in dyslexia and developmental language disorders and an ongoing collaboration with speech therapists to investigate the memory deficits associated with those disorders. Prior to arriving at Oxford, he obtained a M.Phil. in applied linguistics at the University of Cambridge, where he worked on a project that examined the relation between statistical learning and spelling proficiency in a second language.

Joan Mele-McCarthy, D.A., CCC, Executive Director of The Summit School, Edgewater, Maryland

Dr. McCarthy is Executive Director of The Summit School, a school designed for students who have dyslexia and other learning differences. Prior to holding this position, she served as a special assistant to the Assistant Secretary for Special Education/Rehabilitation Services in the U.S. Department of Education and worked on policy issues related to the connections between special education and general education, and English language learners and disabilities. She also has served on university faculties in departments of communication sciences and disorders, owned/directed a private practice that provided direct intervention and school consultation, and worked in public schools. Her work is focused on language-based learning differences and special education policy.

Brett Miller, Ph.D., Program Director, *Eunice Kennedy Shriver* National Institute of Child Health and Human Development (NICHD)

Dr. Miller oversees the Reading, Writing, and Related Learning Disabilities research portfolio at the NICHD, National Institutes of Health, that focuses on developing and supporting research and training initiatives to increase knowledge relevant to the development of reading and written-language abilities for learners with and without disabilities. Dr. Miller also co-directs the Language, Bilingualism, and Biliteracy research program, which focuses on language development and psycholinguistics from infancy through early adulthood; bilingualism and/or second-language acquisition; and reading in bilingual and/or English-language learning children and youth.

Kate Nation, Ph.D., Professor of Experimental Psychology at the University of Oxford and a Fellow of St John's College, Oxford, England

Dr. Nation's research is concerned with language processing, especially reading development. She is interested in how children learn to read words and comprehend text, and more generally, the relationship between spoken language and written language. A key aim at present is to specify some of the mechanisms involved in the transition from novice to expert. She also studies language processing in skilled adults, addressing the issue of how skilled behavior emerges via language learning experience, and reading processes in individuals with developmental disorders that influence reading and language. For more information visit http://www .readoxford.org and follow on Twitter @ReadOxford.

Elizabeth S. Norton, Ph.D., Assistant Professor at Northwestern University, Evanston, Illinois

Dr. Norton leads the Language, Education, and Reading Neuroscience (LEARN) Lab at Northwestern. Her research combines behavioral and brain measures and seeks to understand typical development as well as reading, language, and neurodevelopmental disorders. As a former high school teacher for students with dyslexia, she is particularly interested in understanding individual differences and working toward early identification and intervention for reading disabilities.

Rauno Parrila, Ph.D., Professor of Educational Studies, Macquarie University, Sydney, Australia

Dr. Parrila has co-edited a book on theories of reading development and published more than 100 research papers that have mostly focused on different aspects of home literacy practices, reading acquisition, and reading disabilities. He is the past Editor and Associate Editor (2008–2009) of *Scientific Studies of Reading.* For more than 20 years, Dr. Parrila has trained hundreds of preservice and in-service teachers in Canada to teach reading to struggling readers, and he worked with Dr. Georgiou on developing and delivering professional development on literacy for K–9 teachers.

Nicole Patton Terry, Ph.D., Olive & Manuel Bordas Professor of Education and Associate Director, Florida Center for Reading Research (FCRR), Florida State University, Tallahassee

Dr. Patton Terry's research concerns young children with and without disabilities struggling to acquire language and literacy skills, especially those from culturally and linguistically diverse backgrounds and those living in poverty. Her research has been supported by diverse organizations, including the Spencer Foundation, National Institutes of Health, Institute of Education Sciences, and The Annie E. Casey Foundation. She currently serves as a board member for the Society for the Scientific Study of Reading and an associate editor for the *Journal of Learning Disabilities.* At FCRR, she directs The Village—a division that creates and maintains research partnerships with diverse community stakeholders to promote reading achievement and school success among vulnerable children.

Yaacov Petscher, Ph.D., Associate Director at the Florida Center for Reading Research, Tallahassee, and Deputy Director of the National Center on Improving Literacy

Dr. Petscher's research interests include the study of cross-sectional and longitudinal individual differences in literacy, psychometrics, reading assessment, and research design. He has co-authored more than 150 peer-reviewed publications, book chapters, books, and technical reports, and his work has been recognized by awards from the Society for the Scientific Study of Reading, the International Literacy Association, the American Educational Research Association, and the International Society for Technology in Education. He presently serves as an associate editor for the *Journal of Learning Disabilities* and *Elementary School Journal* and as an editorial board member for other educational journals.

Jay G. Rueckl, Ph.D., Senior Scientist at Haskins Laboratories, New Haven, Connecticut; Director of the University of Connecticut's Brain Imaging Research Center, Storrs; Associate Professor of Psychological Sciences, and Associate Director of the Variable Vowel Collaborative, a National Institutes of Health Learning Disabilities Hub

Since earning a Ph.D. in experimental psychology at the University of Wisconsin, Dr. Rueckl has used behavioral experiments, neuroimaging, and computational modeling to study the neurocomputational processes underlying reading and reading acquisition in a variety of languages (including English, Hebrew, Spanish, and Mandarin) and in ages ranging from beginning readers to young adults.

Elinor Saiegh-Haddad, Ph.D., Professor of Applied Linguistics at Bar-Ilan University, Israel

Dr. Saiegh-Haddad is senior advisor to Israeli authorities in education and technology and has been actively involved in L1 Arabic and L2 English curricula and textbook development. She holds graduate degrees from Reading University, England (M.A.), Bar-Ilan University, Israel (Ph.D.), and the University of Toronto (Rothschild postdoctoral fellow). She maintains strong interest in studying language and reading development and disability in Arabic and focuses on the role of diglossia and the linguistic distance between Arabic written and spoken dialects on literacy. She also studies reading development in English as a second language with a focus on cross-linguistic differences in language and orthography. She has published a large number of articles on reading development in these contexts and is co-editor of the *Handbook of Arabic Literacy* (Springer, 2014).

Joseph Sanfilippo, M.Sc., Ed.M., medical student, Queen's University, Kingston, Canada, and research student working under Dr. Nadine Gaab at Boston Children's Hospital, Massachusetts

Involved in the Gaab Lab for several years, Mr. Sanfilippo is currently the lab's full-time research coordinator. Sanfilippo has coordinated several projects investigating cognitive, language, literacy, and brain development, including a large-scale longitudinal infant dyslexia study in Boston, as well as several international studies (e.g., Bangladesh, Brazil, South Africa). His interests lie at the intersection of medical science and education, including the investigation of the neural bases of language and literacy development, and the implications of this research for practice and policy.

Robert Savage, Ph.D., Professor and Head of the Department of Psychology and Human Development at University College, London, England

Dr. Savage has experience both as a school psychologist and as a classroom teacher and maintains a strong interest in making schools effective learning places for all children. He has published more than 100 research articles exploring children's early reading and spelling strategies. His work includes studies of the neurocognitive processes that are used in reading and spelling, and he is particularly interested in preventing early reading and spelling problems by better teaching of phonics. Together with Drs. Georgiou and Parrila, he is developing and testing a professional development program that helps teachers understand and use phonics effectively to support typically developing and struggling children.

Eliane Segers, Ph.D., Professor, Learning & Technology, Behavioural Science Institute, Radboud University, The Netherlands

Eliane Segers is a professor of Learning & Technology at the Behavioural Science Institute at Radboud University, and she also has a chair by special appointment in Reading and Digital Media at Instructional Science at the University of Twente, both in The Netherlands. Her background is in cognitive science and speech technology, and she has a Ph.D. in social sciences (2003). Her research is focused on understanding individual differences in learning and reading, on learning in technology-based environments, and on optimizing learning in such environments via smart use of technological affordances. The main research focus is children in primary schools.

Christopher T. Stanley, Ph.D., Associate in Research in the Division of Quantitative Methodology and Innovation at Florida State University, Tallahassee

Prior to his current appointment, Dr. Stanley was full-time psychology faculty at Winston-Salem State University and, subsequently, Florida Gulf Coast University. Throughout his career, he has been involved on a variety of collaborative research projects and applied activities related broadly to human development and performance, including factors and outcomes in athletic, health, psychosocial, and educational domains.

Karen A. Steinbach, M.A., C. Psych. Assoc., Program Manager in the Learning Disabilities Research Program at The Hospital for Sick Children, Toronto, Canada

Ms. Steinbach has coordinated several multisite *Eunice Kennedy Shriver* National Institute of Child Health and Human Development– and Institute of Education Sciences–funded intervention research studies over a period of more than 25 years. In addition to her role in research, Ms. Steinbach co-leads the knowledge translation and dissemination initiatives of the evidence-based intervention Empower Reading; she collaborates with school districts in and across Canada and in the United States. She is particularly interested in the literacy outcomes of children in remote, disadvantaged communities and is responsible for coordinating and training teachers in the Cree School Board. She is also a senior teacher trainer and mentor for Empower Reading.

Elizabeth A. Stevens, M.A.Ed., doctoral student, The University of Texas at Austin

Ms. Stevens is studying learning disabilities and behavioral disorders. She received a master's degree in special education from the College of William and Mary and a reading specialist degree from the University of Virginia. She taught special education for 9 years in Arlington County Public Schools. Ms. Stevens currently coordinates a large-scale research project at The Meadows Center for Preventing Educational Risk and provides professional development to teachers in Texas and other states. Her research interests include diagnosis and remediation of learning disability, effective instructional practices for students with reading difficulty or disability, and the role of student explanations and discourse on student outcomes within mathematics and reading interventions.

Carmen Strigel, Director of Technology for Education and Training at RTI International, Durham, North Carolina

Ms. Strigel's work focuses on technology for building capacity, collaboration, and information-based decision making in low- and middle-income countries. Ms. Strigel's passion lies in deploying technology at the intersection of desirability by users, feasibility in the context, and viability for sustainable use. She led the development of Tangerine, open source software facilitating continuous student assessment and program monitoring, which has been deployed in more than 60 countries and 100 languages to date. Specific to inclusive education, she has led groundbreaking research in Ethiopia using carefully designed technology to measurably improve teachers' inclusive instructional practices in regular reading classrooms. Concurrently, Ms. Strigel is conducting doctoral research in educational neuroscience at Johns Hopkins University.

Theodore (Ted) K. Turesky, Ph.D., Postdoctoral Fellow at Boston Children's Hospital (BCH), Massachusetts, and Harvard Medical School, Cambridge, Massachusetts

In graduate training at Georgetown University, Dr. Turesky examined the functional neuroanatomy of the motor system in development, aging, and developmental dyslexia; he was named the Karen Gale Excellent Ph.D. Student in Science. At BCH, he works on structural and functional brain development in early life adversity (e.g., poverty) and reading. His future work will focus on the biological and psychosocial risk factors mediating the relationship between poverty and brain development, and neural correlates of reading fluency and spelling. Dr. Turesky serves as Vice Chair on the Board of Directors for the American Tinnitus Association, providing expertise in neuroscience and advocating for noise health issues.

Sharon Vaughn, Ph.D., Executive Director of The Meadows Center, The University of Texas at Austin

Dr. Vaughn directs The Meadows Center, an organized research unit at The University of Texas at Austin. She is the recipient of the American Educational Research Association Special Interest Groups Distinguished Researcher Award, the International Reading Association Albert J. Harris Award, The University of Texas Distinguished Faculty Award, and the Jeannette E. Fleischner Award for Outstanding Contributions in the Field of Learning Disabilities from the Council for Exceptional Children. She is the author of more than 35 books and 250 research articles. Dr. Vaughn is Principal Investigator on several Institute of Education Sciences, *Eunice Kennedy Shriver* National Institute of Child Health and Human Development, and U.S. Department of Education research grants.

Ludo Verhoeven, Ph.D., Professor, Psychology and Education, Behavior Science Institute at Radboud University, Nijmegen, The Netherlands, and Professor in Educational Policies and Innovation, The University of Curaçao, Willemstad

Currently President of the Scientific Society for the Study of Reading, Dr. Verhoeven's research focuses on language and literacy learning in typically and atypically developing children in culturally and linguistic diverse environments. He has a master's degree in psychology and special education from Radboud University and a Ph.D. in linguistics (honors degree) from the University of Tilburg. Dr. Verhoeven completed his postdoctoral work at the University of California at Berkeley and at Santa Barbara. He has co-authored more than 350 empirical papers in peer-reviewed scientific journals and co-edited 20 books.

Kelly J. Williams, Ph.D., Assistant Professor of Special Education, Department of Curriculum and Instruction, Indiana University

Dr. Williams's research focuses on improving academic and post-secondary outcomes for students at risk for and identified with high-incidence disabilities. She is particularly interested in reading interventions for English learners and adolescents with reading difficulties and disabilities (e.g., learning disabilities) and interventions designed to reduce high school dropout and increase student engagement in school. Previously, Dr. Williams was the project coordinator at The University of Texas at Austin for an Institute of Education Sciences grant investigating the efficacy of a combined dropout prevention reading intervention for ninth- and tenth-grade students with comprehension difficulties.

Henry Wolf VII, Ph.D., Student and National Science Foundation Integrative Graduate Education and Research Traineeship (IGERT) Fellow

Mr. Wolf is the founder of the Deep Learning Research Group at the University of Connecticut. His research involves using image recognition techniques (convolutional neural networks) in computational models of reading. Prior to pursing a Ph.D., Dr. Wolf earned a master's degree in teaching English to speakers of other languages from Teachers College, Columbia University and a bachelor's degree in international business and marketing from the University of Dayton (Ohio).

Dandan Yang, doctoral student, University of California at Irvine (UCI)

Ms. Yang is a second-year Ph.D. student at UCI's School of Education, specializing in Teaching, Learning, and Educational Improvement (TLEI). She holds a B.A. in English language and literature from China University of Mining and Technology and an M.A. in TESOL from the University of Southern California. Prior to entering this program, Ms. Yang taught English and Chinese to students with various linguistic and cultural backgrounds in both China and California. This teaching experience as well as the research practices in Professor Carol Connor's lab at UCI's School of Education led to her interests in language and the literacy development of young learners, executive functioning, and using game-based applications to assist students' learning.

Jason Zevin, Ph.D., Associate Professor of Psychology and Linguistics, the University of Southern California, Los Angeles

Dr. Zevin is affiliated with Haskins Laboratories as a Senior Scientist. He uses a combination of computational modeling, neuroimaging, and other techniques to study the processing of written and spoken words and other aspects of language.

The Dyslexia Foundation and the Extraordinary Brain Series Symposia

In the late 1980s, The Dyslexia Foundation (TDF) was founded by William H. "Will" Baker in collaboration with notable researchers in dyslexia. The concept began in the late 1970s, then came to fruition in 1982, when, through the generosity of the Wm. Underwood Co. and the Baker family, the first Dyslexia Research Laboratory under the direction of Drs. Albert Galaburda and Norman Geshwind at Beth Israel Hospital, Harvard Medical School, Boston, Massachusetts, was established to investigate the neural underpinnings of dyslexia. In 1987, top researchers from cognition, neuroscience, and education were convened in a scientific symposium in Florence, Italy, where ideas were presented and discussed, with sufficient time to disagree, to identify research challenges, and to brainstorm solutions—and the concept of a dyslexia symposium series was born. In the fall of 1989, Baker established the National Dyslexia Research Foundation (later renamed The Dyslexia Foundation) to focus specifically on research. In 1990, the new foundation sponsored a second symposium in Barcelona, Spain. With it, the symposium series was designated as the Extraordinary Brain Series (EBS)!

The EBS symposia began as think tanks of researchers who were encouraged to discuss, disagree, and explore new possibilities. Many have called these symposia the best research meetings they have ever attended because of the depth of discussion and exchange of ideas afforded by a 5-day think tank. Each symposium resulted in a volume to share the research presented and the ideas that grew out of the symposia's deliberations. Educators from independent schools for students with learning differences, interested in hearing the latest research and witnessing these cutting-edge discussions, began to attend and to contribute as TDF sponsors to the meetings. Hearing their cry for bringing current research to their classrooms, in a then-novel outreach activity, TDF instituted 1-day annual educational meetings held on the campus of Harvard Medical School, where educators and allied health practitioners could hear about current research directly from researchers. In 2007, at the 10th EBS symposium in Brazil, educators asked so many questions and were so eager to share their research needs with the researchers present that these educators were given a forum during the meeting, and the research-to-practice efforts of TDF took on a new, higher level. Since that time, educators and practitioners are heard and participate in each EBS symposium, and the interactions among them and researchers have been rich and rewarding. Although it had been part of the TDF philosophy to include not only senior, established researchers but also promising early-stage researchers as participants in the symposia, this has also accelerated. At the 11th symposium in Taiwan, in 2010, Taiwanese researchers invited their graduate students and postdoctoral fellows to display posters of their work during the meeting. Since that time, those invited to present or moderate sessions at EBS symposia are also invited to bring junior colleagues, postdoctoral fellows, and graduate students and to have them present posters—both displaying the posters and giving a very brief explanation of their work during one special session at the symposium.

Over the 3 decades of the existence of TDF and EBS, major strides have been made in not only dyslexia and reading research itself (many researchers have commented that their best new ideas and great new collaborations have grown out of their participation in EBS symposia), but these meetings have also provided a safe venue for the exchange and development of research-to-practice ideas, the mentoring of many new and emerging researchers, and content for the continuing and expanding 1-day research-to-practice meetings for educators and practitioners, which are live-streamed in real time and archived for later viewing.

This volume celebrates the 17th symposium in the EBS. The series volumes make accessible to all researchers and practitioners the thoughts of scholars across various disciplines as they tackle various aspects of the behavior, neurobiology, and genetics of dyslexia and of learning to read and write. The following is a listing of TDF symposia and the related volumes to date:

I.   June 1987, Florence, Italy. Symposium Director: Albert M. Galaburda.

      Galaburda, A. M. (Ed.). (1989). *From reading to neurons.* Cambridge, MA: Bradford Books/MIT Press.

II.   June 1990, Barcelona, Spain. Symposium Director: Albert M. Galaburda.

      Galaburda, A. M. (Ed.). (1993). *Dyslexia and development: Neurobiological aspects of extra-ordinary brains.* Cambridge, MA: Bradford Books/Harvard University Press.

III. June 1992, Santa Fe, NM. Symposium Director: Paula Tallal.

      Chase, C., Rosen, G., & Sherman, G. F. (Eds.). (1996). *Developmental dyslexia: Neural, cognitive, and genetic mechanisms.* Mahwah, NJ: Lawrence Erlbaum Associates.

IV.   June 1994, Kauai, Hawaii. Symposium Director: Benita Blachman.

      Blachman, B. R. (Ed.). (1997). *Foundations of reading acquisition and dyslexia: Implications for early intervention.* Mahwah, NJ: Lawrence Erlbaum Associates.

V.   June 1998, Kona, Hawaii. Symposium Director: Drake Duane.

      Duane, D. (Ed.). (1999). *Reading and attention disorders: Neurobiological correlates.* Baltimore, MD: York Press.

VI.   June 2000, Crete, Greece. Symposium Director: Maryanne Wolf.

       Wolf, M. (Ed.). (2001). *Time, fluency, and dyslexia.* Baltimore, MD: York Press.

VII.   June 2002, Kona, Hawaii. Symposium Director: Barbara Foorman.

       Foorman, B. (Ed.). (2003). *Preventing and remediating reading difficulties: Bringing science to scale.* Baltimore, MD: York Press.

VIII.   October 2002, Johannesburg, South Africa. Symposium Director: Frank Wood.

       Multilingualism and dyslexia. No publication.

IX.   June 2004, Como, Italy. Symposium Director: Glenn Rosen.

       Rosen, G. (Ed.). (2006). *The dyslexic brain: New pathways in neuroscience discovery.* Mahwah, NJ: Lawrence Erlbaum Associates.

X.   June 2007, Campos do Jordão, Brazil. Symposium Directors: Ken Pugh and Peggy McCardle.

       Pugh, K., & McCardle, P. (Eds.). (2009). *How children learn to read: Current issues and new directions in the integration of cognition, neurobiology and genetics of reading and dyslexia research and practice.* New York, NY: Psychology Press, Taylor & Francis Group.

XI.   January 2010, Taipei, Taiwan. Symposium Directors: Peggy McCardle, Ovid Tseng, Jun Ren Lee, and Brett Miller.

       McCardle, P., Miller, B., Lee, J. R., & Tseng, O. (Eds.). (2011). *Dyslexia across languages: Orthography and the brain-gene-behavior link.* Baltimore, MD: Paul H. Brookes Publishing Co.

XII.   June 2010, Cong, Ireland. Symposium Directors: April Benasich and Holly Fitch.

       Benasich, A. A., & Fitch, R. H. (Eds.). (2012). *Developmental dyslexia: Early precursors, neurobehavioral markers, and biological substrates.* Baltimore, MD: Paul H. Brookes Publishing Co.

XIII.   June 2012, Tallinn, Estonia. Symposium Directors: Brett Miller and Laurie Cutting.

       Miller, B., Cutting, L., & McCardle, P. (Eds.). (2013). *Unraveling reading comprehension: Behavioral, neurobiological, and genetic components.* Baltimore, MD: Paul H. Brookes Publishing Co.

XIV.   June 2014, Horta, Faial Island, The Azores. Symposium Directors: Carol Connor and Peggy McCardle.

       Connor, C. M., & McCardle, P. (Eds.). (2015). *Advances in reading intervention: Research to practice to research.* Baltimore, MD: Paul H. Brookes Publishing Co.

XV.   June 2016, Saint Croix, U.S. Virgin Islands. Symposium Directors: Albert Galaburda, Fumiko Hoeft, and Nadine Gaab.

Galaburda, A. M., Gaab, N., Hoeft, F., & McCardle, P. (Eds.). (2017). *Dyslexia and neuroscience: The Geschwind-Galaburda Hypothesis, 30 years later.* Baltimore, MD: Paul H. Brookes Publishing Co.

XVI.   May 2018, St. Petersburg, Russia. Symposium Directors: Elena Grigorenko and Yury Shtyrov.

Grigorenko, E., Shtyrov, Y., & McCardle, P. (Eds.). (2020). *All about language: Science, theory, and practice* (Неделя языка: наука, теория, практика). Baltimore, MD: Paul H. Brookes Publishing Co.

XVII.   June 2018, Cathedral Peak, Drakensburg, South Africa. Symposium Directors: Julie A. Washington and Donald L. Compton.

Washington, J. A., Compton, D. L., & McCardle, P. (Eds.). (2020). *Dyslexia: Revising etiology, diagnosis, treatment, and policy.* Baltimore, MD: Paul H. Brookes Publishing Co.

Preface

This volume is one of two, both based on the Extraordinary Brain Series (EBS) Symposia, and thus both resulting in EBS edited volumes. Although it was unprecedented to hold two such symposia in 1 year, it turned out to be a wonderful convergence of ideas and information on the underpinnings of reading and dyslexia. The first symposium (and eponymous volume, co-edited by Elena Grigorenko, Yury Shtyrov, and Peggy McCardle), *All About Language: Science, Theory, and Practice* (Неделя языка: наука, теория, практика; Paul H. Brookes Publishing Co., 2020), focuses on the evolution and development of language in all its forms—spoken and written, and how typical and atypical language underlie and relate to reading and reading difficulties. The meeting was held in Russia and addressed some of the issues of diagnosis, access to special education services in Russia, the United States, the United Kingdom, and other countries, as well as education policy. The second volume, *Dyslexia: Revisiting Etiology, Diagnosis, Treatment, and Policy* (Paul H. Brookes Publishing Co., 2020), co-edited by Julie A. Washington, Donald L. Compton, and Peggy McCardle, examines how reading develops, what happens when it does not develop typically, and how best to identify and treat those cases, as well as how local and national policies and legislation can help or hinder those trying to do so. This symposium, held in South Africa, also looked beyond the United States, with presenters (and thus authors) from other countries or whose work involves international collaborations. The two meetings had seemingly different foci, but both asked similar questions about how best to understand, treat, and implement proven interventions for those who struggle with reading. Each symposium brought together a group of scholars and clinicians in a think-tank setting to take stock of what is known and what needs to be known. These two groups were largely nonoverlapping, but their timely (almost) co-occurrence allows us to access both sets of information in a very useful complementarity via these two volumes.

The complementarity of these two volumes should enhance our thinking as a field as we move to gain a fuller, more complete understanding of the total picture of reading difficulties, the reading process, the language skills that underlie it, and the individual differences that add to the complexity of this task. EBS symposia (and volumes) bring together scientists from different disciplines and areas of research, and they generally seek to address integratively the neurobiology, genetics, and behavior of reading and reading disabilities, thinking about how skills are learned, why they might not be, what influences are in play across development, and how they change the course of development (be it typical or atypical) as well as how those influences change our interventions (i.e., what we do about teaching individuals to read). Increasingly it is clear that the context—the environment, physical, social, linguistic, cultural, and economic—affects learning.

The environment includes language exposure—in the home, community, and school—whereas school instruction requires knowledge that teachers often do not have on entering the profession. Thus, ensuring that researchers share their reliable findings with educators and other clinicians, and that they seek to answer the questions most pressing for those educators and clinicians, is also an essential goal of the EBS symposium. Each of these volumes contains chapters addressing these issues (with nontechnical summaries to begin each)—and the volumes' integrative section commentaries seek to pull together across chapters the common threads of each thematic section. The final chapter in each volume offers suggestions for the way forward.

Acknowledgments

Many individuals contributed in many ways to making this volume possible. First, it would have been impossible without The Dyslexia Foundation (TDF), sponsor of the symposium that gave rise to it. We owe huge thanks to TDF Founder and President Will Baker, Amelia Baker Lauderdale, and Ben Powers, along with a number of Trustees and Scientific Advisory Board members of TDF. Without them there would be no Extraordinary Brain Symposia (EBS) and thus no EBS series of volumes!

We also wish to acknowledge the authors who traveled to South Africa to present their own work and thoughts; engaged in deep discussions with symposium participants; and wrote and revised chapters for this volume, often meeting stringent deadlines. In addition, we acknowledge the practitioners (teachers, educators, administrators, and clinicians), researchers, graduate students, and postdoctoral fellows who attended and not only listened attentively and thought deeply but discussed, questioned, and commented, helping to inform this volume.

We and TDF offer heartfelt thanks to the following individuals, schools, and businesses that generously supported EBS XVII: Wilson Language Training, Jemicy School, AIM Academy, The Howard School, The Schenck School, The Southport School, Westmark School, Athena Academy, Brehm Preparatory School, Carroll School, Curry Ingram Academy, Marburn Academy, New Community School, The Summit School, Erika and Robyn Ray, and four individuals and two foundations that wish to remain anonymous. In addition, we want to offer a special acknowledgment to the late Joan McNichols, a generous benefactor and dedicated colleague of TDF for more than 30 years.

Finally, thanks go to the flexible, helpful, and very capable editorial and production staff at Paul H. Brookes Publishing Co., especially Astrid Pohl Zuckerman, Tess Hoffman, Nicole Schmidl, and MaryBeth Winkler, who were willing to take on not just one but two EBS volumes at the same time! Thank you for your diligence, excellent help, and patience on this and the EBS XVI book. We loved working with you!

Co-Editors,
Julie A. Washington, Donald L. Compton, and Peggy McCardle

Setting the Stage

CHAPTER 1

An Overview and Introduction to the Volume

Julie A. Washington, Donald L. Compton, and Peggy McCardle

Interest in the root causes, diagnosis, and treatment of dyslexia has a long history, dating back to the late 19th century, when the term *dyslexia* was first coined. The earliest characterizations of children with dyslexia described them as "bright, intelligent and quick" and as having "text blindness" despite intact intellect and speech. Understanding of dyslexia improved exponentially in the 20th century. In the United States, the study of dyslexia was buoyed by the establishment of the Specific Learning Disabilities Act of 1969 (PL 91-230), which was followed by, and included in, the Education for All Handicapped Children Act of 1975 (PL 94-142), a federal law mandating free appropriate public education for all children. Since being renamed the Individuals with Disabilities Education Act (IDEA) of 1990 (PL 101-476) and later the Individuals with Disabilities Education Improvement Act (IDEA) of 2004 (PL 108-446), reauthorizations of the federal law have included 1) expanded definitions of reading disability, 2) increased access to the general curriculum for all students, and 3) guidance for identification and intervention for children struggling with learning disabilities. These changes in the law over time have resulted largely from new advances in the research base.

On a global level, the identification and study of dyslexia and, by implication, the education of children struggling to learn to read have not kept pace. A 2014 report by Dyslexia International confirmed that in wealthier nations such as the United States and the United Kingdom, where public education is available for all children, identification of children with dyslexia and subsequent intervention services, though not perfect, are more likely to occur. In contrast, children in impoverished countries are more likely to go undiagnosed and have their symptoms unaddressed, contributing to significant illiteracy rates. The report cited five major reasons for the gaps in addressing dyslexia in these countries, where public services are more limited: 1) limited knowledge about dyslexia, including its characteristics and treatment; 2) limited teacher training; 3) lack of awareness of cost-effective, modern solutions; 4) poor leadership for establishment of public policies; and 5) a global shortage of teachers. Importantly, many of these same variables have affected the identification of dyslexia in impoverished children in wealthy nations as well.

Overall, this is an exciting time for dyslexia research. Developing knowledge in areas such as genetics, brain imaging, cognitive psychology, and intervention has expanded understanding of dyslexia considerably over the past approximately 15 years. Despite these advances, there continue to be as many disagreements as there are agreements about the definition, etiology, diagnosis, and treatment of dyslexia. For example, researchers generally agree that early detection and intervention are critical, that dyslexia is a specific learning disability with a phonological basis, and that children with dyslexia benefit from ongoing assessment and support. On the other hand, the neurological and genetic bases of dyslexia have provided exciting insights and discoveries but no universal consensus regarding the nature of brain or gene processes. Of importance for the The Dyslexia Foundation (TDF) Extraordinary Brain Symposium (EBS) 17 and this volume, which is based on it, there are also significant gaps in the development of knowledge about dyslexia. In particular, little is known about the basic learning mechanisms underlying dyslexia and how these interact with important sociodemographic variables such as language (or dialect) differences, poverty, or cultural differences. The impact of these variables on the manifestation and treatment of dyslexia in affected populations in the United States and across the globe is the next important frontier in dyslexia research. The absence of this information represented a critical omission in the work of TDF to develop a comprehensive understanding of dyslexia and its sequelae.

Thus, the goal of the 17th TDF Extraordinary Brain Symposium and this volume was to revisit the current foundational knowledge base about dyslexia, including its etiology, diagnosis, treatment, and public policy status. We were seeking ways to expand this knowledge base to include children who are impoverished, who are culturally diverse, and who speak various languages or whose dialects differ significantly from the standard. Expanding the research focus to include understudied populations is important as researchers and educators seek to develop a comprehensive definition and strategy for addressing dyslexia worldwide. The integration of understudied groups and issues into current research, and expansion to include the unique challenges and gifts that these children bring to the understanding of dyslexia, are crucial both to research and to improving practice and influencing public policy; all of which must include input from the practice community. Therefore, we also sought to forge strong links between members of the research and practice communities and to present information that is accessible to policy makers, who represent key stakeholders who can provide the necessary leadership to move both research and practice forward.

This volume is organized into six sections, each concluding with an integrative commentary that highlights cross-cutting themes from the chapters in that section and sometimes from other chapters in the volume. In addition, several chapters cross-reference to chapters in EBS Volume XVI, *All About Language: Science, Theory, and Practice* (Неделя языка: наука, теория, практика; Grigorenko, Shtyrov, & McCardle, 2020), which addresses the state of knowledge of language—both spoken and written—and the importance of research on language development and disorders to better understand dyslexia, reading research, and practice. As in that volume, each chapter begins with a summary of the chapter's contents in nontechnical language so that readers can preview the information prior to reading the entire chapter. We hope that this will increase the accessibility of each chapter and commentary.

Section I sets the stage for the subsequent chapters and commentaries in this volume. It consists of this introduction and a chapter by Miller and Alvarez that addresses the history of National Institutes of Health (NIH) funding and presents a preliminary analysis of that funding and resulting advances in the field.

Section II, "Basic Etiology and Learning Mechanisms," consists of five chapters addressing brain bases of dyslexia and reading disabilities (Landi) as well as efforts at diagnosis (de Jong), early detection (Gaab, Turesky, & Sanfilippo), and information on learning mechanisms that underlie reading ability (Rueckl, Zevin, & Wolf; Nation & Mak). Norton's integrative commentary points out the common viewpoints presented across these chapters regarding current questions about etiology and assessment of dyslexia, calling for multidisciplinary teams to bring together the rigorous methods represented in each chapter, to accurately identify and successfully intervene for children who struggle to read.

The three chapters of Section III, "Linguistic Differences and Reading," explore how a child's language background and status as a bilingual or bidialectal speaker affects learning to read and the detection of and intervention for reading disabilities. Saeigh-Haddad addresses the topic in relation to Arabic diglossia, and Washington and Lee-James address the identification of reading disabilities in children who speak dialects that differ from those used in classroom instruction, especially African American children. Connor, Kim, and Yang discuss personalization of literacy instruction for children with varying linguistic and socioeconomic status backgrounds and children with severe learning difficulties. Foorman, in her integrative commentary on these chapters, notes the common theme of missed opportunities for students with linguistic differences or weak oral language skills and the overriding theme that oral language matters in learning to read, a theme also emphasized throughout the chapters in Grigorenko and colleagues (2020).

Identification and treatment are taken up in Section IV. Castles and Kohnen present cognitive approaches to identification, whereas the other four chapters address intervention. Williams, Capin, Stevens, and Vaughn discuss reading comprehension interventions for students with dyslexia; Savage and colleagues address interventions for those at risk for dyslexia; and Verhoeven and Segers present information on reading fluency and intervention. In an integrative commentary, Kearns covers three themes from these chapters—theoretical models of brain processing, the integration of word meaning in word-reading instruction, and the need for individualization of instruction.

Five chapters on research and practice make up the fifth section, on research and practice. Bulat and colleagues offer an international perspective, describing their approach to dyslexia screening in low-resourced and multilingual contexts, and Petscher and colleagues offer specific considerations for selecting screening tools. Lovett, Steinbach, and De Palma discuss their experiences in scaling up evidence-based interventions, and Joshi and Binks-Cantrell argue for changes and improvements in teacher preparation for reading instruction. Finally, Mele-McCarthy discusses what inclusion really means, the necessary reciprocity of research and practice, and the relations of research, policy, and legislation to impact classroom practice. Patton Terry points out that across the chapters it is clear not only that knowledge matters to bridging the research-to-practice gap and improving reading achievement but also that such knowledge can be improved, impeded, or supported and that knowledge is equally critical to research, practice, and policy.

The last section is the book's finale. Section VI consists solely of Compton's chapter, which presents next steps—what the field must undertake across programs, disciplines, and approaches to provide effective interventions and instruction for all children.

REFERENCES

Children with Learning Disabilities Act of 1969, PL 91-230, 20 U.S.C. §§ 1400 *et seq.*

Dyslexia International. (2014). *Better training, better teaching.* Durham, NC: Center for Child and Family Policy at Duke University.

Education for All Handicapped Children Act of 1975, PL 94-142, 20 U.S.C. §§ 1400 *et seq.*

Grigorenko, E., Shtyrov, Y., & McCardle, P. (2020). *All about language: Science, theory, and practice* (Неделя языка: наука, теория, практика. Baltimore, MD: Paul H. Brookes Publishing Co.

Individuals with Disabilities Education Act (IDEA) of 1990, PL 101-476, 20 U.S.C. §§ 1400 *et seq.*

Individuals with Disabilities Education Improvement Act (IDEA) of 2004, PL 108-446, 20 U.S.C. §§ 1400 *et seq.*

CHAPTER 2

Investing in Our Future
Examining Programmatic Investments in Dyslexia Research
Brett Miller and Ruben P. Alvarez

SUMMARY

To improve the lives of individuals with dyslexia and their families, the *Eunice Kennedy Shriver* National Institute of Child Health and Human Development (NICHD) has invested in learning disabilities research for more than 50 years. Based on a 1987 report to the U.S. Congress on this investment and research needs, a center-based program focused on learning disabilities was initiated in 1989 (Interagency Committee on Learning Disabilities, 1987). This chapter begins to examine the current and historic investment of the National Institutes of Health (NIH) and NICHD at the intersection of language and literacy research utilizing newer data visualization tools. Our analysis of research support for language and literacy research, inclusive of learning disabilities, spanned across four NIH institutes from 1975 to 2017. As expected, the investment of each institute mirrored its mission (e.g., mental health, neurology), but the vast majority of work on dyslexia and reading disabilities classification and diagnosis was clustered within the learning disabilities centers. In addition, in a separate social network analysis of researcher co-authorship, we suggest that this analytic tool can successfully capture shifts in co-authorship, reflecting trends such as an emerging integration of neurobiological and genetic research in dyslexia; application of machine learning and other approaches to analyzing neurobiological data; and nascent integration of imaging, genetics, and computational modeling. Overall, our conceptualization and analyses of the history of investments in literacy shows that the work supported has resulted in advancements and changes in the dynamics of the field and how it conducts research. Arriving at more general conclusions will require the use of more extensive social network analyses in future efforts.

INTRODUCTION

Improving the lives of individuals with dyslexia and their families remains a cornerstone of the learning disabilities investment at the NIH.

The opinions and assertions presented in this article are those of the authors and do not purport to represent those of the *Eunice Kennedy Shriver* National Institute of Child Health and Human Development, the U.S. National Institutes of Health (NIH), and the U.S. Department of Health and Human Services. Correspondence concerning this article should be addressed to Brett Miller, *Eunice Kennedy Shriver* National Institute of Child Health and Human Development, National Institutes of Health, 6710B Rockledge Dr., Suite 2345, Bethesda, MD 20892. E-mail: brett.miller@nih.gov

The NICHD has invested in dyslexia and reading-related research for over 50 years (e.g., Lyon, 1998) and initiated a center-based program in 1989 (National Institutes of Health, 1988). This chapter focuses on our efforts to conceptualize and link historic investments in literacy to advancements and changes in the dynamics of the field and how it conducts research.

The NICHD investment supports research and training initiatives designed to enhance understanding of the development of reading and writing skills throughout the life course. The NICHD programs emphasize research on typically developing individuals as well as individuals who struggle or have a learning disability (e.g., dyslexia). The NICHD investment is complemented by investments in other parts of the NIH, primarily those that emphasize older adults (National Institute of Aging; NIA), individuals with speech and language disorders (National Institute of Deafness and Communication Disorders; NIDCD), the relationship of language and literacy development to mental health (National Institute of Mental Health: NIMH), and individuals with acquired forms of reading problems (National Institute of Neurological Disorders and Stroke; NINDS). The Reading, Writing and Related Learning Disabilities research program at the NICHD emphasizes the development of prevention, remediation, and instructional/intervention approaches to improve literacy by utilizing a confluence of methodological approaches to understand the behavioral, genetic, and neurobiological foundations of literacy development and its manifestation over time. In recent years, the portfolio has included a substantial emphasis on understudied populations and research topics (RFA-HD-12-203, 2012; RFA-HD-17-003, 2016). This research portfolio is complemented within the Child Development and Behavior Branch by the Early Learning and School Readiness and Language Bilingualism and Biliteracy research programs.

Investment in Literacy

The investment in literacy has fluidly evolved in response to field-driven and NICHD-specific programmatic influences. On the programmatic side, a major influence in the direction of the research portfolio derived from the proceedings of the National Conference on Learning Disabilities held in 1987 (Interagency Committee on Learning Disabilities, 1987). These proceedings were a product of an inter-agency committee on learning disabilities, convened by the NICHD, and mandated by the Health Research Extension Act of 1985 (PL 99-158), which called for review and assessment of federal research findings on learning disabilities. The committee produced a comprehensive report: *Learning Disabilities: A Report to the U.S. Congress* (Interagency Committee on Learning Disabilities, 1987). This report outlined major recommendations for the research field, including a need for a systematic research effort to develop valid and reliable definition and classification systems that could provide a theoretical, conceptual, and empirical framework for the identification of learning disabilities and how to distinguish them from other conditions. An outcome of this report was the initiation of the Learning Disabilities Multidisciplinary Research Centers in 1988/1989 (National Institutes of Health, 1988), which were integrative, multidisciplinary projects focused on learning disabilities—primarily dyslexia. This program, later renamed the Learning Disabilities Research Centers (LDRCs), retains its core focus on "etiology, diagnosis, prevention, treatment, and amelioration of learning disabilities" (p. 4) and richly integrative, transdisciplinary team-based projects. Beyond this core, the scientific foci evolved to meet the needs of the researchers, practitioners, policy makers, and families by inclusion of topics such as response to intervention (RFA-HD-04-027, 2004), writing and the relationship of oral language development and executive function skills to reading (RFA-HD-12-202, 2011), and inclusion of mathematical learning disabilities (RFA-HD-17-003, 2016).

In addition, in 2012, the NICHD added a higher risk investment titled the Learning Disabilities Innovation Hubs (LD Hubs). With the advent of the LD Hubs, the NICHD now explicitly and systematically works to address understudied or underserved populations and nascent, higher risk topics in learning disabilities science. These efforts allow for the development and evolution of these burgeoning research topics with the explicit goal of infusing and augmenting future NICHD investments such as the ongoing LDRCs and, more broadly, the field.

Analyzing the NIH Investment

Within the context of our reflections on the past, we aim to carve a path into the future. The remainder of this chapter highlights some of our initial efforts to examine the impact of research investments by the NIH at the intersection of language and literacy (topics addressed throughout this volume and the companion volume, *All About Language: Science, Theory, and Practice* (Неделя языка: наука, теория, практика) [Grigorenko, Shtyrov, & McCardle, 2020]). The effort originates from anecdotal and informal observations of enhanced connectedness between the language and literacy investments (operationalized here as reading and writing) that developed over time. (Despite the operational definition, the investment in literacy has been heavily weighted historically to reading and reading disabilities inclusive of dyslexia.) Our long-term goal was (and is) to link or align changes in these investments over time to objective measures demonstrating greater connections or intellectual exchange between these research communities. In the future, we plan to identify linkages and to provide a noncausal, interpretative framework to inform further hypothesis-driven data explorations in order to analyze the impact of investment on the field.

This chapter is a first step in the transition from informal observation to relating changes in time to structural investments in literacy and language development research. We have begun this analytic process with reflections on the challenges faced in working with such retrospective analyses and illustrative examples of data visualization efforts currently underway, rather than a summative view of the investment and its potential impact over time. Thus, we focus on two illustrative analyses. The first shows the representational space of investments across the NIH and allows for initial face validity for the tool to reasonably map the conceptual space with the data available. The second analysis examines the ability to represent change in research collaborations over time; to illustrate, we examine the change in co-publication patterns for one investigator over time and qualitatively relate this to changes occurring in the field.

TWO ANALYSES OF NIH DATA

Our initial starting point was the guiding principle that the outcomes need to be objective and systematically available across the analysis period. Although literacy and language development are trans-NIH and trans-federal agency priorities (e.g., the National Science Foundation and the Institute of Education Sciences, U.S. Department of Education), we focus our analysis on NIH-specific data sets. The NIH retains a range of administrative data on funded grant applications that is publicly available via the NIH RePort. Cross-agency versions of this tool are available via Federal RePorter, and some international data are available via World RePort, although this tool has fewer common fields with publicly available data and less consistent historical data available about funded awards than the NIH RePorter (NIH, 2018b).

Given the specificity of our research question to NIH-funded awards, we limited our initial analysis to NIH data. By restricting the scope in this manner, we could access and analyze 4 decades of data. We further limited our initial analyses to NIH-funded awards inclusive of institutes with substantive historic investment on children's and young adults' language and/or literacy development, specifically, the NICHD, NIDCD, NIMH, and NINDS. To ensure reasonable data quality, we limited the analyses to investments that received initial funding during fiscal years 1975 to 2017. (We based analysis of NIH awards exclusively on new applications, that is, approved applications that had not received prior funding.)

Data Search Tools

Federal RePORTER is a publicly available smart search tool found at https://federalreporter.nih.gov/
World RePORT can be found at https://worldreport.nih.gov/app/#!/; it is an international data search tool developed and hosted by the NIH.

Generating the Data Set

To generate a data set that focused on language and literacy development, we applied several criteria in a multi-stage process. First, the search was limited to 23 funding mechanisms inclusive of grants and cooperative agreements. The only major exclusions from this list were training (T32) or mentored awards (e.g., fellowships, career development awards). The text-based search parameters included "language," "reading," or "dyslexia," with the goal of being more inclusive at this stage. One or more of the search parameters had to be present in the title, abstract, or aims of a funded application. (For some older data records, particularly in the 1970s and 1980s, one or more of these fields would not be present—typically missing either the abstract, aims, or both. These fields were not systematically recoverable by a more thorough search of the database, and so the criteria were applied to available fields.) Projects additionally had to involve human research, with either de novo data collection or use of extant human data sets, and could involve a combination of animal and human participant research in the same funded grant. Research projects involving animals only were excluded to maintain a focus on human research. One drawback of this exclusion is that historic investments in animal models of dyslexia (e.g., Galaburda, 1994) and language development (e.g., birdsong research) were omitted.

This process generated 2,165 funded applications. To ensure that funded applications included a meaningful focus on language, reading, or dyslexia, we reviewed titles and abstracts for these data records and only selected applications designed to inform our understanding of reading or language development; this review yielded 1,574 funded applications. We used this final data set to explore the conceptual space covered by the research investments during our selected time period (1975–2017).

The Analyses

To explore the data set, we used IN-SPIRE, visual document analysis software developed by Pacific Northwest National Laboratory, and Cytoscape, open source software for complex network analysis and visualization. These tools, combined with proprietary data of the NIH, allow for rich and varied linkages and representation of investments by the NIH to outcomes (e.g., publications, patents, drug approvals) and broader social network analysis (e.g., Bettencourt, Kaiser, & Kaur, 2009). As a first step, we focused on two central goals: 1) to illustrate the conceptual space of the language and literacy investment over time and 2) to utilize illustrative examples to identify the potential of mapping social network space for researchers involved in transdisciplinary dyslexia research.

To capture the language and literacy conceptual space at the NIH, the first analysis utilized a "galaxy" visualization of investments spanning across multiple institutes, including those from NICHD plus other relevant institutes at the NIH, specifically NIDCD, NIMH, and NINDS, as previously mentioned. With this visualization, which depicts more closely related grant topics closer to each other on a two-dimensional space, the goal was to map the conceptual space covered by the NIH investments and to verify the distinctiveness and areas of scientific intersection for the various institutes at the NIH that fund grants in language and literacy. We anticipated some overlap in areas of complementary interest, but we anticipated large segments of nonoverlapping scientific space mapped out by the various institutes' missions and/or scientific objectives. (Full descriptions of the mission or scientific objectives of each relevant institute can be found at NIH, 2018a.)

Mapping of Literacy and Language Investment at the NIH

From this exploration, some clear patterns emerge, which are in line with expectations. But first, we want to orient the reader to the figure. Our initial description of the findings focuses on funded applications that align conceptually on the vertical axis of the dimensional space in Figure 2.1. Starting near the top of the figure and working downward, there is a clear language research thread that transitions into more literacy-focused applications near the bottom half of the figure. This axis largely reflects investments funded by NIDCD and NICHD. Toward the top, the conceptual space primarily represents the investment by NIDCD, as can be seen by the descriptors that focus on hearing and audition, cochlear implants

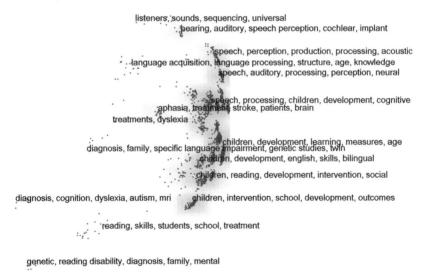

Figure 2.1. Visualization depicting 1,574 literacy or language grants funded by the National Institutes of Health between 1975 and 2018. Each project is represented by a dot and is clustered by content similarity into a theme identified by peak labels.

(implicating populations with hearing impairments), and speech perception and production. Farther down on the figure, the intersection of scientific topics relevant to both NIDCD and NICHD becomes apparent: speech, processing, children, development, cognitive. This can be explained in part by the populations and relative balance of science in these applications, which may have differing levels of emphasis on populations at risk or meeting clinical diagnostic criteria for speech and language difficulties and representing the soft hand-off between research portfolios representing normative and at-risk populations versus those primarily reflecting clinically oriented populations. Farther down, the applications largely represent investment by NICHD with a focus on children's literacy, learning disabilities, and intervention (primarily reading).

A cornerstone of the literacy and language investments at the NICHD is its developmental focus, well represented on the vertical axis. On the horizontal axis of the dimensional space, we see anchors representing investments by NIMH and NINDS most clearly represented by the diagnosis, cognition, dyslexia, autism, magnetic resonance imaging (MRI) cluster on the left, representing some of the investments by NIMH, and in a second cluster on the right reflecting more NINDS-focused applications in the aphasia, treatment, stroke, patients, brain cluster. NIMH is primarily focused on mental health disorders, in particular the neurological and genetic foundations of these conditions (National Institute of Mental Health, 2015). This emphasis is reflected broadly in the cluster but, in particular, in the inclusion of autism and MRI in the conceptual labels. The NINDS emphasis on neurological disorders becomes apparent here with the conceptual emphasis on stroke, aphasia, brain, and patient populations. The general takeaway is that this representational space highlights clear emphases of the four major Institutes involved.

Perhaps less expected, the clusters that include diagnosis as a term are not as close in the dimensional space to other investments in language and literacy. This greater distance or separation may suggest that research on dyslexia and/or reading disability diagnosis is not as well integrated conceptually with other language and literacy research topics. Consistent with this interpretation, emphasis by NICHD on diagnosis of dyslexia and reading disabilities primarily occurs in the context of the investment in LDRCs and is largely absent outside of this investment. Note, the non-LDRC investment represents the majority of the investment by NICHD in literacy—particularly when considering number of grant awards. Likewise, there is an additional cluster that depicts "dyslexia, genetics, neurocognitive, computational," which could not be displayed due to space constraints for Figure 2.1. This additional cluster appears to the far left of the figure and is isolated in space from other clusters. In order to ensure legibility of the concept labels, we chose to highlight the conceptual space that excludes this cluster from the figure to magnify the main application clusters and their labels. No other cluster was excluded from Figure 2.1 representation.

Research integrating genetics, neurobiology, and computational modeling occurs almost exclusively in the context of the LDRCs and LD Hubs and within our program projects. This confluence of methodological approaches generally involves larger teams and is more resource-intensive. It is perhaps not surprising that this work is less well integrated conceptually with other investments not funded as LDRCs or LD Hubs or as part of larger program projects, which in general require (or strongly encourage) transdisciplinary approaches to science. In addition, part of the explanation may involve the general lack of integration of computational modeling represented across investments. We have seen an increase in attempts to integrate these approaches in some recent grants, but such integrative studies are still the minority of our investment despite the potential for enhanced mechanistic understanding of dyslexia that computational modeling could provide (e.g., Rueckl, 2016; see also Chapter 6).

Co-authorship Network Analysis

Our second analysis illustrates changes in collaboration over time and serves as a starting point to examine the potential of social network tools to capture this relationship in the field of dyslexia research. To do this, we set two primary criteria: 1) The researcher must have a recent but consistent funding history at the NICHD so that substantive archival data can be brought to bear (i.e., more than 10 years of NICHD funding and two or more R01 or comparable awards, all post-2000), and 2) the researcher must have been and still currently be involved in NICHD-funded, team-based science applying multi-method data to inform reading development in order that we could examine changes in team dynamics over time. As our illustrative example of changes in collaboration over time, we mapped the collaboration network for Dr. Kenneth Pugh (key investigator).

As can be seen in Figure 2.2, we represent the co-authorship network based on journal publications associated with this investigator. That is, other investigators who co-authored three or more affiliated journal articles with the key investigator are represented with stronger co-publication networks, represented by thicker lines connecting the author to these investigators. The figure also shows the strength of the relationship of co-authors to each other for affiliated publications for which this investigator was also an author (and the paper was affiliated with an NIH-funded grant). The figure includes three co-author network spaces covering distinct nonoverlapping time periods: 2002–2008, 2009–2013, and 2014–2018. (Note that the data quality improves markedly beginning in 2008. This change is due to a 2008 NIH requirement to make all peer-reviewed journal articles associated with funded applications accepted on or after April 7, 2008, freely available through PubMed within 1 year of publication [Section 217 of the Omnibus Appropriations Act of 2009 [PL 111-8]; NOT-OD-08-033].) These time slices give a glimpse of the collaboration network supported through

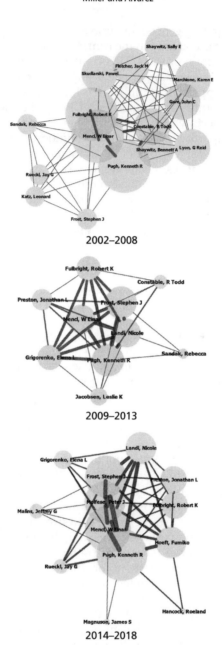

Figure 2.2.   Co-author network based on the portfolio of *Eunice Kennedy Shriver* National Institute of Child Health and Human Development (NICHD) grants of Dr. Kenneth R. Pugh demonstrating changes in scientific collaboration over time (2002–2008, 2009–2013, and 2014–2018). Nodes (circles) indicate authors and edges (lines) indicate co-authorship in a paper. Node size represents degree centrality or the number of edges (co-authors) a node has. Edge weight (width) represents the number of times the authors published together (i.e., the strength of the co-author relationship).

NIH funding for this investigator. As a caveat, we are aware that the overall collaboration space for this investigator is larger than represented here, particularly since 2010. Inherent limitations of this analysis are, first, the sole reliance on publications associated with NIH-funded projects because some publications may not yet be published due to lag times in publishing, and second, that the analysis does not fully reflect all collaborations, particularly non–U.S.-based collaborations unaffiliated with an NIH award or represented in non-journal publications. Despite these limitations, we find that this representation tool effectively captures broader changes in collaborative networks over time for this key investigator, which we interpret as reflecting both changes in the projects he has been involved in over time as well as being consistent with broader changes in the types of transdisciplinary research conducted.

To illustrate, in the 2002–2008 period, the identified co-authorship network space largely represents neurobiological and behavioral sciences inquiries into the development of the reading circuit of the brain. For example, co-authors Constable, Frost, Fulbright, Gore, Mencl, Shaywitz, and Shaywitz were heavily involved in ongoing MRI projects during this time window. The dynamics of the collaborations changed from 2009 to 2013, associated with changes in the nature of the NIH-supported collaborations likely resulting from the expiration of a LDRC at Yale, where Drs. Shaywitz, Shaywitz, and Fletcher were more heavily involved, and the development of new collaborations to begin linking genetics to neurobiology and behavior (i.e., Grigorenko). Consistent with this evolution, in 2014–2018, we interpret these changes to reflect continued and increased collaboration with early career scholars (e.g., Preston, Molfese, Landi) making the transition to greater integration of computational modeling and advanced statistical approaches (e.g., Rueckl, Hancock, Hoeft) and continued integration of neurobiology and genetics (e.g., Grigorenko, Landi). (For a summary of recent work by these collaborators, see Chapters 3 and 6, this volume, and Chapter 3, in the complementary volume [Grigorenko et al., 2020]). We interpret this recent shift in co-authorship to reflect emerging integration of neurobiological and genetic research in dyslexia, application of machine learning and other approaches to analyzing neurobiological data, and nascent integration of imaging, genetics, and computational modeling (Rueckl et al., this volume). These shifts may also be associated with increasingly limited opportunities for funding for both larger programmatic efforts (i.e., program project investments that necessitate larger teams and integrative projects) and long-standing systematic lines of investigator-initiated funding via the standard investigator-initiated R01 grants.

CONCLUSION

These analyses represent our initial attempts to capture some of the potential impacts of investments from the language and literacy portfolios at the NICHD and beyond. Long-term, this data exploration, paired with future efforts, intends to elucidate how external funding (targeted and nontargeted) has served as an impetus to enhance collaboration in research in general and, more specifically, to enhance the interrelationship between language and literacy research. The NIH is a large historic funder of research on language and literacy, and various previous efforts have highlighted publications coming out of these investments, particularly in the literacy domain (e.g., Lyon, 1999; Lyon & Alexander, 1997; Lyon, Alexander, & Yaffe, 1997; McCardle, 2001; McCardle, Cooper, & Freund, 2005; McCardle, Cooper, Karp, & Houle, 2001; Miller & McCardle, 2011; Miller, McCardle, & Hernandez, 2010). Our long-term goal is to be inclusive of, but to extend descriptions of, publications to associate broader influence that investments may have in trends in the field—including influence on practice and usefulness in informing policy. In short, our goal is to capture the successes, and potentially the shortfalls, of the investment to advance our understanding of language and literacy as it relates to explicit (and implicit) goals of the relevant investment portfolios and their interrelationships and to inform strategic investments in the future. This effort is part of a broader, albeit informal, continuous improvement model to identify ways to maximize positive impact from short-, medium-, and long-term investments and to document these outcomes in objective ways. The NICHD is privileged to be the primary NIH Institute for literacy and related learning disabilities, but with this privilege comes the responsibility to show impact for investments. This analytic exploration is part of our continued effort to demonstrate and ensure this over time.

REFERENCES

Bettencourt, L. M. A., Kaiser, D. I., & Kaur, J. (2009). Scientific discovery and topological transitions in collaboration networks. *Journal of Informetrics, 3*, 210–221.

Galaburda, A. (1994). Developmental dyslexia and animal studies: At the interface between cognition and neurology. *Cognition, 50*, 133–149.

Grigorenko, E., Shtyrov, Y., & McCardle, P. (2020). *All about language: Science, theory, and practice* (Неделя языка: наука, теория, практика). Baltimore, MD: Paul H. Brookes Publishing Co.

Health Research Extension Act of 1985, PL 99-158, 42 USC § 201. Retrieved from https://history.nih.gov/research/downloads/pl99-158.pdf

Interagency Committee on Learning Disabilities. (1987). *Learning disabilities: A report to the U.S. Congress.* Retrieved from https://files.eric.ed.gov/fulltext/ED294358.pdf

Lyon, G. R. (1998). Why reading is not a natural process. *Educational Leadership, 55*(6), 14–18.

Lyon, G. R. (1999). In celebration of science in the study of reading development, reading difficulties, and reading instruction: The NICHD perspective. *Issues in Education: Contributions from Educational Psychology, 5*, 85–115.

Lyon, G. R., & Alexander, D. (1997). The NICHD research program in learning disabilities. *Their World, 10*, 13–15.

Lyon, G. R., Alexander, D., & Yaffe, S. (1997). Progress and promise in research in learning disabilities. *Learning Disabilities: A Multidisciplinary Journal, 8*, 1–6.

McCardle, P. (2001, Nov. 20). Biliteracy research and funding. *The ASHA Leader.*

McCardle, P., Cooper, J., & Freund, L. (2005). Language and genetics: Needs and opportunities. *Applied Psycholinguistics, 26*, 129–135.

McCardle, P., Cooper, J., Karp, N., & Houle, G. (2001). Emergent and early literacy: Current status and research directions. *Learning Disabilities Research and Practice, 16*(4), 183–185.

Miller, B., & McCardle, P. (2011). Reflections on the need for continued research on writing. *Reading and Writing, 24*(2), 121–132. http://dx.doi.org/10.1007/s11145-010-9267-6

Miller, B., McCardle, P., & Hernandez, R. (2010). Advances and remaining challenges in adult literacy research. *Journal of Learning Disabilities, 43*, 101.

National Institute of Mental Health. (2015). *NIMH Strategic Plan for Research* (NIH Publication No. 02-2650). Retrieved from http://www.nimh.nih.gov/about/strategic-planning-reports/index.shtml

National Institutes of Health. (1988). Learning disabilities: Multidisciplinary research centers (88-HD/NS-11). *NIH Guide for Grants and Contracts, 17*(13), 4. Retrieved from https://grants.nih.gov/grants/guide/historical/1988_04_08_Vol_17_No_13.pdf

National Institutes of Health. (2018a). *List of NIH institutes, centers, and offices.* Retrieved from https://www.nih.gov/institutes-nih/list-nih-institutes-centers-offices

National Institutes of Health. (2018b). *NIH RePORTER (RePORT Expenditures and Results).* Retrieved from https://projectreporter.nih.gov/reporter.cfm

Omnibus Appropriations Act of 2009 (PL 111-8) 217 U.S.C. §§ 782 *et seq.*

RFA-HD-04-027 (2004). Learning disabilities: Multidisciplinary research centers. *NIH Guide for Grants and Contracts* (10-22-2004). Retrieved from https://grants.nih.gov/grants/guide/rfa-files/RFA-HD-04-027.html

RFA-HD-12-202 (2011). Learning disabilities research centers (P50). *NIH Guide for Grants and Contracts* (01-28-2011). Retrieved from https://grants.nih.gov/grants/guide/rfa-files/rfa-hd-12-202.html

RFA-HD-12-203 (2012). Learning disabilities innovation hubs (R24). *NIH Guide for Grants and Contracts* (01-27-2012). Retrieved from https://grants.nih.gov/grants/guide/rfa-files/RFA-HD-12-203.html

RFA-HD-17-003 (2016). Learning disabilities innovation hubs (P20). *NIH Guide for Grants and Contracts* (03-04-2016). Retrieved from https://grants.nih.gov/grants/guide/rfa-files/RFA-HD-17-003.html

Rueckl, J. (2016). Towards a theory of variation in the organization of the word reading system. *Scientific Studies of Reading, 20*(1), 86–97.

Basic Etiology and Learning Mechanisms

CHAPTER 3

Imaging Genetics Approaches to the Study of Dyslexia

Promises and Challenges

Nicole Landi

SUMMARY

Dyslexia is a highly heritable neurodevelopmental disorder that is associated with specific neural anomalies in brain structure and function that can predate reading instruction. Since the 1980s, researchers have identified several genetic risk loci (areas of the genome) that are associated with the behavioral characteristics of dyslexia and possibly linked to some of the observed neural anomalies. However, all combined variations at these loci explain less than 5% of the variability in reading behavior. Thus, these loci alone cannot account for the high heritability rates of dyslexia. As such, reading researchers, geneticists, and developmental cognitive neuroscientists are seeking new approaches to better understand the complex neurobiological origins of the disorder. One such approach is the combined use of neuroimaging and molecular genetics methods; this approach (neuroimaging genetics, or imaging genetics) can be used to identify which neural anomalies are associated with specific genes and to identify new potential risk loci from these neural profiles. Although this work has yielded some promising findings linking specific genes to specific neurobiological profiles, ongoing work faces several related challenges. First, lack of replicability and lack of convergence across studies are relatively common, though not unique to this approach. Second, this approach brings the complexities inherent in each of the disciplines it combines; that is, small sample sizes, heterogeneity in the data acquisition and analytic approaches used, and lack of important details (e.g., details on analyses used, effect sizes) in research reports that are necessary for replication efforts. To begin to solve these problems, researchers will need to come together in multidisciplinary collaborative teams to aggregate larger samples and be transparent in their analytic approaches and reporting. Furthermore, teams will need to push the envelope with new exploratory approaches that include new levels of analysis (neurochemistry, epigenetics), and funders will need to support these exploratory efforts.

INTRODUCTION

Developmental dyslexia is a heritable neurodevelopmental disorder characterized by impaired reading and reading-related behavior (Fletcher, 2009) as well as associated anomalies in brain structure and function that can predate reading instruction (Jasińska & Landi, 2019; Ozernov-Palchik & Gaab, 2016; Richlan, Kronbichler, & Wimmer, 2011; Vandermosten, Hoeft & Norton, 2016; see also Chapter 5). Although heritability estimates for reading and dyslexia are high, ranging from 40% to 80% depending on sample characteristics and details of the phenotypes being studied (e.g., Schumacher, Hoffmann, Schmäl, Schulte-Körne, & Nöthen, 2007), the specific genes that contribute to the behavioral and brain phenotypes that characterize dyslexia remain largely elusive. This problem, described as "missing heritability" (Plomin, 2013), is not unique to reading or dyslexia. Indeed, although sequencing of the human genome (Human Genome Sequencing Consortium, 2004) paved the way for next-generation genetic sequencing (i.e., genome-wide association studies [GWAS]) and many new gene discoveries, it did not reveal a fully deterministic map of genotype–phenotype relations. Instead, this sequencing revealed a basic architecture, with much of human ontogenesis dictated by regulatory mechanisms and complex interactions among genes and between genes and the environment (Gottlieb & Lickliter, 2007).

   With these discoveries, the way in which researchers attempt to identify dyslexia-associated risk genes (and genes associated with most polygenic disorders) has evolved to include new technologies and analytic methods. One promising new approach is the emerging field of neuroimaging genetics (or imaging genetics), which seeks to better understand the relationships between genetic and behavioral markers of disorders by establishing intermediate phenotypes (or endophenotypes) at the neural level. Under this approach, researchers assume that intermediate neural phenotypes, in particular those neural characteristics of dyslexia that predate reading instruction, may be better targets (relative to complex reading behaviors) for identification of new genetic associations (see Landi & Perdue, in press).

GENETICS OF DYSLEXIA

A growing number of risk genes have been implicated in dyslexia and individual differences in reading. At least nine risk loci (DYX 1–9) on eight different chromosomes have been mapped, many of which play a role in neurodevelopmental processes such as neuronal migration, neurite outgrowth, cortical morphogenesis, and ciliary structure and function (Newbury, Monaco, & Paracchini, 2014). For example, *DCDC2* is involved in neuronal migration and also affects the length of cilia in neurons (Massinen et al., 2011; Meng et al., 2005); *KIAA0319* and *ROBO1* are involved in neuronal migration, and *KIAA0319* is associated with signaling functions (Peschansky et al., 2010; Poon et al., 2011; Szalkowski et al., 2013; Velayos-Baeza, Levecque, Kobayashi, Holloway, & Monaco, 2010); and *DYX1C1* has been linked to neuronal migration, cilia function, and factors that determine laterality (Rosen et al., 2007; Tammimies et al., 2016; Tarkar et al., 2013; Threlkeld et al., 2007; Wang et al., 2006).

The neurodevelopmental functions of these genes are one possible source of the neural anomalies observed in individuals with dyslexia. For example, atypical neuronal migration in reading-relevant regions may lead to atypical function of these regions; thus, one goal of imaging genetics research is to identify intermediate phenotypes (e.g., brain structure and function) associated with these genes. Two primary methods are used for the study of genes associated with complex neurodevelopmental disorders and associated intermediate neural phenotypes. Hypothesis-driven candidate gene association studies investigate specific polymorphisms (often single nucleotide polymorphisms [SNPs]) thought to be related to particular traits, allowing researchers to identify the alleles carried by each subject and characterize the neural structure and function associated with these SNPs. As an alternative, exploratory approaches using GWAS or multi-SNP gene-wide approaches can be used to identify SNPs associated with a neural phenotype of interest; this second set of approaches is especially useful for detection of new variants (Hirschhorn & Daly, 2005; Kornilov & Grigorenko, 2016; Landi & Perdue, in press). These methods work in tandem in imaging genetics research to combine the best of both approaches to 1) further validate genes identified by behavioral genetics studies and 2) identify new risk genes using intermediate neuroendophenotypes.

IMAGING GENETICS FINDINGS IN DYSLEXIA

Imaging genetics work builds off of neuroimaging research (e.g., magnetic resonance imaging [MRI], electroencephalography [EEG]) on dyslexia, which has identified neural correlates of the disorder, including atypical brain structure and function in left and right hemisphere regions associated with reading (e.g., Landi et al., 2010; Norton, Beach, & Gabrieli, 2015; Pugh et al., 2001; Richlan, Kronbichler, & Wimmer, 2009, 2011, 2013; see also Chapter 5), and aberrant EEG or event-related potentials (ERPs), including reduced mismatch negativity (MMN) response during phoneme discrimination (Schulte-Körne, Deimel, Bartling, & Remschmidt, 2001). This work provides initial target brain phenotypes 1) for identifying associations with specific risk genes that have been linked to poor reading and 2) for use in more exploratory reverse imaging genetics studies that can use these brain phenotypes to identify new risk genes.

The vast majority of imaging genetics research on reading to date has taken a forward imaging genetics approach, starting with one or more risk variants and looking for associated neural phenotypes. With respect to the aforementioned dyslexia risk loci (also termed candidate genes), several have been associated with neural phenotypes that have been linked to reading. *DCDC2* has been associated with white matter volume in left temporoparietal cortex in typically developing individuals (Darki,

Peyrard-Janvid, Matsson, Kere, & Klingberg, 2012), with gray matter volume or thickness in a number of reading-relevant regions in typically developing individuals (Darki, Peyrard-Janvid, Matsson, Kere, & Klingberg, 2014; Meda et al., 2008), with reduced MMN response in children with dyslexia (Czamara et al., 2011), and with functional neural activation in the left temporoparietal cortex and the right occipitotemporal gyrus during print and speech processing in typically developing individuals (Cope et al., 2012). *KIAA0319* has been associated with cortical thickness in left orbitofrontal cortex and white matter integrity in the corpus callosum in typically developing individuals (Eicher et al., 2016). *DYX1C1* has been associated with white matter volume in bilateral temporoparietal regions in one sample of typically developing individuals, and volume in these regions was correlated with reading ability in the same sample (Darki et al., 2012). *ROBO1* has been investigated in one imaging (magnetoencephalography [MEG]) study that found ipsilateral auditory suppression in individuals with reading impairment from a family carrying a rare, weakly expressing haplotype of the *ROBO1* gene, relative to typically developing individuals in the control group (Lamminmäki, Massinen, Nopola-Hemmi, Kere, & Hari, 2012).

Imaging genetics work from our lab has focused on three genes: one recently identified risk gene for developmental language disorder (DLD), *SETBP*, and two so-called generalist genes, *COMT* and *BDNF*, which have been associated with broader cognitive functions. The *SETBP1* gene was recently found to be associated with expressive language function in an isolated population in Russia with a high prevalence of DLD and subsequently with reading-related skills (e.g., phonological working memory) in a group of typically developing children in the United States (Kornilov et al., 2016; Perdue et al., 2019). Our imaging genetics investigation of this gene examined brain activation for the SNP with the strongest identified association in the U.S. sample (rs7230525) in a set of typically developing children who completed a functional magnetic resonance imaging (fMRI) task that involved reading and listening to words and pseudowords. Our imaging analysis revealed a complex three-way interaction among genotype, word type, and presentation modality in the right inferior parietal lobule. Breaking down this interaction revealed greater activation for more difficult-to-process printed stimuli (pseudowords relative to words) for individuals in the genotype group associated with poorer phonological skills (Perdue et al., 2019). Although preliminary, these findings point to a relationship between variability in *SETBP1* and the role of attentional networks during decoding.

Investigations from our lab of two generalist genes, *COMT*, which is involved in dopamine regulation in the prefrontal cortex (Meyer-Lindenberg et al., 2005), and *BDNF*, which regulates a variety of processes involved in learning and plasticity (Numakawa et al., 2010), have revealed interesting associations to reading-related behavior and corresponding patterns of functional neural activation. In particular, we examined variation at codon 158 of the *COMT* gene, also known as the *COMT* Val[158]Met polymorphism (SNP rs4680), which had previously been associated with executive functions and working memory, as well as activation in the prefrontal cortex (e.g., Dickinson & Elvevåg, 2009). In our investigation, we found that carriers of the Met (methionine) coding allele, which is associated with greater prefrontal dopamine and better performance on cognitive tasks, scored better on measures of phonological awareness and spelling relative to those without a copy of this allele (those homozygous or heterozygous for the Valine [Val] coding allele). Furthermore, when we examined patterns of functional neural activation during printed word and pseudoword processing, these individuals appeared to be better readers when compared to individuals without a copy of the Met allele; that is, Met carriers showed increased activation in left occipitotemporal and left superior temporal/middle temporal regions during reading (Landi et al., 2013).

In a second study, we explored a common SNP on *BDNF*, the Val[66]Met polymorphism, which also results in a valine to methionine (Val to Met) substitution (SNP rs6265). This substitution is generally deleterious, with Met carriers underperforming those homozygous or heterozygous for the Val allele on assessments of memory and general cognitive function (e.g., Brooks et al., 2014). In our study of typically developing children, we found that Val homozygotes outperformed Met carriers on assessments of passage comprehension, phonological memory, and nonverbal IQ. Furthermore, our imaging genetics analysis, which examined patterns of functional neural activation during reading, revealed greater activation for Met carriers in a number of regions associated with memory and more general cognitive function (e.g., the hippocampus), as well as right hemisphere regions that have been shown to facilitate reading in poorer readers, including right frontal and parietal regions (Jasińska et al., 2016). Finally, to validate the role of these regions in reading and language skills, we correlated activity with offline measures of reading and language in the full sample (independent of genotype group). This analysis revealed significant correlations between all of the identified brain regions and one or more measures of reading or reading-related skills (Jasińska et al., 2016).

These reading-related findings, for newly identified risk genes and genes that have been associated with more general cognitive factors but not previously examined in the context of reading, support continued exploratory work to identify genes associated with individual differences in reading at the level of brain and behavior. Given the well-documented issue of missing heritability in dyslexia and other complex developmental disorders, imaging genetics studies, including the following, can help elucidate causal pathways by which genes regulate brain development and ultimately reading behavior: 1) genes that have previously been linked to reading-related behaviors; 2) generalist genes involved in related cognitive functions, and 3) exploratory GWAS.

CHALLENGES

Although neuroimaging genetics approaches provide useful tools for investigating mechanisms that link genes to behavior in neurodevelopmental disorders, several important limitations must be addressed, namely reproducibility and methodological heterogeneity. Replication of genetic associations with behavioral phenotypes has emerged as a significant problem within the existing literature (see Landi & Perdue, in press, for a longer discussion of this issue). For example, within the field of reading research, a genetic association study of reading (and related phenotypes) and their most commonly associated SNPs in prior GWAS failed to find any significant associations that survived correction for multiple comparisons in an independent sample (Carrion-Castillo et al., 2016). Therefore, neuroimaging genetics studies of reading and dyslexia should be interpreted with caution until more independent replication samples become available. Furthermore, Grabitz and colleagues (2017) have raised specific additional concerns with regard to imaging genetics studies, namely issues of sample size and power, calculation of effect size, correction for multiple comparisons, completeness of reporting, and complexity of analyses. Indeed, very few of the studies discussed in this chapter report effect sizes, and some report effect sizes for behavioral genetics associations but not imaging genetics associations, making it difficult to interpret the magnitude of reported effects.

In addition to issues of replication and power, heterogeneity among study samples, measures, and methods contributes to a perceived lack of replication in imaging genetics studies. However, these issues point to a partially distinct problem: a lack of convergence. Neuroimaging genetics studies of reading and dyslexia include a great deal of variance in selection of samples, genetic markers, and analytic approaches that makes it difficult to compare findings across studies. With respect to sample, some studies include only individuals with dyslexia, some include only those with typical development, some include both, and still others include individuals with other clinical disorders (e.g., schizophrenia). In addition, sample sizes can vary dramatically from study to study, but most have relatively small homogeneous samples, which presents challenges for generalization. With respect to analytic methods, variability exists in the genotyping approach (e.g., single SNP, multi-SNP, GWAS) and in the neuroimaging approach (e.g., whole-brain analysis, region of interest [ROI]-based analysis, structure vs. function). Furthermore, variability exists in the statistical models and corrections applied at each level.

To illustrate one example of lack of convergence, consider a study by Eicher and colleagues (2016), which included a set of behaviorally associated SNPs on DCDC2, but not the DCDC2 intron 2 deletion (DCDC2d), in their neuroimaging genetics analysis. In this study, researchers observed no associations between DCDC2 SNPs and gray matter measures. However, Meda and colleagues (2008) found an association between gray matter volume and the DCDC2d during their imaging genetics work on DCDC2; thus, the omission of the DCDC2d in the Eicher and colleagues (2016) study could have resulted in a perceived lack of convergence with existing imaging genetics literature on DCDC2.

CONCLUSION

The summary and synthesis of imaging genetics findings presented in this chapter demonstrate the complexity of the neurobiology associated with dyslexia. Many studies find promising associations between dyslexia risk genes and intermediate phenotypes that have previously been implicated in standard neuroimaging studies of dyslexia; that is, imaging genetics studies of DCDC2 (Cope et al., 2012; Darki et al., 2012, 2014; Meda et al., 2008), DYX1C1 (Darki et al., 2012), ROBO1 (Lamminmäki et al., 2012), COMT (Landi et al., 2013), BDNF (Jasińska et al., 2016), and SETBP1 (Perdue et al., 2019) all show relations between variation in these genes and variation in brain structure or function in reading-related regions. However, as in the broader field, we observe failures of replication and/or convergence demonstrated by the contrast in DCDC2–gray matter associations found by Meda and colleagues (2008) and Eicher and colleagues (2016). The path toward convergence and identification of new, relevant genes is paved with large-scale projects that utilize diverse samples of individuals (with and without dyslexia) that build in replication samples and plan to utilize the same methodologies for data collection and analysis. This approach will require both exploratory and confirmatory approaches, as well as collaboration among research teams (likely at multiple locations) with diverse skill sets for careful phenotyping, genotyping, and next-generation imaging genetics analyses.

Furthermore, advances in genetic sequencing and in neuroimaging technologies will help to identify relations among genes, brain, and behavior. One promising new imaging approach is the use of magnetic resonance spectroscopy (MRS). This noninvasive tool allows for in vivo measurement of neurometabolites and neurotransmitters, thereby providing a neurochemical level of exploration for identification of connections between genes and neural function. For example, this method could afford human investigation of evidence linking genes and neurochemistry to atypical neural function in animal models. One such model links mutation of the DCDC2 homolog in mice and altered neural activity driven by dysfunction of the neurotransmitter glutamate (Che, Girgenti,

& LoTurco, 2014; Che, Truong, Fitch, & Loturco, 2016). Indeed, some initial work utilizing MRS in humans has identified links between glutamate and choline and dyslexia and formed the basis for the application of the neural noise hypothesis to the study of dyslexia (e.g., Hancock, Pugh, & Hoeft, 2017; Pugh et al., 2014). Future research with this approach may shed light on additional neurometabolic contributions to reading and language difficulties and, by providing an intermediate level of analysis, further our understanding of the relations among genes, neural function, and reading phenotypes.

Finally, it is time to extend imagining genetics approaches in the study of dyslexia by examining educational and other environmental factors. Researchers can begin this work by looking for associations among genes, neural endophentoypes, and children's response to treatment. Combined with longitudinal studies that begin prior to reading acquisition (see Chapter 5), this work may be able to dissociate genes that are associated with risk for developing dyslexia from those associated with other factors (e.g., protective factors) that may be correlated with dyslexia. With regard to environmental factors more broadly, consider the relation between epigenetic variation and neural endophenotypes. Epigenetic variation (broadly defined) consists of changes to proteins within cells (external to the DNA itself) that govern genetic expression and can be inherited. As such, epigenetic variation has the potential to account for substantial variability in the behavioral phenotype of dyslexia. Although some types of epigenetic variation (those that are inherited) may not help to solve the missing heritability problem per se, given high linkage disequilibrium (a measure of covariance) between structural variation and epigenetic variation, studies of the epigenome can contribute to understanding of causal pathways from gene, to brain, to behavior (Slatkin, 2009). Furthermore, epigenetic variation, unlike variation in DNA structure, need not be stable over development, and thus dynamic measures of the epigenome could also be useful as markers of change in response to treatment. Relations between specific environmental factors and epigenetic variation (e.g., methylation profiles) have been useful for understanding causal links between genes and behavior in other fields (e.g., Tong et al., 2015), but they have not been studied in relation to learning disabilities. Adding this level of analysis will facilitate the development of comprehensive models of the neurobiological basis of dyslexia.

REFERENCES

Brooks, S. J., Nilsson, E. K., Jacobsson, J. A., Stein, D. J., Fredriksson, R., Lind, L., & Schiöth, H. B. (2014). *BDNF* polymorphisms are linked to poorer working memory performance, reduced cerebellar and hippocampal volumes and differences in prefrontal cortex in a Swedish elderly population. *PloS One, 9*(1), e82707.

Carrion-Castillo, A., van Bergen, E., Vino, A., van Zuijen, T., de Jong, P. F., Francks, C., & Fisher, S. E. (2016). Evaluation of results from genome-wide studies of language and reading in a novel independent dataset. *Genes, Brain and Behavior, 15*(6), 531–541. http://doi.org/10.1111/gbb.12299

Che, A., Girgenti, M. J., & LoTurco, J. (2014). The dyslexia-associated gene *DCDC2* is required for spike-timing precision in mouse neocortex. *Biological Psychiatry, 76*(5), 387–396. https://doi.org/10.1016/j.biopsych.2013.08.018

Che, A., Truong, D. T., Fitch, R. H., & LoTurco, J. J. (2016). Mutation of the dyslexia-associated gene *DCDC2* enhances glutamatergic synaptic transmission between Layer 4 neurons in mouse neocortex. *Cerebral Cortex, 26*, 3705–3718. https://doi.org/10.1093/cercor/bhv168

Cope, N., Eicher, J. D., Meng, H., Gibson, C. J., Hager, K., Lacadie, C., . . . Gruen, J. R. (2012). Variants in the *DYX2* locus are associated with altered brain activation in reading-related brain regions in subjects with reading disability. *NeuroImage, 63*(1), 148–156. https://doi.org/10.1016/j.neuroimage.2012.06.037

Czamara, D., Bruder, J., Becker, J., Bartling, J., Hoffmann, P., Ludwig, K. U., . . . Schulte-Körne, G. (2011). Association of a rare variant with mismatch negativity in a region between *KIAA0319* and *DCDC2* in dyslexia. *Behavior Genetics, 41*(1), 110–119.

Darki, F., Peyrard-Janvid, M., Matsson, H., Kere, J., & Klingberg, T. (2012). Three dyslexia susceptibility genes, *DYX1C1*, *DCDC2*, and *KIAA0319*, affect temporo-parietal white matter structure. *Biological Psychiatry, 72*(8), 671–676. http://doi.org/10.1016/j.biopsych.2012.05.008

Darki, F., Peyrard-Janvid, M., Matsson, H., Kere, J., & Klingberg, T. (2014). *DCDC2* polymorphism is associated with left temporoparietal gray and white matter structures during development. *Journal of Neuroscience, 34*(43), 14455–14462. https://doi.org/10.1523/JNEUROSCI.1216-14.2014

Dickinson, D., & Elvevåg, B. (2009). Genes, cognition and brain through a *COMT* lens. *Neuroscience, 164*(1), 72–87.

Eicher, J. D., Montgomery, A. M., Akshoomoff, N., Amaral, D. G., Bloss, C. S., Libiger, O., . . . Ernst, T. (2016). Dyslexia and language impairment associated genetic markers influence cortical thickness and white matter in typically developing children. *Brain Imaging and Behavior, 10*(1), 272–282.

Fletcher, J. M. (2009). Dyslexia: The evolution of a scientific concept. *Journal of the International Neuropsychological Society, 15*(4), 501–508.

Gottlieb, G., & Lickliter, R. (2007). Probabilistic epigenesis. *Developmental Science, 10*(1), 1–11. http://doi.org/10.1111/j.1467-7687.2007.00556.x

Grabitz, C. R., Button, K. S., Munafò, M. R., Newbury, D. F., Pernet, C. R., Thompson, P. A., & Bishop, D. V. M. (2017). Logical and methodological issues affecting genetic studies of humans reported in top neuroscience journals. *Journal of Cognitive Neuroscience, 30*(1), 1–18. http://doi.org/10.1162/jocn_a_01192

Hancock, R., Pugh, K. R., & Hoeft, F. (2017). Neural noise hypothesis of developmental dyslexia. *Trends in Cognitive Sciences, 21*(6), 434–448. https://doi.org/10.1016/j.tics.2017.03.008

Hirschhorn, J. N., & Daly, M. J. (2005). Genome-wide association studies for common diseases and complex traits. *Nature Reviews Genetics, 6*, 95–108. http://doi.org/10.1038/nrg1521

Human Genome Sequencing Consortium, I. (2004). Finishing the euchromatic sequence of the human genome. *Nature, 431*(7011), 931–945. http://doi.org/10.1038/nature03001

Jasińska, K., & Landi, N. (2019). Dyslexia and its neurobiological basis. In G. de Zubicaray & N. Schiller (Eds.), *The Oxford handbook of neurolinguistics* (pp. 626–646). New York, NY: Oxford University Press.

Jasińska, K. K., Molfese, P. J., Kornilov, S. A., Mencl, W. E., Frost, S. J., Lee, M., . . . Landi, N. (2016). The *BDNF* Val⁶⁶Met polymorphism influences reading ability and patterns of neural activation in children. *PLoS One, 11*(8), e0157449. http://doi.org/10.1371/journal.pone.0157449

Kornilov, S. A., & Grigorenko, E. L. (2016). Molecular genetics methods for developmental scientists. In D. Cicchetti (Ed.), *Developmental psychopathology* (3rd ed., pp. 378–415). Hoboken, NJ: Wiley.

Kornilov, S. A., Rakhlin, N., Koposov, R., Lee, M., Yrigollen, C., Caglayan, A. O., . . . Grigorenko, E. L. (2016). Genome-wide association and exome sequencing study of language disorder in an isolated population. *Pediatrics, 137*(4).

Lamminmäki, S., Massinen, S., Nopola-Hemmi, J., Kere, J., & Hari, R. (2012). Human *ROBO1* regulates interaural interaction in auditory pathways. *The Journal of Neuroscience, 32*(3), 966–971. http://doi.org/10.1523/JNEUROSCI.4007-11.2012

Landi, N., Frost, S. J., Mencl, W. E., Preston, J. L., Jacobsen, L. K., Lee, M., . . . Grigorenko, E. L. (2013). The *COMT* Val/Met polymorphism is associated with reading-related skills and consistent patterns of functional neural activation. *Developmental Science, 16*(1), 13–23. http://doi.org/10.1111/j.1467-7687.2012.01180.x

Landi, N., Mencl, W. E., Frost, S. J., Sandak, R., Chen, H., & Pugh, K. R. (2010). An fMRI study of multimodal semantic and phonological processing in reading disabled adolescents. *Annals of Dyslexia, 60*(1), 102–121.

Landi, N., & Perdue, M. (in press). Neuroimaging genetic studies of specific reading disability and developmental language disorder: A review. *Language and Linguistics Compass.*

Massinen, S., Hokkanen, M. E., Matsson, H., Tammimies, K., Tapia-Páez, I., Dahlström-Heuser, V., . . . Peyrard-Janvid, M. (2011). Increased expression of the dyslexia candidate gene *DCDC2* affects length and signaling of primary cilia in neurons. *PLoS One, 6*(6), e20580.

Meda, S. A., Gelernter, J., Gruen, J. R., Calhoun, V. D., Meng, H., Cope, N. A., & Pearlson, G. D. (2008). Polymorphism of *DCDC2* reveals differences in cortical morphology of healthy individuals—A preliminary voxel based morphometry study. *Brain Imaging and Behavior, 2*(1), 21–26. http://doi.org/10.1007/s11682-007-9012-1

Meng, H., Smith, S. D., Hager, K., Held, M., Liu, J., Olson, R. K., . . . Sherman Weissman, C. M. (2005). *DCDC2* is associated with reading disability and modulates neuronal development in the brain. *Proceedings of the National Academy of Sciences, 102*(47), 17053–17058. Retrieved from http://www.pnas.org/content/102/47/17053.full.pdf

Meyer-Lindenberg, A., Kohn, P. D., Kolachana, B., Kippenhan, S., McInerney-Leo, A., Nussbaum, R., . . . Berman, K. F. (2005). Midbrain dopamine and prefrontal function in humans: Interaction and modulation by *COMT* genotype. *Nature Neuroscience, 8*(5), 594–596. http://doi.org/10.1038/nn1438

Newbury, D., Monaco, A., & Paracchini, S. (2014). Reading and language disorders: The importance of both quantity and quality. *Genes, 5*(2), 285–309. http://doi.org/10.3390/genes5020285

Norton, E. S., Beach, S. D., & Gabrieli, J. D. E. (2015). Neurobiology of dyslexia. *Current Opinion in Neurobiology, 30*, 73–8. http://doi.org/10.1016/j.conb.2014.09.007

Numakawa, T., Suzuki, S., Kumamaru, E., Adachi, N., Richards, M., & Kunugi, H. (2010). *BDNF* function and intracellular signaling in neurons. *Histology and Histopathology, 25*(2), 237–258. http://doi.org/10.14670/HH-25.237

Ozernov-Palchik, O., & Gaab, N. (2016). Tackling the "dyslexia paradox": Reading brain and behavior for early markers of developmental dyslexia. *Wiley Interdisciplinary Reviews: Cognitive Science, 7*(2), 156–176.

Perdue, M., Mascheretti, S., Kornilov, S. A., Jasińska, K. K., Ryherd, K., Mencl, W. E., . . . Landi, N. (2019). Common variation within the *SETBP1* gene is associated with reading-related skills and patterns of functional neural activation. *Neuropsychologia, 130*, 44–51. https://doi.org/10.1016/j.neuropsychologia.2018.07.015

Peschansky, V. J., Burbridge, T. J., Volz, A. J., Fiondella, C., Wissner-Gross, Z., Galaburda, A. M., . . . Rosen, G. D. (2010). The effect of variation in expression of the candidate dyslexia susceptibility gene homolog Kiaa0319 on neuronal migration and dendritic morphology in the rat. *Cerebral Cortex, 20*(4), 884–897. http://doi.org/10.1093/cercor/bhp154

Plomin, R. (2013). Commentary: Missing heritability, polygenic scores, and gene–environment correlation. *Journal of Child Psychology and Psychiatry, 54*(10), 1147–1149.

Poon, M.-W., Tsang, W.-H., Chan, S.-O., Li, H.-M., Ng, H.-K., & Waye, M. M.-Y. (2011). Dyslexia-associated Kiaa0319-like protein interacts with axon guidance receptor Nogo Receptor 1. *Cellular and Molecular Neurobiology, 31*(1), 27–35. http://doi.org/10.1007/s10571-010-9549-1

Pugh, K. R., Frost, S. J., Rothman, D. L., Hoeft, F., Del Tufo, S. N., Mason, G. F., . . . Preston, J. L. (2014). Glutamate and choline levels predict individual differences in reading ability in emergent readers. *Journal of Neuroscience, 34*(11), 4082–4089.

Pugh, K. R., Mencl, W. E., Jenner, A. R., Katz, L., Frost, S. J., Lee, J. R., . . . Shaywitz, B. A. (2001). Neurobiological studies of reading and reading disability. *Journal of Communication Disorders, 34*(6), 479–492. https://doi.org/10.1016/S0021-9924(01)00060-0

Richlan, F., Kronbichler, M., & Wimmer, H. (2009). Functional abnormalities in the dyslexic brain: A quantitative meta-analysis of neuroimaging studies. *Human Brain Mapping, 30*(10), 3299–3308. https://doi.org/10.1002/hbm.20752

Richlan, F., Kronbichler, M., & Wimmer, H. (2011). Meta-analyzing brain dysfunctions in dyslexic children and adults. *NeuroImage, 56*(3), 1735–1742. doi.10.1016/j.neuroimage .2011.02.040

Richlan, F., Kronbichler, M., & Wimmer, H. (2013). Structural abnormalities in the dyslexic brain: A meta-analysis of voxel-based morphometry studies. *Human Brain Mapping, 34*(11), 3055–3065. https://doi.org/10.1002/hbm.22127

Rosen, G. D., Bai, J., Wang, Y., Fiondella, C. G., Threlkeld, S. W., LoTurco, J. J., & Galaburda, A. M. (2007). Disruption of neuronal migration by RNAi of *Dyx1c1* results in neocortical and hippocampal malformations. *Cerebral Cortex, 17*(11), 2562–2572. https://doi .org/10.1093/cercor/bhl162

Schulte-Körne, G., Deimel, W., Bartling, J., & Remschmidt, H. (2001). Speech perception deficit in dyslexic adults as measured by mismatch negativity (MMN). *International Journal of Psychophysiology, 40*(1), 77–87.

Schumacher, J., Hoffmann, P., Schmäl, C., Schulte-Körne, G., & Nöthen, M. M. (2007). Genetics of dyslexia: The evolving landscape. *Journal of Medical Genetics, 44*(5), 289–297.

Slatkin, M. (2009). Epigenetic inheritance and the missing heritability problem. *Genetics, 182*(3), 845–850.

Szalkowski, C. E., Fiondella, C. F., Truong, D. T., Rosen, G. D., LoTurco, J. J., & Fitch, R. H. (2013). The effects of *Kiaa0319* knockdown on cortical and subcortical anatomy in male rats. *International Journal of Developmental Neuroscience, 31*(2), 116–122. http://doi .org/10.1016/j.ijdevneu.2012.11.008

Tammimies, K., Bieder, A., Lauter, G., Sugiaman-Trapman, D., Torchet, R., Hokkanen, M.-E., . . . Swoboda, P. (2016). Ciliary dyslexia candidate genes *DYX1C1* and *DCDC2* are regulated by Regulatory Factor X (RFX) transcription factors through X-box promoter motifs. *The FASEB Journal, 30*(10), 3578–3587. https://doi.org/10.1096/fj.201500124RR

Tarkar, A., Loges, N. T., Slagle, C. E., Francis, R., Dougherty, G. W., Tamayo, J. V, . . . Omran, H. (2013). *DYX1C1* is required for axonemal dynein assembly and ciliary motility. *Nature Genetics, 45*(9), 995–1003. https://doi.org/10.1038/ng.2707

Threlkeld, S. W., McClure, M. M., Bai, J., Wang, Y., LoTurco, J. J., Rosen, G. D., & Fitch, R. H. (2007). Developmental disruptions and behavioral impairments in rats following in utero RNAi of *Dyx1c1*. *Brain Research Bulletin, 71*(5), 508–514. https://doi.org/10.1016/J .BRAINRESBULL.2006.11.005

Tong, Z., Han, C., Qiang, M., Wang, W., Lv, J., Zhang, S., . . . He, R. (2015). Age-related formaldehyde interferes with DNA methyltransferase function, causing memory loss in Alzheimer's disease. *Neurobiology of Aging, 36*, 100–110. http://dx.doi.org/10.1016/j .neurobiolaging.2014.07.018

Vandermosten, M., Hoeft, F., & Norton, E. S. (2016). Integrating MRI brain imaging studies of pre-reading children with current theories of developmental dyslexia: A review and quantitative meta-analysis. *Current Opinion in Behavioral Sciences, 10*, 155–161. doi:10.1016/j.cobeha.2016.06.007

Velayos-Baeza, A., Levecque, C., Kobayashi, K., Holloway, Z. G., & Monaco, A. P. (2010). The dyslexia-associated KIAA0319 protein undergoes proteolytic processing with {gamma}-secretase-independent intramembrane cleavage. *The Journal of Biological Chemistry, 285*(51), 40148–40162. http://doi.org/10.1074/jbc.M110.145961

Wang, Y., Paramasivam, M., Thomas, A., Bai, J., Kaminen-Ahola, N., Kere, J., . . . LoTurco, J. J. (2006). *DYX1C1* functions in neuronal migration in developing neocortex. *Neuroscience, 143*, 515–522. Retrieved from http://ac.els-cdn.com/S0306452206010918/1-s 2.0-S0306452206010918-main.pdf?_tid=aac0d08a-1581-11e7-b37a-

CHAPTER 4

Diagnosing Dyslexia
How Deep Should We Dig?
Peter F. de Jong

SUMMARY

Poor word-level reading and/or spelling are generally regarded as characteristics of dyslexia, but whether other criteria also should be met to qualify for the disorder is hotly debated. One of these, a discrepancy between the level of reading ability and intelligence, has been mostly discarded. This chapter considers another additional criterion: the presence of cognitive deficits that are believed to cause dyslexia. Two issues are addressed that speak to whether it is valid to withhold a diagnosis of dyslexia from individuals with severe reading and/or spelling problems but without underlying cognitive deficits. The first issue is whether it is safe to assume that all underlying causes of dyslexia are known. Family risk studies of dyslexia suggest that this is not the case. The second issue concerns the status of deficits. Currently a deficit is conceived as a risk factor, which only raises the likelihood that a disorder occurs. As a consequence, by mere chance, there will always be a group of individuals with the disorder but without a deficit. It is also argued that various types of deficits are involved. Some of them cannot be interpreted as risk factors for atypical development, as they reflect the functioning of (parts of) the reading system at a certain moment in its development. Overall, current evidence does not support the use of underlying cognitive deficits as an additional criterion in diagnosing dyslexia. A diagnosis seems warranted in the case of severe reading and/or spelling problems that are not caused by a lack of opportunity to learn to read and spell. In closing, I note that the search for additional criteria to pinpoint dyslexia will continue. Researchers will remain interested in pursuing subtypes that are informative for intervention; public pressure will demand more clarification of the meaning and consequences of the cutoff criteria used to distinguish typical and poor performance in reading and spelling.

INTRODUCTION

From the first case descriptions of dyslexia, there has been a strong urge to make dyslexia special. Pringle Morgan, for example, described the 14-year-old Percy F. as "a bright and intelligent boy" whose reading disorder is "so remarkable and so pronounced" that it must be "due to some congenital deficit" (1896, p. 1387). Implicit in the description is that dyslexia is more than a difficulty in the acquisition of age-appropriate levels of word reading (Parrila & Protopapas, 2017) and/or spelling (de Jong & van Bergen,

31

2017). Pringle Morgan hinted at a discrepancy with intelligence and a specific underlying cause. Over the years, additional criteria have been proposed to define dyslexia (Tannock, 2013). They generally refer to the unexpectedness of the reading (and/or spelling) difficulties and help to distinguish dyslexia from poor reading in general (Fletcher, Lyon, Fuchs, & Barnes, 2007; Parrila & Protopapas, 2017).

Unexpectedness is often conceived as discrepancy. Three types of discrepancies have been proposed. The discrepancy between IQ and reading ability is the oldest. The inclusion of an IQ–reading ability discrepancy in the definition of dyslexia, a long-standing debate, seems to have ended, given overwhelming evidence to discard it (e.g., Fletcher et al., 2007; Tannock, 2013). Indeed, the discrepancy is no longer present in the definition of dyslexia in the *Diagnostic and Statistical Manual of Mental Disorders, Fifth Edition* (DSM-5; American Psychiatric Association, 2013).

The second proposal can be described as a discrepancy between the opportunity to learn to read and the level of reading ability. The response to intervention (RTI) approach is based on this idea (Fletcher et al., 2007; Fuchs, Fuchs, & Compton, 2012). In the RTI approach, a substantial lag in reading (or spelling) is insufficient to obtain a diagnosis of dyslexia (or learning disability in general). Additional criteria are poor growth in reading ability during general education classroom instruction at school (Tier 1) and a lack of response to more specialized and evidence-based interventions in small groups (Tiers 2 and 3). Thus, in the RTI approach, dyslexia is considered as a discrepancy between (poor) growth in reading and the quality of instruction (Fuchs et al., 2012). Dyslexia is likely if reading difficulties persist despite instruction that is of sufficient quality to foster reading acquisition. Another approach that rests on an opportunity–ability discrepancy is the use of exclusionary criteria in addition to the requirement of poor reading. This approach is featured, for example, in definitions in DSM-5 and of the International Dyslexia Association. Exclusionary criteria include the absence of intellectual disabilities, visual and hearing problems, mental or neurological disorders, and inadequate instruction (as in RTI). Clearly such conditions impede the possibility to acquire reading ability and provide compelling alternative explanations for poor reading ability (but see also Chapter 9 for difficulties with these exclusionary criteria).

The third discrepancy concerns a disparity between poor reading ability and the severity of underlying cognitive deficits (Hale et al., 2010). Individuals with poor reading but without any accompanying underlying cognitive deficit do not qualify for a diagnosis of dyslexia. The inclusion of underlying deficits in the diagnosis of dyslexia is clearly reminiscent of the idea by Pringle Morgan (1896) that the reading problems in some children are so remarkable that they must be due to one (or more) specific underlying causes (see also Chapter 11). Some have gone a step further and proposed that there should be a discrepancy between cognitive weaknesses and strengths (e.g., Hale et al., 2010), denoted as cognitive discrepancy models (Taylor, Miciak, Fletcher, & Francis, 2017). Taylor and colleagues (2017) noted that such models are very similar to the reading ability–intelligence discrepancy model for the diagnosis of dyslexia. Indeed, arguments to discard the model are the same: classifications are unreliable and unstable, differences between those with weaknesses with and without strengths are minimal on the underlying causes of dyslexia, and the pattern of strengths and weaknesses is not informative for intervention (Fletcher & Miciak, 2017; Taylor et al., 2017).

In this chapter, I consider the role of underlying cognitive deficits in diagnosing dyslexia. I give two additional reasons why underlying cognitive deficits should not be included in diagnosing dyslexia. Then, I conclude that the diagnosis should be based on the severity of reading and/or spelling problems in combination with sufficient opportunity to acquire these abilities. Notwithstanding this conclusion, I expect a constant need to pinpoint dyslexia will persist; therefore, I briefly consider some alternative possibilities to do this.

UNDERLYING DEFICITS AND THE DIAGNOSIS OF DYSLEXIA

A considerable group of approximately 20%–25% of poor readers seem to have no accompanying underlying cognitive deficits (e.g., Pennington et al., 2012). They would not qualify for the diagnosis of dyslexia if the existence of underlying deficits is demanded. This raises the question of why individuals without such deficits might read poorly. One answer, which could support the use of underlying deficits, is that the causes of reading difficulties in this group are largely environmental, such as poor education or, more generally, a lack of opportunities to learn to read. There are, however, more plausible explanations. One explanation is simply that not all relevant cognitive deficits underlying dyslexia are yet known. Another explanation is that this group is an inevitable consequence of the probabilistic status of cognitive deficits. Both explanations are considered next.

Are All Deficits Known?

At first sight, it seems easy to show that not all underlying cognitive deficits of dyslexia are known. It suffices to state that there is probably no study in which dyslexia status or the full variation in reading ability can be perfectly predicted from cognitive abilities or deficits. This failure to predict might be due to unknown cognitive factors as well as unknown environmental circumstances that also influence the development of reading. A main reason to include underlying deficits in the diagnosis of dyslexia, however, is that this diagnosis is only believed appropriate when it concerns a "congenital deficit" (Pringle Morgan, 1896). The question then becomes whether currently known underlying cognitive abilities capture all genetic variance in reading ability. Family risk studies can shed light on this question.

Family risk studies are based on the finding that having a parent with dyslexia increases the likelihood that a child will develop dyslexia (Snowling & Melby-Lervåg, 2016). Parents pass on genes to their children and provide an environment that might be more or less favorable for the development of reading (Sénéchal, Whissell, & Bildfell, 2017). Thus, in principle, parent–offspring similarities in reading ability can be due to both genetic and cultural transmission. However, there is some evidence to suggest that the correlation between parents' and children's reading ability is mostly due to genetic transmission. First, Wadsworth, Corley, Hewitt, Plomin, and DeFries (2002) found that a parent–offspring relation was absent in adoptive families. In these families, parents and children had no genes in common, and only cultural transmission could explain a relationship between the reading ability of parents and children. Given the absence of a relationship, it seemed that there was no effect of the family environment. This is supported by a more recent study by Swagerman and colleagues (2017), who modeled the relationships of reading ability among twins, their siblings, and their parents. In this twin-family design, genetic and cultural transmission could be nicely separated. Swagerman and colleagues found that the parent–offspring relation was mainly due to genetic transmission. Second, several studies suggested that the home literacy environment of children with a family risk of dyslexia does not differ from the environment of children without family risk (e.g., van Bergen, de Jong, Maassen, & van der Leij, 2014). The increased likelihood in the former group of children to develop dyslexia can therefore be explained only by the genes that parents and children have in common. In all, these findings suggest that the relationship between parents and children's reading ability is mainly genetic.

If all deficits are known and underlying cognitive deficits reflect the genetic roots of dyslexia, then it follows that the parent–offspring relationship, which is largely genetic in origin, should be fully mediated by children's underlying cognitive abilities of reading. Two recent studies suggest that this is not the case. Van Viersen and colleagues (2018) followed children with and without a family risk for dyslexia from kindergarten through Grade 6. In kindergarten, the researchers assessed children's phonological awareness (PA), rapid automatic naming (RAN), and letter knowledge (LK). These cognitive abilities are generally believed to fuel reading development and to be the major deficits underlying dyslexia. PA is the ability to detect and manipulate phonemes in spoken words. RAN refers to the speed of naming symbols (letters, objects, digits). From the beginning of second grade onward, the researchers assessed children's reading accuracy and fluency.

Van Viersen and colleagues (2018) specified a longitudinal model to capture the relationships among all underlying cognitive abilities and reading skills from kindergarten to sixth grade. The relevant part of their model for this chapter is displayed in Figure 4.1. The solid lines show the independent effects of LK, PA, and RAN in kindergarten on individual differences in reading ability in the beginning of second grade. It is noteworthy that LK had an effect on both reading accuracy and fluency, whereas the effects of PA and RAN depended on the measure of reading; PA had an (independent) effect on accuracy, RAN only on fluency. The dotted lines reveal effects of family risk. As expected, FR had an effect on all kindergarten cognitive skills. Children with a family risk for dyslexia had a lower ability to name colors and objects in kindergarten and had less LK and PA. The most interesting results, however, are the direct effects of family risk on reading accuracy and fluency. This implies that the effect of family risk is only partly mediated by the underlying cognitive abilities of reading at the end of kindergarten. Put differently, the genetic relationship between parental reading ability, one or no parent with dyslexia, and children's ability to read is only partly explained by children's underlying cognitive abilities.

This result resonates well with findings from research with twins. Such research enables the estimation of the genetic variance that abilities

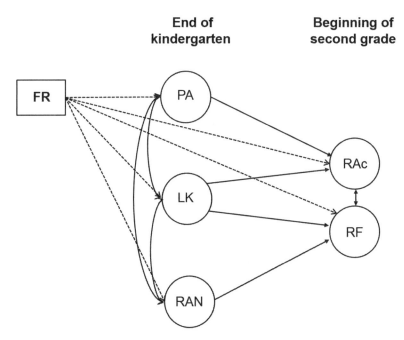

Figure 4.1. Effects of family risk (FR; dotted lines) on cognitive abilities at the end of kindergarten on reading accuracy (RAc) and fluency (RF) at the beginning of second grade. (*Key:* LK, letter knowledge; PA, phonological awareness; RAN, rapid automatic naming). (*Source:* van Viersen et al., 2018).

have in common, roughly the extent to which they are determined by the same genes. Byrne and colleagues (2009) showed that the genetic variance in reading and spelling at the end of second grade could only partly be accounted for by the major underlying abilities of reading development at the end of kindergarten. As reading is acquired, new sources of genetic variability (novel genes) apparently start to exert effects. However, note that neither the study by van Viersen and colleagues (2018) nor the behavior genetic study by Byrne and colleagues (2009) considered underlying deficits and reading ability at the same occasion, as is usual when diagnosing dyslexia.

An earlier study by van Bergen, Bishop, van Zuijen, and de Jong (2015) did look at underlying deficits and reading ability at the same time. They examined the relationship between the reading ability of children from 6 to 16 years and their parents and to what extent this relationship was mediated by the children's underlying cognitive abilities. The study had two novel features. First, van Bergen and colleagues had an unselected sample covering the full range of reading and its underlying cognitive abilities. Second, the study included both parents. In most family risk studies, no distinction is made between the risk of having a father or mother with dyslexia. Underlying cognitive abilities involved PA and RAN but also visual attention span (VAS). VAS was measured as the number of letters that can be reported correctly from a string of letters exposed for 200 milliseconds. Several studies show that VAS has an independent contribution to the prediction of reading (e.g., Bosse, Tainturier, & Valdois, 2007; van den Boer, van Bergen, & de Jong, 2015), although whether the measure is a pure reflection of visual attention is debated.

First, van Bergen and colleagues (2015) considered the parent–offspring relations for fathers and mothers. The results showed that both parents contributed equally to children's reading ability. The observed parent–offspring correlations were about equal to what would be expected in cases of pure genetic transmission, providing further support for the largely genetic origins of the parent–offspring relation in word-reading ability. Next, van Bergen and colleagues examined whether children's cognitive abilities (PA, RAN, and VAS) could account for the parent–child relationship in reading. The result was clear-cut. Indirect effects of parents on their children's reading ability; that is, through children's underlying skills, could account for just over half of the total effects of parental reading ability on their children's reading ability.

Taken together, current evidence suggests that parental reading ability can be conceived as a genetic risk factor for children's reading proficiency. These genetic effects of parents on their children are only partly mediated by the currently known underlying cognitive abilities of reading. This suggests that, as of yet, not all genetically determined cognitive deficits of dyslexia are known.

The Status of Deficits

Developmental disorders, such as dyslexia, are now generally believed to be the outcome of an interplay between many genetic and environmental deficits (or causes) (Pennington, 2006). Causes are no longer considered deterministic but are conceived as risk factors (e.g., Pennington, 2006; van Bergen, van der Leij, & de Jong, 2014). None of the associated deficits is sufficient or necessary to lead to the disorder. The presence of a deficit only raises the probability that a developmental disorder (e.g., dyslexia) will occur. As a consequence, there will always be a group of individuals with dyslexia who do not have the underlying deficit and, vice versa, a group of individuals with the underlying deficit who do not have dyslexia. Given a probabilistic conception of causes, just by mere chance poor readers without underlying cognitive deficits are to be expected.

But can all deficits be regarded as risk factors? If not, what does this imply for the use of cognitive deficits in diagnosing dyslexia? Genetic findings are often mentioned in support of an interpretation of cognitive deficits as risk factors. Gene variants associated with dyslexia are also found, although less often, in individuals without dyslexia (Bishop, 2015). Moreover, the probabilistic conception of causes of dyslexia also fits very well with findings that none of the underlying cognitive abilities are perfectly related to reading ability (de Jong & van Bergen, 2017). These arguments are not entirely convincing. Genes are very distant from reading behavior, and the pathway from genes to reading is poorly understood. In addition, conceiving causes as probabilistic is not the only way that imperfect relationships between cognitive abilities and reading proficiency can occur.

Distal and Proximate Causes   Jackson and Coltheart (2001) made a distinction between distal and proximal causes of atypical reading. Proximal causes refer to components of the reading system. This is the system that is used to read a word, or put differently, the mechanisms that can be used to generate the spoken form of a word from its written counterpart. The components of the reading system are what lung capacity and muscle strength are for the marathon runner: they contribute to the system's overall performance. An example of a (computational) model of the reading system is the Dual-Route Cascaded model specifying various components involved in reading (Coltheart, Rastle, Perry, Langdon, & Ziegler, 2001). All components are needed, but the functioning of each component is only partly related to the outcome of the system. A poor reader can have deficits in one or more of these components (e.g., Kohnen et al., 2018). As long as a component has not been entirely switched off, as in acquired dyslexia, no deficit can be sufficient to cause dyslexia.

Distal causes are related to reading performance but do not concern a component of the reading system. A distal cause influences the *development* of the reading system. Distal causes can be more and less distal to the reading system. This is because each distal cause is dependent on more basic processes, such as phonological awareness on auditory processing (Vellutino, Fletcher, Snowling, & Scanlon, 2004). However, distal causes can also concern more general characteristics of the person that affect reading acquisition, such as socioeconomic status. Distal causes are often part of a causal chain (see Protopapas, 2014). As a cause is farther down the causal chain (i.e., more distant from reading), then its relation with reading ability will be lower. Moreover, because reading development and atypical reading have multiple causes, it is to be expected that each cause is only moderately related to reading.

From a developmental perspective, it makes perfect sense to consider distal causes and aversive environmental factors, as well as (genetic) within-child factors, as risk factors (e.g., Sameroff, 2010). A distal deficit might increase the likelihood of a cascade of developmental processes leading to a negative outcome, but whether these intermediate processes occur is dependent on a range of other distal factors, including protective factors (e.g., Kiuru et al., 2013; Sameroff, 2010) that can lead to resistance to risk factors. Therefore, a distal cause does not determine a specified outcome but only increases its likelihood (Rutter, 2006).

In contrast, proximal deficits do not concern development but are in effect at the moment that the performance of the reading system is measured, for example, through a word-reading test. They are part of the system and contribute to its overall outcome, just as lung capacity is one of the factors that determines running performance. In essence, proximal causes are deterministic and not probabilistic. Proximal causes co-determine reading proficiency.

Thus, not all deficits are alike. Distal deficits refer to antecedents of reading development. Proximal deficits are part of the reading system that is the outcome of development. Moreover, distal deficits are probabilistic, whereas proximal deficits are not. If causes or deficits are probabilistic, just by chance a group of individuals with reading problems but without accompanying deficits will be found. However, with respect to proximal deficits, the existence of such a group can only mean that all relevant components of the reading system are not yet known.

Phonological Awareness and Rapid Automatic Naming   Two major deficits generally believed to underlie dyslexia are PA and RAN. The question is how these deficits should be qualified. PA concerns language processing and not reading; therefore, it can be regarded as a distal deficit. But what about RAN?

From a theoretical point of view, RAN has often been tied to the reading system. For example, Norton and Wolf (2012) stated that RAN acts as "a microcosm of the processes involved in reading" (p. 427). RAN and reading aloud are similar in many respects, such as multi-element sequence processing (Protopapas, Katopodi, Altani, & Georgiou, 2018). Recent evidence

Table 4.1.   Correlations between rapid automatic naming and the reading of short, high-frequency words for Dutch, English, and Greek children

Format	Dutch[a]	English[a]	Greek[b]
Serial	.76	.70	.66
Discrete	.80	.86	.78

[a]*Source:* van den Boer, Georgiou, & de Jong (2016); [b]*Source:* Protopapas, Katopodi, Altani, & Georgiou (2018).

tends to provide support for the similarity of RAN and reading. Van den Boer, Georgiou, and de Jong (2016) gave a reading task and a RAN task to groups of fifth-grade readers from the Netherlands who were learning to read in Dutch and from Canada who were learning to read in English. The reading task for each group consisted of high-frequency four-letter words in their own language. Both the reading and the RAN task were given in two formats: the traditional serial format of rows of words or symbols (digits and letters) and a discrete format in which the words and symbols were presented one by one. The results were striking (see Table 4.1). In the serial format, correlations between RAN and reading were .70 or higher. Correlations were even above 0.80 in the discrete format. Similar results were found by Protopapas and colleagues (2018) with Greek sixth-grade children, although the correlations were somewhat lower, possibly due to the use of two-syllable instead of one-syllable words.

What these findings show is that under certain conditions, that is, with short high- frequency words, reading and RAN are almost the same. Their relationship is about as high as between two reading tasks. This suggests that RAN reflects a component of the reading system. By analogy, running performance would be only dependent on lung capacity if no other relevant differences among runners existed.

In sum, the two major cognitive deficits underlying dyslexia are of a different type. PA is a distal deficit. It is a risk factor that affects the development of the reading system. RAN is a proximal deficit, indicative of the functioning of a component of this system. It does not make sense conceptually to include such disparate deficits in the diagnosis of dyslexia.

PINPOINTING DYSLEXIA: CLOSING REMARKS

There is not sufficient evidence to grant the diagnosis of dyslexia exclusively to individuals with specific underlying cognitive deficits. Reading problems without known underlying cognitive deficits are not more likely to be due to environmental causes. Moreover, as with the IQ–achievement discrepancy, the distinction of different groups of poor readers is unreliable, stability is poor, and the distinction is not informative for intervention (Fletcher et al., 2007; Schatschneider, Wagner, Hart, & Tighe, 2016;

Taylor et al., 2017). The developmental pathways toward poor reading are insufficiently understood to predict the outcome from underlying causes. Likewise, researchers do not yet have the necessary knowledge of the reading system to determine in all cases why it breaks down. Therefore, the next best option is to confine the term *dyslexia* to the lower end of the reading ability distribution (with an arbitrary cut off) and, in addition, ensure that the reading and/or spelling problems are not environmentally caused, that is, by a lack of opportunity to acquire reading.

Lack of opportunity can be determined by a form of RTI (see the Hybrid model of Spencer et al., 2014) or by considering exclusionary factors (e.g., DSM-5) or both, but neither is without problems. RTI seems promising but comes with a lot of practical problems (e.g., de Jong & van Bergen, 2017; Fuchs et al., 2012). The choice of the proper exclusionary criteria is not without problems either. In DSM-5, a lack of proficiency in the language of instruction is on the list of exclusionary criteria. This criterion can be debated. Whether insufficient knowledge of the language of instruction has an effect on the acquisition of basic reading skills is not yet clear (e.g., Agirdag & Vanlaar, 2018). Moreover, this criterion tends to exclude from a diagnosis of dyslexia substantial numbers of children who come from families that speak heritage languages or dialects at home (see Chapter 9). Also, for these children, instruction in school should be sufficient for reading acquisition. Therefore, apart from structural neurological restrictions, inadequate instruction at school should suffice as an exclusion criterion. However, note that despite the fact that poor-quality instruction may lead to withholding the diagnosis of dyslexia, this group of poor readers and/ or spellers still needs help.

The recurring attempts to pinpoint dyslexia to a special group show that it is hard to accept that no distinction can be made among groups of poor readers. In closing, I mention three reasons for this and accompanying issues for future consideration. First, researchers remain interested in finding subtypes of dyslexia that can inform treatment (Kohnen et al., 2018; Norton & Wolf, 2012; see also Chapter 11). Several subtypes have been proposed, but the most promising seem to be those that are tied to the proximal causes of reading. Still, we are far from knowing which subtypes to distinguish and how they respond to different kinds of instruction. Second, there is ongoing public pressure to keep the costs of dyslexia low and make sure that treatment is given to only those who really need it. Therefore, it seems hardly acceptable that dyslexia be restricted to the lower end of the distribution of reading disability with an arbitrary cutoff. The problem is aggravated by the cutoffs that are currently in use, 1.5 or 2 standard deviations below the population mean. Such cutoffs are devoid of meaning. It is important to substantiate cutoffs, for example by showing the negative consequences of the various levels of reading ability for daily literate functioning. Dyslexia is not only a disability but also a handicap, the negative impact of the disability (Elbro, 2010).

As a related reason, public pressure to pinpoint dyslexia is also due to the observation that some people seem not to be affected by their poor reading ability. Large individual differences exist in how dyslexia is experienced and how persons with dyslexia cope with its potentially negative consequences. More knowledge is needed about the origins of these differences: why some seem to cope quite well whereas many experience great difficulties.

REFERENCES

Agirdag, O., & Vanlaar, G. (2018). Does mere exposure to the language of instruction lead to higher academic achievement? A cross-national examination. *International Journal of Bilingualism, 22,* 123–137.

American Psychiatric Association. (2013). *Diagnostic and statistical manual of mental disorders* (5th ed.). Arlington, VA: Author.

Bishop, D. V. M. (2015). The interface between genetics and psychology: Lessons from developmental dyslexia. *Proceedings of the Royal Society B: Biological Sciences, 282*(1806), 1–8. http://dx.doi.org/10.1098/rspb.2014.3139

Bosse, M., Tainturier, M. J., & Valdois, S. (2007). Developmental dyslexia: The visual attention span deficit hypothesis. *Cognition, 104*(2), 198–230. http://dx.doi.org/10.1016/j.cognition.2006.05.009

Byrne, B., Coventry, W. L., Olson, R. K., Samuelsson, S., Corley, R., Willcutt, E. G., . . . DeFries, J. C. (2009). Genetic and environmental influences on aspects of literacy and language in early childhood: Continuity and change from preschool to Grade 2. *Journal of Neurolinguistics, 22*(3), 219–236. http://dx.doi.org/10.1016/j.jneuroling.2008.09.003

Coltheart, M., Rastle, K., Perry, C., Langdon, R., & Ziegler, J. (2001). DRC: A Dual Route Cascaded model of visual word recognition and reading aloud. *Psychological Review, 108,* 204–256.

de Jong, P. F., & van Bergen, E. (2017). Issues in diagnosing dyslexia. In E. Segers & P. W. van den Broek (Eds.), *Developmental perspectives in written language and literacy* (pp. 349–361). Amsterdam, The Netherlands: John Benjamins.

Elbro, C. (2010). Dyslexia as disability or handicap: When does vocabulary matter? *Journal of Learning Disabilities, 43,* 469–478. http://dx.doi.org/10.1177/0022219409357349

Fletcher, J., Lyon, G. R., Fuchs, L., & Barnes, M. (2007). *Learning disabilities: From identification to intervention.* New York, NY: Guilford Press.

Fletcher, J. M., & Miciak, J. (2017). Comprehensive cognitive assessments are not necessary for the identification and treatment of learning disabilities. *Archives of Clinical Neuropsychology, 32*(1), 2–7. doi:10.1093/arclin/acw103

Fuchs, D., Fuchs, L. S., & Compton, D. L. (2012). Smart RTI: A next generation approach to multilevel prevention. *Exceptional Children, 78,* 263–279.

Hale, J., Alfonso, V., Berninger, V., Bracken, B., Christo, C., Clark, E., . . . Yalof, J. (2010). Critical issues in response-to-intervention, comprehensive evaluation, and specific learning disabilities identification and intervention: An expert white paper consensus. *Learning Disability Quarterly, 33*(3), 223–236. http://dx.doi.org/10.1177/073194871003300310

Jackson, N. E., & Coltheart, M. (2001). *Routes to reading success and failure.* New York, NY: Psychology Press.

Kiuru, N., Lerkkanen, M., Niemi, P., Poskiparta, E., Ahonen, T., Poikkeus, A., & Nurmi, J. (2013). The role of reading disability risk and environmental protective factors in students' reading fluency in Grade 4. *Reading Research Quarterly, 48,* 349–368.

Kohnen, S., Nickels, L., Geigis, L., Coltheart, M., McArthur, G., & Castles, A. (2018). Variations within a subtype: Developmental surface dyslexias in English. *Cortex, 106,* 151–163.

Norton, E. S., & Wolf, M. (2012). Rapid automatized naming (RAN) and reading fluency: Implications for understanding and treatment of reading disabilities. *Annual Review of Psychology, 63,* 427–452.

Parrila, R. K., & Protopapas, A. (2017). Dyslexia and word reading problems. In K. Cain, D. Compton, & R. Parrila (Eds.), *Theories of reading development* (pp. 333–358). Philadelphia, PA: John Benjamins.

Pennington, B. F. (2006). From single to multiple deficit models of developmental disorders. *Cognition, 101*(2), 385–413.

Pennington, B. F., Santerre-Lemmon, L., Rosenberg, J., MacDonald, B., Boada, R., Friend, A., . . . Willcutt, E. G. (2012). Individual prediction of dyslexia by single versus multiple deficit models. *Journal of Abnormal Psychology, 121*(1), 212–224.

Pringle Morgan, W. (1896). A case of congenital word blindness. *British Medical Journal, 7*, 1378.

Protopapas, A. (2014). From temporal processing to developmental language disorders: Mind the gap. *Philosophical Transactions of the Royal Society B: Biological Sciences, 369*, 1–11.

Protopapas, A., Katopodi, K., Altani, A., & Georgiou, G. K. (2018). Word reading fluency as a serial naming task. *Scientific Studies of Reading, 22*, 248–263.

Rutter, M. (2006). *Genes and behavior: Nature–nurture interplay explained.* Oxford, England: Blackwell.

Sameroff, A. (2010). A unified theory of development: A dialectic integration of nature and nurture. *Child Development, 81*, 6–22.

Schatschneider, C., Wagner, R. K., Hart, S. A., & Tighe, E. L. (2016). Using simulations to investigate the longitudinal stability of alternative schemes for classifying and identifying children with reading disabilities. *Scientific Studies of Reading, 20*(1), 34–48.

Sénéchal, M., Whissell, J., & Bildfell, A. (2017). Starting from home: Home literacy practices that make a difference. In K. Cain, D. Compton, & R. Parrila (Eds.), *Theories of reading development* (pp. 383–407). Philadelphia, PA: John Benjamins.

Snowling, M. J., & Melby-Lervåg, M. (2016). Oral language deficits in familial dyslexia: A meta-analysis and review. *Psychological Bulletin, 142*, 498–545. http://dx.doi.org/10.1037/bul0000037

Spencer, M., Wagner, R. K., Schatschneider, C., Quinn, J. M., Lopez, D., & Petscher, Y. (2014). Incorporating RTI in a hybrid model of reading disability. *Learning Disability Quarterly, 37*, 161–171. http://dx.doi.org/10.1177/0731948714530967

Swagerman, S. C., van Bergen, E., Dolan, C., de Geus, E. J. C., Koenis, M. M. G., Hulshoff Pol, H. E., & Boomsma, D. I. (2017). Genetic transmission of reading ability. *Brain and Language, 172*, 3–8.

Tannock, R. (2013). Rethinking ADHD and LD in DSM-5: Proposed changes in diagnostic criteria. *Journal of Learning Disabilities, 46*(1), 5–25.

Taylor, W. P., Miciak, J., Fletcher, J. M., & Francis, D. J. (2017). Cognitive discrepancy models for specific learning disabilities identification: Simulations of psychometric limitations. *Psychological Assessment, 29*(4), 446–457. http://dx.doi.org/10.1037/pas0000356.

van Bergen, E., Bishop, D., van Zuijen, T., & de Jong, P. F. (2015). How does parental reading influence children's reading? A study of cognitive mediation. *Scientific Studies of Reading, 19*(5), 325–339. https://doi.org/10.1080/10888438.2015.1050103

van Bergen, E., de Jong, P. F., Maassen, B., & van der Leij, A. (2014). The effects of parents' literacy and children's preliteracy skills on the risk of dyslexia. *Journal of Abnormal Child Psychology, 42*, 1187–1200.

van Bergen, E., van der Leij, A., & de Jong, P. F. (2014). The intergenerational multiple deficit model and the case of dyslexia. *Frontiers in Human Neuroscience, 8*(346), 1–13. http://dx.doi.org/10.3389/fnhum.2014.00346

van den Boer, M., Georgiou, G. K., & de Jong, P. F. (2016). Naming of short words is (almost) the same as naming of alphanumeric symbols: Evidence from two orthographies. *Journal of Experimental Child Psychology, 144*, 152–165.

van den Boer, M., van Bergen, E., & de Jong, P. F. (2015). The specific relation of visual attention span with reading and spelling in Dutch. *Learning and Individual Differences, 39*, 141–149. http://dx.doi.org/10.1016/j.lindif.2015.03.017

van Viersen, S., de Bree, E. H., Zee, M., Maassen, B., van der Leij, A., & de Jong, P. F. (2018). Pathways into literacy: The role of early oral language abilities and family risk for dyslexia. *Psychological Science, 29*, 418–428.

Vellutino, F. R., Fletcher, J. M., Snowling, M. J., & Scanlon, D. M. (2004). Specific reading disability (dyslexia): What have we learned in the past four decades? *Journal of Child Psychology and Psychiatry, 45*(1), 2–40.

Wadsworth, S., Corley, R., Hewitt, J., Plomin, R., & DeFries, J. (2002). Parent–offspring resemblance for reading performance at 7, 12 and 16 years of age in the Colorado adoption project. *Journal of Child Psychology and Psychiatry, 43*(6), 769–774.

CHAPTER 5

Early Identification of Children at Risk for Reading Difficulty
Neurobiology, Screening and Evidence-Based Response, and Educational Technology

Nadine Gaab, Ted K. Turesky, and Joseph Sanfilippo

SUMMARY

Proficiency in reading is crucial for academic and vocational success. In the United States, 63% of children in the fourth grade are reading below grade level, and about 5%–12% are diagnosed with dyslexia. Many of these children are not "flagged" in the school system until after reading instruction has begun and they have repeatedly failed in learning to read. This is often detrimental to the child's development because repeated failure to learn to read can lead to severe academic and psychological harm. Also, reading interventions are more effective in curbing reading failure when begun early (see Lovett et al., 2017), when the gap in proficiency compared to typically developing children is still small and the secondary implications of reading failure (e.g., reduced vocabulary, reduced background knowledge) are minimal. Atypical brain development in certain brain regions has been evinced in prereading children who subsequently manifested reading disability, which has helped to shed light on the underlying mechanisms of reading failure and provided an impetus for the development of early screening programs to identify children at risk for reading impairments. Screening children individually for risk of reading disability can be accomplished through behavioral assessment of preliteracy abilities, which are strong predictors of later reading disability, including phonological awareness, letter–sound knowledge, rapid automatic naming (RAN), vocabulary, and oral language comprehension. As such, the first step toward preventing reading failure is to assess these abilities in children prior to formal reading instruction. The second step is for educators to be immediately directed to an evidence-based response to screening protocol (EBRS), similar to a response to intervention (RTI) multi-tiered approach that is customized to the specific preliteracy deficits identified in the screening step, and then monitored for progress. Thus, the "failure model" of screening and intervention is replaced by a "support model." This proactive support model is paramount in preventing both repeated failures in learning to read and the academic and psychosocial consequences of those failures.

INTRODUCTION

The development of skilled reading requires a complex network of competencies. Beginning in utero and through the first years of life, children typically start developing skills that lay the groundwork for later literacy. A child's auditory and visual processing skills develop through interactions with the environment, and these become a cornerstone for the acquisition of oral language skills, including phonological processing skills and letter recognition ability—critical precursors to reading—as the child approaches school age. Children discern the relationship between the sounds of words and the letters that represent them (known as phoneme–grapheme mapping); this underpins decoding and recognition of single words. These word recognition skills become increasingly automatic and coalesce with developing language skills (e.g., mastery of complex syntax, semantics, vocabulary); together, these skills serve as the foundation for fluent reading of sentences and complex text for comprehension. In this way, reading can be thought of as a rope composed of many fine strands woven inextricably together to produce skilled reading (Scarborough, 2001). Through this developmental process, children can progress from effortful training in reading, to using reading as a tool to facilitate new learning. In simpler terms, they can progress from a stage of learning to read, to a stage of reading to learn. The completion of this transition is crucial for later life success, both academic and vocational.

Indeed, the development of basic reading skills is one of the primary goals of elementary education. However, a National Assessment of Educational Progress (NAEP) report conducted by the National Center for Education Statistics (NCES) in the United States indicated that 63% of children in fourth grade are reading below grade-level proficiency, and fourth-grade reading levels in the United States have been consistently below proficiency since 1992 (NCES, 2017). In addition, 70% of children who are poor readers at the start of elementary school remain poor readers in eighth grade (Foorman, Francis, Shaywitz, Shaywitz, & Fletcher, 1997). Reading difficulty has been shown to lead to a cascade of socioemotional difficulties in children, including low self-esteem; depression; and feelings of shame, inadequacy, and helplessness (Valas, 1999). Children with learning disabilities are less likely to complete high school and are increasingly at risk of entering the juvenile justice system (Mallett, Stoddard-Dare, & Workman-Crewnshaw, 2011). Even larger scale socioeconomic effects of reading failure have been noted: 92% of those with learning disabilities have annual incomes of less than $50,000 (USD) within 8 years of finishing high school, and 67% earn less than $25,000 per year (Cortiella & Horowitz, 2014). A screening and early intervention system that identifies children at risk for reading difficulty with high sensitivity and specificity and works to preemptively counteract reading failure in school through EBRS in preschool and early kindergarten would thus be of great long-term benefit to these students.

The etiologies of reading disability are complex, and there is a debate as to the classification of reading disabilities (*The Dyslexia Debate*; see Elliott & Grigorenko, 2014) and the use of terms such as *dyslexia* and *reading disability* (e.g., Ramus, 2014). Developmental dyslexia is described as a specific and heritable learning disability with a known neurobiological origin, affecting 5%–10% of children. It is characterized by deficits in phonological processing and cannot be explained by any sensory deficit or lack of opportunity or motivation (Fisher & DeFries, 2002). In the past, a diagnosis of dyslexia was contingent on a discrepancy between IQ and reading scores, so children with high IQ and low reading scores received a diagnosis but children with low IQ and low reading scores did not. It is important to note, however, that behavioral and neuroimaging evidence has indicated that poor readers experience similar patterns of reading difficulty regardless of IQ (e.g., Fletcher, 2009).

Reading difficulty in general, unlike dyslexia, is more often thought of as the result of perceptual, cognitive, or environmental deficits or impoverishment. For example, 80% of fourth-grade students from low socioeconomic status (SES) backgrounds have been shown to read below grade-level proficiency (NCES, 2017). We will not solve the dyslexia debate in this chapter, as atypical reading development is variable and multifactorial, with biological, psychological, and/or environmental causes and, as such, requires multifactorial strategies for screening and accommodation (Catts & Petscher, 2018). However, we have the responsibility to find every struggling reader regardless of the cause of the difficulty and to design screening and EBRS with this variability in mind. Regardless of the way in which a reading disability is classified, all children who experience reading failure experience similar psychosocial implications and are often responsive to the same interventions (Kilpatrick, 2018).

Research has shown that the most effective window for early reading interventions is in kindergarten and first grade (Wanzek & Vaughn, 2007), most likely even earlier. However, a child with a reading disability is often not diagnosed and does not receive intensive services until several years after formal reading instruction begins (see overview in Ozernov-Palchik, Norton, et al., 2016), when the child has already failed to learn to read and the most effective intervention window has passed. By this time, per the Matthew effect (Stanovich, 1986), the child has already fallen behind his or her peers both in reading ability and in the use of reading to learn new content; as time passes, it becomes continuously more difficult for the child to catch up. Conversely, when at-risk beginning readers received intensive reading instruction, 56%–92% (across six research studies) achieved average reading ability (Torgesen, 2004).

A crucial component of alleviating the burden of reading disability is to design, implement, and scale efficient and effective screening and intervention programs for at-risk children. The failure of some existing RTI programs can be partially attributed to inappropriate universal screening instruments, poor sensitivity and specificity of screening methods, and/or inadequate or unspecific response to screening (e.g., providing remedial training in phonological awareness when the child's deficit is a lack of developmentally appropriate vocabulary), or the delivery method, quantity, and/or quality of the early intervention. Although RTI is crucial for implementing targeted instruction and monitoring ongoing student progress, EBRS resources can proceed and supplement RTI by empowering the general education teacher and can provide professional development that will benefit the quality and fidelity of RTI approaches.

ATYPICAL READING DEVELOPMENT AND ITS NEUROBIOLOGY

Reading is a cultural invention, dating back roughly 5,400 years. Because this is relatively recent, it is highly unlikely that specific brain regions or mechanisms evolved for reading (Dehaene, 2004; Wolf, 2008). Instead, researchers think that brain regions or mechanisms that evolved to serve other functions were repurposed for reading (Dehaene, 2004). This "neuronal recycling" hypothesis has since been evinced by studies of adults who were formerly illiterate but learned to read later in life; they exhibited greater activation in response to orthographic stimuli in the same brain region and weaker activation in response to objects and faces compared to people who had been literate since childhood (Dehaene et al., 2010).

Reading in typically developing children and adults is primarily supported by left hemisphere brain areas (Martin, Schurz, Kronbichler, & Richlan, 2015), including inferior frontal cortex for phonological and semantic processing of words, temporoparietal cortex for grapheme–phoneme conversion, and occipitotemporal cortex for whole-word recognition (Eden, Olulade, Evans, Krafnick, & Alkire, 2016). Developmental dyslexia has been consistently associated with structural and functional atypicalities in these brain regions (Ozernov-Palchik & Gaab, 2016), including reduced gray matter volume (Richlan, Kronbichler, & Wimmer, 2013), hypoactivations in response to reading-related functional magnetic resonance imaging (fMRI) tasks (Richlan, Kronbichler, & Wimmer, 2011), and weaker functional connectivity (Schurz et al., 2015). These hypoactivations were present in children with low reading scores, some of whom had low and some high IQ scores, thereby opposing discrepancy-based definitions of dyslexia (Tanaka et al., 2011). In addition, white matter tracts connecting these brain regions have also exhibited atypicalities, most consistently reduced microstructure in the left arcuate fasciculus (AF) as well as superior longitudinal fasciculus (SLF) and inferior longitudinal fasciculus (ILF) (Vandermosten, Boets, Wouters, & Ghesquière, 2012).

A remaining question in understanding the brain bases of dyslexia is whether these observed atypicalities reflect the underlying cause of dyslexia or the consequence of reduced reading experience that often accompanies reading difficulty. Reading level–matched designs, in which a cohort of children with dyslexia is contrasted with a cohort matched for reading ability rather than age, have been employed to address this question. For instance, one study reported that children with dyslexia exhibited similar reductions in activation of left temporoparietal and occipitotempo-ral regions and reductions of gray matter volume in the left temporopa-rietal cortex when compared with both age- and reading level–matched (younger by 2–4 years) children (Hoeft et al., 2007). This was bolstered by a finding showing atypical gray and white matter morphology common to children with different types of reading disability (e.g., poor compre-hension, poor decoding), suggesting that qualitatively different reading experiences under the umbrella of reading impairments do not alter the brain bases of reading disability (Eckert et al., 2017). Overall, these find-ings point to dyslexia as caused by a fundamental difference in the devel-opmental trajectories of certain brain regions and altered developmental trajectories as a consequence of reduced reading experience.

EARLY MARKERS OF READING DIFFICULTIES BEFORE READING ONSET

Another means of disambiguating cause and consequence is to conduct studies in prereading children and infants with hereditary risk of devel-opmental dyslexia. Family studies suggest that dyslexia is strongly her-itable, occurring on average in 45% of children who have a first-degree relative with dyslexia (Snowling & Melby-Lervåg, 2016). Consistent with this, several genes have been reported as candidates for dyslexia suscep-tibility, and it has been suggested that the majority of these genes play a role in early brain development (Galaburda, LoTurco, Ramus, Fitch, & Rosen, 2006). Furthermore, there are indications that these genes are also associated with language processes other than phonological processing or reading specifically (i.e., pleiotropy; Mascheretti et al., 2014; Stein et al., 2004), which fits with the concept of multiple cognitive profiles of early reading (Ozernov-Palchik, Norton, et al., 2016) and bolsters the hypothesis that dyslexia arises from multiple cognitive deficits (Ozernov-Palchik, Yu, Wang, & Gaab, 2016; Pennington, 2006; van Bergen, van der Leij, & de Jong, 2014). Given the complicated and highly debated role of genes in dyslexia (Paracchini, Scerri, & Monaco, 2007), it is critical to examine early and pre-natally determined developmental trajectories.

Given the heritability estimates of 0.4–0.6 for dyslexia, this can be (partially) accomplished by examining brain function and structure in preschool-age prereading children with (FHD+) and without (FHD−) family history of dyslexia. In studies of brain function, we have observed that FHD+ children exhibited reduced activation on a task of phonological processing in left temporoparietal and bilateral occipitotemporal regions compared with FHD− prereaders (Raschle, Zuk, & Gaab, 2012). Likewise, studies of brain structure have indicated that FHD+ prereaders exhibited reduced gray matter volume in bilateral temporoparietal and occipito-temporal cortices compared with FHD− prereaders (Raschle, Chang, & Gaab, 2011). Also, compared with children without dyslexia, children with dyslexia and FHD+ prereaders exhibited decreased similarity in the sulcal pattern (Im, Raschle, Smith, Grant, & Gaab, 2016), a feature of the human brain determined primarily prenatally (Chi, Dooling, & Gilles, 1977) and hypothesized to relate to optimal organization of cortical function and white matter connectivity (e.g., Van Essen, 1997); furthermore, sulcal pattern similarity estimates positively correlated with reading ability, suggesting that atypicalities in dyslexia may begin in utero (Im et al., 2016).

White matter pathways commonly related to reading, including left AF, inferior fronto-occipital fasciculus (IFOF), ILF, and SLF, have also been examined. Using diffusion tensor imaging (DTI), these pathways were assessed on measures of fractional anisotropy (FA), which are thought to reflect microstructural measures, including tract density, myelination, and axonal diameter. Prereading FHD+ children (~5 years of age) exhibited lower (uncorrected) FA in left IFOF compared with age-matched FHD− children (Vandermosten et al., 2015). Left hemisphere atypicalities were again found as part of a longitudinal study (with time points at prereading, beginning reading, and fluent reading stages); here, FHD+ children exhibited reduced FA in the left AF compared with FHD− children at all time points. In addition, the rate of FA development in the left AF 1) correlated with gains in reading performance and 2) differed between FHD+ children who subsequently became good or poor readers (Wang et al., 2017). Consistent with this, earlier studies have demonstrated that auditory event-related potential (ERP) responses to speech and nonspeech stimuli measured in FHD+ prereaders predict reading skills at school-age (Hämäläinen et al., 2013; Maurer et al., 2009). Furthermore, reading ability outcomes have been modeled using familial risk of dyslexia, psychometric measures at the prereading stage, and rates of FA development in left AF and SLF (Wang et al., 2017) or ERP responses (Maurer et al., 2009).

Although these models capture the heritability component of dyslexia, they do not incorporate the adverse environmental circumstances that can contribute to reading disability. Another study through a collaboration between our group and Massachusetts Institute of Technology (Project READ) consisted of a socioeconomically and ethnically diverse sample. This study showed that prevalence of prereading skill profiles differs based on SES (Ozernov-Palchik, Norton, et al., 2016), but white matter microstructural measures in this study showed a strong correlation with phonological awareness in kindergarten, suggesting similar atypical brain development in this very diverse sample of children (Saygin et al., 2013). Previous work has demonstrated that SES is associated with alterations in brain structure (Noble, Houston, Kan, & Sowell, 2012) and function (Kim et al., 2013). In a recent study, we showed a positive association between SES and FA in bilateral ILF in kindergarten (Ozernov-Palchik et al., 2018). Furthermore, SES moderated the association between kindergarten FA in ILF and second-grade reading performance such that the association was positive in children with lower SES but not significant in children with higher SES.

DETECTING INFANTS AT RISK FOR LATER READING DIFFICULTY

Although it has been demonstrated that preschool-age children at risk for dyslexia exhibit atypicalities in brain function and structure compared with children not at risk for dyslexia, it is unclear whether these result from 1) atypical development beginning in the first years of life in close interaction with language development, 2) a congenitally less optimal brain to learn to read, or 3) a combination of the two. Several studies have identified brain-based atypicalities related to dyslexia in infants. For instance, atypical ERP responses to basic speech sounds have been observed in FHD+ infants compared with FHD− infants (Lyytinen et al., 2004; van Leeuwen et al., 2008), and in infants later characterized as having dyslexia or being poor readers compared with infants later characterized as being typically developing or good readers (Molfese, 2000; van Zuijen, Plakas, Maassen, Maurits, & van der Leij, 2013). Nevertheless, how the effects observed in infancy develop into the structural and functional atypicalities observed later in children with dyslexia (i.e., developmental trajectories) remains unknown.

We started to examine this with a series of longitudinal MRI measurements in children from infancy to school age using the natural sleep paradigm for infants (Raschle, Zuk, Ortiz-Mantilla, et al., 2012). So far, white matter atypicalities have been identified in FHD+ 5- to 17-month-old infants (Langer et al., 2017), suggesting that the white matter atypicalities observed in preschool-age children (Wang et al., 2017) are present as early as infancy. Taken together, many brain regions shown to exhibit FHD-related atypicalities in brain structure and function at preschool age and later exhibit similar atypicalities in infancy.

Although it is expected that further understanding of the emergence of these atypicalities will be gleaned once it is known which of the infants participating in these longitudinal studies develop dyslexia, it is unlikely that brain imaging methods described here are capable of the sensitivity or specificity required to effectively screen for reading disability. Therefore, efforts should be aimed toward improving sensitivity and specificity of behavioral screening approaches, which have already been shown to predict reading disability with some success (see the next section for details) and are far less expensive.

EARLY SCREENING AND EVIDENCE-BASED RESPONSE TO SCREENING

Although the underlying mechanisms of atypical reading development have been illuminated by neurobiological evidence, studies of behavior indicate that many cognitive, linguistic, and preliteracy characteristics that are predictive of later reading problems can be observed at a pre-reading age. Prereading children who go on to develop reading disability tend to struggle with phonological awareness, pseudoword repetition, letter–sound knowledge, RAN, expressive and receptive vocabulary, and oral language comprehension, and they tend to have less literacy-rich home environments (e.g., Compton, Fuchs, Fuchs, & Bryant, 2006). Letter–sound knowledge and RAN determine a child's ability to associate a visual cue with an auditory representation; RAN further assesses automaticity of retrieval paired with an oral output and has been shown to be a strong predictor of later reading fluency. Oral language comprehension and vocabulary tasks test language skills that serve as the foundation for word decoding and reading comprehension, fluency, and automaticity. Phonological awareness and pseudoword repetition tasks assess ability to manipulate the aural components of words. Thus, a weakness in any of these tasks indicates a susceptibility to later reading disability. Given that children at risk for dyslexia begin school with brains that are less optimized to learn to read, and that some indicators of later reading difficulties can be identified well before reading instruction begins, society has the responsibility to identify these children before reading instruction begins so that appropriate and timely interventions can be put into place to facilitate literacy development.

Although early screeners do exist, most lack the sensitivity and specificity to be effective in identifying children at risk for reading disability. That is, they yield an unacceptably high rate of false negatives (poor sensitivity; i.e., children who are at risk but are not identified as such) and false positives (poor specificity; i.e., children who are not at risk but are identified as being at risk). Many screeners do not comprehensively assess all the predictive components of reading disability (or strands that make up the "reading rope"). A screener that identifies specific deficits in prereading cognitive and linguistic abilities offers the opportunity to target those specific deficits as early as possible. A comprehensive screener would also reduce the number of false negatives in screening; by reducing the number of "misses," a comprehensive screener ensures that more students who would benefit from EBRS will receive the appropriate resources in the classroom. However, a comprehensive screener still may present the problem of poor specificity, or overidentification of children at risk for reading disability. Although this is a concern, ultimately it is more egregious to fail to identify a child with reading disability than it is to provide extra resources to a child needlessly, and the problem of poor specificity can be mitigated by strategic allocation of resources in the classroom (Poulsen, 2018).

Other screeners have been designed for children who have already begun to develop some reading skills, although ideally screeners would be designed for younger children whose problems can be addressed before reading instruction begins. Just as a patient at risk for heart disease should be screened and monitored over time and should be provided the behavioral changes/intervention necessary to prevent or mitigate heart disease to every extent possible, so too should children at risk for reading

disability be identified prior to the onset of reading difficulty and re-
sponded to in an attempt to prevent reading disability. The few screeners that are sufficiently comprehensive and administered early enough are
also often prohibitively lengthy or expensive, rendering them inaccessible
to the majority of children. An effective screener will comprehensively
assess proficiency in the evidence-based preliteracy predictors listed previously: it will be developmentally appropriate (i.e., a screener designed
for a 4-year-old will assess preliteracy skills typical of a 4-year-old and
not reading comprehension or nonword reading); be normed among an
appropriate, diverse, norming group; be quick and inexpensive; and be
readily accessible such that it could be administered at home, at school, in
the pediatrician's office, or elsewhere. A screener with these characteristics
has the potential to benefit all children at risk for developing problems
with reading (e.g., Kilpatrick, 2018). In selecting the appropriate screener,
a school district or other organization should also consider contextual factors, such as financial resources, demographics of the student population
(e.g., socioeconomic factors, the number of English language learners, the
number of dialect speakers), personnel available to administer screening
and intervention approaches, and assessment tools and other resources
already available within the institution.

Of course, screening is only impactful when followed up with EBRS
and intervention approaches. An EBRS program can provide parents and
teachers with resources and strategies to address any identified preliteracy
weakness, even without a formal diagnosis of dyslexia or reading disability and before reading instruction begins. Such a strategy will create a
support model that will facilitate a child's reading development beginning
at a prereading age. EBRS can proceed and supplement an RTI framework,
which involves follow-up screening at appropriate intervals to monitor
progress, which can identify improvements in skills (or lack thereof) as
well as new deficits that may appear as skills develop (Poulsen, 2018). The
advent of computer-assisted technology has provided the potential to create screening and response-to-screening platforms that are more comprehensive than ever (e.g., by allowing for the automatic recording and scoring
of spoken responses) and has provided a platform for gamification, which
can facilitate user motivation and enjoyment (Catts & Petscher, 2018).

The primary goal of a widespread early literacy screening and EBRS
and intervention regimen should be to identify and reduce the number of
children who experience reading difficulty. Children identified as being at
risk do not need to be sent to special education; rather, evidenced-based,
structured, explicit, and cumulative instruction should be implemented
in the general education curriculum by empowered and trained general
education teachers. A successful program could engender many clinical,
educational, and economic benefits. For instance, it is more cost effective
to provide professional development to general education teachers so that
they can teach children at risk rather than addressing reading disability

after it has manifested and secondary mental health issues after they have arisen. This instruction will benefit all children in the classroom, not just those who are at risk. Policy changes that arise from successful early screening would lead to resource savings, in addition to the economic benefits derived from higher rates of literacy among populations.

Perhaps the most immediate implication of successful screening and intervention of reading difficulty will be mitigation or even prevention of the harmful social and psychological effects of reading failure. By allocating resources to children at risk for reading difficulty even before reading instruction begins, supports can be put in place to prevent reading failure in school and to prevent the Matthew effect that subjects struggling readers to a series of compounding social, educational, and vocational disadvantages. An improvement in literacy would thus not only facilitate academic success among students, but it would also promote a healthier and more productive society.

REFERENCES

Catts, H., & Petscher, Y. (2018). Early identification of dyslexia: Current advancements and future directions. *Perspectives on Language and Literacy, 44*(3), 33–36.

Chi, J. G., Dooling, E. C., & Gilles, F. H. (1977). Gyral development of the human brain. *Annals of Neurology, 1*(1), 86–93. http://doi.org/10.1002/ana.410010109

Compton, D. L., Fuchs, D., Fuchs, L. S., & Bryant, J. D. (2006). Selecting at-risk readers in first grade for early intervention: A two-year longitudinal study of decision rules and procedures. *Journal of Educational Psychology, 98*(2), 394–409.

Cortiella, C., & Horowitz, S. H. (2014). *The state of learning disabilities: Facts, trends and emerging issues* (3rd ed.) New York, NY: National Center for Learning Disabilities.

Dehaene, S. (2004). Evolution of human cortical circuits for reading and arithmetic: The "neuronal recycling" hypothesis. *Evolution, 34,* 133–157.

Dehaene, S., Pegado, F., Braga, L. W., Ventura, P., Filho, G. N., Jobert, A., . . . Cohen, L. (2010). How learning to read changes the cortical networks for vision and language. *Science, 1359*(6009), 1359–1364.

Eckert, M. A., Vaden, K. I., Maxwell, A. B., Cute, S. L., Gebregziabher, M., Berninger, V. W., . . . Wandell, B. (2017). Common brain structure findings across children with varied reading disability profiles. *Scientific Reports, 7*(1), 1–10.

Eden, G. F., Olulade, O. A., Evans, T. M., Krafnick, A. J., & Alkire, D. R. (2016). Developmental dyslexia. In G. Hickok & S. Small (Eds.), *The neurobiology of language* (pp. 815–826). Amsterdam, The Netherlands: Elsevier.

Elliott, J., & Grigorenko, E. L. (2014). *The dyslexia debate.* New York, NY: Cambridge University Press.

Fisher, S. E., & DeFries, J. C. (2002). Developmental dyslexia: Genetic dissection of a complex cognitive trait. *Nature Reviews Neuroscience, 3*(10), 767–780.

Fletcher, J. M. (2009). Dyslexia: The evolution of a scientific concept. *Journal of the International Neuropsychological Society, 15*(4), 501–508.

Foorman, B., Francis, D., Shaywitz, S., Shaywitz, B., & Fletcher, J. (1997). The case for early reading intervention. In B. Blachman (Ed.), *Foundations of reading acquisition and dyslexia: Implications for early intervention* (pp. 243–64). Mahwah, NJ: Lawrence Erlbaum Associates.

Galaburda, A. M., LoTurco, J., Ramus, F., Fitch, R. H., & Rosen, G. D. (2006). From genes to behavior in developmental dyslexia. *Nature Neuroscience, 9*(10), 1213–1217.

Hämäläinen, J. A., Guttorm, T. K., Richardson, U., Alku, P., Lyytinen, H., & Leppänen, P. H. T. (2013). Auditory event-related potentials measured in kindergarten predict later reading problems at school age. *Developmental Neuropsychology, 38*(8), 550–566.

Hoeft, F., Meyler, A., Hernandez, A., Juel, C., Taylor-Hill, H., Martindale, J. L., . . . Gabrieli, J. D. E. (2007). Functional and morphometric brain dissociation between dyslexia and reading ability. *Proceedings of the National Academy of Sciences, 104*(10), 4234–4239.

Im, K., Raschle, N., Smith, S. A., Grant, P. E., & Gaab, N. (2016). Atypical sulcal pattern in children with developmental dyslexia and at-risk kindergarteners. *Cerebral Cortex, 26*(3), 1138–1148.

Kilpatrick, D. A. (2018). Genetics, the environment, and poor instruction as contributors to word-level reading difficulties: Does it matter for early identification and instruction? *Perspectives on Language and Literacy, 44*(3), 25–28.

Kim, P., Evans, G. W., Angstadt, M., Ho, S. S., Sripada, C. S., Swain, J. E., . . . Phan, K. L. (2013). Effects of childhood poverty and chronic stress on emotion regulatory brain function in adulthood. *Proceedings of the National Academy of Sciences, 110*(46), 18442–18447.

Langer, N., Peysakhovich, B., Zuk, J., Drottar, M., Sliva, D. D., Smith, S., . . . Gaab, N. (2017). White matter alterations in infants at risk for developmental dyslexia. *Cerebral Cortex, 27*(2), 1027–1036.

Lovett, M. W., Frijters, J. C., Wolf, M., Steinbach, K. A., Sevcik, R. A., Morris, R. D., . . . Lovett, W. (2017). Early intervention for children at risk for reading disabilities: The impact of grade at intervention and individual differences on intervention outcomes. *Association, 109*(7), 889–914.

Lyytinen, H., Aro, M., Eklund, K., Erskine, J., Guttorm, T., Laakso, M. L., . . . Torppa, M. (2004). The development of children at familial risk for dyslexia: Birth to early school age. *Annals of Dyslexia, 54*(2), 184–220.

Mallett, C. A., Stoddard-Dare, P., & Workman-Crewnshaw, L. (2011). Special education disabilities and juvenile delinquency: A unique challenge for school social work. *School Social Work Journal, 36*(1), 26–40.

Martin, A., Schurz, M., Kronbichler, M., & Richlan, F. (2015). Reading in the brain of children and adults: A meta-analysis of 40 functional magnetic resonance imaging studies. *Human Brain Mapping, 36*(5), 1963–1981.

Mascheretti, S., Riva, V., Giorda, R., Beri, S., Lanzoni, L. F. E., Cellino, M. R., & Marino, C. (2014). KIAA0319 and ROBO1: Evidence on association with reading and pleiotropic effects on language and mathematics abilities in developmental dyslexia. *Journal of Human Genetics, 59*(4), 189–197.

Maurer, U., Bucher, K., Brem, S., Benz, R., Kranz, F., Schulz, E., . . . Brandeis, D. (2009). Neurophysiology in preschool improves behavioral prediction of reading ability throughout primary school. *Biological Psychiatry, 66*(4), 341–348.

Molfese, D. L. (2000). Predicting dyslexia at 8 years of age using neonatal brain responses. *Brain and Language, 72*(3), 238–245. http://doi.org/10.1006/brln.2000.2287

National Center for Education Statistics (NCES). (2017). *National Assessment of Educational Progress (NAEP) 1992, 1994, 1998, 2000, 2002, 2003, 2005, 2007, 2009, 2011, 2013, 2015, and 2017 Reading Assessments.* Retrieved from https://nces.ed.gov/nationsreportcard /naepdata/

Noble, K. G., Houston, S. M., Kan, E., & Sowell, E. R. (2012). Neural correlates of socio-economic status in the developing human brain. *Developmental Science, 15*(4), 516–527.

Ozernov-Palchik, O., & Gaab, N. (2016). Tackling the "dyslexia paradox": Reading brain and behavior for early markers of developmental dyslexia. *Wiley Interdisciplinary Reviews: Cognitive Science, 7*(2), 156–176.

Ozernov-Palchik, O., Norton, E. S., Sideridis, G., Beach, S. D., Wolf, M., Gabrieli, J. D. E., & Gaab, N. (2016). Longitudinal stability of pre-reading skill profiles of kindergarten children: Implications for early screening and theories of reading. *Developmental Science, 20*(5), 1–18.

Ozernov-Palchik, O., Norton, E. S., Wang, Y., Beach, S. D., Wolf, M., Gabrieli, J. D. E., & Gaab, N. (2018). The relationship between socioeconomic status and white matter microstructure in pre-reading children: A longitudinal investigation. *Human Brain Mapping, 40*(3), 741–754. http://dx.doi.org/10.1002/hbm.24407

Ozernov-Palchik, O., Yu, X., Wang, Y., & Gaab, N. (2016, Aug.). Lessons to be learned: How a comprehensive neurobiological framework of atypical reading development can inform educational practice. *Current Opinion in Behavioral Sciences, 10*, 45–58.

Paracchini, S., Scerri, T., & Monaco, A. P. (2007). The genetic lexicon of dyslexia. *Annual Review of Genomics and Human Genetics, 8*(1), 57–79.

Pennington, B. F. (2006). From single to multiple deficit models of developmental disorders. *Cognition, 101*(2), 385–413.

Poulsen, M. (2018). The challenge of early identification of later reading difficulties. *Perspectives on Language and Literacy, 44*(3), 11–14.

Ramus, F. (2014). Should there really be a "dyslexia debate"? *Brain, 137*(12), 3371–3374.

Raschle, N. M., Chang, M., & Gaab, N. (2011). Structural brain alterations associated with dyslexia predate reading onset. *NeuroImage, 57*(3), 742–749.

Raschle, N., Zuk, J., & Gaab, N. (2012). Functional characteristics of developmental dyslexia in left-hemispheric posterior brain regions predate reading onset. *Proceedings of the National Academy of Sciences, 109*(6), 2156–2161.

Raschle, N., Zuk, J., Ortiz-Mantilla, S., Sliva, D. D., Franceschi, A., Grant, P. E., . . . Gaab, N. (2012). Pediatric neuroimaging in early childhood and infancy: Challenges and practical guidelines. *Annals of the New York Academy of Sciences, 1252*(1), 43–50.

Richlan, F., Kronbichler, M., & Wimmer, H. (2011). Meta-analyzing brain dysfunctions in dyslexic children and adults. *NeuroImage, 56*(3), 1735–1742.

Richlan, F., Kronbichler, M., & Wimmer, H. (2013). Structural abnormalities in the dyslexic brain: A meta-analysis of voxel-based morphometry studies. *Human Brain Mapping, 34*(11), 3055–3065.

Saygin, Z. M., Norton, E. S., Osher, D. E., Beach, S. D., Cyr, A. B., Ozernov-Palchik, O., . . . Gabrieli, J. D. E. (2013). Tracking the roots of reading ability: White matter volume and integrity correlate with phonological awareness in prereading and early-reading kindergarten children. *Journal of Neuroscience, 33*(33), 13251–13258.

Scarborough, H. S. (2001). Connecting early language and literacy to later reading (dis)abilities: Evidence, theory, and practice. In S. Neuman & D. Dickinson (Eds.), *Handbook of early literacy research* (pp. 97–110). New York, NY: Guilford Press.

Schurz, M., Wimmer, H., Richlan, F., Ludersdorfer, P., Klackl, J., & Kronbichler, M. (2015). Resting-state and task-based functional brain connectivity in developmental dyslexia. *Cerebral Cortex, 25*(10), 3502–3514.

Snowling, M. J., & Melby-Lervåg, M. (2016). Oral language deficits in familial dyslexia: A meta-analysis and review. *Psychological Bulletin, 142*(5), 498–545.

Stanovich, K. E. (1986). Matthew effects in reading: Some consequences of individual differences in the acquisition of literacy. *Reading Research, 21*(4), 360–407.

Stein, C. M., Schick, J. H., Gerry Taylor, H., Shriberg, L. D., Millard, C., Kundtz-Kluge, A., . . . Iyengar, S. K. (2004). Pleiotropic effects of a chromosome 3 locus on speech-sound disorder and reading. *The American Journal of Human Genetics, 74*(2), 283–297.

Tanaka, H., Black, J. M., Hulme, C., Stanley, L. M., Kesler, S. R., Whitfield-Gabrieli, S., . . . Hoeft, F. (2011). The brain basis of the phonological deficit in dyslexia is independent of IQ. *Psychological Science, 22*(11), 1442–1451.

Torgesen, J. K. (2004). Lessons learned from research on interventions for students who have difficulty learning to read. In P. McCardle & V. Chhabra (Eds.), *The voice of evidence in reading research* (pp. 355–382). Baltimore, MD: Paul H. Brookes Publishing Co.

Valas, H. (1999). Students with learning disabilities and low-achieving students: Peer acceptance, loneliness, self-esteem, and depression. *Social Psychology of Education, 3*(3), 173–192.

van Bergen, E., van der Leij, A., & de Jong, P. F. (2014, June). The intergenerational multiple deficit model and the case of dyslexia. *Frontiers in Human Neuroscience, 8*, 1–13.

Van Essen, D. (1997). A tension-based theory of morphogenesis and compact wiring in the central nervous system. *Nature, 385*, 313–318.

van Leeuwen, T., Been, P., van Herten, M., Zwarts, F., Maassen, B., & van der Leij, A. (2008). Two-month-old infants at risk for dyslexia do not discriminate /bAk/ from /dAk/: A brain-mapping study. *Journal of Neurolinguistics, 21*(4), 333–348.

van Zuijen, T. L., Plakas, A., Maassen, B. A. M., Maurits, N. M., & van der Leij, A. (2013). Infant ERPs separate children at risk of dyslexia who become good readers from those who become poor readers. *Developmental Science, 16*(4), 554–563.

Vandermosten, M., Boets, B., Wouters, J., & Ghesquière, P. (2012). A qualitative and quantitative review of diffusion tensor imaging studies in reading and dyslexia. *Neuroscience and Biobehavioral Reviews, 36*(6), 1532–1552.

Vandermosten, M., Vanderauwera, J., Theys, C., De Vos, A., Vanvooren, S., Sunaert, S., . . . Ghesquière, P. (2015). A DTI tractography study in pre-readers at risk for dyslexia. *Developmental Cognitive Neuroscience, 14,* 8–15.

Wang, Y., Mauer, M. V., Raney, T., Peysakhovich, B., Becker, B. L. C., Sliva, D. D., & Gaab, N. (2017). Development of tract-specific white matter pathways during early reading development in at-risk children and typical controls. *Cerebral Cortex, 27*(4), 2469–2485.

Wanzek, J., & Vaughn, S. (2007). Research-based implications from extensive early reading interventions. *School Psychology Review, 36*(4), 541–561.

Wolf, M. (2008). *Proust and the squid: The story and science of the reading brain.* New York, NY: Cambridge Icon.

CHAPTER 6

Using Computational Techniques to Model and Better Understand Developmental Dyslexia

Jay G. Rueckl, Jason Zevin, and Henry Wolf VII

SUMMARY

When described in sufficient detail, mechanistic theories of the neuro-cognitive processes underlying word reading and reading acquisition can be simulated on a computer. These theories can then be evaluated by asking whether the behavior of the simulated models captures important aspects of reading behavior observed experimentally. In this chapter, we briefly describe one such theory (the triangle model) and provide a preliminary report of computational simulations related to developmental dyslexia. A number of experimental studies have demonstrated that subsets of children with dyslexia exhibit different patterns of impairment. Of particular interest is the finding that relative to age-matched controls, children with phonological dyslexia have more impairments when reading unfamiliar nonwords (e.g., *zill*) than irregular words (words such as *pint* that violate the spelling–sound rules of English). In contrast, children with surface dyslexia experience more impairments with irregular words. Our results provide further support for two hypotheses about this contrast. One hypothesis is that these subtypes of dyslexia have different underlying causes. Specifically, phonological dyslexia is associated with difficulties in the system responsible for processing the spoken properties of words, whereas surface dyslexia is associated with differences in the mechanisms that translate written words into their spoken forms. The second hypothesis is that whereas phonological dyslexia reflects an aberrant developmental trajectory, surface dyslexia is better characterized as a form of developmental delay: Children in this group exhibit a slower growth rate along the trajectory followed by typically developing readers. In addition to supporting these hypotheses, our simulations also highlight some conceptual and methodological issues that need to be addressed in future research.

Research reported in this publication was supported by the *Eunice Kennedy Shriver* National Institute of Child Health & Human Development of the National Institutes of Health under Awards P01HD070837, P20HD091013, and P01HD001994. The content is solely the responsibility of the authors and does not necessarily represent the official views of the National Institutes of Health.

INTRODUCTION

Computational models provide a highly mechanistic account of the neurocognitive processes involved in reading. Typically, these theories are primarily concerned with "one second of reading" (Gough, 1972)—the millisecond-scale processes that are engaged during the processing of an individual printed word. Although many of these theories are static, in that they do not seek to model the processes that occur at the longer time scale of learning and development, this is not universally so. Some models (e.g., Harm & Seidenberg, 2004; Pritchard, Coltheart, Marinus, & Castles, 2018) explicitly incorporate a learning mechanism and thus have the potential to provide insights about reading acquisition and related issues (e.g., the bases of dyslexia, the impact of different methods for instruction and remediation) of direct interest to educators, clinicians, and other practitioners. In this chapter, we illustrate this approach in the context of a simulation study of developmental dyslexia.

THE TRIANGLE MODEL

The triangle model (Harm & Seidenberg, 2004; Plaut, McClelland, Seidenberg, & Patterson, 1996; Seidenberg & McClelland, 1989) is an artificial neural network model composed of many simple, neuron-like processing units (*nodes*) that communicate by sending excitatory and inhibitory signals to one another. The activation value of a given node (the equivalent of the firing rate of a neuron) is determined by the sum of the excitatory and inhibitory inputs it receives, and this value in turn determines the strength of the excitatory and inhibitory signals it sends to other nodes. Each signal is weighted by the strength of the connection it is sent across. Like neural synapses, the connections in a network are plastic, and a learning algorithm is used to adjust their strengths (or *weights*) to improve the speed and accuracy of the performance of the network.

As illustrated in Figure 6.1, the nodes in the network are organized into distinct layers, including layers responsible for representing the various linguistic properties (orthographic, phonological, semantic) of a word, as well as layers of hidden units (the smaller ovals in Figure 6.1) that function to mediate the associative mappings between the orthographic, phonological, and semantic layers. Seeing a word causes a pattern of activation over the orthographic layer specific to that word. This results in a cascading flow of excitatory and inhibitory signals throughout the network, and over time the network settles into a stable pattern of activation that serves as the representation of that word.

The speed and accuracy of the behavior of the network can be assessed by determining how long it takes to settle into a stable pattern and whether this pattern is an appropriate one given the input. Behavioral performance is a consequence of the flow of activation within the network, and the flow of activation is itself a consequence of the strength of the connections

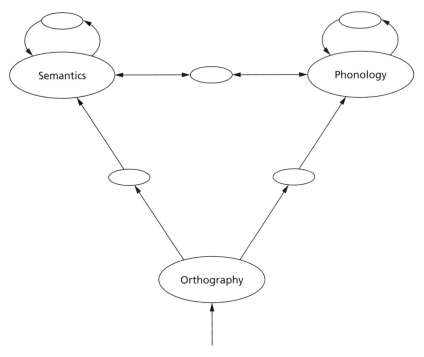

Figure 6.1. The triangle model.

between the nodes. A simple learning algorithm (*backpropagation*) is used to determine these connection strengths. Each time a word is presented, the resulting pattern of activation is compared to a target pattern (a pattern representing the correct pronunciation and meaning of that word) and the weights are changed to reduce the difference between these patterns. The changes made as a consequence of any particular learning event are small. As these changes accumulate and the network moves through its "weight space" (the high-dimensional space of all possible patterns of connectivity in the network), its behavior changes systematically. After a sufficient amount of experience (and under appropriate conditions— discussed below), the behavior of the network closely resembles that of skilled readers.

INDIVIDUAL DIFFERENCES

Simulations of the triangle model have been used to address a wide variety of reading phenomena. (See Rueckl, 2016, and Seidenberg, 2017, for reviews.) As with other computational models of word reading, these simulations have primarily focused on capturing the behavior of typical

readers. One reason for this is that these models are rooted in the literature on skilled adult reading, where (until recently) experimental data are
primarily characterized by measures of central tendency, and individual
differences are usually treated as little more than a source of observational
noise. Moreover, because many computational models lack a learning
mechanism, they offer limited means of capturing individual differences,
such as exploring how variation in the parameters of a model gives rise
to variations in behavior (see Ziegler et al., 2008, for an illustrative example). As a consequence, such theories provide little insight about the processes that give rise to differences among readers—a matter of particular
relevance for those who seek to understand, diagnose, and treat reading
disability.

In this light, it is noteworthy that although relatively few simulations of
the triangle model have directly addressed such differences (see Welbourne,
Woollams, Crisp, & Lambon Ralph, 2011, and Zevin & Seidenberg, 2006,
for notable exceptions), the theoretical principles of central importance to
the model's account of individual differences among readers can be articulated. First, the organization of the reading system changes incrementally
as it moves through its weight space as a consequence of experience with
written words. Thus, changes in organization are both continuous in form
and gradual in time.

Second, these trajectories through weight space vary from individual to individual. There are numerous factors that give rise to this variation, including 1) nonsystematic factors such as random variation in the
initial pattern of connectivity or the order in which words are encountered, 2) extrinsic (experiential) factors such as differences in instruction or
language-specific properties of the writing system, and 3) intrinsic factors
that constrain the processes underlying word reading and learning. In the
model, these factors are *control parameters*—values that specify either the
structure of the network (e.g., the number of units in a particular layer) or
the characteristics of the learning and activation functions (e.g., the degree
to which each function is deterministic or noisy).

Third, although the organization of an individual network can be
equated with its position in weight space, at the level of a population of
individuals this equivalence is technically and practically problematic.
These problems can be addressed by characterizing reading organization
in terms of higher order *dimensions of variation*. Some such dimensions are
primarily associated with the internal activation dynamics of the network
(e.g., the componentiality of the system representations [Plaut et al., 1996],
the relative importance of orthographic–semantic and orthographic–
phonological processes in word reading [Harm & Seidenberg, 2004]). Others index a reader's sensitivity to the statistical and structural properties of
the writing system, including orthographic–phonological correspondences
at the level of graphemes and phonemes; word bodies and word rimes;
or whole words, morphological structure, and semantic imageability.

(See Rueckl, 2016, for further discussion.) This approach is exemplified by a set of computational simulations, described below, in which we model not only differences between typically developing readers and those with dyslexia but also variation within each group.

Developmental Dyslexia

Researchers generally agree that developmental dyslexia does not have a single cause (see Chapter 11). Rather, there appear to be numerous developmental pathways that result in reading disability, as suggested by the variety of risk factors—genetic, neurobiological, cognitive, and environmental—associated with dyslexia. Many of the efforts to subtype reading disability (e.g., Morris et al., 1998) can be understood as efforts to reveal these distinct developmental pathways. This approach typically involves the classification of individuals on the basis of *cognitive profiles*— scores on measures that do not assess reading performance directly but rather index the language-specific and domain-general cognitive processes that reading and reading acquisition are dependent on.

Classification schemes of this type leave open the possibility that the various developmental pathways associated with reading disability all converge on a common outcome—an organization of the reading system that is less than optimal and that differs from the organization of typically developing readers. However, a parallel line of research suggests that there are important dimensions of variation in the organization of readers with dyslexia. These results suggest that individuals with dyslexia can be meaningfully classified on the basis of reading profiles—scores on a set of measures of reading that index the processes directly involved in word recognition. For example, researchers have argued that individual differences in the naming of irregular words (*pint*) and nonwords (*zill*) reveal differences in the proficiency of lexical and sublexical components of the reading system (Baron & Strawson, 1976). On the basis of this framework, Castles and Coltheart (1993) distinguished between individuals with phonological dyslexia, who exhibit a greater deficit on nonword naming than irregular word naming, and individuals with surface dyslexia, whose deficits on irregular word naming are more pronounced.

However, several subsequent developments have raised questions about the differences between phonological and surface dyslexia. First, although Manis, Seidenberg, Doi, McBride-Chang, and Peterson (1996) also observed that children with dyslexia differ with regard to whether they have more impairments in nonword or irregular word naming, they also noted that most readers with dyslexia have impairments on both measures relative to age-matched typically developing readers. Although this observation is not necessarily incompatible with the validity of the phonological/surface distinction, it does call into question the notion that these conditions arise due to the selective impairment of sublexical versus lexical processing mechanisms. Second, Manis and colleagues also concluded that the performance of children classified as having surface dyslexia closely matches that of younger typically developing readers. Manis and colleagues argued that whereas phonological dyslexia is associated with an atypical trajectory of reading development, surface dyslexia is a kind of developmental delay: Children classified as having surface dyslexia follow the same trajectory as typically developing readers but move along this trajectory at a slower rate.

Harm and Seidenberg (1999) reported computational modeling results that supported and extended the conclusions of Manis and colleagues (1996). The simulations of Harm and Seidenberg implemented the phonological pathway of the triangle model (the direct pathway from orthography to phonology in Figure 6.1). The model was trained on a set of English words and learned to map representations of how those words are spelled to representations of how they are pronounced. To simulate developmental dyslexia, Harm and Seidenberg manipulated several control parameters of the model. In general, varying these parameters systematically changes how a network behaves (Rueckl, 2016). Harm and Seidenberg found that phonological dyslexia resulted from parameter manipulations that degraded phonological representations of the model and that manipulations that produced more severe deficits in nonword naming resulted in larger deficits in irregular word naming as well. They also found that a different set of manipulations (those that impaired the capacity of the network to represent statistical regularities in the mapping from orthography to phonology or to learn these regularities efficiently) impaired irregular word naming more than nonword naming. Moreover, they demonstrated that the behavior of the networks with surface dyslexia closely resembled that of unimpaired networks earlier in training—as would be expected from the conclusion of Manis and colleagues (1996) that surface dyslexia is a form of developmental delay.

One important limitation of the study by Harm and Seidenberg (1999) is that they conducted different simulations to investigate the effects of each control variable. As a consequence, they did not explore potential interactions between these manipulations. In addition, different control parameters were associated with different degrees of impairment; although this may suggest subtypes within subtypes (i.e., different causal bases for mild, moderate, and severe phonological dyslexia), it may also reflect the small number of simulations conducted with each manipulation—a limitation owing to the relatively limited computational technology of the time. In the next section, we report the results of a large-scale simulation study replicating and extending the Harm and Seidenberg (1999) study.

Preliminary Results of a Large-Scale Simulation Study

The simulations reported here were conducted in the service of two ongoing projects investigating the effects of instruction and treatment on children spanning a range of grades and skill levels. One goal of the present simulations was to provide a more systematic exploration of the parameter space of the model than Harm and Seidenberg were able to perform. Thus, we conducted more than 2,000 simulations of the model, independently varying three control parameters: the amount of noise added to the activation of the phonological units, the number of hidden units mediating the mapping from orthography to phonology, and the parameter scaling the step size of the weight changes resulting from each learning trial. In the Harm and Seidenberg (1999) simulations, increasing the phonological noise parameter resulted in the pattern of impairment associated with phonological dyslexia, whereas reducing the number of hidden units or the learning step size resulted in surface dyslexia.

We manipulated each of the three control parameters more than 7–10 levels, and most of the possible combinations of the settings of the three parameters are represented in the results. (Some networks with extreme values of more than one parameter exhibited minimal learning. We excluded these networks from the analyses.) We trained each run of the model for 1 million trials with a training set that included 5,870 monosyllabic words. We evaluated the model at 19 points over the course of training using a test set that included a subset of the trained words as well as a list of nonwords taken from Treiman, Kessler, Zevin, Bick, and Davis (2006). No learning occurred during these tests.

Although an extensive report of the results is beyond the scope of this chapter, several general findings are worth noting. Not surprising, accuracy increased over the course of training. Moreover, performance varied as a function of stimulus type in a manner consistent with both human and previous simulation data. The simulations read high-frequency words more accurately than low frequency words. Likewise, the simulations read spelling–sound consistent words (e.g., *mint*) more accurately than irregular words (e.g., *pint*). On average, the simulations read words more accurately than nonwords, although the magnitude and direction of the lexicality effect varied somewhat depending on specific stimulus properties as well as the amount of training. Finally, each of the control parameter manipulations affected overall performance in a manner consistent with the results of previous simulations. On average, accuracy decreased as the amount of phonological noise increased, the number of hidden units decreased, and the learning step size diminished.[1] In addition to these main effects, the results also revealed two-way interactions of each combination of manipulations as well as a three-way interaction. A simple summary of

---

[1] These patterns depend in part on the range of parameter values employed. Thus, although performance was on average monotonically related to both the number of hidden units and the learning step size, there is reason to believe that performance will begin to degrade as either of these parameters gets sufficiently large. Indeed, the manipulation of the phonological noise parameter had a nonmonotonic effect: performance was worse with no noise than with small amounts of noise, although a high level of noise was quite disruptive.

these interactions is that the costs of a suboptimal setting of one parameter are magnified by suboptimal settings of the other parameters.

With these results as a backdrop, we now turn to the question of what these simulations reveal about the contrast between phonological and surface dyslexia. As it turns out, to address this question we must first wrestle with several conceptual issues about how to relate the simulation results to human data. First, on what basis should a network be classified as typically developing or dyslexic? In previous simulations (e.g., Harm & Seidenberg, 1999), this classification was based on the value of the control parameters: An initial exploration of parameter space was used to identify a set of parameter settings yielding behavior approximating that of typically developing children, and dyslexic networks were created by changing one or more of these values in a way that impaired performance. In the present simulations, each parameter varied over a range of values, and the impact of a given parameter depended in part on the values of the other parameters. Therefore, classification into reading groups on the basis of the control parameters is problematic.

One alternative is to use a performance-based classification strategy, but there are issues with this approach as well. For example, it would be possible to take a distributional approach and classify a particular network as dyslexic if, say, it performed more than 1.5 standard deviations below the mean (of the 2,000 networks in the population) on some measure of performance. One problem is that the means and standard deviations of any such measure are dependent on the distribution of control parameter combinations. In our simulations, we selected control parameter values to sample a wide range of possible combinations and not based on any assumptions about their distributions in human populations.

Another strategy would be to classify the networks as dyslexic or not based on a comparison to human data. One problem with this approach is that whereas dyslexia is generally defined in terms of age-appropriate reading achievement, networks do not have a chronological age in any meaningful way. On the contrary, precise information about the amount of reading experience is available for a network, whereas measures of reading experience (e.g., print exposure) are relatively imprecise and, more important, are generally not central to age-based definitions of reading disability. Thus, there is no a priori way to decide which point in training corresponds to, say, second grade. One possible approach is to use performance measures to make this decision. This is not an unreasonable approach. However, as noted previously, the learning trajectories for different types of stimuli vary systematically (in both growth rate and asymptotic performance) as a function of factors such as lexicality, frequency, and phonological consistency. This is particularly problematic given the hypothesis that different types of dyslexia are associated with the differential impairment of word or nonword reading. Which of these measures should be used to compare networks to children or to compare dyslexic networks

with skill-matched controls? It quickly became apparent that different conclusions could be supported by selecting different performance metrics
applied at different points in training.

In light of these considerations, we adopted a strategy that was geared
toward revealing the overall pattern in the data in a manner that minimized
the number of underlying assumptions and was unlikely to skew the data
one way or the other with regard to the questions of primary interest. There
are two key aspects to our approach. First, we opted not to classify each
network as typically developing or dyslexic; instead, we rank-ordered the
networks based on an overall measure of reading performance (average
accuracy across all stimulus types and all testing sessions). Although this
makes the connection between the simulation and human data more abstract, it provides a straightforward way to investigate the reading of irregular words and nonwords in relatively good versus relatively poor learners
(within the population of simulations). Second, we plotted each network behavior in a "performance space" such that each dimension of this space corresponds to a particular stimulus class and the position of a network along
each dimension corresponds to its accuracy in naming a set of test items
defined by that class. Assessing behavior in this way minimizes potential
issues due to the complicated relationship between chronological age and
amount of reading experience, and it allows us to characterize learning trajectories without reference to changes over time or amount of experience.

In the analyses reported here, we focus on naming stimuli that are
most relevant to the contrast between phonological and surface dyslexia:
irregular words and nonwords.[2] In Figure 6.2, nonword naming accuracy
is plotted as a function of irregular word naming accuracy. Each data point
represents the behavior of a particular network at a particular point in
training, and separate panels partition the data based on overall rank.
Three aspects of the results displayed in Figure 6.2 are of note. First, nonword accuracy and irregular word accuracy are (not surprising) positively
correlated. Second, the overall pattern is somewhat S-shaped: At low levels of accuracy, words tend to be named more accurately than nonwords;
at intermediate levels, nonwords tend to have the advantage; and at high
levels of performance, there is again a word advantage.[3] Third, this pattern is modulated by rank. For example, when irregular word accuracy is
50%, the proportion of networks naming more than 50% of the nonwords
correctly is highest for the networks ranked in the top 25%.

---

[2]The words and nonwords used to test the model were taken from the materials of
two ongoing projects investigating the effects of word exposure and remediation and
were selected based on their suitability for second- through fifth-grade students across a
wide range of reading abilities.

[3]Note that aspects of this pattern are contingent on the relative difficulty of the words
and nonwords. However, there are reasons to believe that the overall shape of the distribution is robust over materials, and it is of theoretical interest that this pattern bears some
relationship to Frith's (1986) stage theory of learning to read.

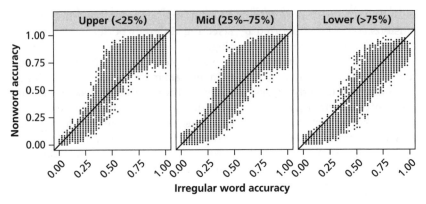

Figure 6.2. The distribution of test observations in performance space, portioned by rank.

These results are consistent with the general idea that poor readers tend to struggle with nonword reading in particular—the pattern associated with phonological dyslexia. But what about the converse pattern—the relative difficulty with nonword naming characteristic of surface dyslexia? Given the results of Harm and Seidenberg (1999), we would expect that these patterns result from different combinations of control parameters. In Figure 6.3, we break out the data based on these parameters. (Due to space limitations, only a theoretically relevant subset of the data is presented.) The left panel displays the results from networks with parameter settings similar to those of the network considered typically developing by Harm and Seidenberg (1999). All of these networks were in the top 25%

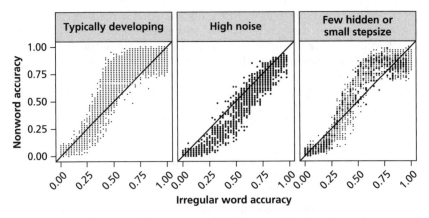

Figure 6.3. Distributions in performance space for different combinations of control parameters. (Larger points: Data from networks ranked in the bottom 25% of the population on overall accuracy.)

of the population in overall accuracy, and as can be seen, there is a strong S-shaped pattern with a pronounced nonword advantage at intermediate levels of word accuracy. The center panel displays the data from networks with relatively high levels of phonological noise. These networks generally name irregular words more accurately than they name nonwords, and compared to networks ranked in the top 75% in overall performance (see Figure 6.2), their nonword naming appears to be impaired across the range of irregular word–reading accuracy. The right panel of Figure 6.3 presents the data from networks with low levels of noise combined with low learning rates and/or small numbers of hidden units (according to Harm & Seidenberg, 1999, circumstances that give rise to surface dyslexia). Approximately half of these networks were ranked in the bottom 25% of the sample. The distributions of the lower and higher ranked networks in this subset are virtually indistinguishable. This pattern is consistent with the interpretation of surface dyslexia as a form of developmental delay: The lower-ranked networks in this subset were slower to learn (hence, their lower overall ranking), but their learning trajectories appear to be typical when plotted in performance space.

Although the question of whether surface dyslexia is a form of developmental delay is fundamentally a question about learning trajectories, it is difficult to plot a large number of trajectories in a concise and understandable way. Thus, in Figures 6.2 and 6.3 we plotted the data as distributions of what is in essence cross-sectional data. However, the shapes of these distributions are reflective of the underlying trajectories. To illustrate this point, in Figure 6.4 we plotted the trajectories of 10 networks from each of the subsets of networks corresponding to the three panels of Figure 6.3. Note the similarity between these trajectories and the shapes of their corresponding distributions in Figure 6.3.

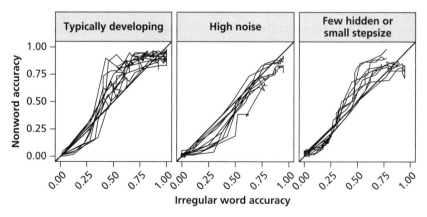

Figure 6.4. Representative learning trajectories.

CONCLUSION

The simulations reported here extend the Harm and Seidenberg (1999) study in several ways: We simulated a far larger population of networks (thanks in part to technological advances that occurred in the intervening years); we systematically and concurrently manipulated three control parameters, allowing for a more systematic exploration of behavioral consequences of these manipulations; and finally, we adopted an analytic strategy that sidestepped thorny issues about both the classification of networks as either typically developing or not and the relationship between chronological age and amount of reading experience. Despite these differences, our results are consistent with the major findings of Harm and Seidenberg: 1) among the networks that learned the slowest, some exhibited poorer performance on nonwords than on irregular words, and others exhibited the opposite pattern; 2) these differences were systematically related to the control parameters in that networks with high levels of phonological noise tended to name nonwords poorly, whereas networks with too few hidden units or step sizes that were too small had more impairments when naming irregular words; and 3) deficits in nonword naming were associated with learning trajectories that differed from those of most of the better learning networks, whereas the trajectories of slow-learning networks that struggled more with irregular words were similar to the trajectories of networks that learned at a faster rate.

One caveat should be noted here. As Figure 6.2 suggests, there was substantial variability in the learning trajectories of even the fastest learning networks. Indeed, we found that some networks with high levels of phonological noise were relatively fast learning but followed trajectories similar to the phonological dyslexia trajectory in Figure 6.4. These results suggest that this trajectory may be more diagnostic of a condition that gives rise to phonological dyslexia (namely, a noisy phonological system) than it is of phonological dyslexia per se.

Our results are suggestive of a number of theoretical issues that should be addressed in future research. First, in the simulations, we used nonword and irregular word naming to index two dimensions of variation relevant to individual differences in reading. What other dimensions should be investigated, and how should these dimensions be measured? Second, can theories be used to derive predictions about the distribution of individuals on these dimensions? Is a child's location on one dimension predictive of his or her location on other dimensions? Third, can the control parameters of the model be linked to genetic, neurobiological, or cognitive risk factors (Pennington, 2006) that may be predictive of reading achievement? (See Rueckl, 2016, for further discussion of these and other issues.)

Our results also have implications for empirical investigations of reading and reading acquisition. Perhaps the most important of these concerns is the variable relationship between chronological age and amount of experience. There are undoubtedly maturational and environmental factors that are tied to age (and not amount of reading experience) and that are relevant to reading acquisition. That said, from the perspective of a mechanistic theory, the primary driver of reading acquisition is reading experience. Although practices involving comparisons based on chronological age may be appropriate in some settings, they are likely to be problematic in others, especially in the context of research investigating the differences between typically developing and struggling readers in general (Huettig, Lachmann, Reis, & Petersson, 2018) and between children with phonological and surface dyslexia in particular (see, e.g., Peterson, Pennington, & Olson, 2013; Sprenger-Charolles, Siegel, Jimenez, & Ziegler, 2011). One way to avoid the problems associated with age matching is to match readers on measures indexing reading experience (e.g., Cunningham & Stanovich, 1990; Mol & Bus, 2011). An alternative strategy is the performance-space approach exemplified by the analyses discussed in this chapter.

REFERENCES

Baron, J., & Strawson, C. (1976). Use of orthographic and word-specific knowledge in reading words aloud. *Journal of Experimental Psychology: Human Perception and Performance, 2*(3), 386–393.

Castles, A., & Coltheart, M. (1993). Varieties of developmental dyslexia. *Cognition, 47*, 149–180.

Cunningham, A. E., & Stanovich, K. E. (1990). Assessing print exposure and orthographic processing skill in children: A quick measure of reading experience. *Journal of Educational Psychology, 82*, 733.

Frith, U. (1986). A developmental framework for developmental dyslexia. *Annals of Dyslexia, 36*, 67–81.

Gough, P. B. (1972). One second of reading. In J. F. Kavanagh & I. G. Mattingly (Eds.), *Language by ear and by eye: The relationship between speech and reading.* Cambridge, MA: MIT Press.

Harm, M. W., & Seidenberg, M. S. (1999). Phonology, reading acquisition, and dyslexia: Insights from connectionist models. *Psychological Review, 106*, 491–528.

Harm, M. W., & Seidenberg, M. S. (2004). Computing the meanings of words in reading: Cooperative division of labor between visual and phonological processes. *Psychological Review, 111*, 662–720.

Huettig, F., Lachmann, T., Reis, A., & Petersson, K. M. (2018). Distinguishing cause from effect—Many deficits associated with developmental dyslexia may be a consequence of reduced and suboptimal reading experience. *Language, Cognition and Neuroscience, 33*(3), 333–350.

Manis, F., Seidenberg, M., Doi, L., McBride-Chang, C., & Peterson, A. (1996). On the basis of two subtypes of developmental dyslexia. *Cognition, 58*, 157–195.

Mol, S. E., & Bus, A. G. (2011). To read or not to read: A meta-analysis of print exposure from infancy to early adulthood. *Psychological Bulletin, 137*(2), 267.

Morris, R. D., Stuebing, K. K., Fletcher, J. M., Shaywitz, S. E., Lyon, G. R., Shankweiler, D. P., . . . Shaywitz, B. A. (1998). Subtypes of reading disability: Variability around a phonological core. *Journal of Educational Psychology, 90*(3), 347–373.

Pennington, B. F. (2006). From single to multiple deficit models of developmental disorders. *Cognition, 101*(2), 385–413.

Peterson, R. L., Pennington, B. F., & Olson, R. K. (2013). Subtypes of developmental dyslexia: Testing the predictions of the dual-route and connectionist frameworks. *Cognition, 126*(1), 20–38.

Plaut, D. C., McClelland, J. L., Seidenberg, M. S., & Patterson, K. (1996). Understanding normal and impaired word reading: Computational principles in quasi-regular domains. *Psychological Review, 103,* 56–115.

Pritchard, S. C., Coltheart, M., Marinus, E., & Castles, A. (2018). A computational model of the self-teaching based on the dual-route cascaded model of reading. *Cognitive Science, 42*(3), 722–770.

Rueckl, J. G. (2016). Toward a theory of variation in the organization of the word reading system. *Scientific Studies of Reading, 20*(1), 86–97.

Seidenberg, M. (2017). *Language at the speed of sight: How we read, why so many can't, and what can be done about it.* New York, NY: Basic Books.

Seidenberg, M. S., & McClelland, J. L. (1989). A distributed, developmental model of word recognition and naming. *Psychological Review, 96,* 523–568.

Sprenger-Charolles, L., Siegel, L. S., Jimenez, J. E., & Ziegler, J. C. (2011). Prevalence and reliability of phonological, surface, and mixed profiles in dyslexia: A review of studies conducted in languages varying in orthographic depth. *Scientific Studies of Reading, 15*(6), 498–521.

Treiman, R., Kessler, B., Zevin, J. D., Bick, S., & Davis, M. (2006). Influence of consonantal context on the reading of vowels: Evidence from children. *Journal of Experimental Child Psychology, 93,* 1–24.

Welbourne, S. R., Woollams, A. M., Crisp, J., & Lambon Ralph, M. A. (2011). The role of plasticity-related functional reorganization in the explanation of central dyslexias. *Cognitive Neuropsychology, 28,* 65–108.

Zevin, J. D., & Seidenberg, M. S. (2006). Consistency effects and individual differences in nonword naming: A comparison of current models. *Journal of Memory and Language, 54,* 145–160.

Ziegler, J. C., Castel, C., Pech-Georgel, C., George, F., Alario, F.-X., & Perry, C. (2008). Developmental dyslexia and the dual route model of reading: Simulating individual differences and subtypes. *Cognition, 107,* 151–178.

CHAPTER 7

Orthographic Learning and Learning to Read

Implications for Developmental Dyslexia

Kate Nation and Matthew H. C. Mak

SUMMARY

Orthographic learning refers to the processes and knowledge that enable a person to make the transition from a novice to an expert reader. In this chapter, we examine the extent to which developmental dyslexia can be viewed as a failure of orthographic learning. The first section discusses dyslexia within the context of the self-teaching framework. It posits that translating letters to speech sounds (phonological decoding) is the core process required for orthographic learning. Furthermore, it predicts that because developmental dyslexia is characterized by consistently poor phonological skills, children with dyslexia should be poor at orthographic learning. Although few would dispute this causal chain, we review evidence that phonological deficits are unlikely to be the sole factor that leads to poor orthographic learning in dyslexia. In the following sections, we consider other factors that might contribute to orthographic learning. We first focus on paired-associate learning (PAL; the ability to learn arbitrary associations between two or more items), which has been shown to contribute independently to literacy acquisition in typical development. We then consider statistical learning (the ability to detect regularities in perceptual inputs), which sees orthographic learning as the acquisition of statistical regularities embedded in written languages. Although there is some evidence to suggest that differences in PAL and statistical learning ability are associated with individual differences in reading and with dyslexia, we argue that there are important theoretical and methodological issues that need to be clarified before strong conclusions can be made.

INTRODUCTION

Researchers recognize that beginning readers must ultimately move from having a reading system that is heavily reliant on phonological decoding to one that recognizes words rapidly via access to rich, high-quality lexical representations. This requires instruction and a good deal of reading

Acknowledgments: This chapter was prepared with the support of The Economic and Social Research Council to the first author, grant reference ES/M009998/1. Matthew H. C. Mak is supported by a scholarship from the Drs. Richard Charles and Esther Yewpick Lee Charitable Foundation.

experience (for review, see Castles, Rastle, & Nation, 2018). Developmental dyslexia represents a difficulty with learning to read. In this chapter, we consider dyslexia in the context of *orthographic learning*—the term used to refer to the processes or knowledge that needs to be acquired for a child to move from novice to expert (Castles & Nation, 2006; Nation & Castles, 2017).

At the heart of orthographic learning is the need for a child to understand how his or her writing system works. Learning how letters relate to sounds is not easy in English because the relationship between orthography and phonology is not straightforward. For example, the words *beat, street, ski, theme,* and *thief* all contain the same vowel pronunciation but look different, whereas *steak* and *teak* look very similar yet sound very different, and despite looking different and having distinct meanings, *weak* and *week* have identical pronunciations. English is quasi-regular—there is much consistency but with exceptions. Some spellings are truly exceptional, such as the "ot" sound in *yacht,* whereas others are much more predictable. For example, graphemes representing English vowels are notoriously variable in terms of how they are pronounced, but the consonant context in which a particular vowel appears does much to narrow things down (e.g., Treiman, Kessler, Zevin, Bick, & Davis, 2006). Alongside orthographic regularities (e.g., Gingras & Sénéchal, 2019; Pacton, Perruchet, Fayol, & Cleeremans, 2001), connections between orthography and morphology are quasi-regular (e.g., Rastle, 2019; Rueckl, 2010), as is the assignment of lexical stress when reading aloud (e.g., Arciuli, Monaghan, & Seva, 2010). At multiple levels, therefore, written language is a system, and each written language has its own unique statistical structure. As children learn to read and experience print, they become increasingly familiar with the distributional properties that characterize their orthographic system. Learning to read is about internalizing these statistics such that a person's orthographic knowledge embodies the conventions of how his or her written language works.

By definition, dyslexia represents difficulty with learning to read. For whatever reason, the reading system struggles to move from novice to expert. It is possible to address what is meant by "whatever reason" in diverse ways and at multiple levels of explanation, from genetic (see Chapter 3) to neural pathways (see Chapter 5), and from detailed cognitive models (see Chapter 11) to computational instantiations (see Chapter 6). Our approach is to consider whether dyslexia is, for whatever reason, a failure of orthographic learning. To do this, we need to consider orthographic learning in typical development before asking what might be different in children with dyslexia.

PHONOLOGICAL DECODING AND ORTHOGRAPHIC LEARNING VIA SELF-TEACHING

The self-teaching hypothesis (Share, 1999) has phonological decoding at its core. Translating from print to sound provides children with a means of accessing the spoken form of a word from its written form. Early on in reading development, decoding might be slow and effortful; however, it encourages children to focus on the letters in the word and their sequence and how they relate to spoken language. The consequence of this for reading development is twofold. First, it provides an opportunity to learn word-specific knowledge that constitutes the orthographic form of a word. This knowledge will then be available on future encounters with the word, lessening the reliance on phonological decoding and instead supporting direct connections between orthography and meaning. Second, it provides the substrate from which more general knowledge about the writing system begins to emerge. As Nation and Castles (2017) noted, "This includes knowledge of regularities and sub-regularities, orthographic conventions and exceptions to those conventions, statistics which sum over time to provide each individual child with their own experience-based database of orthographic knowledge" (p. 150).

Phonological decoding being at the core of orthographic learning has obvious implications for dyslexia as it is generally accepted that children with dyslexia find decoding difficult. This is illustrated most clearly by the nonword-reading deficit—the observation that most individuals with dyslexia have disproportionate difficulty with reading nonwords (e.g., Rack, Snowling & Olson, 1992; but see also Chapter 11) as a consequence of underlying phonological deficits—difficulty with perceiving, manipulating, or processing speech sounds (e.g., Snowling & Hulme, 1994). If poor phonological skills lead to problems with decoding, what follows, according to the principles of the self-teaching hypothesis, is a deficit in orthographic learning. This makes sense and is well-evidenced, given dyslexia is defined as a difficulty learning to read, which at a broad level must be associated with differences in orthographic learning.

This straightforward causal chain, however, is unlikely to be the whole story. At one extreme, consider those children with severe phonological dyslexia (i.e., children who find phonological decoding extraordinarily difficult and whose nonword-reading deficits manifest across the life span). If phonological decoding is the only foundation required for orthographic learning, it follows that children with phonological dyslexia would never learn to read words. This clearly is not the case: Such children do learn to read words, albeit more slowly and effortfully than their peers. This suggests that other factors also contribute to orthographic learning.

At the other extreme, consider children described as surface dyslexic. Such children have all the hallmarks of poor orthographic learning, including poor spelling and lack of word-specific orthographic knowledge. Yet, for some children with surface dyslexia, there is no evidence of them having or ever having had problems with phonological decoding (see Chapter 11). For these children, then, why have their strong phonological decoding skills not fueled equally strong orthographic learning?

To shed light on these paradoxes, some studies have attempted to chart orthographic learning directly in children with dyslexia, using a variation of Share's self-teaching paradigm (e.g., Bailey, Manis, Pederson, & Seidenberg, 2004; Wang, Marinus, Nickels & Castles, 2014; Wang, Nickels, & Castles, 2015). It is hard to draw strong conclusions, given the small literature and the small samples that characterize some studies. What is clear, however, is that there is variation in orthographic learning via self-teaching, and this variation does not neatly align with the nature or severity of a child's decoding difficulties. There is more to orthographic learning than phonological decoding, a conclusion that chimes with evidence from studies of reading development more generally. Less clear is which other cognitive skills play a causal role in orthographic learning, beyond phonological decoding itself, or factors that are the direct product of phonological decoding (for discussion, see Nation & Castles, 2017).

Written words are a particular class of stimuli, and the self-teaching hypothesis is a specific hypothesis about learning to read words. Another approach to understanding reading acquisition and dyslexia is to situate learning to read in the context of learning and memory mechanisms more generally (e.g., Nation & Castles, 2017; Sawi & Rueckl, 2019). With this in mind, we now turn to consider PAL and statistical learning with respect to reading development and dyslexia.

IMPAIRED PAIRED-ASSOCIATE LEARNING AS A CAUSE OF DYSLEXIA?

Given that the ability to learn the mappings between a written language system (orthography) and a spoken language system (i.e., phonology) forms a crucial basis for the development of literacy, it is no surprise that PAL has garnered much interest in our field. PAL tasks typically require a child to learn an arbitrary association between a stimulus item and a response item. Children who are good on PAL tasks tend to be good at reading too, and PAL shares a unique relationship with reading that cannot be readily accounted for by other known cognitive predictors of reading, including, for example, phonological awareness (e.g., Warmington & Hulme, 2012). There is some evidence that PAL predicts progress in reading development longitudinally across Grades 1–5 (e.g., Poulsen & Elbro, 2018; but see Lervåg, Bråten, & Hulme, 2009); PAL performance also predicts how well children acquire novel orthographic representations in an orthographic learning task (Wang, Wass, & Castles, 2017). In line with these relationships in typical development, children with dyslexia are poor at PAL (e.g., Messbauer & de Jong, 2006). Therefore, whatever causes children with dyslexia to perform poorly on PAL tasks might also be the root of their reading problem.

It is possible to contrast two theoretical accounts of the PAL–reading relationship, both with implications for understanding dyslexia. According to the cross-modal theory, the PAL–reading relationship is driven by a cross-modal (i.e., visual—verbal) associative learning mechanism that is crucial for the acquisition of orthographic knowledge (Hulme, Goetz,

Gooch, Adams, & Snowling, 2007). According to this view, children with dyslexia might have difficulty with learning to read because this mechanism is not working well. In contrast, the verbal theory asserts that the PAL–reading relationship is driven by the verbal component of the task and that the verbal skills tapped by this component are strongly related to reading ability (Litt, de Jong, van Bergen, & Nation, 2013). On this view, children with dyslexia are poor at PAL (and at reading) because of underlying verbal-phonological deficits. Evidence is accumulating for the latter hypothesis (e.g., Clayton, Sears, Davis, & Hulme, 2018), with differences in phonological learning being key for helping researchers understand why variations in PAL are associated with variations in learning to read (Litt & Nation, 2014; Litt, Wang, Sailah, Badcock, & Castles, 2019).

It seems clear that PAL is a correlate of reading, but discussion continues as to the nature of the role it might play in reading development and in dyslexia. Is it a cause, correlate, or consequence? One important question concerns specificity. In the PAL literature, evidence is emerging to show that poor PAL in dyslexia is attributable to phonological learning— that difficulty in learning new phonological forms constrains how well these can then be associated with another stimulus (e.g., Litt & Nation, 2014). Although this variance is statistically distinct from "known culprits" implicated in dyslexia, such as phonological awareness and rapid naming, problems with phonological learning clearly sit comfortably within the phonological deficit hypothesis. It is also possible to emphasize the arbitrary nature of the associations to be learned in classic PAL tasks, in line with the view that PAL is a marker of declarative learning. However, the finding that phonological learning explains the ease with which children are able to learn stimulus–verbal response associations requires researchers to ask why there is variation in phonological learning. One possibility is that this aligns with variation in procedural learning—children's ability to implicitly learn information that is sequential and structured probabilistically, such as phonological information. Relevant to this point are speculations that statistical learning ability is related to learning to read and is causally implicated in developmental dyslexia.

IMPAIRED STATISTICAL LEARNING AS A CAUSE OF DYSLEXIA?

As discussed previously, learning to read can be described as learning the statistical structure that characterizes written language. Being good at reading means that an individual has good knowledge of the statistics that capture the writing system; he or she has internalized the orthographic conventions of his or her language and can use this knowledge to recognize words and as the basis for generalizing to new words. For example, given the nonword *poom*, most people generate a pronunciation rhyming with *room*; by contrast, most people pronounce the nonword *pook* as rhyming with *book* or *spook* (Treiman, Kessler, & Bick, 2003).

If learning to read is, at least in part, a consequence of learning the distributional properties that characterize the orthographic system, might it be the case that some people are poor at reading because they are poor at learning relationships between stimuli that are graded and probabilistic? This would not be a reading problem in a specific sense but more of a domain-general problem that nevertheless has serious implications for learning to read. Preliminary evidence consistent with this hypothesis comes from studies that take an individual differences approach to discover whether statistical learning ability is associated with reading development. For example, Arciuli and Simpson (2012) reported a modest correlation between word-reading ability and how well people can track covert statistics across sequentially occurring visual images in a visual statistical learning task. Spencer, Kaschak, Jones, and Lonigan (2015) reported similar findings. Taken together, these studies lend support to the idea that the ability to implicitly detect statistical patterns across visual input is a skill that contributes independently to reading development.

This leads naturally to the question of whether statistical learning difficulties might cause dyslexia. To address this question, researchers have examined statistical learning in groups of individuals with dyslexia, comparing their performance with that of a control group. There is some evidence that there may be impairments in statistical learning in dyslexia. For example, Szmalec, Loncke, Page, and Duyck (2011) found reduced learning in a Hebb repetition task among individuals with dyslexia, suggesting a lack of sensitivity to sequential information. Likewise, some studies have found individuals with dyslexia to perform less well on serial reaction time tasks—another type of task that taps sequential learning (for review, see Lum, Ullman, & Conti-Ramsden, 2013).

Not all studies report consistent findings, however, making it impossible to draw strong conclusions on the basis of the existing literature (for review, see Schmalz, Altoè, & Mulatti, 2017). For example, Steacy and colleagues (2019) found essentially no correlation between a measure of visual statistical learning (as developed by Arciuli & Simpson, 2012) and a range of reading and reading-related variables in their study with 96 children in second to fifth grade. Alongside lack of replication between studies, how well a person performs on one putative measure of statistical learning does not predict how well he or she will perform on another. For example, Schmalz, Moll, Mulatti, and Schulte-Körne (2019) found no correlation between two measures of statistical learning in typically reading adults, mirroring the lack of correlation between Hebb learning and serial reaction time performance in dyslexia (Henderson & Warmington, 2017). This lack of cross-task correlation might reflect poor task reliability (e.g., Siegelman, Bogaerts, & Frost, 2017; West, Vadillo, Shanks, & Hulme, 2017). A more positive explanation might be that different tasks tap different aspects of statistical learning ability (Frost, Armstrong, Siegelman, & Christiansen, 2015). On this view, statistical learning is componential, not a unitary and domain-general learning mechanism (e.g., Siegelman, Bogaerts, Christiansen, & Frost, 2017).

Returning to the relationship between statistical learning and reading, Sawi and Rueckl (2019) argued that as reading processes are shaped by the statistical structure of the writing system, learning to read is "fundamentally a form of statistical learning." They also stated that it remains an open question as to whether statistical learning in this context is at all related to statistical learning as captured by tasks such as serial reaction time, given lack of replication of the reading–statistical learning relationship across studies, as well as methodological concerns regarding reliability. Building on the notion that statistical learning is componential and multi-faceted, they offered some speculative hypotheses about how it may relate to reading, learning to read, and to dyslexia, drawing on the division of labor between two pathways involved in word reading (Harm & Seidenberg, 2004). They suggested that different types of statistical learning might underpin different components of the reading system, with the capacity to learn arbitrary mappings characterizing the semantic pathway, served by the memory systems in the medial temporal lobe, whereas more frontal-striatal procedural memory systems are critical for acquiring the more systematic and structured mappings that characterize the phonological pathway. They further speculated that heterogeneity in dyslexia might be associated with differences in specific components of statistical learning, leading to differences in reading behavior across varieties or subtypes of dyslexia (see Chapter 11).

These are theoretically plausible suggestions that await further evidence. At present, there are reasons to remain somewhat cautious. For example, Steacy and colleagues (2019) found that children used more sophisticated and context-dependent vowel pronunciations with increasing levels of reading experience, consistent with their becoming increasingly tuned to variations in grapheme–phoneme correspondence statistics. However, this development was not at all predicted by performance on a visual statistical learning task. Thus, while reading acquisition can be usefully described as learning the statistical structure of one's writing system, more work is needed to understand how (or indeed whether) this relates to concepts of statistical learning ability, distal to the reading system itself.

In summary, there is some evidence to suggest that it might be meaningful to talk about individual differences in statistical learning ability that influence reading development. However, there are critical issues with replication. These might reflect solvable methodological issues, or they might reflect the fact that it is not meaningful to consider statistical learning as a domain-general capacity with respect to reading. Another possibility is that there are more specific aspects of statistical learning that do relate to aspects of reading. However, the more statistical tasks resemble the task in hand—reading—the harder it is to maintain a distinction between statistical learning as a cause of individual differences in reading versus a finer level description of them. Researchers are tackling issues regarding the reliability and specificity of statistical learning measures and of individual differences in statistical learning (Siegelman et al., 2017). An important next step will be to consider in more detail how (and whether) these specific indices relate to learning to read and failures of learning to read in theoretically meaningful ways.

CONCLUSION

Critical to developing orthographic expertise is the accumulation of knowledge about the writing system. For this to happen, reading experience is clearly needed. Reading provides an opportunity to experience specific words; reading also provides the substrate from which probabilistic knowledge is extracted, built, and refined, based on what has been learned and experienced by the child to date. In short, reading experience generates the statistics: a child's own orthographic database, based on his or her own lexical history (Nation, 2017). By definition, children with dyslexia struggle to learn to read, and for these children, their statistics will be compromised relative to peers who have read more. In some sense, then, dyslexia represents nonoptimal orthographic learning, resulting in a reading system that inadequately reflects the statistical structure of the writing system. In this chapter, we explored why this might be.

The self-teaching hypothesis outlines how the reading system begins, with phonological decoding providing the necessary foundation. This account provides a natural explanation of some children's poor orthographic learning, given the severe difficulties with phonological decoding that are commonly seen in dyslexia. However, data from studies of both typical development and of dyslexia suggest that other factors are likely to be important too, although these factors are not yet understood (e.g., Nation & Castles, 2017; Share, 2008). We reviewed two factors, PAL and statistical learning, and we asked whether it is useful to consider learning to read within the context of learning and memory more generally. With this as a backdrop, we can then ask whether individuals with dyslexia differ in these domains and whether these differences might be causally implicated in their poor reading. Although there is some evidence consistent with there being more domain-general learning differences associated with dyslexia, we have also seen that there are many open questions—some methodological, some theoretical. These questions need to be addressed before we can fully understand the nature and origins of individual differences in orthographic learning.

REFERENCES

Arciuli, J., Monaghan, P., & Seva, N. (2010). Learning to assign lexical stress during reading aloud: Corpus, behavioral, and computational investigations. *Journal of Memory and Language, 63*(2), 180–196. http://dx.doi.org/10.1016/j.jml.2010.03.005

Arciuli, J., & Simpson, I. C. (2012). Statistical learning is related to reading ability in children and adults. *Cognitive Science, 36*(2), 286–304. http://dx.doi.org/10.1111/j.1551 -6709.2011.01200.x

Bailey, C., Manis, F., Pedersen, W., & Seidenberg, M. (2004). Variation among developmental dyslexics: Evidence from a printed-word-learning task. *Journal of Experimental Psychology, 87,* 125–154.

Castles, A., & Nation, K. (2006). How does orthographic learning happen? In S. Andrews (Ed.), *From inkmarks to ideas: Challenges and controversies about word recognition and reading* (pp. 151–179). London, England: Psychology Press.

Castles, A., Rastle, K., & Nation, K. (2018). Ending the reading wars: Reading acquisition from novice to expert. *Psychological Science in the Public Interest, 19*(1), 5–51. http://dx.doi .org/10.1177/1529100618772271

Clayton, F. J., Sears, C., Davis, A., & Hulme, C. (2018). Verbal task demands are key in explaining the relationship between paired-associate learning and reading ability. *Journal of Experimental Child Psychology, 171,* 46–54. http://dx.doi.org/10.1016/j.jecp.2018.01.004

Frost, R., Armstrong, B. C., Siegelman, N., & Christiansen, M. H. (2015). Domain generality versus modality specificity: The paradox of statistical learning. *Trends in Cognitive Sciences, 19*(3), 117–125.

Gingras, M., & Sénéchal, M. (2019). Evidence of statistical learning of orthographic representations in grades 1–5: The case of silent letters and double consonants in French. *Scientific Studies of Reading, 23*(1), 37–48. http://dx.doi.org/10.1080/10888438.2018 .1482303

Harm, M. W., & Seidenberg, M. S. (2004). Computing the meanings of words in reading: Cooperative division of labor between visual and phonological processes. *Psychological Review, 111,* 662–720. http://dx.doi.org/10.1037/0033-295X.111.3.662

Henderson, L. M., & Warmington, M. (2017). A sequence learning impairment in dyslexia? It depends on the task. *Research in Developmental Disabilities, 60,* 198–210. http:// dx.doi.org/10.1016/j.ridd.2016.11.002

Hulme, C., Goetz, K., Gooch, D., Adams, J., & Snowling, M. J. (2007). Paired-associate learning, phoneme awareness, and learning to read. *Journal of Experimental Child Psychology, 96*(2), 150–166.

Lervåg, A., Bråten, I., & Hulme, C. (2009). The cognitive and linguistic foundations of early reading development: A Norwegian latent variable longitudinal study. *Developmental Psychology, 45*(3), 764–781. http://dx.doi.org/10.1037/a0014132

Litt, R. A., de Jong, P. F., van Bergen, E., & Nation, K. (2013). Dissociating crossmodal and verbal demands in paired associate learning (PAL): What drives the PAL–reading relationship? *Journal of Experimental Child Psychology, 115,* 137–149. http://dx.doi .org/10.1016/j.jecp.2012.11.012

Litt, R. A., & Nation, K. (2014). The nature and specificity of paired associate learning deficits in children with dyslexia. *Journal of Memory and Language, 71*(1), 71–88. http:// dx.doi.org/10.1016/j.jml.2013.10.005

Litt, R. A., Wang, H.-C., Sailah, J., Badcock, N. A., & Castles, A. (2019). Paired associate learning deficits in poor readers: The contribution of phonological input and output processes. *Quarterly Journal of Experimental Psychology, 72*(3), 616–613. http://dx.doi .org/10.1177/1747021818762669

Lum, J. A. G., Ullman, M. T., & Conti-Ramsden, G. (2013). Procedural learning is impaired in dyslexia: Evidence from a meta-analysis of serial reaction time studies. *Research in Developmental Disabilities, 34*(10), 3460–3476. http://dx.doi.org/10.1016/j. ridd.2013.07.017

Messbauer, V. C. L., & de Jong, P. F. (2006). Effects of visual and phonological distinctness on visual-verbal paired-associate learning in Dutch dyslexic and normal readers. *Reading and Writing, 19,* 393–426. http://dx.doi.org/10.1007/s11145-005-5121-7

Nation, K. (2017). Nurturing a lexical legacy: Reading experience is critical for the development of word reading skill. *NPJ Science of Learning, 2*(1), 3. http://dx.doi.org/10.1038/s41539-017-0004-7

Nation, K., & Castles, A. (2017). Putting the learning in to orthographic learning. In K. Cain, D. Compton, & R. Parrila (Eds.), *Theories of reading development* (pp. 147–168). Amsterdam, The Netherlands: John Benjamins. http://dx.doi.org/10.1075/swll.15

Pacton, S., Perruchet, P., Fayol, M., & Cleeremans, A. (2001). Implicit learning out of the lab: The case of orthographic regularities. *Journal of Experimental Psychology: General, 130*, 401–426. http://dx.doi.org/10.1037/0096-3445.130.3.401

Poulsen, M., & Elbro, C. (2018). The short- and long-term predictions of reading accuracy and speed from paired-associate learning. *Journal of Experimental Child Psychology, 174*, 77–89.

Rack, J. P., Snowling, M. J., & Olson, R. K. (1992). The nonword reading deficit in developmental dyslexia: A review. *Reading Research Quarterly, 27*(1), 28–53. http://dx.doi.org/10.2307/747832

Rastle, K. (2019). Writing systems, reading, and language. The EPS Mid-Career Award Lecture. *Quarterly Journal of Experimental Psychology, 72*(4), 677–692. https://doi.org/10.1177/1747021819829696

Rueckl, J. G. (2010). Connectionism and the role of morphology in visual word recognition. *The Mental Lexicon, 5*(3), 371–400. http://dx.doi.org/10.1075/ml.5.3.07rue

Sawi, O. M., & Rueckl, J. (2019). Reading and the neurocognitive bases of statistical learning. *Scientific Studies of Reading, 23*(1), 8–23. http://dx.doi.org/10.1080/10888438.2018.1457681

Schmalz, X., Altoè, G., & Mulatti, C. (2017). Statistical learning and dyslexia: A systematic review. *Annals of Dyslexia, 67*(2), 147–162. http://dx.doi.org/10.1007/s11881-016-0136-0

Schmalz, X., Moll, K., Mulatti, C., & Schulte-Körne, G. (2019). Is statistical learning ability related to reading ability, and if so, why? *Scientific Studies of Reading, 23*(1), 64–76. http://dx.doi.org/10.1080/10888438.2018.1482304

Share, D. L. (1999). Phonological recoding and orthographic learning: A direct test of the self-teaching hypothesis. *Journal of Experimental Child Psychology, 72*(2), 95–129. http://dx.doi.org/10.1006/jecp.1998.2481

Share, D. L. (2008). On the Anglocentricities of current reading research and practice: The perils of overreliance on an "outlier" orthography. *Psychological Bulletin, 134*, 584–615.

Siegelman, N., Bogaerts, L., Christiansen, M. H., & Frost, R. (2017). Towards a theory of individual differences in statistical learning. *Philosophical Transactions of the Royal Society. Series B: Biological Sciences, 372*(1711), 20160059. http://dx.doi.org/10.1098/rstb.2016.0059

Siegelman, N., Bogaerts, L., & Frost, R. (2017). Measuring individual differences in statistical learning: Current pitfalls and possible solutions. *Behavior Research Methods, 49*(2), 418–432. http://dx.doi.org/10.3758/s13428-016-0719-z

Snowling, M. J., & Hulme, C. (1994). The development of phonological skills. *Philosophical Transactions of the Royal Society. Series B: Biological Sciences, 346*(1315), 21–28. http://dx.doi.org/10.1098/rstb.1994.0124

Spencer, M., Kaschak, M. P., Jones, J. L., & Lonigan, C. J. (2015). Statistical learning is related to early literacy-related skills. *Reading and Writing, 28*(4), 467–490. http://dx.doi.org/10.1007/s11145-014-9533-0

Steacy, L. M., Compton, D., Petscher, Y., Elliott, J. D., Smith, K., Rueckl, J. G., . . . Pugh, K. R. (2019). Development and prediction of context-dependent vowel pronunciation in elementary readers. *Scientific Studies of Reading, 23*(1), 49–63. http://dx.doi.org/10.1080/10888438.2018.1466303

Szmalec, A., Loncke, M., Page, M. P., & Duyck, W. (2011). Order or disorder? Impaired Hebb learning in dyslexia. *Journal of Experimental Psychology: Learning, Memory and Cognition, 37*(5), 1270–1279. http://dx.doi.org/10.1037/a0023820

Treiman, R., Kessler, B., & Bick, S. (2003). Influence of consonantal context on the pronunciation of vowels: A comparison of human readers and computational models. *Cognition, 88*, 49–78. http://dx.doi.org/10.1016/S0010-0277(03)00003-9

Treiman, R., Kessler, B., Zevin, J., Bick, S., & Davis, M. (2006). Influence of consonantal context on the reading of vowels: Evidence from children. *Journal of Experimental Child Psychology, 93*, 1–24. http://dx.doi.org/10.1016/j.jecp.2005.06.008

Wang, H. C., Marinus, E., Nickels, L., & Castles, A. (2014). Tracking orthographic learning in children with different profiles of reading difficulty. *Frontiers in Human Neuroscience, 8*(July), 1–14. http://dx.doi.org/10.3389/fnhum.2014.00468

Wang, H. C., Nickels, L., & Castles, A. (2015). Orthographic learning in developmental surface and phonological dyslexia. *Cognitive Neuropsychology, 32*(2), 58–79. http://dx.doi.org/10.1080/02643294.2014.1003536

Wang, H. C., Wass, M., & Castles, A. (2017). Paired-associate learning ability accounts for unique variance in orthographic learning. *Scientific Studies of Reading, 21*(1), 5–16. http://dx.doi.org/10.1080/10888438.2016.1231686

Warmington, M., & Hulme, C. (2012). Phoneme awareness, visual-verbal paired-associate learning, and rapid automatized naming as predictors of individual differences in reading ability. *Scientific Studies of Reading, 16*(1), 45–62. http://dx.doi.org/10.1080/10888438.2010.534832

West, G., Vadillo, M. A., Shanks, D. R., & Hulme, C. (2017). The procedural learning deficit hypothesis of language learning disorders: We see some problems. *Developmental Science, 21*(2), e12552. http://dx.doi.org/10.1111/desc.12552

Bringing Together Multiple Methods and Measurements to Improve Our Understanding of Dyslexia

Elizabeth S. Norton

F or as many processes and levels as there are involved in skilled reading, there are equally as many approaches to studying reading development and how it differs in dyslexia, from behavioral profiles to brain scans, genes, or computer simulations of reading. The chapters in Section II review some of the extensive work that has been done in each of these areas, yielding converging evidence for some concepts, such as the need to consider these multiple processes that must interact smoothly to produce fluent reading. Despite their varying backgrounds, the authors share several common viewpoints on how the field might resolve the outstanding questions regarding the etiology and assessment of dyslexia. Understanding the multiple linguistic, cognitive, and learning processes that comprise reading ability and the heterogeneity of individual profiles that these many factors can produce will be crucial for accurate understanding and diagnosis of dyslexia. In addition to assessing behavior at multiple levels, characterizing a child's genetic-epigenetic-neurobiological profile as well as the child's environment is important. Then, measuring how each of these factors changes and interacts over time will provide the most comprehensive picture of the causes and correlates of dyslexia. It will take multidisciplinary teams who can bring together expertise in all of these areas with rigorous methods and large data sets to address the longstanding questions of the cause(s) of dyslexia, how best to identify children accurately, and how to provide successful intervention.

INTRODUCTION

Despite the substantial research related to dyslexia, a plethora of basic and applied questions remain unanswered. In this section, authors from diverse research perspectives—behavioral, genetic, neuroimaging, and computational—provide summaries of the state of our field in understanding the etiology, expression, and best practices for diagnosis of dyslexia. Indeed, each chapter provides insights into basic facets of dyslexia that are still evolving, as was the goal of The Dyslexia Foundation meeting that inspired this volume.

THE COMPLEX BIOLOGICAL BASIS OF DYSLEXIA

In Chapter 3, Landi summarizes the research relating genetics of dyslexia to brain and behavior measures and lays out the challenges the field faces in this area. Despite the high heritability of dyslexia, the genes that have been identified to date only account for a very small amount of variation in behavior. Thus, researchers have attempted to bridge the gap between genetics and behavior by looking at links between genes and the brain, which are likely to be more directly related. Even so, the picture remains quite complicated. The studies reviewed in the chapter differ not only in the candidate dyslexia genes examined but in the imaging methods, languages studied, and criteria for dyslexia; thus, the heterogeneity in results that is observed across studies is not surprising. In work from Landi's lab looking at more "generalist" genes that broadly affect cognition and reading, the results are still quite complex. Given that dyslexia is, by definition, genetic and brain based, how can researchers reconcile this ambiguity among genes, brain, and behavior? In an effort to move the field toward a clearer picture of these complex associations that support reading, Landi lays out a series of key challenges related to reproducibility and the need for converging evidence from multiple large-scale studies. Finally, Landi calls for imaging genetics studies to begin to examine the broader educational and environmental factors that shape reading over time through varied mechanisms, including epigenetic factors, which change dynamically during an individual's lifetime.

CONSIDERATIONS FOR DIAGNOSIS AND ASSESSMENT

Diagnosing dyslexia is often a crucial first step in obtaining services and helping improve a child's reading ability. The seemingly straightforward concept of which factors should be considered in diagnosis is discussed by de Jong in Chapter 4. Though the field has moved away from an IQ–reading ability discrepancy criterion, debate remains as to whether unexpectedness of reading ability given an individual's reading-related cognitive abilities (e.g., phonological awareness, rapid automatized naming [RAN] ability) is required for a diagnosis of dyslexia—or is useful in practice. De Jong asserts that classifications of reading-related cognitive abilities can be unstable among individuals and may not be informative for intervention. In the same way that there seems to be a missing link between genetic profiles and reading ability, there is a similar lack of direct correspondence between an individual's profile in terms of reading-related cognitive abilities and the individual's reading ability. De Jong suggests that this apparent disconnect may arise from an incomplete understanding of the deficits underlying dyslexia. Furthermore, he presents a framework that differentiates these cognitive deficits as being either distal and noncausal risk factors, or proximal and causal indicators of reading ability. These notions are worthy of further study. De Jong then discusses evidence for using multicomponential assessment as a method to detect the rare cases when an individual may be feigning dyslexia in order to access beneficial accommodations. Taken together, the arguments in this chapter shed light on the need for continued examination of the component abilities that underlie reading, their assessment and change over time as these relate to reading, and how they meaningfully affect day-to-day function and outcomes across the spectrum of reading ability.

Despite the inconsistency in diagnostic criteria and terms that are still very present in the field, Gaab, Turesky, and Sanfilippo present a case for early assessment of reading-related skills, as well as the need for a framework to respond to screening, in Chapter 5. Studies of children at risk for poor reading using magnetic resonance imaging (MRI) show that they differ from their typically reading peers in terms of the brain's regional gray matter volume, white matter connections, sulcal folding patterns, functional activity, and functional connectivity. Gaab's research team has led efforts to assess many of these factors much earlier in life and to examine the unfolding longitudinal patterns of brain and behavior within individuals. Though new preliminary analyses described in the chapter show that structural and functional measures from MRI differ in babies with versus without family history of dyslexia, Gaab and colleagues assert that MRI neuroimaging approaches are unlikely to reach the levels of sensitivity and specificity needed to achieve widespread practical use for dyslexia screening. Thus, they call for the development of high-quality behavioral screeners, emphasizing the need for these measures to be multicomponential (assessing all the key reading- and language-related skills that work together to support reading, e.g., Katzir et al., 2006), accessible, and well designed and normed so as to achieve high diagnostic accuracy. Such a tool could help identify children at risk for dyslexia, as well as those who will struggle with reading due to a lack of supportive home language and literacy environments. The authors note that this individualized and comprehensive assessment must be followed by individualized remediation based on each child's profile and that this may be possible with well-trained general classroom teachers. This vision for integrated research-based screening and remediation of reading problems early would be a paradigm shift for the field of education.

UNDERSTANDING DYSLEXIA
THROUGH MODELING AND LEARNING PROCESSES

Studies that inform the understanding of the etiology of dyslexia and the trajectories of reading development can be carried out in the MRI scanner and the classroom, but the evolving theories of reading and dyslexia can be combined with modern technological power to create computational models of reading. In Chapter 6, Rueckl, Zevin, and Wolf provide a view of how computational modeling can inform several of the key issues in developmental dyslexia discussed in other chapters, such as the nature of the deficits underlying dyslexia, the challenges of deciding on diagnostic criteria, and the need to assess individual profiles and longitudinal change. They present data that replicate and extend findings from previous work by Harm & Seidenberg (1999), Seidenberg & McClelland (1989), and Plaut and colleagues (1996) on the triangle model of reading, which is based on interactions among phonological, orthographic, and semantic processes. Their models show interesting parallels with findings from studies of children developing reading, such as unique and shared variance between nonword and irregular word reading, and interactions among multiple unique deficits that can cause various subtypes or profiles of reading ability (e.g., Pennington et al., 2012). They also find that there is a diversity of longitudinal profiles among the various networks (which can be considered similar to an individual child learning to read), with some that are qualitatively similar to "typical" trajectories and others that are qualitatively different. They suggest that both computational and human studies may avoid some challenges and methodological confounds by matching participants on reading experience or multiple indices of underlying abilities (a "performance space").

In Chapter 7, Nation and Mak describe the complex learning processes that are needed for successful development of reading. Learning the associations between phonological and orthographic representations is sometimes thought of as straightforward, but there are many complex ways in which these two systems interact and develop to produce reading expertise. The authors present a continuum of frameworks in which to consider orthographic learning and the acquisition of reading expertise, from the domain-specific phonological recoding (self-teaching hypothesis; Share, 1995), to modality-specific visual-auditory paired associate learning, to domain-general statistical learning processes. Studies focusing on measures of learning at each of these levels have found correlations with reading ability, so a major challenge moving forward is to disentangle them. Even within studies examining domain-general statistical learning in dyslexia, the authors report that there is noticeable inconsistency among studies. Whether the tasks used to measure these learning processes are unreliable or not representative of true individual characteristics or whether the tasks tap different aspects of a more multifaceted statistical learning construct is an open question. Clarifying the nature of the learning deficit or deficits in dyslexia is central to knowing how to intervene, and again, measurement at the right levels and multiple measurements over time may provide new answers.

CONCLUSION

Several common threads emerge among the diverse lines of research discussed in this section. First, most authors agree that there is a need to assess the many factors that are involved in reading and to consider individual

profiles or subtypes, both in research and practice. There are clearly various profiles of performance on different measures that seem relatively
stable over time (Ozernov-Palchik et al., 2017) and different brain activation patterns for children with different profiles (Norton et al., 2014). In the
same way that Rueckl and colleagues (see Chapter 6) can plot characteristics of each network in a "performance space" with multiple dimensions,
Gaab and colleagues (see Chapter 5) aim to develop a multidimensionally
defined picture of each child's abilities at kindergarten screening. Genetic
studies are moving toward examining component skills in reading rather
than broad diagnostic categories. However, as de Jong (see Chapter 4)
points out, this type of nuanced assessment is only useful in practice if it
can be translated into more effective intervention. A thorough assessment
ideally is the starting point for implementing evidence-based interventions to address the root cause of the child's reading difficulty.

A second theme in this section is the value of rich longitudinal data
at multiple levels. Reading development unfolds over time, and a child's
ability at any given moment may not be as informative as his or her trajectory. This is the basis of response to intervention approaches in education.
Tracking an individual's trajectory longitudinally may be highly informative for research as well. Rueckl and colleagues' (see Chapter 6) computational networks showed not only a variety of endpoints but variation
in their individual trajectories. Understanding the learning processes that
support reading that Nation and Mak (see Chapter 7) describe depends
on charting the learning process as it unfolds over time. Knowing where
a child begins, not only on a single measure of reading, but on the component processes involved, the broader home and educational environment
and literacy experiences (as highlighted in Chapters 3 [Landi], 6 [Rueckl
et al.], and 5 [Gaab et al.]), and how this changes over time gives the most
comprehensive picture of reading development. Studies that chart the
growth of individuals across domains may provide new insight into the
processes that inform the etiology of dyslexia at the levels of genetics, epigenetics, and the brain.

Despite technologies that allow researchers to easily classify genetic
profiles in large samples, track minute changes in function of the brain in
infants and children, and run thousands of model simulations on their
desktops, no one approach has been able to answer the fundamental questions about the etiology of dyslexia. There is a clear need for cooperation
among labs and methods and for rigorous science that uses reliable measurements and is replicated across data sets. Richer collaborations among
different researchers may provide new insights more than a single focus.
Imagine taking data on multiple indicators of an individual's reading-
related skills (including traditional measures, e.g., phonological awareness
and RAN, as well as more cutting-edge measurements of things like statistical learning and environmental factors) over time and then using a model
to predict how that individual may respond to a particular intervention.

Integrating this with neural, genetic, and epigenetic data could provide insights into the etiology of reading problems and help identify the best parameters for early and accurate identification. These bridges are being built across labs and approaches, and large data sets are beginning to be used, such as the neuroimaging Dyslexia Data Consortium (e.g., Eckert et al., 2017), and genetic NeuroDys Consortium (e.g., Becker et al., 2014). Given that there seems to be no single behavioral profile, single brain region, or single gene that is the cause of dyslexia, the approaches that appreciate this complexity are most likely to be fruitful in the future.

REFERENCES

Becker, J., Czamara, D., Scerri, T. S., Ramus, F., Csépe, V., Talcott, J. B., . . . Honbolygó, F. (2014). Genetic analysis of dyslexia candidate genes in the European cross-linguistic NeuroDys cohort. *European Journal of Human Genetics, 22*(5), 675.

Eckert, M. A., Vaden, K. I., Maxwell, A. B., Cute, S. L., Gebregziabher, M., . . . Dyslexia Data Consortium. (2017). Common brain structure findings across children with varied reading disability profiles. *Scientific Reports, 7*(1). http://dx.doi.org/10.1038/s41598-017-05691-5

Harm, M. W., & Seidenberg, M. S. (1999). Phonology, reading acquisition, and dyslexia: Insights from connectionist models. *Psychological Review, 106,* 491–528.

Katzir, T., Kim, Y., Wolf, M., O'Brien, B., Kennedy, B., Lovett, M., & Morris, R. (2006). Reading fluency: The whole is more than the parts. *Annals of Dyslexia, 56,* 51–82.

Norton, E. S., Black, J. M., Stanley, L. M., Tanaka, H., Gabrieli, J. D. E., Sawyer, C., & Hoeft, F. (2014). Functional neuroanatomical evidence for the double-deficit hypothesis of developmental dyslexia. *Neuropsychologia, 61,* 235–246.

Ozernov-Palchik, O., Norton, E. S., Sideridis, G., Beach, S. D., Gabrieli, J. D. E., & Gaab, N. (2017). Early-reading profiles of children at kindergarten and longitudinally: Implications for early screening and theories of reading. *Developmental Science, 20*(5). http://dx.doi.org/10.1111/desc.12471

Pennington, B. F., Santerre-Lemmon, L., Rosenberg, J., MacDonald, B., Boada, R., Friend, A., . . . Olson, R. K. (2012). Individual prediction of dyslexia by single versus multiple deficit models. *Journal of Abnormal Psychology, 121,* 212–224. http://dx.doi.org/10.1037/a0025823

Plaut, D. C., McClelland, J. L., Seidenberg, M. S., & Patterson, K. (1996). Understanding normal and impaired word reading: Computational principles in quasi-regular domains. *Psychological Review, 103,* 56–115.

Seidenberg, M. S., & McClelland, J. L. (1989). A distributed, developmental model of word recognition and naming. *Psychological Review, 96,* 523–568.

Share, D. L. (1995). Phonological recoding and self-teaching: Sine qua non of reading acquisition. *Cognition, 55,* 151–218. http://dx.doi.org/10.1016/0010-0277(94)00645-2

Linguistic Differences and Reading

CHAPTER 8

The Impact of Linguistic Distance on Dyslexia in Dialect Speakers

The Case of Arabic Diglossia

Elinor Saiegh-Haddad

SUMMARY

Arabic native speaking children across the world grow up in a sociolinguistic context called *diglossia* (Ferguson, 1959). In this context, two language varieties are used within the same speech community for two sets of complementary functions: spoken Arabic (SpA) for informal speech and (modern) standard Arabic (MSA, StA) for formal speech and reading/writing. As a consequence, all Arabic-speaking children learn to read in a language variety that is different from the spoken variety/dialect they use for everyday speech. The two language varieties are linguistically related, yet different in all domains of language, notably in phonology and lexicon. Research addressing typical reading in Arabic reveals the impact of linguistic distance (specifically lexical–phonological) on reading skills development. The chapter reviews research addressing the impact of linguistic distance on dyslexia. By manipulating linguistic affiliation and comparing the processing of words and pseudowords that preserve the same lexico-phonological form in SpA and in StA against those that are different in the two language varieties, researchers demonstrated a significant and persistent effect of linguistic distance on word-level reading (accuracy and fluency), phonological memory, and word learning in Arabic-speaking children with dyslexia as compared to age-matched controls. These results imply that the linguistic distance between the written language variety and the spoken dialect is a factor of complexity that interferes with linguistic processing and with reading in Arabic dialect speakers with dyslexia.

INTRODUCTION

Many factors have an impact on children's acquisition of reading. These include cognitive-linguistic, instructional, and environmental factors (Binks-Cantrell, Washburn, Joshi, & Hougan, 2012; Castles, Rastle, & Nation, 2018; McCardle, Scarborough, & Catts, 2001). Linguistic distance between the child's spoken lect (language or dialect) and the language of literacy is another factor that can have a strong influence on children's acquisition of literacy (Charity, Scarborough, & Griffin, 2004; Saiegh-Haddad, 2018). Linguistic distance characterizes the acquisition of literacy in standard-with-dialect contexts, such as the African American context in the United States or the Swiss-German context in Switzerland, as well as many other unilingual and multilingual contexts in which children learn to read first in a language that is different from the dialect they use for everyday speech. The nature of literacy development in these dialectal contexts has only recently started to attract attention (e.g., Brown, Sibley, Washington, & Seidenberg, 2015; Bühler, von Oertzen, McBride, Stoll, & Maurer, 2018).

Linguistic distance between the dialect children first acquire for use in everyday spoken interactions and the language encoded in print is a conspicuous feature of literacy acquisition in all Arabic-speaking children, regardless of the geographic region they reside in or the specific dialect they speak. These children are always faced with the task of learning to read and write in a language variety that they do not use for everyday speech. This variety is referred to as (modern) standard Arabic and is remarkably different in phonology, morphology, lexicon, and syntax from all spoken vernaculars, referred to collectively as colloquial or spoken Arabic. The question that emerges then pertains to the impact of linguistic distance on the acquisition of literacy in these children.

ARABIC DIGLOSSIA: SOCIOLINGUISTIC FEATURES AND LINGUISTIC MANIFESTATIONS

Arabic is a typical case of diglossia, defined by Ferguson as

> A relatively stable language situation in which, in addition to the primary dialects of the language . . . there is a very divergent, highly codified (often grammatically more complex) superposed variety . . . . which is learned largely by formal education and is used for most written and formal spoken purposes but is not used by any section of the community for ordinary conversation. (1959, p. 336)

This definition, outlined some 6 decades ago, still applies to the linguistic context of Arabic today. Everyday conversation in all Arabic-speaking regions is conducted using a local vernacular of spoken Arabic. This variety is acquired naturally as a mother tongue but has no conventional written form. In contrast, standard Arabic, the language of conventional literacy and formal speech, and a largely uniform variety across the Arabic-speaking world, is acquired mainly in the formal classroom context. Despite a deceivingly dichotomous context, and despite the fact that SpA is undoubtedly the primary spoken language, native speakers of Arabic, including young children, are constantly engaged with StA as well; they pray, read stories and books, and do all their schoolwork in StA; they also watch many TV programs in this variety. Thus, from an early age, linguistic development in Arabic involves concurrent acquisition of SpA and StA.

A conspicuous linguistic manifestation of diglossia in Arabic is a phonological and a lexical distance between StA and SpA (for a discussion, see Saiegh-Haddad & Henkin-Roitfarb, 2014). This distance takes various forms in different Arabic-speaking regions and among speakers of different spoken vernaculars. Nonetheless, no spoken vernacular shares the exact set of linguistic units or lexical items with standard Arabic. For instance, StA comprises 28 consonantal phonemes and six vowel phonemes, and all words in standard Arabic must begin with a single consonant followed by a vowel. In contrast, SpA vernaculars usually comprise a smaller set of consonants and a larger set of vowels and allow complex onsets. To illustrate, interdental consonants are not within the phonemic inventory of many urban dialects of Palestinian Arabic spoken in the north of Israel. Thus, cognate words, namely StA words also used in these spoken dialects, acquire a different phonological form in SpA, with StA interdental phonemes substituted for by corresponding SpA phonemes (e.g., StA /θaʕlab/; SpA /taʕlab/ "fox").

The lexical distance between standard and spoken Arabic is another pervasive manifestation of Arabic diglossia. Saiegh-Haddad and Spolsky (2014) found that only 21.2% of the words in the children's spoken lexicon had an identical lexico-phonological form in both SpA and StA (e.g., /naːm/ "slept"; /daftar/ "notebook"), whereas the remaining words were approximately evenly divided between cognate words (i.e., words shared by the two varieties but with only partially overlapping phonological forms; e.g., SpA /dahab/ vs. StA /ðahab/ "gold"), and unique SpA words (i.e., having a unique lexico-phonological form in SpA completely different from its form in StA, such as SpA /ʒuzdaːn/ vs. StA /ħaqiːba/ "bag"). Such a remarkable orality–literacy gap is expected to profoundly influence reading development in Arabic (for reviews, see Saiegh-Haddad, 2017, 2018).

LINGUISTIC DISTANCE AND TYPICAL READING DEVELOPMENT IN ARABIC DIGLOSSIA

Researchers have tested the impact of the linguistic distance between SpA and StA on the acquisition of literacy in typically developing children by systematically comparing linguistic processing and reading of parallel linguistic structures that are either shared by SpA and StA or only used in StA. For instance, Saiegh-Haddad and colleagues (e.g., Saiegh-Haddad, 2003, 2004, 2007; Saiegh-Haddad & Ghawi-Dakwar, 2017; Saiegh-Haddad & Haj, 2018; Saiegh-Haddad, Levin, Hende, & Ziv, 2011; Saiegh-Haddad & Schiff, 2016) investigated the impact of linguistic distance on phonological representations, phonological awareness, pseudoword decoding, and word-reading accuracy and fluency. They found that phonological representations and processing in StA were negatively affected by the phonological distance between SpA and StA, with children showing consistently lower scores when asked to process StA linguistic structures that are not within their spoken dialect. Moreover, the acquisition of word-reading accuracy and fluency was influenced by the phonological and lexical distance between the two language varieties.

Thus, the linguistic distance between SpA and StA hinders the processing of StA linguistic units that are not within SpA. This is despite evidence that linguistic processing in SpA shows cross-dialectal transfer and predicts metalinguistic processing and reading in StA (Schiff & Saiegh-Haddad, 2018). The impact of linguistic distance appears to be attributed, at least partly, to difficulty among Arabic-speaking children in constructing high-quality phonological representations for StA linguistic units not within their dialect (Saiegh-Haddad & Ghawi-Dakwar, 2017; Saiegh-Haddad & Haj, 2018; Saiegh-Haddad et al., 2011), with detrimental consequences for language and literacy development. The pending question pertains to the influence that linguistic distance has on language and reading development in Arabic speakers with dyslexia.

LINGUISTIC DISTANCE AND DYSLEXIA IN ARABIC DIGLOSSIA

Developmental reading disability or dyslexia manifests as unexpected difficulties in acquiring basic reading subskills, such as word identification and alphabetic decoding, and is accompanied by deficits in other linguistic domains (Vellutino, Fletcher, Snowling, & Scanlon, 2004). The most widely held view is that, among those linguistic deficits, most children with reading disabilities have a core phonological deficit that interferes with their ability to develop phonological skills critical for reading, including phonological awareness and word decoding (e.g., Liberman, Shankweiler, & Liberman, 1989; Stanovich & Siegel, 1994).

Diglossia makes it difficult to identify children with dyslexia because the developmental trajectories of typical language and reading in SpA (i.e., for linguistic units that are shared by SpA and StA) are different from those of typical development in StA (Saiegh-Haddad & Schiff, 2016; Schiff & Saiegh-Haddad, 2018). These differences might stem from differences in age of acquisition or age of exposure to the two linguistic systems (De Houwer, 2017) with subsequent differences in representational quality (Saiegh-Haddad, 2017; Saiegh-Haddad & Ghawi-Dakwar, 2017; Saiegh-Haddad & Haj, 2018; Saiegh-Haddad et al., 2011). This results in either underdiagnosis (i.e., the erroneous interpretation of genuine signs of disability as reflecting the fact that assessment is in an unfamiliar nonspoken language that has not yet been acquired or mastered) or overdiagnosis. As such, assessment is often based on StA and does not take linguistic distance into account, thus potentially leading to erroneous interpretation of normative developmental delays, resulting from linguistic distance, as indicators of disability. For instance, phonemic awareness for phonemes not within the spoken vernacular of children is challenging and is acquired later than awareness of StA phonemes (Schiff & Saiegh-Haddad, 2018). This is because children have not been sufficiently exposed to StA phonology and therefore have failed to construct accurate phonological representations (e.g., Saiegh-Haddad, 2003; Saiegh-Haddad et al., 2011). Likewise, learning the sounds of some letters in kindergarten may be difficult simply because they represent phonemes that do not exist in the spoken vernacular of children (Levin, Saiegh-Haddad, Hende, & Ziv, 2008). Both forms of misidentification reflect lack of appropriate assessment tools sensitive to and tailored for the dialects that children speak (Khamis-Dakwar & Makhul, 2014).

Research on reading disability in Arabic is scarce (e.g., Al-Mannai & Everatt, 2005; Saiegh-Haddad & Taha, 2017) and has not addressed the role of linguistic distance. The following section reviews research addressing this question. The context of the research reviewed below is Arabic-speaking Palestinian citizens of Israel, who speak various dialects of Palestinian Arabic as their mother tongue. These children grow up monolingual living in Arab towns and villages; only 10% of the Arabs in Israel live in Arab-Jewish "mixed cities," and even there they tend to concentrate in isolated territories (Kipnis & Schnell, 1978). The great majority of Palestinian children in Israel enroll in Arabic-medium schools (preschool through high school) in which Arabic is the sole language of instruction. Hebrew and English are taught as additional languages starting in the third and fourth grades, respectively (for more, see Saiegh-Haddad & Everatt, 2017).

Schiff and Saiegh-Haddad (2017) were the first to directly test the impact of the linguistic distance between SpA and StA on dyslexia in Arabic. They tested word and pseudoword decoding accuracy and fluency in sixth-grade children with reading difficulties and compared them with age-matched typically developing controls and with two groups of younger typically developing readers (second- and fourth-grade students). Schiff and Saiegh-Haddad operationalized reading in SpA by targeting identical words, which maintain an identical lexico-phonological form in SpA and StA. They tested reading in StA by targeting cognate and unique words. They matched words for frequency, phonological length, and complexity and presented them in the voweled orthography (which uses diacritics to map all phonological information necessary for accurate word decoding) and in the unvoweled orthography (a consonantal system that only uses letters to map the consonants and the long vowels and is, therefore, a phonologically underspecified orthography). The results from the word-reading accuracy task in sixth-grade children with dyslexia ("reading disabilities," or RD) versus age-matched and younger second-grade typically developing (TD) controls are summarized in Figure 8.1.

The study showed that the reading accuracy and fluency of words and pseudowords among the sixth-grade students with dyslexia was similar to the levels observed in the typically developing second-grade students but significantly lower than that in the typically developing sixth-grade students. More important for the current discussion is that the reading accuracy and fluency of words and pseudowords were significantly higher for SpA than for StA words, both among the sixth-grade students with dyslexia and in the younger control children. In contrast, this difference fell below significance in the age-matched sixth-grade control group.

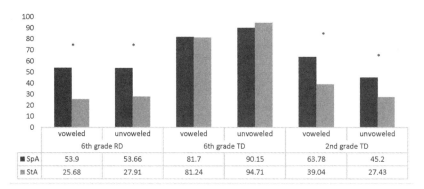

	voweled	unvoweled	voweled	unvoweled	voweled	unvoweled
	6th grade RD		6th grade TD		2nd grade TD	
■ SpA	53.9	53.66	81.7	90.15	63.78	45.2
▩ StA	25.68	27.91	81.24	94.71	39.04	27.43

Figure 8.1. Means of word-reading accuracy for voweled and unvoweled words by language variety (spoken Arabic [SpA], standard Arabic [StA]) and group (sixth-grade children with dyslexia [RD], sixth-grade typically developing children [TD], and second-grade typically developing children [TD]). *p < .05.

Moreover, differences in reading in favor of SpA words were significant both in the voweled and in the unvoweled orthography.

These results are compelling because they show that the linguistic distance between SpA and StA exerts a significant influence on word-reading accuracy and fluency in middle school children with reading disability but not in age-matched peers. In turn, it indicates sensitivity in the children with reading disability to linguistic affiliation of the word with SpA or StA, also referred to as *diglossia-effect* (Saiegh-Haddad, 2018), namely a processing advantage for words that are within their dialect. Finally, the finding that the diglossia-effect was significant in the group of children with reading disability both in the voweled and in the unvoweled orthography implies that linguistic distance is a source of complexity for this group of children that pervades orthographic depth.

As explicated previously, one critical manifestation of Arabic diglossia is a remarkable phonological distance between the formal StA and the everyday SpA. One manifestation of this phonological distance is a set of phonemes that are only used in StA but not in SpA. Saiegh-Haddad and Hanna-Irsheid (ms.) studied the impact of this phonemic distance between SpA and StA on the acquisition of phonological processing skills in children with developmental reading difficulties, targeting two phonological skills known to be compromised in dyslexia: phonological memory operationalized as pseudoword (or nonword) repetition and pseudoword learning, using a paired-associate or a fast-mapping task (e.g., Brady, Shankweiler, & Mann, 1983; Catts, 1986; Hulme & Snowling, 1992). All items employed pronounceable pseudowords (1–4 syllables long) that abided by the phonotactics of SpA and manipulated linguistic affiliation or distance: pseudowords encoding only SpA phonemes versus pseudowords encoding one StA phoneme each. Saiegh-Haddad and Hanna-Irsheid predicted that

linguistic affiliation with SpA versus StA would have a significant impact
on phonological processing in children with reading difficulties, probably
more than in typically developing children, whose phonological processing skills are supposed to be intact. This question was tested in a group of
third-grade (average age 8 years) and fifth-grade Arabic-speaking children
with reading disability and in age-matched typically developing children
(Total $N = 100$; 25/group/grade).

The results from the pseudoword repetition task showed that typically developing readers outperformed children with reading disability,
and older children outperformed younger children. More important,
pseudowords encoding StA phonemes yielded significantly lower repetition scores than pseudowords encoding only SpA phonemes. Moreover,
results showed that although items encoding StA phonemes yielded generally lower repetition scores in both groups, the difference between the
two types of words was not significant in either grade in the typically developing children, yet younger children with reading disability showed
the lowest scores among all groups when StA words were involved. This
finding mimics the patterns observed among younger children with language impairment (Saiegh-Haddad & Ghawi-Dakwar, 2017), and it implies
representational phonological memory deficits in Arabic-speaking children with dyslexia, namely difficulty creating and accessing accurate phonological representations for StA phonological units that are not within
their dialect. This difficulty continues to surface in the third grade, even
after 3 years of intensive exposure to StA at school, and it persists into the
fifth grade. This finding is summarized in Figure 8.2.

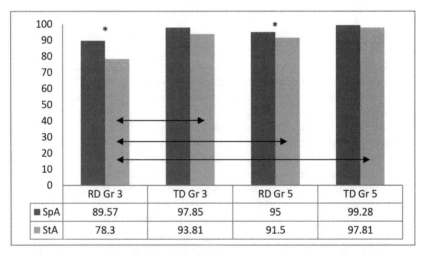

Figure 8.2. Interaction of language variety (spoken Arabic [SpA], standard Arabic [StA]) by grade
(third-grade [Gr 3], fifth-grade [Gr 5]) and by group (children with reading disability [RD], typically developing readers [TD]) on nonword repetition. *p < .05; double-headed arrows = p < .05.

The second skill that was tested in this study was pseudoword learning recognition. The results from this task showed again that older children outperformed younger ones and that typically developing readers outperformed children with reading disability. Moreover, pseudowords encoding StA phonemes were more difficult for all children to learn than pseudowords encoding only SpA phonemes. Yet, the difficulty in learning new words encoding StA phonemes was not limited to the children with reading disability but extended to their age-matched controls. Moreover, differences between children with reading difficulties and age-matched controls, in both third and fifth grade, were significant when words encoded both SpA and StA phonemes. Yet, developmental differences (between third and fifth grades) in the children with reading difficulties were only significant when pseudowords encoded SpA phonemes but not when they encoded StA phonemes. In contrast, in the age-matched control groups, developmental differences were significant for words encoding SpA and those encoding StA phonemes. These results imply that phonological distance interfered with and complicated the task of word learning both in children with and without dyslexia. Yet, they also show that the impact of linguistic distance on word learning is developmentally more persistent in children with dyslexia, resulting in no developmental differences in this group in the learning of words encoding StA words. These results are summarized in Figure 8.3.

Altogether, the results show that the phonological distance between StA and SpA affects phonological memory and word learning in children with dyslexia and that phonological distance is an additional phonological complexity factor impeding phonological processing in these children.

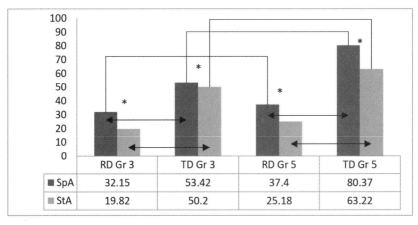

Figure 8.3. Interaction of language variety (spoken Arabic [SpA], standard Arabic [StA]) by grade (third-grade [Gr 3], fifth-grade [Gr 5]) and by group (children with reading disability [RD], typically developing readers [TD]) on nonword learning. *p < .05; double-headed arrows and connecting lines = p < .05.

The results showed that the impact of phonological distance on pseudoword repetition emerged in children with dyslexia in the third grade and persisted in this group into the fifth grade. In contrast, in typically developing children, this effect was not observed in either grade. With respect to word learning, the impact of phonological distance was observed in children with dyslexia and in typically developing controls in both grades. Moreover, whereas differences between children with dyslexia and their typically developing age-matched peers was significant on all words: SpA and StA, developmental differences (between the third and fifth grades) in the ability to learn words with StA phonemes persisted and did not improve significantly with grade in children with dyslexia, but it did improve in typically developing controls. This implies that although phonological distance presents a challenge for both groups of children, with and without dyslexia, its effect on learning words with StA phonemes is developmentally more persistent in children with dyslexia than in typically developing controls.

CONCLUSION

In light of earlier evidence demonstrating a strong impact of the phonological distance between SpA and StA on phonological processing skills in StA among typically developing SpA dialect speakers, researchers predicted that children with reading disability would show a similar, and probably an even stronger impact of phonological distance than that observed in typically developing children when required to process phonological structures that are not within their spoken dialect. This is because phonological distance is a factor of complexity that is expected to challenge the fragile phonological representation and processing skills of children with dyslexia. The results reported in this chapter support this prediction and show that the linguistic distance between SpA and StA has a strong impact on reading accuracy and fluency in children with dyslexia. Moreover, it has a significant and persistent impact on phonological memory and word learning in these children. The impact of linguistic distance is manifest as lower scores on word and pseudoword reading, pseudoword repetition, and pseudoword learning when items encode linguistic units that are not within the spoken dialect. On some tasks, such as word learning, this impact further manifests as developmentally more elongated and persistent difficulties among children with dyslexia when items contain phonological structures not within their spoken dialect.

The findings outlined previously imply that phonological distance is an additional phonological complexity factor that undermines phonological processing in dialect speakers with dyslexia. Furthermore, they imply that dialect speakers with dyslexia might have a dual deficit: 1) a general phonological deficit observed on all phonological processing items, including those that encode linguistic units within their dialect, and 2) a specific phonological distance deficit that emerges when the task requires the processing of phonological units not within their dialect. The double deficit manifests as significant difficulty with words encoding nonspoken units and conversely as an advantage for words that encode only dialect structures. It also manifests as persistent difficulties over time. Unlike their typically developing peers, children with dyslexia fail to show significant growth with age or grade when StA words are involved.

The results reported in this study support the psychological reality of a novel linguistic factor that should be taken seriously in assessment and intervention with dialect-speaking children with dyslexia (Saiegh-Haddad & Everatt, 2017). These results have important implications for theory and practice. They imply that theories of dyslexia should incorporate linguistic distance as another linguistic risk factor affecting processing in dialect speakers with dyslexia. The results reveal that dialect speakers with dyslexia, who are required to develop language and literacy in a language variety they do not speak, present with particular difficulty creating and accessing novel phonological structures not within their dialect, and this manifests as difficulty representing these structures and utilizing them in word decoding and in word learning. These findings have serious practical implications, especially because linguistic distance is often not heeded in assessment or intervention (Saiegh-Haddad, 2019; Russak & Saiegh-Haddad, 2011, 2017).

REFERENCES

Al-Mannai, H., & Everatt, J. (2005). Phonological processing skills as predictors of literacy amongst Arabic speaking Bahraini children. *Dyslexia, 11*, 269–291.

Binks-Cantrell, E., Washburn, E., Joshi, R. M., & Hougan, M. (2012). Peter effect in the preparation of reading teachers. *Scientific Studies of Reading, 16*, 526–536

Brady, S., Shankweiler, D., & Mann, V. (1983). Speech perception and memory coding in relation to reading ability. *Journal of Experimental Child Psychology, 35*, 345–367.

Brown, M. C., Sibley, D. E., Washington, J., & Seidenberg, M. (2015). Impact of dialect use on a basic component of learning to read. *Frontiers in Psychology, 6*, 1–16.

Bühler, J. C., von Oertzen, T., McBride, C. A., Stoll, S., & Maurer, U. (2018). Influence of dialect use on early reading and spelling acquisition in German-speaking children in Grade 1. *Journal of Cognitive Psychology, 30*, 336–360. https://doi.org/10.1080/20445911.2018.1444614

Castles, A., Rastle, K., & Nation, K. (2018). Ending the reading wars: Reading acquisition from novice to expert. *Psychological Science in the Public Interest, 19*, 5–51.

Catts, H. W. (1986). Speech production/phonological deficits in reading-disordered children. *Journal of Learning Disabilities, 19*, 504–508.

Charity, A. H., Scarborough, H. S., & Griffin, D. M. (2004). Familiarity with school English in African American children and its relation to early reading achievement. *Child Development, 75*, 1340–1356.

De Houwer, A. (2017). The role of language input environments for language outcomes and language acquisition in young bilingual children. In D. Miller, N. Denhovska, & F. Bayram (Eds.), *Bilingual cognition and language: The state of the science across its subfields* (pp. 127–153). Amsterdam, The Netherlands: John Benjamins.

Ferguson, C. A. (1959). Diglossia. *Word, 14*, 47–56.

Hulme, C., & Snowling, M. J. (1992). Deficits in output phonology: An explanation of reading failure? *Cognitive Neuropsychology, 9*, 47–72.

Khamis-Dakwar, R., & Makhul, B. (2014). The development of ADAT (Arabic Diglossic Knowledge and Awareness Test): A theoretical and clinical overview. In E. Saiegh-Haddad & M. Joshi (Eds.), *Handbook of Arabic literacy: Insights and perspectives* (pp. 279–300). Dordrecht, The Netherlands: Springer.

Kipnis, B. A., & Schnell, I. (1978). Changes in the distribution of Arabs in mixed Jewish-Arab cities in Israel. *Economic Geography, 54,* 168–180.

Levin, I., Saiegh-Haddad, E., Hende, N., & Ziv, M. (2008). Early literacy in Arabic: An intervention with Israeli Palestinian kindergarteners. *Applied Psycholinguistics, 29,* 413–436.

Liberman, I. Y., Shankweiler, D., & Liberman, A. M. (1989). The alphabetic principle and learning to read. In D. Shankweiler & I. Y. Liberman (Eds.), *Phonology and reading disability: Solving the reading puzzle* (pp. 1–33). Ann Arbor: University of Michigan Press.

McCardle, P., Scarborough, H. S., & Catts, H. W. (2001). Predicting, explaining, and preventing children's reading difficulties. *Learning Disabilities Research & Practice, 16,* 230–239.

Russak, S., & Saiegh-Haddad, E. (2011). Phonological awareness in Hebrew (L1) and English (L2) in normal and disabled readers. *Reading & Writing: An Interdisciplinary Journal, 24,* 427–440.

Russak, S., & Saiegh-Haddad, E. (2017). What do phonological segmentation errors tell us about phonological representations? *Second Language Research, 34,* 1–14.

Saiegh-Haddad, E. (2003). Linguistic distance and initial reading acquisition: The case of Arabic diglossia. *Applied Psycholinguistics, 24,* 431–451.

Saiegh-Haddad, E. (2004). The impact of phonemic and lexical distance on the phonological analysis of words and pseudowords in a diglossic context. *Applied Psycholinguistics, 25,* 495–512.

Saiegh-Haddad, E. (2007). Linguistic constraints on children's ability to isolate phonemes in Arabic. *Applied Psycholinguistics, 28,* 605–625.

Saiegh-Haddad, E. (2017). Learning to read in Arabic. In L. Verhoeven & C. Perfetti (Eds.), *Reading acquisition across languages and writing systems: An international handbook* (pp. 127–154). New York, NY: Cambridge University Press.

Saiegh-Haddad, E. (2018). MAWRID: A Model of Arabic Word Reading In Development. *Journal of Learning Disabilities, 51,* 454–462.

Saiegh-Haddad, E. (2019). What is phonological awareness in L2? *Journal of Neurolinguistics, 50,* 17–27. https://doi.org/10.1016/j.jneuroling.2017.11.001

Saiegh-Haddad, E., & Everatt, J. (2017). Literacy education in Arabic. In N. Kucirkova, C. Snow, V. Grover, & C. McBride-Chang (Eds.), *The Routledge international handbook of early literacy education* (pp. 185–199). New York, NY: Taylor & Francis Routledge.

Saiegh-Haddad, E., & Ghawi-Dakwar, O. (2017). Impact of diglossia on word and nonword repetition among language impaired and typically developing Arabic native speaking children. *Frontiers in Psychology, 8,* 2010. http://dx.doi.org/10.3389/fpsyg.2017.02010

Saiegh-Haddad, E., & Haj, L. (2018). Does phonological distance impact quality of phonological representations? Evidence from Arabic diglossia. *Journal of Child Language, 45*(6):1377–1399. http://dx.doi.org/10.1017/S0305000918000302

Saiegh-Haddad, E., & Hanna-Irshied, H. (n.d.). *The impact of linguistic distance on dyslexia in L1 and in L2.* Manuscript submitted for publication.

Saiegh-Haddad, E., & Henkin-Roitfarb, R. (2014). The structure of Arabic language and orthography. In E. Saiegh-Haddad & M. Joshi (Eds.), *Handbook of Arabic literacy: Insights and perspectives* (pp. 3–28). Dordrecht, The Netherlands: Springer.

Saiegh-Haddad, E., Levin, I., Hende, N., & Ziv, M. (2011). The Linguistic Affiliation Constraint and phoneme recognition in diglossic Arabic. *Journal of Child Language, 38,* 297–315.

Saiegh-Haddad, E., & Schiff, R. (2016). The impact of diglossia on voweled and unvoweled word reading in Arabic: A developmental study from childhood to adolescence. *Scientific Studies of Reading, 20,* 311–324.

Saiegh-Haddad, E., & Spolsky, B. (2014). Acquiring literacy in a diglossic context: Problems and prospects. In E. Saiegh-Haddad & M. Joshi (Eds.), *Handbook of Arabic literacy: Insights and perspectives* (pp. 225–240). Dordrecht, The Netherlands: Springer.

Saiegh-Haddad, E., & Taha, T. (2017). The role of phonological and morphological awareness in the early development of word reading and spelling in typical and disabled
Arabic readers. *Dyslexia, 23,* 345–371.

Schiff, R., & Saiegh-Haddad, E. (2017). When diglossia meets dyslexia: The effect of
diglossia on voweled and unvoweled word reading among native Arabic-speaking
dyslexic children. *Reading & Writing: An Interdisciplinary Journal, 30,* 1089–1113.

Schiff, R., & Saiegh-Haddad, E. (2018). Development and relationships between phonological awareness, morphological awareness and word reading in spoken and standard Arabic. *Frontiers in Psychology, 9,* 356. https://doi.org/10.3389/fpsyg.2018.00356

Stanovich, K. E., & Siegel, L. S. (1994). Phenotypic performance profiles of children with
reading disabilities: A regression-based test of the phonological-core variable difference model. *Journal of Educational Psychology, 86,* 24–53.

Vellutino, F. R., Fletcher, J. M., Snowling, M. J., & Scanlon, D. M. (2004). Specific reading
disability (dyslexia): What have we learned in the past four decades? *Journal of Child
Psychology and Psychiatry, 45,* 2–40.

CHAPTER 9

Intersection of Race, Poverty, and Diagnostic Accuracy

Identifying Reading Disabilities in African American Children

Julie A. Washington and Ryan Lee-James

SUMMARY

A significant area of emphasis in learning disabilities (LDs) research with young children has been accurate and timely identification and diagnosis of LDs (see Chapter 5). The importance of attaining an appropriate diagnosis is critical to both academic and clinical planning and to prevention efforts such as those described by Gaab and colleagues (see Chapter 5). Diagnostic accuracy is significantly affected by, and confounded with, many sociodemographic variables, including race, socioeconomic status (SES), and linguistic differences. As a consequence, children who are impoverished, are minorities, and who speak dialects or languages that differ from mainstream American English (MAE), are reportedly underdiagnosed among children identified as having LDs (Morgan, Farkas, Hillemeier, Mattison, et al., 2015). This chapter focuses on the unintended consequences of the exclusionary language in the Individuals with Disabilities Education Act (IDEA) of 2004 (PL 108-446). As it stands, by definition, in order to be diagnosed as having LDs, and subsequently reading impairment, children have to be from a higher income background and have had sufficient learning opportunities and instruction. For African American and other impoverished children, this is often not the case. In addition, impoverished African American children often use cultural language forms that may contribute to reading difficulties. Existing diagnostic instruments lack sensitivity when used with these children in practice and in research (Craig & Washington, 2000; Washington & Craig, 2004). Whereas current research on reading disabilities, including dyslexia, largely excludes impoverished and African American children, future research must ask the question, "What are the characteristics of reading disabilities in the presence of poverty, disadvantage, and dialectal variation?" Furthermore, development of standardized reading instruments that are sensitive enough to help researchers to distinguish disadvantage from disability should be a priority. Attention to these important issues will go a long way toward development of definitions and interventions that are inclusive of all children who present reading differences and disabilities.

INTRODUCTION

Despite the fact that more than 80% of African American children and 70% of Hispanic children read at a basic level or below, they are unlikely to be identified with reading or math disabilities. As a result, these children may not receive the appropriate interventions needed to become proficient in reading, writing, and mathematics. Educators frequently assume, especially in schools, that the children's learning difficulties result from poverty and its sequelae, rather than from underlying, possibly neurological, learning difficulty. African American children in particular are frequently underrepresented in mild- and high-incidence disability categories, such as LDs and speech and language impairments, and are significantly over-represented in the most severe disability categories, including cognitive and emotional impairment (Bronson, 2014). Indeed, African American and Hispanic children are among those most likely to be misdiagnosed. The long-term consequences are well documented for their impact well into adulthood (e.g., Feinberg et al., 2016; Harman, 1970; Walter, 1999).

Misdiagnosis may be attributable to several factors, most of which are exacerbated by factors related to poverty. Currently policy, research, and practice have combined to create an environment in which impoverished and minority children are highly unlikely to receive special education interventions designed to address LDs, including reading disabilities. In IDEA 2004, specific learning disability (SLD) is defined as

> A disorder in one more of the basic psychological processes involved in understanding or in using language, spoken or written, which disorder may manifest itself in the imperfect ability to listen, think, speak, read, write, spell, or do mathematical calculations. (IDEA 2004, 34 CFR 300.307)

Most important for impoverished and minority children, the exclusionary criteria in the same section state that "such term does not include a learning problem that is primarily the result of visual, hearing, or motor disabilities, of mental retardation, of emotional disturbance, or of *environmental, cultural, or economic disadvantage*" (IDEA 2004; emphasis ours). The last five words of the statute have had unintended negative consequences for both research and practice for identification and diagnosis of LD in impoverished and minority children. The original intent may have been to avoid overrepresentation and identification based on disadvantage, but the outcomes have proven to be far different. Why can't children be both impoverished and have LDs?

We propose that the exclusionary criteria in IDEA 2004 are an important and primary reason that children who are underprivileged have not been included routinely in research studies focused on identification of and/or intervention for reading disabilities. Definitions drive research. Researchers' questions, methods, and interpretations are shaped by their assumptions and definitions. De Jong (see Chapter 4) describes a type of opportunity–ability discrepancy created by the SLD exclusionary criteria in which the extremely poor reading ability of a child from a disadvantaged background is not sufficient for a diagnosis of SLD (or in De Jong's example, dyslexia). Instead, the burden of proof for children from disadvantaged backgrounds rests with the teacher or researcher who must demonstrate that the child's reading deficits are not simply due to poor opportunity but rather to a true reading disability in order for that child to be diagnosed and more important to be eligible for the interventions designed to address reading disability. Most germane here, these exclusionary criteria effectively bar impoverished, minority children from being the focus of research designed to understand the educational and neurological underpinnings of reading disabilities within their respective populations.

Researchers often assume that low-income, minority children are poor readers because they are impoverished and have substandard teaching. In the United States, minority children are disproportionately impoverished, making them most affected by the disparities created by researchers' current thinking. This phenomenon led Blanchett and colleagues to lament that LD has become a privileged disability category that primarily serves children who are white and middle to upper middle class (Blanchett, 2010; Blanchett, Klinger, & Harry, 2009). In fairness to researchers, the lack of sensitivity of their instruments also is problematic because they cannot distinguish performance based on disability from performance resulting from disadvantage or differences. This is a longstanding concern in language research (e.g., Seymour, Bland-Stewart, & Green, 1998; Stockman, 2010) and has been a driver in the development of disability policy designed to avoid disproportionality. Among impoverished and minority children, these policies have had the unfortunate consequence of permitting distal causes of reading deficits (e.g., SES and substandard instruction) to drive both research and practice. They have discouraged simultaneous examination of the proximal causes to get at the root of and to improve researchers' ability to identify and diagnose reading disabilities in children from disadvantaged backgrounds. It is absurd to conclude that students who are impoverished cannot have LDs, so why are researchers not asking, "In the face of poor opportunity, what does LD look like?"

UNDERREPRESENTATION IN THE LEARNING DISABILITY CATEGORY

There is an emerging recognition that the exclusionary criteria adopted in the reauthorization of IDEA have contributed to a pendulum swing in educational diagnosis from overrepresentation to underrepresentation of minority children identified as having LDs. Despite a long-standing belief that African American children are disproportionately overrepresented in special education, more recent research suggests that the direction of disproportionality differs by disability category. African American children reportedly are overrepresented in high-incidence categories, including emotional disturbance and intellectual disability (e.g., Blanchett et al., 2009; Oswald, Coutinho, Best, & Nguyen, 2011; Skiba, Feggins-Azziz, & Chung, 2005). However, they are underrepresented in disability categories most critical for language and reading (Hibel, Farkas, & Morgan, 2010; Morgan, Farkas, et al., 2016; Morgan, Farkas, Hillemeier, Hammer, & Maczuga, 2015).

Three papers demonstrated that the direction of disproportionality may be influenced by the age or grade of the child. African American children were disproportionately underrepresented in speech-language delay or impairment from birth to age 5 years (Morgan, Hammer, et al., 2016), in elementary school (Hibel et al., 2010), and throughout middle school (Morgan, Farkas, Hillemeier, Mattison, et al., 2015) compared to white children, after controlling for factors such as prior academic achievement and SES. The same pattern was reported for LD in elementary and middle school (Hibel et al., 2010; Morgan, Farkas, Hillemeier, Mattison, et al., 2015). Though identification rates for both African American and Hispanic students were significantly lower than for white children, African American children were less likely than both groups to be identified as having either speech-language impairments or LD, regardless of age (Morgan, Farkas, Hillemeier, Mattison, et al., 2015). Children with limited English proficiency were underrepresented in the LD category in elementary school and proportionately represented in secondary grades, compared to African American children, for whom proportionality was not achieved at any age. Disproportionate representation cannot solely be explained by race, however, because African American and Hispanic students are more likely to attend low-performing, low-SES, and majority-minority schools. Children attending majority-minority schools are less likely to be identified as having any disability (Hibel et al., 2010).

Another factor that has long been associated with poor diagnostic accuracy for African American children is lack of available culturally and linguistically appropriate assessments (e.g., Craig & Washington, 2000, 2004; Stockman, Newkirk-Turner, Swartzlander, & Morris, 2016; Washington & Craig, 2004). Publishers of widely used assessments have aimed to increase diagnostic accuracy through revisions generally focused on 1) developing norms based on a representative sample, 2) exclusion of items that may pose cultural or linguistic bias, and 3) scoring corrections. In spite of these adjustments, there is still a desperate need for assessments with improved discriminative ability that more successfully identify children from different cultural, linguistic, and economic backgrounds.

Taken together, recent work on disproportionality challenges the status quo and suggests it is time to update current thinking. Although there is no reason to assume one group is more vulnerable to disabilities than another, the reality in the United States is that African American children are more likely to be impoverished and attend high-poverty schools (Bohrnstedt, Kitmitto, Ogut, & Chan, 2015), more likely to have risk factors for disabilities (e.g., low birth weight), and less likely to have access to quality health care and quality education. These risk variables make them less likely to be diagnosed with LD because poverty and its sequelae

Table 9.1. Factors contributing to disproportionality in special education in the United States

Intrinsic factors	Extrinsic factors
Caregiver English language proficiency	Access to quality health care
Child English language proficiency	Access to quality early childhood education
Age/grade level	School demographics (i.e., percentage of minority enrollment, overall socioeconomic status)
Previous academic achievement	IDEA definition of learning disability Lack of sensitivity of assessment instruments Lack of familiarity of the examiner with language and cultural norms of the child Oversensitivity of teachers to language and cultural differences Teacher expectations (influenced by norms in their setting)

Key: IDEA, Individuals with Disabilities Education Improvement Act (IDEA) of 2004 (PL 108-446).

can be overwhelming and obscure disabilities. (See Table 9.1 for additional factors that contribute to disproportionality.) An important question for future research is "In a population in which 8 of 10 children will be struggling readers, who has a reading disability, and how does it manifest?"

EXPOSURE TO MAINSTREAM AMERICAN ENGLISH

Though languages and dialects may be theoretically distinct, conceptually the argument that rates of disproportionately vary in either direction based on English proficiency has implications for African American English (AAE) speakers as a linguistically diverse group whose primary language system differs significantly from the language used at school (*Martin Luther King Junior Elementary School Children et al. v. Ann Arbor School District,* 1979). Learning to read in English can be an arduous task, even for children who are typically developing. Alphabetic languages with deep orthographies, such as English, have variable letter–sound correspondence compared with languages such as Welsh, where letter–sound correspondence is more consistent (Ellis & Hooper, 2001). Being able to decode written text in English requires that children understand more than the alphabetic principle; reading accuracy is also highly dependent on stored phonological representations of the sounds in spoken words and the orthographic manifestations of those sounds (see Chapter 7). For reading comprehension, morphological and syntactic knowledge are critical because making sense of written text requires an understanding of derivations and inflections, base words and their derived forms, relationships between words, and complex grammatical structures (Kamhi & Catts, 2012). Because reading relies heavily on language, learning to read can be exceptionally difficult for children whose linguistic systems vary from the language of written text.

The most recent National Assessment of Educational Progress (NAEP) data indicated that only 18% of African American children read at or above proficient levels in fourth grade, and in eighth grade, this proportion drops to 16% (Bohrnstedt et al., 2015). A recent longitudinal study confirmed that this reality disproportionately affects African American boys. Washington, Branum-Martin, Lee-James, and Sun (2019) reported gender differences in reading (favoring girls) at each grade—most notably divergence in growth trajectories, with girls growing faster in reading comprehension and boys decelerating slightly in fluency. Although a host of factors have been identified as contributing to reading failure among African American children, oral language differences have been implicated as an important factor to consider. AAE dialect varies from MAE in all language domains but most notably in phonology and morphosyntax (see Craig, Thompson, Washington, & Potter, 2003; Oetting & McDonald, 2001), making learning to read a challenge for students. Generally speaking, AAE is characterized primarily by phonological and morphosyntactic deletions (e.g., His han_ is big; He kick_ the girl yesterday) and substitutions (e.g., pin/pen, ax/ask; They was eating; They is tired). (See Table 9.2 for a list of AAE forms.)

The rate of dialect use, or dialect density, seems to be predictive of reading outcomes (Craig & Washington, 2004; Gatlin & Wanzek, 2015; Terry et al., 2010) in that children with high density demonstrate lower reading achievement than their peers who use dialect less frequently (Washington, Branum-Martin, Sun, & Lee-James, 2018). Using simulated cases, a recent paper demonstrated that it actually takes longer to achieve reading mastery as dialect feature production increases (Brown et al., 2015). The relationship between density and reading failure disproportionately affects African American children reared in poverty (Terry et al., 2010) because they are more likely to use greater amounts of dialect in their speech compared to their same-age middle-income peers (Washington, Craig, & Kushmaul, 1998). These findings have fueled an increase in the movement to teach African American children to dialect-shift (Johnson, Terry, Connor, & Thomas-Tate, 2017; Wheeler & Swords, 2004).

Evidence from a longitudinal investigation examined the impact of dialect density on the growth of language and reading achievement over time in a sample of approximately 900 children in first through fifth grades (Washington et al., 2018). Like other studies in the extant literature, this study found an overall negative relationship between dialect density and language and dialect density and reading. However, the impact of dialect density did not affect rate of growth in language but affected rate of growth in reading such that children with higher dialect density demonstrated slower growth

Table 9.2.   Features of African American English

Phonological features	Examples
Consonant cluster reduction	/hæn/ for /hænd/
Consonant cluster movement	/æks/ for /æsk/
"g" dropping	/wetn/ for wetŋ/
Postvocalic consonant reduction	mau for mouth
Substitution for interdental fricatives	/dɪs/ for /ðɪs/ /bof/ for /boθ/
Variable production of vowels	/pɪn/ for /pɛn/ /kent/ for /kænt/

Morphosyntactic features	Examples
Omission of auxiliary *do*	How ___ you get up here?
Omission of auxiliary *have*	I ___ only been there once.
Noninversion of Wh-questions	Why this one won't sit?
Substitution of *was* for *were*	They was going to the store.
Substitution of *is* for *are*	They is running fast.
Zero BE	They ___ hungry. This one ___ yours?[a]
Zero plural	I have twenty-five cent ___.
Zero possessive	That's daddy' ___ coat.
Zero regular past tense	The boy kick ___ the ball.
Zero third person	They cat eat ___ his food.

Note: Phonological features included are based on Craig, Thompson, Washington, and Porter (2003).
Morphosyntactic features are based on Oetting and McDonald (2001). Reference these for a comprehensive list of phonological and morphosyntactic features.

[a]African American English speakers may also omit the auxiliary and copula verbs in questions.

in reading over time whereas children with strong reading skills decreased their dialect density over time. These findings indicate a reciprocal relationship between dialect and reading, suggesting that intervention efforts targeting reading skills (rather than dialect shifting) should lead to spontaneous reduction in overall dialect use. This study found that children decreased their dialect density as grade increased; however, the rate of decrease slowed over time, which suggests that building oral language and foundational reading skills early will be critical for supporting dialect shifting in later years.

Although AAE clearly affects reading development, there is no empirical evidence that it adversely affects identification or diagnosis of reading impairment. Instead, it is more likely to have an impact on phonemic- and phonologically based interventions. There is some evidence that children's perception of mainstream phonology is affected by their use of AAE phonology such that they may have difficulty discriminating phonemes in their dialect that contrast with MAE (Seymour et al., 1998). Therefore, current approaches to teaching reading that rely heavily on phonology may be affected by these perceptual differences. An important question related to dialect may be whether a child's use of dialect makes it more difficult for researchers and educators to identify phonological and phonemic differences that result from disability versus those that result from linguistic difference. Furthermore, heavy dialect use is associated with poverty in African American children, making it more likely that dialect use in impoverished children could be confused with language and literacy impairments, or vice versa. Longitudinal studies are needed to be able to examine the contribution of poverty and dialect to language and reading achievement in order to develop evidence-based instruction.

CONCLUSION

Given that definitions drive research, the exclusionary criteria outlined in IDEA 2004 are a major challenge in that the statute influences the likelihood that impoverished minority children will be included in studies of reading disability. As such, very little is known about how LD manifests in African American children from economically disadvantaged backgrounds. In research and in practice, impoverished minority children are considered special populations, though current data suggests they should be treated as the rule—not the exception. In the United States, 43% of children are from low-income households, and 21% are living below the poverty line (National Center for Children in Poverty, 2018); these children are largely from minority backgrounds. Because low-income children are not generally the focus of disabilities research, methods designed for and normed on mainstream children are inappropriately applied to them, which undoubtedly contributes to disproportionality in special education. A critical area for future research will be to continue to unpack unbalanced representation across special education categories to ensure that children are accurately diagnosed and receiving appropriate service.

An unintended consequence of IDEA 2004 is that it decreases the likelihood that African American children will receive a diagnosis of LD and appropriate intervention, if it is believed that reading, writing or mathematics deficits can be better explained by cultural or linguistic differences and/or economic disadvantage. Though the impact of poverty on development is unquestionable, the assumption that all impoverished children are reared in substandard language and literacy environments, and that attending

Title I schools automatically results in poor opportunity or poor instruction, is biased and simply not true. Thus, researchers cannot, in every case, attribute reading failure to the student's culture, home, or school environments.

The language used in IDEA 2004 has led to binary thinking on the part of educators and researchers about disability and difference as mutually exclusive, instead of recognizing that LD does exist in the context of differences and disadvantage. Given the fact that the extant literature base is saturated with studies on the adverse impact of poverty on development, it may be hard for some educators and researchers to conceive that a child's reading failure could be the result of neurological underpinnings rather than a symptom of growing up in poverty. Future research should seek to change binary thinking by unpacking a profile of reading disabilities in impoverished and minority children in order to encourage a shift in practices and policies.

The conversation regarding disabilities existing within differences has recently resurfaced as a topic of interest in the field of language disorders (Oetting, Gregory, & Riviere, 2016). For decades, researchers were focused on distinguishing linguistic difference from language disorder, often posing the question, "Is the child presenting with a language difference OR is the child presenting with a language disorder?" Cultural, linguistic, and economic differences contribute significantly to language development, as they do to reading. In many instances, differences in oral language, especially for AAE speakers, may present as language disorder because the typical patterns of the dialect overlap, to some extent, with clinical indicators of language impairment. It wasn't until the late 1990s (Craig & Washington, 2000; Seymour et al., 1998; Stockman, 2006; Washington & Craig, 2004) that researchers began to ask how language disorder manifests in children who speak African American English, arguing that no child, regardless of cultural or linguistic background, is immune to language disorders; ignoring this fact systematically places students of color at a disadvantage. Participants in these studies were from low-income backgrounds. Given that oral language is the foundation for reading acquisition, adopting the perspective of disability within difference, as opposed to current thinking that focuses on disability versus difference, should serve to improve diagnostic accuracy for reading disabilities in minority children from economically disadvantaged backgrounds.

Improving reading achievement in African American children will require that researchers intentionally include minority children in studies focused on accurate identification of reading disabilities. Continuing to subscribe to the idea that LD cannot exist in the face of difference and disadvantage is absurd and unethical, and it contributes to the current educational debt among impoverished and minority children in the United States. Future research directions should emphasize development of a profile of LD that includes minority children from economically disadvantaged backgrounds, with a specific focus on determining what LDs looks like in the face of poor opportunity.

REFERENCES

Blanchett, W. J. (2010). Telling it like it is: The role of race, class, & culture in the perpetuation of learning disability as a privileged category for the white middle class. *Disability Studies Quarterly, 30*(2).

Blanchett, W. J., Klinger, J. K., & Harry, B. (2009). The intersection of race, culture, language, and disability. *Urban Education, 44*(4), 389–409.

Bohrnstedt, G., Kitmitto, S., Ogut, B., & Chan, D. (2015). *School composition and the Black–White achievement gap* (NCES 2015-018). Washington, DC: U.S. Department of Education, National Center for Education Statistics. Retrieved from http://nces.ed.gov/pubsearch

Bronson, J. (2014). The overrepresentation of Black children in special education and the human right to education. In M. Gill & C. J. Schlund-Vials (Eds.), *Disability, human rights and the limits of humanitarianism* (pp. 205–217). Burlington, VT: Ashgate.

Brown, M. C., Sibley, D. E., Washington, J. A., Rogers, T. T., Edwards, J. R., MacDonald, M. C., & Seidenberg, M. S. (2015). Impact of dialect use on a basic component of learning to read. *Frontiers in Psychology, 6,* 196. http://dx.doi.org/10.3389/fpsyg.2015.00196

Craig, H., Thompson, C. A., Washington, J. A., & Potter, S. L. (2003). Phonological features of child African American English. *Journal of Speech, Language, and Hearing Research, 46,* 623–635.

Craig, H., & Washington, J. A. (2000). An assessment battery for identifying language impairments in African American children. *Journal of Speech, Language, and Hearing Research, 43,* 366–379.

Craig, H., & Washington, J. A. (2004). Grade-related changes in the production of African American English. *Journal of Speech, Language, and Hearing Research, 47,* 450–463.

Ellis, N. C., & Hooper, A. M. (2001). Why learning to read is easier in Welsh than in English: Orthographic transparency effects evinced with frequency-matched tests. *Applied Linguistics, 22,* 571–599.

Feinberg, I., Frijters, J., Johnson-Lawrence, V., Greenberg, D., Nightingale, E., & Moodie, C. (2016). Examining associations between health information seeking behavior and adult education status in the US: An analysis of the 2012 PIAAC Data. *PloS One, 11*(2), e0148751.

Gatlin, B., & Wanzek, J. (2015). Relations among children's use of dialect and literacy skills: A meta-analysis. *Journal of Speech Language Hearing Research, 58*(4), 1306–1318. http://dx.doi.org/10.1044/2015_JSLHR-L-14-0311

Harman, D. (1970). Illiteracy: An overview. *Harvard Educational Review, 40*(2), 226–243.

Hibel, J., Farkas, G., & Morgan, P. L. (2010). Who is placed into special education? *Sociology of Education, 83*(4), 312–332. http://dx.doi.org/10.1177/0038040710383518

Individuals with Disabilities Education Improvement Act (IDEA) of 2004, PL 108-446, 20 U.S.C. §§ 1400 *et seq.*

Johnson, L., Terry, N. P., Connor, C. M., & Thomas-Tate, S. (2017). The effects of dialect awareness instruction on nonmainstream American English speakers. *Reading and Writing, 30*(9), 2009–2038. http://dx.doi.org/10.1007/s11145-017-9764-y

Kamhi, A. G., & Catts, H. W. (2012). *Language and reading disabilities* (3rd ed.). Boston, MA: Pearson.

Martin Luther King Junior Elementary School Children et al. v. Ann Arbor School District, 73 F. Supp. 1371 (E.D. Mich. 1979).

Morgan, P. L., Farkas, G., Cook, M., Strassfeld, N. M., Hillemeier, M. M., Pun, W. H., & Schussler, D. L. (2016). Are Black children disproportionately overrepresented in special education? A best-evidence synthesis. *Exceptional Children, 83*(2), 181–198. http://dx.doi.org/10.1177/0014402916664042

Morgan, P. L., Farkas, G., Hillemeier, M. M., Hammer, C. S., & Maczuga, S. (2015). 24-month-old children with larger oral vocabularies display greater academic and behavioral functioning at kindergarten entry. *Child Development, 86*(5), 1351–1370. http://dx.doi.org/10.1111/cdev.12398

Morgan, P. L., Farkas, G., Hillemeier, M. M., Mattison, R., Maczuga, S., Li, H., & Cook, M. (2015). Minorities are disproportionately underrepresented in special education: Longitudinal evidence across five disability conditions. *Educational Research, 44*(5), 278–292. http://dx.doi.org/10.3102/0013189X15591157

Morgan, P. L., Hammer, C. S., Farkas, G., Hillemeier, M. M., Maczuga, S., Cook, M., & Morano, S. (2016). Who receives speech/language services by 5 years of in the United States? *American Journal of Speech-Language Pathology, 25*, 183–199.

National Center for Children in Poverty. (2018). *Child poverty*. Retrieved from http://www.nccp.org/topics/childpoverty.html

Oetting, J. B., Gregory, K. D., & Riviere, A. M. (2016). Changing how speech-language pathologists think and talk about dialect variation. *Perspectives on the ASHA Special Interest Group 16, 1*, 28–37. http://dx.doi.org/10.1044/persp1.SIG16.28

Oetting, J. B., & McDonald, J. L. (2001). Nonmainstream dialect use and specific language impairment. *Journal of Speech Language and Hearing Research, 44*, 207–223.

Oswald, D. P., Coutinho, M. J., Best, A. M., & Nguyen, N. (2011). Impact of sociodemographic characteristics on the identification rates of minority students as having mental retardation. *Mental Retardation, 39*(5), 351–367.

Seymour, H. N., Bland-Stewart, L., & Green, L. J. (1998). Difference versus deficit in child African American English. *Language, Speech, and Hearing Services in Schools, 29*, 96–108.

Skiba, R. J., Feggins-Azziz, R., & Chung, C. G. (2005). Unproven links: Can poverty explain ethnic disproportionality in special education. *The Journal of Special Education, 39*(3), 130–144.

Stockman, I. J. (2006). Alveolar bias in the final consonant deletion patterns of African American children. *Language Speech and Hearing Services in Schools, 37*, 85–95.

Stockman, I. J. (2010). A review of developmental and applied language research on African American children: From a deficit to difference perspective on dialect differences. *Language, Speech, and Hearing Services in Schools, 41*(1), 23–38.

Stockman, I. J., Newkirk-Turner, B. L., Swartzlander, E., & Morris, L. R. (2016). Comparison of African American children's performances on a minimal competence core for morphosyntax and the index of productive syntax. *American Journal of Speech Language Pathology, 25*(1), 80–96. http://dx.doi.org/10.1044/2015_AJSLP-14-0207

Terry, N. P., Connor, C. M., Thomas-Tate, S., & Love, M. (2010). Examining relationships among dialect variation, literacy skills, and school context in first grade. *Journal of Speech, Language, and Hearing Research, 53*, 126–145.

Walter, P. (1999). Defining literacy and its consequences in the developing world. *International Journal of Lifelong Education, 18*(1), 31–48.

Washington, J. A., Branum-Martin, L., Lee-James, R., & Sun, C. (2019). Reading and language performance of low-income, African American boys in Grades 1–5. *Reading and Writing Quarterly, 35*(1), 42–64 .

Washington, J. A., Branum-Martin, L., Sun, C., & Lee-James, R. (2018). The impact of dialect density on the growth of language and reading in African American children. *Language Speech and Hearing Services in the Schools, 49*(2), 232–247. http://dx.doi.org/10.1044/2018_LSHSS-17-0063

Washington, J. A., & Craig, H. K. (2004). A language screening protocol for use with young African American children in urban settings. *American Journal of Speech-Language Pathology, 13*, 329–340.

Washington, J. A., Craig, H. K., & Kushmaul, A. J. (1998). Variable use of African American English across two language sampling contexts. *Journal of Speech, Language, and Hearing Research, 41*, 1115–1124.

Wheeler, R. S., & Swords, R. (2004). Codeswitching: Tools of language and culture transform the dialectally diverse classroom. *Language Arts, 81*(6), 470–480.

CHAPTER 10

Personalizing Literacy Instruction for Diverse Learners and Children With Severe Literacy Difficulties
Carol McDonald Connor, Young-Suk Grace Kim, and Dandan Yang

SUMMARY

Improving technology promises truly personalized reading instruction for diverse learners. This chapter focuses on Assessment-to-Instruction (A2i), a teacher professional support technology that provides recommendations for individualized (or differentiated) literacy instruction using dynamic forecasting intervention (DFI) algorithms. The A2i DFI algorithms compute the recommended amounts of instruction for each student based on language and literacy assessment scores. In this chapter, we synthesize four studies that are helping us refine the A2i algorithms for students at risk or with dyslexia and dysgraphia. In the first study, we developed A2i algorithms for pre-kindergarten (PK) students that incorporated play as a learning opportunity to build language skills. In the second study, we found that teachers who used A2i were more accurate in judging their students' academic competence and were less influenced by factors such as socioeconomic status (SES) than were control teachers. In the third study, we identified child characteristics in first grade that predicted severe literacy difficulties at the end of second grade. Key risk predictors included difficulties in self-regulation, smaller gains in reading, lower initial reading skills, and not receiving A2i individualized literacy instruction. In the fourth study, we found complex child self-regulation-by-instruction interaction effects on first grade students' literacy gains. Overall, first-grade students with weaker self-regulation made smaller gains in literacy, holding all other characteristics constant. Together, these four studies offer recommendations for serving children who are at risk for dyslexia in general education classrooms, ensuring that these children participate in learning opportunities that are effective for them.

Acknowledgments: We gratefully acknowledge the contributions of the members of the Individualizing Student Instruction (iSi) lab, the Learning Disabilities Multidisciplinary Research Center (LDRC) team, the families, teachers, and school administrators, without whom this research would not have been possible. We thank our funders: The National Institute of Child Health and Human Development Grants P50 HD052120 and R01 HD48539, and the Department of Education, Institute of Education Sciences Grants R305N160050, R305A160404, R305B070074, R305H040013, R305F100027, and the Office of Innovation and Technology Grant U411A17011. University of California, Irvine, has reviewed Dr. Connor's conflict of interest with Learning Ovations and has determined that safeguards are in place to preserve the integrity of the research presented.

INTRODUCTION

Over the past decade (Connor, Morrison, Fishman, Schatschneider, & Underwood, 2007), we have learned that data-driven A2i DFI algorithms can reliably compute effective recommended amounts (minutes/day) of different types of literacy instruction (kindergarten through third grade). When implemented, these recommendations lead to stronger reading outcomes for typically developing children with a range of skills, including children living in poverty, children who are English language learners, children in the individualized education programs (IEPs), and children who belong to minority groups. Meeting What Works Clearinghouse Standards without Reservations (https://ies.ed.gov/ncee/wwc/), using A2i, a teacher professional support technology system that incorporates the A2i DFI algorithms, is associated with significantly greater gains in literacy skills compared to randomly assigned control groups of students whose teachers do not use A2i (Al Otaiba et al., 2011; Connor et al., 2013; Connor et al., 2011) from kindergarten through third grade.

The current A2i DFI algorithms were developed for kindergarten through third grade and rely on the simple view of reading—that proficient reading is the product of fluent decoding and listening comprehension (Hoover & Gough, 1990). Newer, more dynamic models of literacy development, such as the lattice model (Connor, 2016) and models described by Nation (see Chapter 7), Rueckl (see Chapter 6), and others (Direct and Indirect Effect model of Reading, Kim, 2017, in review; Spencer et al., 2014), suggest that other child characteristics are important to the development of literacy skills. These include social, cognitive, and regulatory processes. Thus, when improving the A2i DFI algorithms, there may be other child characteristics to consider, particularly for children whose skills fall at the lowest tail of the literacy continuum, including children with dyslexia and dysgraphia. Dyslexia is frequently comorbid with attention-deficit/ hyperactivity disorder (ADHD), weak self-regulation and executive functioning, and anxiety (Chapter 12).

Using what we have learned over the past 13 years of developing the A2i DFI algorithms and conducting randomized controlled trials (RCTs) to test their precision and efficacy, we hypothesized that we could extend the A2i algorithms down to PK. We also hypothesized that by including measures of self-regulation, for example, we could improve the extent to which the A2i DFI algorithms could identify optimal amounts of several types of literacy instruction for students with or at risk of dyslexia: code or meaning focused, with the teacher, with peers, or alone. Note that we define self-regulation as the coordination of more basic executive function skills, including working memory, attention, effortful control, and task switching, to complete a learning activity (Lin, Coburn, & Eisenberg, 2016). In this chapter, we discuss four studies that test these hypotheses. In the first study, we describe the developed PK algorithms, which have implications for how we conceptualize the role of instruction and play with young children. In the second, we review the findings of an A2i RCT that investigated the impact of teachers' perceptions of children's academic competence on children's literacy achievement (Gatlin et al., in review). We then review the results of a longitudinal study, which used logistic regression to examine first-grade child characteristics to estimate the probability that children will have seriously delayed reading skills (more than one standard deviation below the national norm) at the end of second grade. Finally, we describe a study that explores first-grade students' self-regulation-by-instruction interaction effects on reading gains, which has implications for refining the A2i algorithms and for early diagnostic screening.

NEW PRE-KINDERGARTEN A2i DYNAMIC FORECASTING INTERVENTION ALGORITHMS

The rationale for adding PK DFI algorithms to A2i was to encourage earlier identification of children at risk for dyslexia (see Chapter 5). By closely matching PK learning opportunities to children's learning needs, we can improve the efficacy of these opportunities, thus potentially preventing the onset of reading difficulties. By providing valid and reliable progress monitoring assessments, we can identify PK children who are not gaining critical early literacy and language skills relative to peers and expected norms, even when provided appropriate learning opportunities.

To develop the new algorithms for PK children, we returned to data collected for a study on child characteristic-by-instruction (CXI) interaction effects in PK (Connor, Morrison, & Slominski, 2006). The results of this longitudinal correlational study revealed several CXI interaction effects on children's early literacy and vocabulary skills; three were of interest for incorporating into A2i.

In the current study (and in all the A2i studies), we conceptualize language and literacy instruction multidimensionally across content and context from PK through third grade following the simple view of reading (Hoover & Gough, 1990) and models of play (Roskos & Christie, 2000). For example, literacy activities focused on teaching children letters and letter sounds are considered code-focused instruction (see Table 10.1). In contrast, meaning-focused instruction builds language and comprehension skills—for example, reading to children and asking questions. For young children, play also builds language skills (Dickinson & Porche, 2011; Roskos & Christie, 2000). For context, children might be with a teacher or adult, with peers, or alone, and instruction can be provided to the entire class, to small groups of children, or individually to one child. You can conceive of this as a three-dimensional grid, which is easier to understand if you just consider two dimensions: content and who the child is interacting with; keeping in mind that the activities can be whole class, small group, or individual (not displayed in Table 10.1).

Table 10.1. Multidimensional conceptualization of language and literacy instruction

	With the teacher	With peers	Alone
Code focused	The kindergarten teacher is working with the children on counting phonemes in words. Teacher: "How many sounds in c-a-t?" Everybody: (Children chorally respond and count on their fingers.)	First-grade students are practicing sight word fluency flash cards in pairs.	The student is working on a worksheet on the phonic rules for the spelling of the phoneme /a/.
Meaning focused	The teacher is reading a book to preschool students and asking questions as he or she goes along.	Second-grade students are working together to peer-review in Writers' Workshop.	A third-grade student is reading a book of his or her choice silently during center time.
Play	The pre-kindergarten teacher is facilitating sociodramatic play about going to the doctor's office. Each student has a role.	Kindergarten students are playing together with blocks. They have constructed a town and are using blocks as cars and trucks.	A preschool student is playing alone in the sandbox.

We found that children with weaker early literacy skills in the fall made greater gains in early literacy by spring when they participated in more code-focused instruction with their teacher (e.g., teacher explaining how letters form words, teacher teaching letters and letter sounds). However, there was no effect of this type of instruction for children with stronger early literacy skills in the fall.

For meaning-focused instruction with the teacher (e.g., teacher reading aloud to children and asking questions), we found that more time in this type of instruction was associated with stronger vocabulary gains for all children, with a stronger effect for children with weaker fall vocabulary skills. There were also effects on early literacy gains but only for children with stronger fall early literacy skills. There was a significant negative effect of meaning-focused instruction with the teacher for children with weaker early literacy skills in the fall. This was unexpected. However, because the PK day is limited, it might be that more time in meaning-focused instruction meant less time in code-focused instruction.

We also examined the effect of free-choice playful learning opportunities (e.g., centers), which we describe as *play* (e.g., blocks, sociodramatic play centers). When such opportunities were facilitated by the teacher, children with weaker initial vocabulary skills made significant gains in vocabulary. However, there was no effect for children with stronger vocabulary skills.

Using the data, we reverse-engineered the hierarchical linear models that elucidated the CXI interactions. The Y_{ij} in the hierarchical linear model equation (i.e., target outcome) was set at the mean for the sample, which was the same as the nationally normed test standardization sample mean. We then ran simulations using the coefficients of the model—trimmed to the extent possible. The resulting DFI algorithms are provided in Figure 10.1.

The teacher/child-managed meaning-focused (TCMMF) DFI algorithm incorporates the amount of time recommended for teacher-managed code-focused (TMCF) instruction, which helps to control for the zero-sum nature of the length of the PK day. The recommended amounts vary as a function of both early literacy skills and vocabulary. The play algorithm is more straightforward and relies only on the vocabulary score. Minimum and maximum amounts for each type of instruction were based on the range of amounts of instruction actually observed. That is, there were not more than 30 minutes of TCMMF observed in the PK classrooms. Because there were no CXI interactions for the child and peer-managed instruction, they were set at the mean delivered by the teachers in the sample, which was 5 minutes per day.

Examining these DFI algorithm recommendations, in the context of classroom observation, reveals that if these algorithms are accurate, many

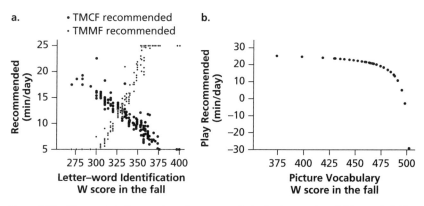

Figure 10.1. The y-axis is the number of recommended minutes per day. a) The x-axis is the early reading W score (Woodcock-Johnson III Tests of Achievement Letter-word Identification; Woodcock, McGrew, & Mather, 2001). The small black dots are the recommended amount of teacher-managed code-focused instruction (min/day) as a function of fall early reading score; the larger black dots are the recommended amount of teacher-managed meaning-focused instruction. Each dot represents a child in the sample using his or her individual Letter-word and Vocabulary scores. b) The x-axis is the Woodcock-Johnson III Tests of Achievement Picture Vocabulary W score (Woodcock, McGrew, & Mather, 2001). Each dot represents the recommended amount of Play for each child based on his or her individual Vocabulary score.

children were not participating in sufficient amounts of play and early literacy to ensure they reached their potential. On average, about 3 minutes per day of code-focused instruction with the teacher were observed ($SD = 3.8$) and only about 11 minutes of play ($SD = 15$). Of course, these observations were conducted in 2002 to 2003. Times have changed, and we have learned more about what children need to learn to become proficient readers. However, a newer PK classroom observation study (Connor et al., 2018) showed that many PK children in 2017 to 2018 were not participating in enough meaningful learning activities.

TEACHER PERCEPTIONS AND DATA-INFORMED INSTRUCTION

Data-driven instruction that is tailored to each student's learning needs, such as instruction informed by A2i, is more effective than one-size-fits-all instruction observed in many studies (Al Otaiba et al., 2011), and why this is the case deserves close attention. One working hypothesis is that teachers' expectations and accurate assessment of children's academic abilities may influence the effectiveness of the instruction teachers provide. In a previous study (Tani & Connor, 2011), we found that teachers systematically rated African American boys as weaker in academic competence than their white peers and girls, even considering children's actual achievement. To examine whether easy access to assessment information might elicit more accurate teacher judgments of academic competence, we used data from an RCT in which teachers were randomly assigned to use A2i or to an alternative treatment control group (Gatlin et al., in review). In this sample, almost 30% of the students qualified for the National School Lunch Program (NSLP), a widely used indicator of family poverty. Most of the children were white, with about 16% reported as African American, Hispanic, Asian, or multiracial.

We found that teachers in first-grade A2i classrooms, when asked to rate students' academic competence, were more accurate than control teachers (i.e., their ratings correlated more highly with standardized literacy assessment scores). Moreover, teachers in the A2i condition were less likely to be influenced by child characteristics (e.g., SES, behavior problems) than were control teachers. Neither SES nor behavior problems significantly predicted actual literacy achievement. Figure 10.2 shows how teachers' ($n = 28$) ratings of students' ($n = 438$) academic competence (standard score in which mean = 100) differed as a function of students' SES status by school context after controlling for actual literacy and math skills measured using standardized measures, literacy gains, math gains, and behavior problems. Overall, teachers in the A2i group rated their students as more academically competent (controlling for actual achievement), and they judged the academic competence of students who qualified for the NSLP as similar to students who did not qualify. Teachers in the control classrooms rated students who qualified for the

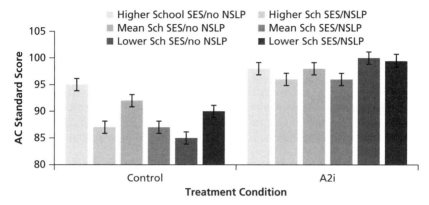

Figure 10.2. Teachers' rating of students' academic competence on the Social Skills Rating System Scale (AC Standard Score, Gresham & Elliot, 1990) as a function of treatment condition (control and Assessment-to-Instruction [A2i]), percentage of students at the school who qualified for the National School Lunch Program (NSLP; modeled at the 25th [light gray], 50th [medium gray], and 75th [dark gray–from more disadvantaged backgrounds] percentile of the sample, in which the mean school socioeconomic status [Mean Sch SES] was 37%), and student eligibility for the NSLP (*yes* = 1; *no* = 0).

NSLP significantly less academically competent than students who did not qualify for the NSLP. However, this varied by school context, with the greatest gap at the more affluent schools. These findings have important implications for children from disadvantaged backgrounds and suggest that effective use of assessment might help make teacher expectations more precise and not dependent on child characteristics, which are not malleable. This may be particularly true for impoverished children at affluent schools in which they are more likely to stand out as different from their more affluent peers.

IDENTIFYING STUDENT CHARACTERISTICS ASSOCIATED WITH RISK FOR READING DISABILITIES

Using data from the longitudinal efficacy study on Individualizing Student Instruction (ISI) (Connor et al., 2013), we conducted logistic regression using a dichotomous outcome in which a serious reading problem at the end of second grade was defined as performance below 1 standard deviation (a standard score of 85 or less = 1, scores above 85 = 0) on the Passage Comprehension test of the Woodcock-Johnson III (Woodcock, McGrew, & Mather, 2001; Yang & Connor, 2019). Only 5% of 373 students were identified as having weak reading skills at the end of second grade. Hierarchical linear modeling with a Bernoulli outcome allowed us to calculate the probability that, given weaknesses in specific skills at the beginning or during first grade, children would be at greater risk for dyslexia.

Results are provided in Figure 10.3. Overall, first-grade students in A2i classrooms were less likely to develop severe reading problems than were students in control classrooms. The weaker a student's self-regulation skills (Ponitz et al., 2008), the greater the risk of demonstrating a very low reading score at the end of second grade. In addition, there were child CXI interaction effects on risk. Children with weaker phonological awareness were more likely to be at risk for serious reading problems at the end of second grade if they were in control classrooms rather than A2i classrooms. The weaker their initial vocabulary skills

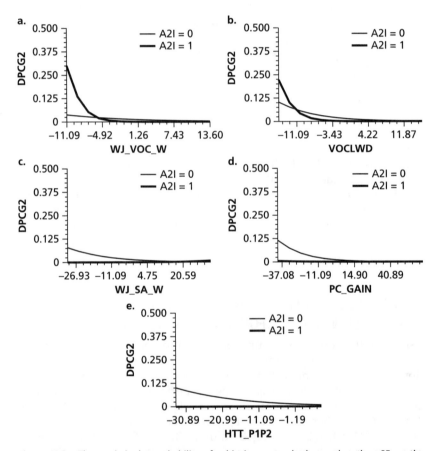

Figure 10.3. The *y*-axis is the probability of achieving a standard score less than 85 on the Woodcock-Johnson III Passage Comprehension (Woodcock, McGrew, & Mather, 2001) in the spring of second grade. The *x*-axis is a) first-grade fall vocabulary, b) the difference between vocabulary and word reading, c) sound awareness, d) gains in passage comprehension from the beginning to the end of first grade, and e) self-regulation measured by the Head-to-Toes task. A2I = 1 (the bold line) refers to students who were in A2i treatment group; A2I = 0 refers to students who were in the control group.

overall, the greater the risk of developing serious reading problems at later grades. Although the probabilities of achieving very low reading scores were small and may not be educationally meaningful, some refinement of the A2i DFI algorithms may be desirable, for example, adding self-regulation to the algorithms (Ponitz et al., 2008). Overall, weak gains in reading skills, weak vocabulary skills and weak self-regulation, as well as weak phonological awareness at the beginning of first grade may signal early risk for dyslexia.

ADDING SELF-REGULATION TO THE FIRST-GRADE A2i DFI ALGORITHMS

The first step in developing DFI algorithms is to examine the child characteristics that moderate students' outcomes in the contexts of particular types of literacy instruction; we ask what types of literacy learning activities are effective for which children in which contexts (see Chapter 12). Based on the results of the logistic regression, we decided to examine whether there might be self-regulation by instruction interaction effects on literacy gains in first grade. There is accumulating evidence that weaker executive function (highly related to self-regulation) is associated with dyslexia and perhaps dysgraphia (Eason, Goldberg, Young, Geist, & Cutting, 2012). Using data from Connor and colleagues (2011), which included the *Head-Toes-Knees-Shoulders* measure of self-regulation (Ponitz et al., 2008), we reanalyzed the data to examine the relation of self-regulation to students' reading gains.

After replicating the original findings, we added fall self-regulation to the models and tested for interactions. We found an overall effect of self-regulation on spring reading gains; in general, first-grade students with weaker self-regulation demonstrated smaller gains in reading compared to peers with stronger self-regulation. There were also child CXI interactions (see Figure 10.4). Overall, more time in whole-class and small-group meaning-focused instruction with the teacher was associated with greater gains for first-grade students with stronger self-regulation, but was less effective for students with weaker self-regulation, particularly in whole-class settings. For code-focused instruction, small-group instruction with the teacher was generally more effective for first-grade students with weaker self-regulation and had no effect for students with stronger self-regulation, holding all other child characteristics constant. There was no interaction effect for whole-class code-focused instruction with the teacher. Our next step will be to incorporate self-regulation scores into the current A2i DFI algorithms and examine in new samples whether they predict more of the variability in children's reading gains than the current algorithms do. If they do, we will then conduct a prospective study to examine the efficacy of using new algorithms.

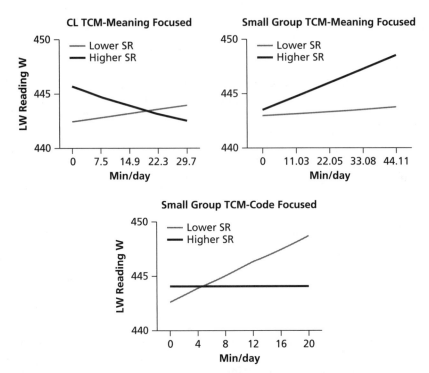

Figure 10.4. Child self-regulation (SR) by instruction interaction effects on first-grade gains in letter-word reading scores (LW Reading W). a) Whole-class (CL) meaning-focused instruction with the teacher (TCM). b) Small-group meaning-focused instruction with the teacher. c) Small-group code-focused instruction with the teacher.

CONCLUSION

The title of this book is *Dyslexia: Revisiting Etiology, Diagnosis, Treatment, and Policy*. In this chapter, we discuss early diagnosis, treatment, and prevention of dyslexia and suggest new models of literacy that include instruction (and play) and students' self-regulation skills as important sources of influence on children's literacy development—keeping in mind that the impact of instruction depends on the constellation of skills students bring to the classroom. For example, effective instruction for a first-grade student with stronger self-regulation may be less effective for a student with weaker self-regulation. Self-regulation provides the foundation for learning, including oral language, reading, and writing (Kim, 2017; Kim & Schatschneider, 2017). One might speculate that the reason whole-class instruction is not as effective for children with weaker self-regulation (see Figure 10.4, top left), whereas it is effective (especially meaning-focused instruction) for children with stronger self-regulation, is that trying to learn in the more complex and complicated setting of whole-class instruction taxes children's weak self-regulation. In contrast, small-group learning contexts are generally more effective for children with weaker self-regulation, likely because the teacher can more easily provide support—bringing children back to the task, encouraging focused attention by asking questions, and monitoring understanding. And there are fewer distractions. There is accumulating evidence that self-regulation is malleable, and it improves as children learn to read (Connor et al., 2016; Connor et al., 2010). Encouraging teachers to be cognizant of more effective learning contexts for children with weaker self-regulation should also support learning, particularly for children with or at risk of dyslexia.

Supporting the lattice model, the consideration of self-regulation and executive function (cognitive and regulatory skills), in addition to linguistic and text-specific processes in the context of instruction, suggests that researchers should move beyond the simplicity of the simple view of reading (Hoover & Gough, 1990) and models that do not consider instruction and learning as important sources of influence on children's developing literacy. Whereas these fundamental models are important and lay the foundation for better understanding dyslexia and routes for remediation, the studies presented in this chapter clearly show the power of effective assessment-informed personalized instruction and intervention to prevent or reduce the sequelae of dyslexia. As we consider the chapters by Washington (Chapter 1) and by Patton Terry (Integrative Commentary 4), we have to ask, how many children could positively benefit from instruction tailored to their unique learning needs? As Yang and Connor (2019) showed, participating in effective A2i classrooms with assessment-informed individualized and personalized instruction significantly reduced the risk of developing severe reading disorders by the end of second grade.

Context matters, including teachers' perceptions of students' academic competence. When teachers use child characteristics that are not malleable, such as child SES, race, and gender, to make judgments of students' capabilities, the true capabilities of students from disadvantaged backgrounds may be underestimated, and these children may not be provided with appropriately challenging learning opportunities. In our study, teachers' perceptions of students' academic competence predicted outcomes independently of actual achievement. Yet, those teachers who used A2i, which made using assessment to inform instruction transparent and meaningful, generally did not use SES to judge students' abilities, whereas control teachers did. Many schools are rejecting assessment, and no wonder. Rather than being used to improve instruction, it is being used to evaluate teacher performance, which the Gates study (Gates & Gates, 2018; Iasevoli, 2018) showed does not lead to significantly stronger student outcomes. Assessment is a powerful tool for student achievement when used appropriately to inform personalized instruction and when coupled with support and training for teachers as professionals.

In this chapter, we also presented the idea that play is an important instructional context for improving early language skills. Early literacy instruction also predicted stronger student outcomes. Thus, both high-quality play and early literacy instruction have their places in the early childhood

PK classroom. Plus, there is the possibility that early literacy activities presented in playful contexts might be particularly effective for young children, and this deserves further study. The classroom observations conducted in 2002 to 2003 suggested that most PK classrooms did not provide enough time in either high-quality play or early literacy learning activities for children with the weakest language and early literacy skills. More recent classroom observations of PK classrooms in 2017 to 2018 revealed very little change over the past 15 years (Connor et al., 2018); many children are not spending enough time in meaningful learning opportunities, particularly those children with the weakest language and early literacy skills.

As we consider the important advances in understanding dyslexia over the past decades, we have come far in developing effective interventions (see Chapters 12, 13, and 17), understanding the difficulties children encounter as they turn written symbols into meaningful language (see Chapter 13)—and understanding that the distance between the language they speak and the language they read has direct implications for their learning (see Chapters 1 and 8). As Mele-McCarthy (see Chapter 19) and Bulat and colleagues (see Chapter 15) note, none of this knowledge will truly help children learn until it is widely used in classrooms around the world. Researchers have an obligation to disseminate their findings to the stakeholders—not just other researchers (see Chapters 18 and 20). It is our hope that as we use basic research to improve our models of literacy (e.g., Chapters 3 and 5), develop effective instructional regimes, and improve communication with stakeholders, from parents to teachers to policy makers, we can improve the lives of children from disadvantaged backgrounds and with dyslexia, and that A2i and all kinds of assessment-informed personalized instruction can help facilitate this.

REFERENCES

Al Otaiba, S., Connor, C. M., Folsom, J. S., Greulich, L., Meadows, J., & Li, Z. (2011). Assessment data-informed guidance to individualize kindergarten reading instruction: Findings from a cluster-randomized control field trial. *Elementary School Journal, 111*(4), 535–560. http://dx.doi.org/10.1086/659031

Connor, C. M. (2016). A lattice model of the development of reading comprehension. *Child Development Perspectives, 10*(4), 269–274. http://dx.doi.org/10.1111/cdep.12200

Connor, C. M., Adams, A., Zargar, E., Wood, T. S., Hernandez, B. E., & Vandell, D. L. (under review). Policy and funding streams: Observing differences for individual children in early childhood classrooms using OLOS. *Special Issue, Early Learning Research Quarterly.* Manuscript submitted for publication.

Connor, C. M., Day, S. L., Phillips, B., Sparapani, N., Ingebrand, S. W., McLean, L., . . . Kaschak, M. P. (2016). Reciprocal effects of self-regulation, semantic knowledge, and reading comprehension in early elementary school. *Child Development, 87*(6), 1813–1824. http://dx.doi.org/10.1111/cdev.12570

Connor, C. M., Morrison, F. J., Fishman, B. J., Crowe, E. C., Al Otaiba, S., & Schatschneider, C. (2013). A longitudinal cluster-randomized controlled study on the accumulating effects of individualized literacy instruction on students' reading from first through third grade. *Psychological Science, 24*(8), 1408–1419. http://dx.doi.org/10.1177/0956797612472204

Connor, C. M., Morrison, F. J., Schatschneider, C., Toste, J., Lundblom, E. G., Crowe, E., & Fishman, B. (2011). Effective classroom instruction: Implications of child characteristic by instruction interactions on first graders' word reading achievement. *Journal of Research on Educational Effectiveness, 4*(3), 173–207. http://dx.doi.org/10.1080/19345747.2010.510179

Connor, C. M., Morrison, F. J., Fishman, B. J., Schatschneider, C., & Underwood, P. (2007). Algorithm-guided individualized reading instruction. *Science, 315*(5811), 464–465.

Connor, C. M., Morrison, F. J., & Slominski, L. (2006). Preschool instruction and children's emergent literacy growth. *Journal of Educational Psychology, 98*(4), 665–689.

Connor, C. M., Ponitz, C. E. C., Phillips, B., Travis, Q. M., Day, S. G., & Morrison, F. J. (2010). First graders' literacy and self-regulation gains: The effect of individualizing instruction. *Journal of School Psychology, 48*, 433–455. http://dx.doi.org/10.1016/j.jsp.2010.06.003

Dickinson, D. K., & Porche, M. V. (2011). Relation between language experiences in preschool classrooms and children's kindergarten and fourth-grade language and reading abilities. *Child Development, 82*(3), 870–886. http://dx.doi.org/10.1111/j.1467-8624.2011.01576.x

Eason, S. H., Goldberg, L. F., Young, K. M., Geist, M. C., & Cutting, L. E. (2012). Reader–text interactions: How differential text and question types influence cognitive skills needed for reading comprehension. *Journal of Educational Psychology, 104*(3), 515–528. http://dx.doi.org/10.1037/a0027182

Gates, B., & Gates, M. (2018). *Annual letter 2018: The 10 toughest questions we get.* Retrieved from https://www.gatesnotes.com/2018-Annual-Letter

Gatlin, B., Hwang, J. K., Powell, K. B., Tani, N. E., Wood, T. S., Yang, D., . . . Connor, C. M. (in review). Using assessment to improve the precision of teachers' perception of students' academic competence.

Gresham, F. M., & Elliot, S. N. (1990). *Social Skills Rating System–Secondary.* Circle Pines, MN: American Guidance Service.

Hoover, W. A., & Gough, P. B. (1990). The simple view of reading. *Reading and Writing: An Interdisciplinary Journal, 2*(2), 127–160. http://dx.doi.org/10.1007/BF00401799

Iasevoli, B. (2018). Teacher-evaluation efforts haven't shown results, say Bill and Melinda Gates. *Education Week.* Retrieved from http://blogs.edweek.org/edweek/teacherbeat/2018/02/teacher_evaluation_efforts_haven't_shown_results_bill_melinda_gates.html

Kim, Y.-S. (2017). Why the simple view of reading is not simplistic: Unpacking the simple view of reading using a Direct and Indirect Effect model of Reading (DIER). *Scientific Studies of Reading, 21*, 310–333. http://dx.doi.org/10.1080/10888438.2017.1291643

Kim, Y.-S. (in review). Structural and dynamic relations of component skills to reading comprehension: Evidence from a longitudinal study. Manuscript submitted for publication.

Kim, Y.-S. G., & Schatschneider, C. (2017). Expanding the developmental models of writing: A direct and indirect effects model of developmental writing (DIEW). *Journal of Educational Psychology, 109*, 35–50.

Lin, B., Coburn, S. S., & Eisenberg, N. (2016). Self-regulation and reading achievement. In C. M. Connor (Ed.), *The cognitive development of reading and reading comprehension* (pp. 67–86). New York, NY: Routledge.

Ponitz, C. E. C., McClelland, M. M., Jewkes, A. M., Connor, C. M., Farris, C. L., & Morrison, F. J. (2008). Touch your toes! Developing a behavioral measure of preschool self-regulation. *Early Childhood Research Quarterly, 23*, 141–158.

Roskos, K. A., & Christie, J. F. (Eds.). (2000). *Play and literacy in early childhood.* Mahwah, NJ: Lawrence Erlbaum Publishers.

Spencer, M., Wagner, R. K., Schatschneider, C., Quinn, J. M., Lopez, D., & Petscher, Y. (2014). Incorporating RTI in a hybrid model of reading disability. *Learning Disability Quarterly.* http://dx.doi.org/10.1177/0731948714530967

Tani, N., & Connor, C. M. (2011). *Association of teacher perceptions on with second graders' behavior and academic achievement: Examining race and gender differences.* Paper presented at the Annual Meeting of the Society for the Scientific Study of Reading, St. Pete's Beach, FL.

Woodcock, R. W., McGrew, K. S., & Mather, N. (2001). *Woodcock-Johnson III Tests of Achievement.* Itasca, IL: Riverside.

Yang, D., & Connor, C. M. (2019). *Child characteristics which can predict dyslexia in the context of an effective intervention.* Poster presented at the Society for Research in Child Development Biennial Meeting, Baltimore, MD.

Language Matters to Reading Success and Linguistic Differences Deserve More Attention

Barbara R. Foorman

The three chapters in this section emphasize the importance of language in learning to read and the critical role that linguistic differences play can play in reading disabilities. Chapter 9, by Washington and Lee-James, describes the features of African American English (AAE) and makes the case that exclusionary criteria in the Individuals with Disabilities Education Act of 2004 (IDEA 2004; PL 108-446) lead to underidentification of children who speak AAE as having a learning disability (LD), specifically a reading disability. Chapter 8, by Saiegh-Haddad, describes how Arabic diglossia—where two dialects are used within the same speech community for informal versus formal speech, reading, and writing—creates linguistic distance that presents a challenge to children learning to read Arabic, especially for children with reading disabilities. Saiegh-Haddad's measurement of this linguistic distance offers a tool for diagnosing reading disabilities as due to a general phonological deficit or to the additional challenge of a mismatch between a dialect and a standard language. Chapter 10, by Connor, Kim, and Yang, describes professional support technology that can improve teachers' predictions of reading risk and provide accurate data for differentiating instruction. All three chapters point out the missed opportunities for students with linguistic differences or weak oral language skills to learn to read in primary-grade classrooms. Altogether, these three chapters offer the knowledge and tools to assist teachers in accurately identifying and instructing children with linguistic differences and reading difficulties so that their students achieve reading success.

INTRODUCTION

Comprehending written language requires knowledge about the formal language of text—knowledge of vocabulary that is less frequent than in oral language, more complex grammatical structures, and discourse strategies that make text cohesive and coherent. This formal language of text also marks the language of discussion around text that occurs in school and in literate households and stands in contrast to the colloquial language spoken in informal settings at home, at school, and in the community. Linguistic gaps between colloquial language and formal language are bridged in literate households through such activities as shared book reading with toddlers and 3- and 4-year-olds (e.g., Cameron-Faulkner & Noble, 2013; Hart & Risley, 1995, 1999; Montag, Jones, & Smith, 2015). Preschool is increasingly offered in public education as a way to bridge this gap prior to formal reading instruction. However, the preschool movement is by no means universal, and preschool and elementary school curricula rarely emphasize formal language skills in inferencing, narrative production, and academic vocabulary. Therefore, as the authors in this section, Linguistic Differences and Reading, point out, educators are largely unaware of the crucial role that language plays in learning to read, and as a consequence, there are many missed opportunities for language learning to inform reading success.

This commentary is divided into four sections. The first section briefly outlines the linguistic differences that Washington and Lee-James and Saiegh-Haddad have identified. The second section highlights the missed opportunities for language learning that these two chapters, as well as the chapter by Connor, Kim, and Yang, discuss. The third section addresses the need to improve assessment if struggling readers with linguistic differences are to be served. Finally, the fourth section emphasizes the importance of improving teacher professional development in preservice and in-service education to equip educators with the knowledge and skills to teach students with linguistic differences to read.

LINGUISTIC DIFFERENCES THAT AFFECT READING DEVELOPMENT

Washington and Lee-James (see Chapter 9) discuss how AAE affects identification of speakers of this dialect as having LD, specifically reading disabilities. Saiegh-Haddad (see Chapter 8) discusses how Arabic diglossia creates linguistic distance that presents a challenge in learning to read Arabic, especially for children who have reading disabilities.

Chapter by Washington and Lee-James

Washington and Lee-James point out that the AAE dialect differs from mainstream American English in all language domains but most notably in morphosyntax and phonology. In addition, dialect density predicts reading outcomes. The authors report a reciprocal relation between dialect and reading in a longitudinal study of approximately 900 children in elementary school. This finding suggests that rather than teaching dialect shifting, interventions that focus on teaching oral language and reading will lead to spontaneous reduction in dialect use. This is good advice for all beginning readers, as we found when we decomposed the total variance explained in 2,938 students' reading comprehension scores in 1st–10th grades into unique decoding, unique language, and variance shared by decoding and language (Foorman, Petscher, & Herrera, 2018). In first grade, decoding explained 14% of the variance and language explained 8% of the variance, but the common variance between decoding and language explained 46% of the variance in reading comprehension. This suggests that in order to improve comprehension, first-grade teachers need to integrate language skills into the teaching of word reading (i.e., phonics) so as to build knowledge of words' linguistic features—multiple meanings across contexts, pronunciations, spellings, morphological structure, synonyms and antonyms, and related words. In addition, the role of language in predicting reading comprehension increased across the grades such that by sixth-grade language uniquely explained 58% of the variance (with 40% explained by the common variance and less than 1% by decoding), and by 10th-grade language uniquely explained 67% of the variance (with 32% explained by the common variance and less than 1% by decoding). Thus, by 10th grade, variation in reading comprehension scores is explained by language and the common variance between language and decoding.

Washington and Lee-James also raise an important question: Why can't children be both impoverished and have LD? The authors argue that the answer lies in the exclusionary criteria in the IDEA 2004 statute that prohibits a diagnosis of specific learning disability if the disability can be attributed to environmental, cultural, or economic disadvantage. Thus, many children from underprivileged backgrounds are excluded from a diagnosis of LD, and those who do receive the label tend to be from more privileged backgrounds. This underrepresentation of impoverished children in the LD category leads the authors to ask, "In the face of inadequate opportunity, what does LD look like?"

The authors recommend a shift in thinking away from considering linguistic differences and having a disability as mutually exclusive and toward recognition that LD can occur in the context of differences and disadvantage. They suggest that future research examine profiles of reading disabilities in impoverished and minority children in order to better address policy and instructional practice. I agree and encourage the use of latent profiles of reading and language skills, validated by their relation to reading comprehension, to guide instructional decisions for all struggling readers (Foorman, Petscher, Stanley, & Truckenmiller, 2017), and impoverished and minority children in particular.

Chapter by Saiegh-Haddad

Like Washington and Lee-James, Saiegh-Haddad (see Chapter 8) is interested in contexts in which children learn to read in a standard language that differs from the dialect used in everyday speech. Whereas Washington and Lee-James are interested in how poverty and race interact with linguistic differences to distort diagnosis and treatment, Saiegh-Haddad is interested in examining how the distance between colloquial and standard Arabic is associated with the diagnosis of reading disabilities. Standard Arabic (StA) differs in phonology, morphology, semantics, and syntax from all spoken dialects of colloquial or spoken Arabic (SpA). StA is acquired primarily in school, but even young children are exposed to it in the home and community through books and media. An additional feature of StA is that it can be represented in the voweled orthography, which uses diacritics to map all phonological information necessary for accurate word decoding, as well as in an unvoweled orthography, a consonantal system that uses only letters to map the consonants and long vowels. The former is used as a support for beginning readers as they learn the more morphologically based reading system; the latter is considered a phonologically underspecified, deep orthography (see Daniels & Share, 2018).

To examine the influence of linguistic distance, Saiegh-Haddad created pairs of words that represented reading in SpA (identical lexico-phonological form in SpA and StA) and reading in StA (cognate and unique words that have overlapping and unique form in the two dialects). Words were matched in frequency, phonological length, and complexity and presented in the voweled and in the unvoweled orthography. These word pairs were presented to sixth-grade students with reading disabilities, to age-matched controls (i.e., typically developing sixth-grade students), and to reading-matched controls (i.e., typically developing second- and fourth-grade readers). Saiegh-Haddad found that reading accuracy and fluency scores in the sixth-grade students with reading disabilities and in the younger students in the control group were significantly higher for SpA than StA words but not significantly different in the age-matched control group. This suggests a processing advantage for words in the colloquial dialect. This advantage was apparent in both the voweled and unvoweled orthography, a finding that implies that linguistic distance affects word reading in spite of orthographic depth.

In another study, however, Schiff and Saiegh-Haddad (2017) found that the sixth-grade students with reading disabilities were not using the diacritics encoded in the voweled words to facilitate word reading. Finally, in a study with students with reading disabilities and age-matched controls in third grade and fifth grade, Saiegh-Haddad found that phonological distance affected nonword repetition scores for the students with reading disabilities in both third and fifth grades but not for the age-matched control group. Phonological distance also affected word learning such that students with reading disabilities performed better in SpA compared to StA in both grades. In contrast, the age-matched control group performed better at reading StA words in fifth grade compared to third grade.

Saiegh-Haddad concludes that Arabic dialect speakers with reading disabilities have a dual deficit—a general phonological deficit that affects processing of all phonological items, including those within their dialect and a specific phonological distance deficit that manifests when items require processing of phonological items not in their dialect. Saiegh-Haddad recommends that this dual deficit be taken into account when designing assessments and intervention.

MISSED OPPORTUNITIES FOR LANGUAGE LEARNING TO INFORM READING SUCCESS

Washington and Lee-James (see Chapter 9) point out that if teachers teach oral language and reading skills, dialect use will spontaneously decline and dialect-shifting does not need to be explicitly taught. A challenge is the oral language part of this recommendation. Relatively little oral language instruction occurs in elementary classrooms (Foorman & Schatschneider, 2003), unless it is in a class specifically labeled English language development (Saunders, Foorman, & Carlson, 2006). In observing 112 first- and second-grade classrooms in two inner cities, Foorman and Schatschneider (2003) found that, on average, 5%–18% of the designated 90-minute reading/language arts block (that ranged from 79 to 180 actual minutes) was devoted to oral language activities and that variability was related to the instructional materials used. However, highly rated teachers in classrooms with students with low initial status in reading spent on average 27% of their time teaching oral language skills (with about 30% on reading comprehension skills).

Connor and colleagues (see Chapter 10) report that in observations of preschool classrooms in 2002–2003, only 3 minutes/day of code-focused instruction with the teacher was observed (SD = 3.8) and only 11 minutes of play (SD = 15). More recent observations in 2017–2018 did not show much change from these numbers. Playful learning included such center activities as socio-dramatic play. When play was mediated by the teacher, children with weaker initial vocabulary skills made significant gains in vocabulary. The more time that the teacher engaged in such meaning-focused instruction as reading aloud to the children and asking questions, the greater the vocabulary gains for all children and especially for children with lower vocabulary scores in the fall. Likewise, a task that measures self-regulation—the Head-to-Toes task—interacted with first-grade students' literacy gains such that students with weaker self-regulation made smaller gains in literacy, holding all other characteristics constant. Connor and colleagues conclude that including a measure of self-regulation in their predictive algorithms might aid in identification of risk for those students at the low end of the continuum of skills. This finding also has implications for including language routines that foster self-regulation in literacy interventions.

In addition to missed opportunities in the classroom for oral language instruction in general and vocabulary instruction in particular, there are missed opportunities for written language instruction that emphasizes word knowledge, lexical quality, and discourse cohesion (Lawrence, Crossen, Paré-Blagoev, & Snow, 2015; Lesaux, Kieffer, Kelley, & Harris, 2014).

IMPROVING ASSESSMENT

The authors of all three of these chapters recommend changes to assessments to better identify at-risk readers and to personalize literacy instruction. Connor and colleagues (see Chapter 10) describe their A2i system, which uses dynamic forecasting algorithms based on language and literacy scores to recommend amounts of instruction for individual students. They also used the A2i algorithms to identify characteristics of students in first grade that predicted the probability of demonstrating a reading disability at the end of second grade.

Saiegh-Haddad (see Chapter 8) and Washington and Lee-James (see Chapter 9) call for better assessments to ascertain whether children with language differences have reading disabilities. The experimental techniques that Saiegh-Haddad used in her studies to measure linguistic distance could be used to develop a screener in Arabic to identify children with a core phonological deficit and those who have an additional challenge in learning to read due to a mismatch between their spoken dialect (SpA) and written language (StA). This strategy could also be applied to AAE speakers to differentiate those who have a core phonological deficit and an additional challenge due to the mismatch between AAE and standard English. Researchers could construct pairs of words in both AAE and standard English and words where the AAE representation differs from the standard. AAE speakers with low initial status in word reading could be given a nonword repetition task and the word pair task to identify AAE speakers who have a general phonological deficit and those with the additional challenge of a mismatch between their dialect and standard English.

All students who struggle with reading due to a general phonological deficit can benefit from intervention in phonological awareness and phonics. AAE speakers who struggle with reading due to the additional challenge of the mismatch between their dialect and standard English might benefit from an intervention in both oral language and in reading in which the teacher points out distinctions between oral and written forms of words in addition to instruction in alphabetics, decoding/encoding, vocabulary, word analysis, and comprehension. All students struggling to learn to read can benefit from such instruction, including English language learners with phonological deficits (Baker et al., 2014; Foorman, Beyler, et al., 2016).

Finally, assessments need to measure oral language as well as written language skills and include linguistic minorities in the norming samples. Computer-adaptive assessments have advantages in precision, efficiency, and range of abilities covered (e.g., Foorman, Espinosa, Jackson, & Wu, 2016).

IMPROVING PROFESSIONAL DEVELOPMENT

Preservice and in-service training for educators needs to include more information on language development, intervention, and assessment for all students and for linguistically different students, in particular. Because core reading programs have the standard Midwestern dialect for key words and sound–spelling relations (Foorman, Francis, Davidson, Harm, & Griffin, 2004), teachers need to become aware of their own dialect, the dialect of their students, and the dialect of the core reading programs.

Furthermore, preservice and in-service training should address how to select and administer reading assessments and how to interpret and translate the resulting data to instruction. In a randomized controlled trial, Connor and her colleagues (see Chapter 10) found that teachers who used A2i were more accurate in judging their students' academic competence, compared to teachers in the control group who did not use A2i. Accurate identification of students' abilities is essential if teachers are to develop the appropriate and differentiated instruction necessary to foster individual learning.

CONCLUSION

The three chapters in this section make the case that oral language matters in learning to read written language and that linguistic differences deserve more attention if at-risk students are to be accurately identified and served. Washington and Lee-James (see Chapter 9) point out that exclusionary criteria in IDEA 2004 lead to underidentification of children who speak AAE as having LD and hence reading disabilities. Saiegh-Haddad's (see Chapter 8) measurement of the linguistic distance between colloquial Arabic and standard Arabic offers a tool for diagnosing reading disabilities as due to a general phonological deficit or to the additional challenge of a mismatch between dialect and the standard language. Connor and colleagues (see Chapter 10) offer teachers professional support technology that can improve predictions of reading risk and provide accurate data for differentiating instruction. These tools can begin to identify those students who have both linguistic differences and reading difficulties, and this knowledge and technology can help teachers provide them with the instruction most likely to enable them to succeed in reading! Now, all teachers have to do is use these tools.

REFERENCES

Baker, S., Lesaux, N., Jayanthi, M., Dimino, J., Proctor, C. P., Morris, J., ... Newman-Gonchar, R. (2014). *Teaching academic content and literacy to English learners in elementary and middle school* (NCEE 2014-4012). Washington, DC: U.S. Department of Education, Institute of Education Sciences, National Center for Education Evaluation and Regional Assistance (NCEE).
Cameron-Faulkner, T., & Noble, C. (2013). A comparison of book text and child directed speech. *First Language, 33,* 269–279. http://dx.doi.org/10.1177/0142723713487613

Daniels, P. T., & Share, D. L. (2018). Writing system variation and its consequences for reading and dyslexia. *Scientific Studies of Reading, 22*(1), 101–116.

Foorman, B., Beyler, N., Borradaile, K., Coyne, M., Denton, C., Dimino, J., ... Wissel, S. (2016). *Foundational skills to support reading for understanding in kindergarten through 3rd grade* (NCEE 2016-4008). Washington, DC: U.S. Department of Education, Institute of Education Sciences, National Center for Education Evaluation and Regional Assistance (NCEE).

Foorman, B., Espinosa, A., Jackson, C., & Wu, Y. (2016). *Using computer-adaptive literacy assessments to monitor the progress of English language learner students* (REL 2016-149). Washington, DC: U.S. Department of Education, Institute of Education Sciences, National Center for Education Evaluation and Regional Assistance, Regional Educational Laboratory Southeast.

Foorman, B. R., Francis, D. J., Davidson, K., Harm, M., & Griffin, J. (2004). Variability in text features in six Grade 1 basal reading programs. *Scientific Studies in Reading, 8*(2), 167–197. http://dx.doi.org/10.1207/s1532799xssr0802_4

Foorman, B., Petscher, Y., & Herrera, S. (2018). Unique and common effects of oral language in predicting reading comprehension in Grades 1–10. *Learning and Individual Differences, 63*, 12–23. http://dx.doi.org/10.1016/j.lindif.2018.02.011

Foorman, B., Petscher, Y., Stanley, C., & Truckenmiller, A. (2017). Latent profiles of reading and language and their association with standardized reading outcomes in kindergarten through tenth grade. *Journal of Research on Educational Effectiveness, 10*(3), 619–645. http://dx.doi.org/10.1080/19345747.2016.1237597

Foorman, B. R., & Schatschneider, C. (2003). Measurement of teaching practices during reading/language arts instruction and its relationship to student achievement. In S. Vaughn & K. L. Briggs (Eds.), *Reading in the classroom: Systems for the observation of teaching and learning* (pp. 1–30). Baltimore, MD: Paul H. Brookes Publishing Co.

Hart, B., & Risley, T. R. (1995). *Meaningful differences in the everyday experience of young American children.* Baltimore, MD: Paul H. Brookes Publishing Co.

Hart, B., & Risley, T. R. (1999). *The social world of children learning to talk.* Baltimore, MD: Paul H. Brookes Publishing Co.

Individuals with Disabilities Education Improvement Act (IDEA) of 2004, PL 108-446, 20 U.S.C. §§ 1400 *et seq.*

Lawrence, J., Crosson, A., Paré-Blagoev, E., & Snow, C. (2015). Word generation randomized trial: Discussion mediates the impact of program treatment on academic word learning. *American Educational Research Journal, 52*(4), 750–786 http://dx.doi.org/10.3102/0002831215579485

Lesaux, N. K., Kieffer, M. J., Kelley, J. G., & Harris, J. (2014). Effects of academic vocabulary instruction for linguistically diverse adolescents: Evidence from a randomized field trial. *American Educational Research Journal, 51*(6), 1159–1194. http://dx.doi.org/10.3102/0002831214532165

Montag, J., Jones, M., & Smith, L. (2015). The words children hear. *Psychological Science, 26*, 1489–1496. http://dx.doi.org/10.1177/0956797615594361

Saunders, W. M., Foorman, B. R., & Carlson, C. D. (2006). Do we need a separate block of time for oral English language development in programs for English learners? *Elementary School Journal, 107*(2), 181–198.

Schiff, R., & Saiegh-Haddad, E. (2017). When diglossia meets dyslexia: The impact of diglossia on reading among Arabic native speaking dyslexic children. Arabic. *Reading & Writing: An Interdisciplinary Journal, 30*, 1089–1113.

Identification and Treatment

CHAPTER 11

Cognitive Approaches to the Identification of Children With Dyslexia

Anne Castles and Saskia Kohnen

SUMMARY

Dyslexia is a highly heterogeneous disorder. In this chapter, we argue that the application of cognitive models of reading is key to making sense of this heterogeneity. Using the examples of three well-described profiles of dyslexia—phonological dyslexia, surface dyslexia, and letter position dyslexia—we demonstrate how cognitive models have helped in formulating clear hypotheses about the types of impairments that should be seen within these profiles, which each contain complexities, and report on research we have carried out testing these hypotheses based on our view that it is time to move beyond these broad categories. We conclude that cognitive models can assist teachers and clinicians to have clearer expectations about the types of problems they might expect to see in a poor reader, thus guiding assessment protocols and ultimately improving treatment recommendations.

INTRODUCTION

The term *dyslexia* is widely used to describe the condition of children with a reading difficulty that is unexpected given their educational opportunities. However, researchers and clinicians have long been aware that dyslexia is not a single syndrome but is highly heterogeneous (Castles & Coltheart, 1993; Manis & Bailey, 2008; McArthur, Kohnen, et al., 2013; Ziegler et al., 2008). This is not surprising because reading is a complex, multifaceted skill. A large amount of variability is present both in the nature of the reading impairment itself (sometimes referred to as the proximal level; Jackson & Coltheart, 2001) and in its underlying causes (the distal level). (A similar distinction is the term *symptomatology* for proximal and *etiology* for distal causes.) In this chapter, we argue that in order to capture this heterogeneity, the assessment and identification of dyslexia should be carried out in the context of detailed cognitive models of reading. This allows for precise specification of the nature of the reading difficulty at the proximal level, which can then support more targeted treatment of the dyslexia as well as more directed investigations of its distal causes.

Supporting our case, we provide examples of specific patterns of reading impairment in dyslexia that would not have been identified if not for the application of cognitive models. These examples are drawn from three major profiles of dyslexia: surface dyslexia, phonological dyslexia, and letter position dyslexia. Our review commences with an overview of the cognitive model on which our research has been based and a brief history of the research into subtypes of dyslexia.

DUAL-ROUTE MODEL AND SUBTYPES OF DYSLEXIA

In 1993, Castles and Coltheart reported evidence for subtypes of developmental dyslexia based on predictions derived from the Dual-Route Model of reading aloud (Coltheart, Curtis, Atkins, & Haller, 1993; Coltheart, Rastle, Perry, Langdon, & Ziegler, 2001; see Figure 11.1). This model proposes two major routes for converting print to sound, referred to as the lexical and nonlexical routes. The lexical route, composed of the processing pathways on the left of Figure 11.1, involves accessing orthographic representations of familiar printed words in a mental lexicon (orthographic lexicon), and proceeding via these to the words' meaning (semantics) and pronunciation (phonological lexicon). The nonlexical route, the processing pathway on the right side of Figure 11.1, involves

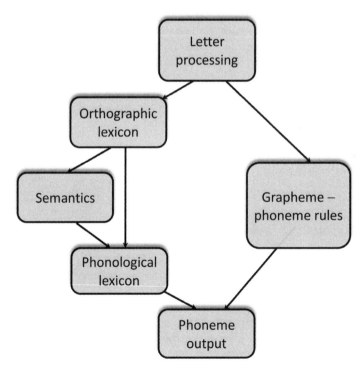

Figure 11.1. Two major routes for converting print to sound: the lexical route, comprising the processing pathways on the left side of the figure, and the nonlexical route, comprising the processing pathways shown on the right side of the figure.

applying knowledge of grapheme–phoneme rules to generate a pronunciation for a presented letter string. Both routes share an initial letter processing stage, in which the identity and position of letters in words are
determined, and a phoneme output stage, in which phonemes are held in
a phonological short-term memory store and blended together to produce
a spoken output. Researchers typically assess functioning of the lexical
route by asking children to read irregular words such as *yacht* or *tomb*
because they can only pronounce these words correctly if they are stored
in their lexicon. Researchers assess nonlexical skills by asking children
to read nonwords such as *gop* and *jeath* because they can only pronounce
these made-up words correctly if they are able to successfully apply
grapheme-to-phoneme rules.

Castles and Coltheart (1993) predicted that, if the lexical and nonlexical routes of the model are indeed partially independent (they are not
completely independent because they share the common letter recognition
and phoneme output processes), then there should also be some indepen-
dence in the acquisition of these routes; that is, there should be children
who have particular difficulty acquiring one route but not the other.
This means that difficulties in acquiring these routes must have different
distal causes, including possibly differing genetic, neurological, and cognitive underpinnings (see Castles, Kohnen, Nickels, & Brock, 2014). Building
on some individual case studies already in the literature (e.g., Coltheart,
Masterson, Byng, Prior, & Riddoch, 1983; Temple & Marshall, 1983), they
tested a group of more than 50 children with reported reading difficulties
on their reading of irregular words and nonwords and compared their
performance with that of typically developing readers of the same age in
the control group. Although many of the poor readers had impairments
on both types of item, a significant proportion showed a clear dissociation
between the two, indicating a particular problem either with the acquisition of nonlexical skills (referred to as phonological dyslexia) or with the
acquisition of lexical skills (surface dyslexia). This finding has since been
replicated several times and, although the interpretation of the results has
varied based on the specific model of reading being applied and on the
choice of control group comparison, the existence of these broad profiles of
heterogeneity is widely agreed on (for review, see Peterson, Pennington, &
Olson, 2013). As Peterson and colleagues stated, "At least half of dyslexic
children in English, French, or Spanish . . . can be classified as belonging to
one of these two subtypes" (2013, p. 21).

These findings are important, in our view, not just because of the identification of the subtypes *per se* but because they demonstrate the value of
using cognitive models to account for the heterogeneity observed in dyslexia and to guide the process of assessment and identification. Indeed,
we would argue that it is time for the field to move beyond the broad
categories of surface and phonological dyslexia because they themselves
are likely to be complex and heterogeneous. If the model presented in

Figure 11.1 is accurate, then there should be as many different subtypes of dyslexia as there are boxes (and arrows) in the model. Instead, what is needed is a move away from categorical thinking and a focus on comprehensive model-based profiling of individual children with reading difficulties. Drawing on genetic terminology, we need to specify the phenotype that the child presents with as precisely as possible in order for diagnosis and subsequent treatment of the dyslexia to be most effective (see Castles et al., 2014). In the following sections, we outline research we have carried out that has taken this approach.

Heterogeneity in Phonological Dyslexia

A significant proportion of children with dyslexia have difficulty reading unfamiliar words. On testing, this presents as impaired reading of nonwords, such as *glinch,* and in many instances nonword reading is significantly poorer than word reading—the phonological dyslexic profile. Indeed, this has even been seen as the defining profile of dyslexia (Rack, Snowling, & Olson, 1992). Broadly speaking, these children are proposed to have difficulty learning the mappings between graphemes and phonemes and using them to read unfamiliar words. However, examination of the nonlexical route in Figure 11.1 reveals three potential sources of difficulty that could result in poor performance on a nonword-reading task: 1) a problem with *letter processing,* 2) a problem with knowledge of the *grapheme–phoneme rules* themselves, or 3) a problem at the *phoneme output* stage; that is, with blending individual phonemes together or with holding those phonemes in memory for a sufficient time to produce a spoken output. In the case of an impairment in Source 1, the child would be expected also to have difficulty reading words because this initial component is shared with the lexical route. However, an impairment in either Source 2 or Source 3 could each produce a selective difficulty in reading nonwords. In the case of Source 2, this process is specific to the nonlexical route, so difficulties would only arise for the child when he or she is trying to read a novel or unfamiliar item such as a nonword; he or she could successfully read familiar words via the lexical route. In the case of Source 3, although this component is common across the two routes, researchers generally think that reading nonwords places heavier demands on the phoneme output system than reading words because there is no top-down support coming from the phonological lexicon in the former case (Shallice, Rumiati, & Zadini, 2000). So, again, an impairment here could produce a selective difficulty in reading nonwords.

We explored whether poor nonword reading in phonological dyslexia can indeed have different proximal causes within the reading system. The participants were 19 children ranging from 7 to 12 years old, who all showed a selective impairment in reading nonwords aloud. Their standardized scores on the nonword-reading measure of the Castles and

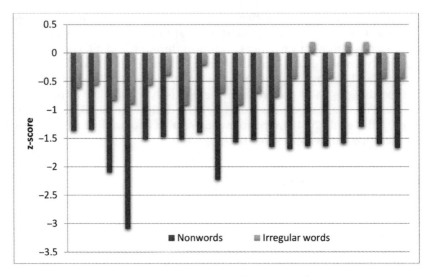

Figure 11.2. Standardized scores on the nonword-reading measure of the Castles and Coltheart 2 test (Castles et al., 2009) relative to the irregular word–reading measure, for 19 children ranging from 7 to 12 years old, who all showed a selective impairment in reading nonwords aloud.

Coltheart 2 test (CC2; Castles et al., 2009) relative to the irregular word–reading measure are presented in Figure 11.2.

We assessed each of the children on the following measures:

- *Letter recognition:* We assessed this using a cross-case matching task in which the children had to identify which of two alternatives (e.g., *a* and *o*) was the same letter as a presented target (e.g., *A*).

- *Knowledge of grapheme–phoneme correspondences:* We assessed this by asking the children to provide the sound of single letters and frequent digraphs presented individually on flash cards.

- *Phoneme blending:* We used the Blending Nonwords subtest from the Comprehensive Test of Phonological Processing (CTOPP; Wagner, Torgesen, & Rashotte, 1999), in which the children listened to nonwords separated into two to eight phonemes (e.g., "k-oo-m-a-g") and were required to blend them to produce a wordlike response ("koomag").

- *Phonological short-term memory:* We used the Repetition of Nonsense Words subtest from the NEPSY (Korkman, Kirk, & Kemp, 1998), in which we asked the children to repeat spoken nonsense words increasing in length (e.g., "crumsee").

As predicted based on the model, none of the children showed impairments relative to age-matched controls on letter recognition (although we should note that there were ceiling effects on this task). However, there was heterogeneity among the participants in whether they showed impairments at the level of knowledge of grapheme–phoneme correspondences or at the level of phonemic storage and output (i.e., phonological short-term memory and blending): some children only had impairments at the former level, some children only at the latter level, and some at both levels. This has important implications for the choice of intervention for children displaying a phonological dyslexic profile; for example, there is clearly little value in intensively teaching individual grapheme–phoneme correspondences to a child whose knowledge of these mappings is at an age-appropriate level, even though this would often be a first line of response to the treatment of a nonword-reading deficit.

Findings such as this demonstrate the value of taking a model-based approach to assessment and identification of dyslexia. Such an approach has also been taken to examining heterogeneity within the broad profile of surface dyslexia.

Heterogeneity in Surface Dyslexia

In contrast to phonological reading problems, children with a surface dyslexic profile show selective impairments in the lexical route of the model presented in Figure 11.1. As noted, in English their difficulties are typically diagnosed using irregular word–reading tasks: for example, they may read *yacht* as "yatched" at an age when their peers can typically read this word accurately. In transparent orthographies, such children may be accurate but very slow at reading, reflecting the fact that they are relying on effortful phonological decoding rather than rapid and automatic word recognition (Sprenger-Charolles, Siegel, Jiménez, & Ziegler, 2011).

Once again, however, examination of the cognitive model of reading presented in Figure 11.1 informs that there may be different proximal reasons for the impairment within the population of children who perform poorly on standardized irregular word–reading tasks. The difficulty may be associated with deficits at the level of the orthographic lexicon itself, or with impaired access from the printed word to its meaning (semantics) and/or spoken form (phonological lexicon). If the problem is in the orthographic lexicon, the child will not be able to recognize a printed word as familiar at all and will not be able to retrieve the pronunciation or meaning of the word from print; however, if the problem is localized at a later stage of processing along the lexical route, the child may recognize the printed word as familiar but still not be able to understand it or read it aloud (even though he or she knows the word and its meaning in oral form).

Friedmann and Lukov (2008) tested these model predictions in a group of 17 Hebrew-speaking individuals with surface dyslexia (all had impairments in reading irregular words). They carried out three tests to tease apart the loci of the participants' impairments along the lexical route. The first test was a lexical decision task to assess functioning of the orthographic lexicon. Participants selected the correct item from a pair consisting of an irregular printed word (e.g., the Hebrew version of a word such as *chef* in English) and its pseudohomophone (a nonword that sounds like the word if decoded phonologically; e.g., *shef*). Because phonological decoding via the nonlexical route will produce the incorrect response here, this task can only be performed correctly via access to the orthographic lexicon. The second test was a homophone comprehension task to assess access to meaning from print in which participants were required to decide which of two printed homophones (e.g., *bear* and *beer*) matched another word in meaning (e.g., *drink*). They were not required to read the words aloud. Finally, a picture naming task was used to assess the functioning of the phonological lexicon.

Once again, Friedmann and Lukov found evidence for a large degree of heterogeneity, this time within the broad profile of surface dyslexia. Approximately half of the participants had a deficit that appeared to be located in the orthographic lexicon itself. They performed poorly on the lexical decision task, and as would be expected for an impairment that interrupts processing at this level, they also performed poorly on the homophone comprehension task. The remaining participants showed no impairment on the lexical decision task, indicating that their irregular word–reading problem had a different locus than the orthographic lexicon. Some had impairments on the homophone comprehension task, pointing to impaired access to semantics from an intact orthographic lexicon. Others showed no impairment on either the lexical decision or the homophone comprehension tasks (despite being poor at reading aloud irregular words), suggesting that these individuals were able to access the meanings of words via their intact orthographic lexicon but for some reason were unable to proceed to the words' pronunciations. Only one participant showed impairments in picture naming, ruling out an impairment within the phonological lexicon itself.

We have carried out similar investigations in a group of English-speaking children with surface dyslexia and also found evidence for a high degree of heterogeneity in the loci of impairment that is consistent with impairments in different processes within the lexical route (Kohnen et al., 2018; see also Sotiropoulos & Hanley, 2017, in Greek). There is clearly much still to be learned about the proximal causes of surface dyslexia and indeed its underlying distal causes. However, the application of a cognitive model has provided a roadmap for investigating individuals with this profile, giving direction as to what aspects of functioning need to be assessed and stimulating the development of targeted tests such as the homophone comprehension task that might not otherwise have been considered. This is also the case for another profile of dyslexia that has been the subject of much attention: letter position dyslexia.

Heterogeneity in Letter Processing Difficulties: Letter Position Dyslexia

The very first stage of successfully reading a word involves letter processing. Although this is represented as a single component in Figure 11.1, letter processing in fact involves at least two subprocesses. The reader must determine the identity of each letter in the word and must resolve letter order. It is easy to underestimate the complexity of this task: A reader must abstract a single letter identity across different cases (*A* versus *a*) and fonts (a versus ə), and must resolve letter position precisely to avoid confusing *tap, pat,* and *apt.* Although some children with dyslexia are known to struggle with letter-level processing (e.g., Brunsdon, Coltheart, & Nickels, 2007), it has been the subject of relatively little research attention compared to other types of reading impairment.

There has been, however, increased focus on children who appear to have specific difficulties in processing letter position within words—motivated by the representation of this aspect of reading in detailed cognitive models. Following on reports in Hebrew-speaking individuals (Friedmann & Rahamim, 2007), we described the first three cases of selective letter position dyslexia in English (Kohnen, Nickels, Castles, Friedmann, & McArthur, 2012). Although the parents and teachers of these children were concerned about their reading, the standard tests had not revealed any deficit: The children performed at age expectations on irregular word– and nonword-reading tasks. Their problem was only detected when they received the appropriate assessment—in this instance, a test of reading aloud anagram words (which make another word when the letters are reordered, such as *slime/smile*). In all three cases, the children made far more errors on these words than did other children their age, with their predominant type of error being to produce the anagram partner of the word. Some examples of the errors made by one of the cases, EL, are provided in Table 11.1.

Table 11.1.   Anagram errors made by a case of letter position dyslexia

Target word	Response
blot	*bolt*
blows	*bowls*
tried	*tired*
trail	*trial*
pirates	*parties*
cruelty	*cutlery*
files	*flies*
from	*form*
stale	*slate*
warp	*wrap*

Source: Kohnen, Nickels, Castles, Friedmann, & McArthur (2012).

Further investigations revealed a number of interesting features of this profile. The children made anagram errors, not just in reading aloud but also in their silent reading. In a lexical decision task, they were much more likely than children in the control group to err in accepting an anagram nonword as a word (e.g., accepting *bron* or *snept,* in which the letters migrate to *born* and *spent,* as words). Their processing impairment also affected their comprehension of the words: When asked to define an anagram word (e.g., *diary*), they were more prone than children in the control group to provide a definition of the anagram partner of the word (e.g., "something from a cow"). In contrast, they did not make phonemically based anagram errors in spoken word production and did not misorder letters in their spelling. This allowed us to localize the deficit at the level of early letter processing and its interaction with the orthographic lexicon. Research attention is now being focussed on determining how best to assist children who experience these kinds of reading difficulties (Friedmann & Rahamim, 2014).

CONCLUSION

In summary, we conclude that the application of cognitive models of reading to dyslexia is extremely important for diagnosis and can help to ensure that treatments are appropriately targeted. Such models provide a roadmap for researchers and clinicians, allowing them to make some sense of the enormous heterogeneity known to be present within the population of individuals with dyslexia. Patterns of impairment observed in dyslexia can, in turn, be highly informative for testing and constraining cognitive models. Letter position dyslexia represents a good example: Some computational models of reading use a "slot coding" system for the initial processing of letters, in which a single mechanism encodes both the identity of the letter and its position within the word (McClelland & Rumelhart, 1981). It is difficult for such a mechanism to produce the dissociation between letter identity and letter position processing observed in letter position dyslexia. Therefore, this as well as findings of imprecise letter position coding in typically developing readers has lent support to alternative systems of letter processing that decouple the coding of identity and position (e.g., Davis & Bowers, 2006; Gomez, Ratcliff, & Perea, 2008). Thus, a close interplay between cognitive modeling and the detailed observation of patterns of dyslexia can be mutually beneficial to both theory and practice.

How, then, can cognitive models of reading be directly used to support the assessment and diagnosis of dyslexia? In our view, it is important that assessment protocols be informed by a model such as the one in Figure 11.1 and that they ensure that the integrity of each of its components is checked. However, in doing so, the protocols should not overtest a child or involve more assessments than are absolutely necessary. The extent and range of bespoke tests available makes this feasible. Some tests, such as measures of the reading aloud of nonwords or irregular words, serve as "omnibus" assessments, capturing multiple components of the model at once. For example, examination of Figure 11.1 reveals that successful reading aloud of nonwords (i.e., performance that is within normal range for age) establishes the integrity of the letter processing, grapheme–phoneme rules, and phoneme output components of the model; an impairment in any one of these components would result in impaired performance on this task. Likewise, normal-for-age performance on an irregular word–reading task would establish the integrity of the letter processing, orthographic lexicon, phonological lexicon, and phoneme output components. Finally, unimpaired performance on a test of reading comprehension would demonstrate typical functioning of the semantics component, meaning that, with just these three tests, the integrity of all components of the model will have been established.

Of course, if performance on one or more of these omnibus tests is impaired, further investigation is necessary. As we have outlined, poor-for-age performance on a nonword-reading task or an irregular word–reading task could be attributable to impaired functioning of a number of different processes within the model. What is required at this point, therefore, is the administration of tests that allow a clinician to "drill down" and discover where a particular child's difficulties lie. These difficulties may be quite specific to one component of the model or may involve a number of components, but once a clinician determines this, he or she can give a clear diagnosis and develop a personalized intervention plan.

To assist in this assessment process, we have developed a suite of model-based reading (and spelling) tests and made them freely available on an online web resource, *MOTIf* (http://www.motif.org.au). The suite includes the three omnibus reading tests described in this chapter that are required for a comprehensive initial assessment: irregular word and nonword reading (as part of the *CC2* battery; Castles et al., 2009), and reading comprehension (TERC: Test of Everyday Reading Comprehension; McArthur, Jones, et al., 2013). It also includes a range of targeted tests of specific processes that can be used to specify a child's difficulties more precisely. For example, the Letter-Sound Test (LeST: Letter Sound Test; Larsen, Kohnen, Nickels, & McArthur, 2015) is designed to be used as a follow-up assessment for a child who is performing poorly on nonword reading for their age. Containing 51 items comprising all the single-letter graphemes of English as well as the most frequent digraphs, it allows evaluation of which specific graphemes the child can sound out in isolation and which he or she cannot. Based on the results, a teacher or clinician can focus on training those grapheme–phoneme correspondences that the child is struggling with. Also available are a range of other targeted tests of lexical and nonlexical route functioning, as well as separate tests of letter identification and letter position processing.

In summary, using the examples of three well-described profiles of dyslexia, we have shown that cognitive models of reading play a crucial role in guiding both researchers and clinicians. Cognitive models help in formulating clear hypotheses about the types of impairments we should see in dyslexia, thus explaining, at least to some degree, why dyslexia is such a heterogeneous disorder. Cognitive models also help clinicians have clearer expectations about the types of problems they should expect in a poor reader, thus guiding assessment protocols and ultimately improving treatment recommendations.

REFERENCES

Brunsdon, R., Coltheart, M., & Nickels, L. (2007). Severe developmental letter-processing impairment: A treatment case study. *Cognitive Neuropsychology, 23,* 795–821.

Castles, A., & Coltheart, M. (1993). Varieties of developmental dyslexia. *Cognition, 47,* 149–180.

Castles, A., Coltheart, M., Larsen, L., Jones, P., Saunders, S., & McArthur, G. (2009). Assessing the basic components of reading: A revision of the Castles and Coltheart test with new norms. *Australian Journal of Learning Difficulties, 14,* 67–88.

Castles, A., Kohnen, S., Nickels, L., & Brock, J. (2014). Developmental disorders: What can be learned from cognitive neuropsychology? *Philosophical Transactions of the Royal Society B, 369*(1634), 1–9.

Coltheart, M., Curtis, B., Atkins, P., & Haller, M. (1993). Models of reading aloud: Dual-route and parallel- distributed-processing approaches. *Psychological Review, 100,* 589–608.

Coltheart, M., Masterson, J., Byng, S., Prior, M., & Riddoch, J. (1983). Surface dyslexia. *Quarterly Journal of Experimental Psychology Section A—Human Experimental Psychology, 35,* 469–495.

Coltheart, M., Rastle, K., Perry, C., Langdon, R., & Ziegler, J. (2001). DRC: A dual route cascaded model of visual word recognition and reading aloud. *Psychological Review, 108,* 204–256.

Davis, C. J. & Bowers, J. S. (2006). Contrasting five different theories of letter position coding: Evidence from orthographic similarity effects. *Journal of Experimental Psychology: Human Perception and Performance, 32,* 535–557.

Friedmann, N., & Lukov, L. (2008). Developmental surface dyslexias. *Cortex, 44,* 1146–1160.

Friedmann, N., & Rahamim, E. (2014). Developmental letter position dyslexia. *Journal of Neuropsychology, 1,* 201–236.

Gomez, P., Ratcliff, R., & Perea, M. (2008). The overlap model: A model of letter position coding. *Psychological Review, 115,* 577–600.

Jackson, N. E., & Coltheart, M. (2001). *Routes to reading success and failure: Toward an integrated cognitive psychology of atypical reading.* New York, NY: Psychology Press.

Kohnen, S., Nickels, L., Castles, A., Friedmann, N., & McArthur, G. (2012). When "slime" becomes "smile": Developmental letter position dyslexia in English. *Neuropsychologia, 50,* 3681–3692.

Kohnen, S., Nickels, L., Geigis, L., Coltheart, M., McArthur, G., & Castles, A. (2018). Variations within a subtype: Developmental surface dyslexias in English. *Cortex, 106,* 151–163.

Korkman, M., Kirk, U., & Kemp, S. (1998). *NEPSY: A developmental neuropsychological assessment.* San Antonio, TX: Psychological Corp.

Larsen, L., Kohnen, S., Nickels, L., & McArthur, G. (2015). The Letter-Sound Test (LeST): A reliable and valid comprehensive measure of grapheme–phoneme knowledge. *Australian Journal of Learning Difficulties, 20*(2), 129–142.

Manis, F. R., & Bailey, C. E. (2008). Exploring heterogeneity in developmental dyslexia: A longitudinal investigation. In G. Reid, A. J. Fawcett, L. S. Siegel, & F. Manis (Eds.), *The Sage handbook of dyslexia* (pp. 149–173). London: Sage Publications.

McArthur, G., Jones, K., Anandakumar, T., Larsen, L., Castles, A., & Coltheart, M. (2013). A Test of Everyday Reading Comprehension (TERC). *Australian Journal of Learning Difficulties, 18*, 35–85

McArthur, G., Kohnen, S., Larsen, L., Jones, K., Anandakumar, T., Banales, E., & Castles, A. (2013). Getting to grips with the heterogeneity of developmental dyslexia. *Cognitive Neuropsychology, 30*, 1–24.

McClelland, J. L., & Rumelhart, D. E. (1981). An interactive activation model of context effects in letter perception: I. An account of basic findings. *Psychological Review, 88*(5), 375–407.

Peterson, R. L., Pennington, B., & Olson, R. K. (2013). Subtypes of developmental dyslexia: Testing the predictions of the dual-route and connectionist frameworks. *Cognition, 126*, 2–38.

Rack, J., Snowling, M. J., & Olson, R. K. (1992). The nonword reading deficit in developmental dyslexia: A review. *Reading Research Quarterly, 27*, 28–53.

Shallice, T., Rumiati, R. I., & Zadini, A. (2000). The selective impairment of the phonological output buffer. *Cognitive Neuropsychology, 17*, 517–546.

Sotiropoulos, A., & Hanley, J. R. (2017). Lexical decision performance in developmental surface dysgraphia: Evidence for a unitary orthographic system that is used in both reading and spelling. *Cognitive Neuropsychology, 34*, 144–162.

Sprenger-Charolles, L., Siegel, L. S., Jiménez, J. E., & Ziegler, J. C. (2011). Prevalence and reliability of phonological, surface, and mixed profiles in dyslexia: A review of studies conducted in languages varying in orthographic depth. *Scientific Studies of Reading, 15*, 498–521.

Temple, C. M., & Marshall, J. C. (1983). A case-study of developmental phonological dyslexia. *British Journal of Psychology, 74*, 517–533.

Wagner, R. K., Torgesen, J. K., & Rashotte, C. A. (1999). *Comprehensive Test of Phonological Processing (CTOPP)*. Austin, TX: PRO-ED.

Ziegler, J. C., Castel, C., Pech-Georgel, C., George, F., Alario, F. X., & Perry, C. (2008). Developmental dyslexia and the dual route model of reading: Simulating individual differences and subtypes. *Cognition, 107*, 151–178.

CHAPTER 12

Reading Comprehension Interventions for Individuals With Dyslexia in Grades 4–8

Kelly J. Williams, Philip Capin, Elizabeth A. Stevens, and Sharon Vaughn

SUMMARY

Students with dyslexia have difficulties with decoding and word recognition; however, by the time these students reach the upper-elementary and middle school grades, many also begin to experience challenges with comprehension. We developed and evaluated the impact of multiyear, multicomponent reading interventions on reading outcomes in a series of studies conducted with students with dyslexia in Grades 4–8. In the studies conducted in Grades 4 and 5, students who received reading intervention from our research team did not perform significantly better than business-as-usual students on standardized measures of reading comprehension; however, students in the business-as-usual condition received similar amounts of reading intervention delivered by school personnel. In contrast, in the series of studies conducted with students in the middle school grades (i.e., Grades 6–8), students who received 3 years of continued intervention throughout middle school performed significantly higher on a standardized measure of reading comprehension than those in the business-as-usual condition. Students who received intervention did not actually catch up to the reading performance of their peers without dyslexia, and the achievement gap became wider for students in the business-as-usual group. Findings from these studies highlight the challenges of improving reading comprehension outcomes for this population. Students with dyslexia in Grades 4–8 may need continued intervention across multiple years in order to substantially improve their reading performance. Based on this research, we provide several suggestions for implementing reading interventions.

INTRODUCTION

Fourth grade is a particularly important period in reading development because it represents a time when some students begin to exhibit

This research was supported by Award Number P50 HD052117, Texas Center for Learning Disabilities, from the *Eunice Kennedy Shriver* National Institute of Child Health & Human Development to the University of Houston. The content is solely the responsibility of the authors and does not necessarily represent the official views of the *Eunice Kennedy Shriver* National Institute of Child Health & Human Development or the National Institutes of Health.

reading difficulties. In the early elementary grades (i.e., kindergarten to Grade 3), students learn how to read and focus on developing proficiency in decoding and fluency (Chall, 1996). They read highly constrained texts, meaning that the vocabulary used and background knowledge required to understand concepts in the texts are those with which students are familiar. However, once students reach fourth grade, they are no longer taught foundational skills and are now expected to be proficient readers and apply those foundational skills to content-area texts (Chall, 1996). Content-area texts are more challenging and complex and frequently include vocabulary words and concepts that may be unfamiliar to students. Unfamiliar concepts are problematic because students may not have the prerequisite background knowledge essential for comprehension. Due to the changing demands of reading, the shifting emphasis toward text comprehension, and the importance of background and vocabulary knowledge, some students who were previously considered good readers may begin to have difficulty understanding what they read (Chall & Jacobs, 1983; Compton, Fuchs, Fuchs, Elleman, & Gilbert, 2008). This seemingly sudden onset of comprehension difficulties after third grade is often referred to as a late-emerging reading disability because many of these students demonstrate little evidence of reading difficulty prior to the upper elementary grades (Catts, Compton, Tomblin, & Bridges, 2012; Compton et al., 2008; Leach, Rescorla, & Scarborough, 2003).

Considerable research has been conducted in the early elementary grades for students with dyslexia, and it is well established that reading interventions provided in kindergarten through Grade 3 are associated with improved reading outcomes, particularly for foundational reading skills (Wanzek, Vaughn, et al., 2016; Wanzek et al., 2018). However, reading interventions for older students with dyslexia have consistently yielded lower effect sizes on reading outcomes (Scammacca et al., 2016; Wanzek, Wexler, Vaughn, & Ciullo, 2010). In a synthesis of reading interventions for students with reading difficulties and disabilities in Grades 4 and 5, Wanzek and colleagues (2010) found that interventions that targeted vocabulary and comprehension had a moderate to large effect on researcher-created comprehension outcome measures, but no studies included standardized, norm-referenced measures. Since the publication of the 2010 synthesis by Wanzek and colleagues, five additional upper-elementary reading intervention studies were conducted featuring high-quality research design elements and standardized reading comprehension measures (Ritchey, Silverman, Montanaro, Speece, & Schatschneider, 2012; Toste, Capin, Vaughn, Roberts, & Kearns, 2016; Toste, Capin, Williams, Cho, & Vaughn, 2017; Wanzek, Petscher et al., 2016; Wanzek & Roberts, 2012). Of note, none of these studies found significant differences between treatment and control conditions on norm-referenced measures of reading comprehension, except Toste and colleagues (2017), which found significant differences between treatment and control conditions on the Gates-MacGinitie Reading

Tests–4 (MacGinitie, MacGinitie, Maria, Dreyer, & Hughes, 2000). Similar to the upper elementary reading intervention research, there has been limited research conducted in the middle school grades, and the existing research shows that improving reading comprehension with older students is a formidable task. Wanzek and colleagues (2013) investigated the impact of extensive (i.e., 75 sessions or more) reading interventions on reading outcomes for students in Grades 4–12 and determined that extensive reading interventions were associated with small positive effects on reading outcomes (effect size [ES] = 0.10–0.16).

We can draw several conclusions after considering the results of the aforementioned research. First, there are a limited number of high-quality studies examining the impact of reading interventions in the upper-elementary and middle grades. Second, the current studies are associated with small effects on reading outcomes. These small effects may be due to the fact that improving reading comprehension in these grades is more difficult than in the early elementary grades because reading comprehension is more complex and relies on background knowledge and vocabulary to a greater extent than does word reading. In addition, students in the upper-elementary and middle grades often have difficulties in both word reading and reading comprehension (e.g., Cirino et al., 2013), which makes it particularly difficult to make large gains in reading comprehension. Due to the heterogenous needs of these students, reading interventions for students with dyslexia need to address multiple components of reading (e.g., word reading, vocabulary, background knowledge) in order to improve reading outcomes.

READING COMPREHENSION
INTERVENTIONS INFORMED BY READING THEORIES

According to Gough and Tunmer (1986), the Simple View of Reading (SVR) posits that reading comprehension is the product of reading decoding (the ability to read words in isolation with automaticity and accuracy) and linguistic comprehension (the interpretation of words, sentences, and connected text). In order to comprehend what is read, individuals also need automaticity in word reading, which allows them to focus on higher order processes such as comprehension (Perfetti, 2011). In a longitudinal study of the decoding skills and linguistic comprehension of students in Grades 2, 4, and 8, Catts, Hogan, and Adolf (2005) found that for students in second grade, decoding skills explained much of the variance in reading comprehension (27%); however, by the time students were in eighth grade, much more of the variance (36%) in reading comprehension was associated with linguistic comprehension (Catts et al., 2005). This suggests that word reading is a significant factor associated with comprehension in the early grades when the meaning of text is less dependent on knowing the meaning of obscure vocabulary words or having adequate background knowledge;

however, in the later grades, linguistic comprehension contributes more to reading comprehension, and both vocabulary and background knowledge are also necessary for students to comprehend text.

Kintsch and van Dijk (1978) proposed the Construction Integration Model of reading comprehension processing, which suggested that readers actively construct meaning as they read. The reader's understanding, or Situation Model, is constructed by integrating ideas across sections of text. This process occurs naturally as the reader incorporates new information with previously read information and the reader's background knowledge. The Situation Model is constantly revised as the reader continues reading and integrating new information with the existing model.

Our group developed multicomponent reading interventions were informed by SVR and the Construction Integration Model of reading comprehension processing, and we targeted word reading, background knowledge, vocabulary knowledge, and the integration of ideas across texts. The interventions included the domains of word reading (i.e., decoding) and vocabulary or world knowledge (i.e., linguistic comprehension), in addition to a third domain we refer to as text-processing strategies, which also address linguistic comprehension. To address word reading, intervention lessons included decoding multisyllabic words and developing automaticity at the word, phrase, and sentence levels. Students developed word knowledge through robust, explicit vocabulary instruction that corresponded with the texts read in each unit. We selected high-utility words and gave students student-friendly definitions, visual representations, synonyms and antonyms, and discussion activities for each word. Tutors reviewed the words throughout each unit of instruction. To develop students' ability to process text, tutors had students engage in text-based reading, which included the reading of stretch texts (i.e., texts on grade level) or fluency texts (i.e., texts on students' reading level). Stretch-text instruction used expository social studies text, and students stopped at predetermined points and explained what was happening in the text. Tutors asked students text-based questions that required them to use information from different parts of the text. Fluency instruction consisted of students reading a text repeatedly to build fluency and automaticity. After reading, students summarized the text and completed an activity in which they read sentences to determine if they made sense.

Impact of Reading Interventions
in the Upper-Elementary Grades

We examined the efficacy of the aforementioned multicomponent reading interventions through a series of studies conducted with struggling readers, including those with dyslexia, in the upper-elementary grades (Miciak et al., 2017; Roberts et al., 2018; Vaughn, Roberts, Miciak, Taylor, & Fletcher, 2018; Vaughn, Solis, Miciak, Taylor, & Fletcher, 2016). Vaughn and colleagues (2016) examined the impact of a reading intervention on reading outcomes for struggling readers in fourth grade. In Year 1, they assigned students to one of three conditions: intervention delivered by the research team for either 1 year or 2 years, or a comparison condition in which reading intervention was provided by the school (Vaughn et al., 2016). In the researcher-provided conditions, students met daily with trained tutors in small groups of four or five students over 16 weeks. Each 35-minute lesson included word reading, vocabulary knowledge, and text-processing strategies, as outlined previously. Students assigned to the comparison condition received intervention provided by their schools, typically implemented for 2–5 days per week for 10–60 minutes per session. The content of the intervention varied by classroom and school but included instruction in reading test preparation, word reading, fluency, and comprehension. After 1 year of intervention, students assigned to both researcher-provided intervention groups performed similarly to the students in the school-provided intervention on all measures (i.e., decoding, spelling, fluency, and comprehension), with no statistically significant differences between groups; however, all groups made significant standard score growth from pretest to posttest on decoding, fluency, and reading comprehension measures.

In Year 2, students assigned to the 2-year researcher-provided intervention condition (n = 162) received 30–40 minutes of supplemental reading instruction daily for 16 weeks (Miciak et al., 2017). These sessions included the same components as in the first year of intervention (Vaughn et al., 2016), plus a self-regulation component. The self-regulation component taught students to set goals for reading and to monitor those goals using a visual prompt. Students in the comparison condition and 1-year researcher-delivered intervention continued to receive reading interventions provided by school personnel. Although students who received 2 years of the reading intervention delivered by researchers had significantly greater growth in word reading and reading fluency compared to students who received 1 year of intervention and the comparison group, there were no significant differences among the groups on standardized measures of reading comprehension.

This 2-year study (Miciak et al., 2017; Vaughn et al., 2016) demonstrates the challenges of implementing school-based research. Because participating schools elected to provide a reading intervention to the comparison students, it was not possible to examine the additive effects of a supplemental reading intervention developed and implemented by the research team. The school-provided comparison condition varied greatly in terms of type of interventions received and the number of hours of intervention provided. Yet, students in all conditions (i.e., researcher-provided and school-provided) received similar amounts of instruction across both years, which may suggest that providing supplemental small-group reading interventions—regardless of the specific reading components addressed in the interventions—may lead to growth in reading comprehension.

Next, we examined the efficacy of a word- and text-based intervention for fourth- and fifth-grade students with significant reading comprehension difficulties. We randomly assigned eligible students (n = 280) to either the reading intervention or to a business-as-usual (BaU) comparison condition. Students who received the reading intervention met with trained tutors daily for 30- to 45-minute lessons in small groups of three to six students. During the first phase of intervention, students worked on word study and fluency in order to develop automaticity at the word and sentence level. In the second and third phases, students read expository, narrative, and hybrid text and focused on setting goals, monitoring their understanding, and answering comprehension questions. Students who received the reading intervention performed significantly better than students in the BaU condition on measures of experimental word reading and oral reading fluency.

In our final study with upper elementary students, we examined the impact of an after-school reading intervention for struggling readers in Grades 3–5 (Roberts et al., 2018). By conducting the treatment after school, we sought to assess the effects of providing supplemental instruction outside of school hours. We randomly assigned eligible students (n = 419) to one of three conditions: 1) text-processing with foundational reading skills (TP + FS), 2) text-processing (TP), or 3) BaU comparison group. Students received intervention 4–5 days per week through 60-minute sessions. Students in the TP + FS condition received 30 minutes of individualized, computerized instruction that focused on phonemic awareness, phonics, grammar, fluency, listening vocabulary, and reading comprehension. During the second 30 minutes, students worked in small groups with a tutor on word reading, fluency, and text comprehension. The lessons also integrated self-regulation and writing instruction within the reading practices. In the TP condition, students also worked on a computer program for 30 minutes in which they read a text and completed multiple choice questions for that text. Then, during the second 30 minutes of the lesson, they worked in small groups in a book club format, where they read narrative and expository texts. Students worked on making predictions and answering comprehension questions, in addition to self-regulation and writing activities.

We encountered challenges with attendance and attrition; on average, students attended approximately 44 lessons (SD = 28.11), although some students assigned to the treatment condition never attended a single session (16.1%). Students in the BaU condition were not assigned to an after-school group and did not receive any supplemental reading instruction after school. Across all three groups, students performed similarly on measures of reading comprehension, and there were no statistically significant differences; however, both the low dosage and the high attrition in the treatment group make it difficult to interpret the actual impact of the interventions.

Impact of Reading Interventions in the Middle Grades

We also investigated the impact of tiered reading interventions in a series of studies conducted with struggling readers in Grades 6–8 (Vaughn et al., 2010; Vaughn et al., 2012; Vaughn et al., 2011). Vaughn and colleagues (2010) identified sixth-grade students with reading difficulties (n = 327) and randomly assigned them to a researcher-developed reading intervention or a BaU condition. The reading intervention was implemented for a full school year for 50 minutes daily with groups of 10–15 students, and it emphasized word study, fluency, vocabulary, and comprehension. In the first phase of the intervention, students focused on word study, fluency, vocabulary, and comprehension strategies. In Phase II, students continued to work on word study and fluency but the intervention placed greater emphasis on vocabulary and comprehension of expository (social studies) and narrative text. In the third phase, the intervention emphasized comprehension, and students applied previously learned strategies (e.g., multiple choice, main idea, summarizing, synthesizing) to content-area text. Students who received the reading intervention outperformed students in the comparison condition on measures of word attack, spelling, comprehension, and phonemic decoding efficiency; however, the effects were relatively small (median d = 0.16), and the intervention did not substantially close the gap between the struggling readers and typically developing readers.

Building on the previous study, the research team then identified participants (n = 182) from the sixth-grade study who were demonstrating inadequate response as measured by failing scores on the state assessment in reading (Vaughn et al., 2011). Researchers randomly assigned inadequate responders to receive a standardized intervention or an individualized intervention protocol in Grade 7. The standardized protocol used a prescribed program and sequence of instruction for all students in that condition, and the individualized protocol adjusted instruction based on student progress monitoring data and response to instruction. Inadequate responders in the comparison group in sixth grade remained in the comparison group in seventh grade. Participants in treatment received intervention for 50 minutes daily in groups of four to five students, and intervention focused on fluency, word study, vocabulary, and comprehension. The individualized condition identified students with higher and lower level word-reading skills and adjusted intervention techniques accordingly. Those with higher word-reading skills spent more time on comprehension and text reading, whereas those with lower word-reading skills spent more time on word study and text-reading instruction.

The standardized condition had three phases of instruction. Phase I placed an emphasis on advanced decoding strategies, vocabulary, and text comprehension. In Phase II, students continued to review previously learned word study and fluency strategies, but there was more of an emphasis on vocabulary and comprehension instruction. In the third phase, students applied the strategies they had learned to expository text. At posttest, there were no significant differences between the two treatment groups (i.e., individualized and standardized) on any outcome measures. There were also no significant differences between the two treatment groups combined and the comparison group on measures of word reading, word attack, or reading fluency, but there was a moderate, significant effect on reading comprehension ($ES = 0.56$).

Students who continued to show inadequate response after 2 years of intervention participated in yet another study in which students were assigned to receive a third year of reading intervention ($n = 28$) or a comparison condition ($n = 13$; Vaughn et al., 2012), which was contingent on their original group assignment in Grade 6. Students in treatment received a daily, 50-minute reading intervention in groups of two to four students, and interventionists customized instruction to meet the needs of the students based on diagnostic and progress monitoring data. Students in treatment significantly outperformed comparison students on measures of reading comprehension ($ES = 1.20$) and word identification ($ES = 0.49$).

A separate analysis examined the overall reading achievement of students who received treatment across all 3 years of the intervention (Grades 6–8) and analyzed the performance of these students compared to their typically developing peers (Roberts, Vaughn, Fletcher, Stuebing, & Barth, 2013). Students who received 3 years of treatment significantly outperformed students in the comparison condition ($ES = 0.26$) on overall reading achievement. However, the seemingly large effects seen on comprehension outcomes in this set of studies was due to the fact that students in the comparison condition actually declined with regard to their reading performance. The students in treatment did not actually catch up to their typically developing peers, and the achievement gap widened for students in the comparison group.

Lessons Learned From Our Reading Intervention Studies

Overall, our studies conducted in the upper-elementary and middle grades highlight several important findings. First, we found that improving scores on reading comprehension measures for students with dyslexia was difficult. Most of our studies showed gains in standard scores but not differential gains between treatment and comparison conditions. In our middle school studies, we did see a significant effect of the reading treatment on reading comprehension outcomes; however, the comparison group actually experienced declines in their reading performance relative to the treatment group. This suggests that students with dyslexia may need continued access to intervention over multiple years just to maintain current reading levels. Furthermore, students who received intervention for multiple years did not actually catch up to their typically developing peers on reading comprehension measures, indicating that sustained ongoing interventions are necessary to reduce this achievement gap.

In addition, these studies highlight the importance of considering the counterfactual or comparison condition in light of the findings. In the upper-elementary studies, students in the comparison condition actually received school-provided interventions that varied greatly in content and length, making it difficult to interpret the true impact of our researcher-provided interventions. On the other hand, the students in the comparison group in the middle grades did not receive school-provided interventions, which may have caused the larger effects on comprehension outcomes. Because all students in the upper-elementary studies were receiving interventions (school or researcher provided), they made significant standard score growth relative to the normative population, whereas students in the comparison condition, who were not receiving equal amounts of instruction that focused on word reading and comprehension, actually declined in their standard score performance relative to the normative population.

Implications for Practice

The interventions we implemented in the upper-elementary and middle grades incorporated several "essential ingredients" based on Chall's (1996) stages of development, the SVR (Gough & Tunmer, 1986), and the Construction Integration Model of reading comprehension processing (Kintsch & van Dijk, 1978). Tutors in the interventions emphasized 1) word reading (i.e., developing automaticity with high-frequency and multisyllable words), 2) vocabulary and background knowledge, and 3) text-processing strategies (i.e., idea integration through main ideas and summarizing). In this section, we describe these components with specific attention to how they can be implemented in authentic educational settings.

Because many older students with dyslexia also have difficulties at the word level, our interventions all included an instructional phase with a strong emphasis on developing proficiency in decoding multisyllabic words. The goal of this first phase was to help students learn strategies to successfully decode multisyllabic words in isolation, phrases, and sentences and for students to develop automaticity in reading these and other high-frequency sight words. Students first learned how to decode vowel sounds (e.g., *ea, ai, oa*) and affixes (e.g., *-tion, pre-, re-*) in isolation and then practiced reading these patterns in lists of words. Teachers developed these based on the individual needs of the students. Teachers modeled how to pronounce the words, and students had multiple opportunities to practice reading these lists with affirmative or corrective feedback from the teachers and other students. Students tracked their progress on the lists and recorded their mastery. As students mastered each list, they progressed to more difficult lists. In addition, the first phase emphasized fluency at the sentence and text level in order to help students develop automaticity.

Sentences and texts included words with previously taught patterns, and students had multiple opportunities to read these with feedback. The lessons also incorporated morphology and vocabulary instruction on the parts that were taught.

Students with underdeveloped language skills often exhibit difficulties with the rule-governed structure of language and do not acquire the meanings of words as quickly as their peers. They also may have difficulty interpreting and remembering the meaning of words. Thus, our interventions included explicit teaching of vocabulary and background knowledge, and our procedures were informed by prior research on vocabulary instruction (Beck, McKeown, & Kucan, 2013; Elleman, Lindo, Morphy, & Compton, 2009). We selected words for explicit vocabulary instruction from text by identifying words that 1) will be frequently seen in other texts and content areas, 2) are related to the main idea of a passage, 3) are unknown by the students, and 4) cannot be learned using context clues or through structural analysis (Beck et al., 2013; Vaughn Gross Center for Reading and Language Arts [VGCRLA], 2013). Tutors taught the words prior to text reading using the following procedure (VGCRLA, 2010):

1. Have students pronounce the word.

2. Provide a student-friendly definition with visual.

3. Ask students to discuss what is known about the word.

4. Provide examples and nonexamples.

5. Engage in deep processing activities.

6. Have students create powerful sentences with the new word.

Tutors reviewed these words daily throughout the unit, and students engaged in meaningful deep-processing activities to support their vocabulary learning, which included completing graphic organizers such as word maps, identifying word relatives (e.g., *classify, classification, classifying, reclassify*), and participating in structured question prompts that allow students to practice using the word in conversation. An example of a structured question prompt for the word *classify* might be, "Turn to your partner and explain something you can classify. Start your sentence by saying, 'I can classify. . . .'" This helps provide additional language support for students with language-related reading difficulties.

The third component of our interventions was text processing, in which students read different types of text and engaged in discussions about the text with tutors, which also helped foster linguistic comprehension. This explicit practice is aligned with the Construction Integration model because it helps students make connections across sections of text. The first type of text used in lessons was stretch text, which was typically expository text that was on students' grade level, not their reading level. Students read texts aloud in various formats (e.g., choral, partner, echo) and stopped at predetermined points to summarize the text and answer questions. Tutors scaffolded this activity by directing students to specific sections of the text necessary to answer the questions. Tutors also incorporated self-regulation into these lessons by having students set goals before reading and then having students reflect on whether they were understanding the text and meeting their goals. Students used a self-monitoring sheet to determine if they had met their goals.

CONCLUSION

The upper-elementary and middle grades represent a critical time in the development of reading proficiency. As texts become more challenging and the focus of instruction shifts, students begin having more difficulty with comprehending text. These difficulties are deeply entrenched, meaning that they are often difficult to remediate. Our studies, which are based on several models of reading comprehension, demonstrate the complexity of providing intensive, multiyear reading interventions and the challenges with implementing them in authentic school contexts. Comprehension is a product of word reading and linguistic comprehension and is affected by background knowledge. By the time students with dyslexia reach the middle grades, they have had many years of inadequate opportunities to read and learn from text, reducing their access to linguistic comprehension and background knowledge, thus further diminishing their success at reading comprehension. We interpret reading comprehension interventions for students with dyslexia as requiring ongoing and sustained instruction over many years, perhaps most of their schooling, in order to improve and sustain text reading and comprehension.

REFERENCES

Beck, I. L., McKeown, M. G., & Kucan, L. (2013). *Bringing words to life: Robust vocabulary instruction.* New York, NY: Guilford Press.
Catts, H. W., Compton, D., Tomblin, J. B., & Bridges, M. S. (2012). Prevalence and nature of late-emerging poor readers. *Journal of Educational Psychology, 104*(1), 166–181.
Catts, H. W., Hogan, T. P., & Adolf, S. M. (2005). Developmental changes in reading and reading disabilities. In H. Catts & A. Kamhi (Eds.), *The connections between language and reading disabilities* (pp. 38–51). Mahwah, NJ: Lawrence Erlbaum Associates.
Chall, J. S. (1996). *Stages of reading development* (2nd ed.). Fort Worth, TX: Harcourt Brace.
Chall, J. S., & Jacobs, V. A. (1983). Writing and reading in the elementary grades: Developmental trends among low-SES children. *Language Arts, 60*(5), 617–626.
Cirino, P. T., Romain, M. A., Barth, A. E., Tolar, T. D., Fletcher, J. M., & Vaughn, S. (2013). Reading skill components and impairments in middle school struggling readers. *Reading and Writing, 26*(7), 1059–1086. http://dx.doi.org/10.1007/s11145-012-9406-3
Compton, D. L., Fuchs, D., Fuchs, L. S., Elleman, A. M., & Gilbert, J. K. (2008). Tracking children who fly below the radar: Latent transition modeling of students with late-emerging reading disability. *Learning and Individual Differences, 18,* 329–337.
Elleman, A. M., Lindo, E. J., Morphy, P., & Compton, D. L. (2009). The impact of vocabulary instruction on passage-level comprehension of school-age children: A meta-analysis. *Journal of Research on Educational Effectiveness, 2*(1), 1–44. http://dx.doi.org/10.1080/19345740802539200
Gough, P. B., & Tunmer, W. E. (1986). Decoding, reading, and reading disability. *Remedial and Special Education, 7*(1), 6–10.

Kintsch, W., & van Dijk, T. A. (1978). Toward a model of text comprehension and production. *Psychological Review, 85*(5), 363–394. http://dx.doi.org/10.1037/0033-295X .85.5.363

Leach, J. M., Rescorla, L., & Scarborough, H. S. (2003). Late-emerging reading disabilities. *Journal of Educational Psychology, 95*(2), 211–224. http://dx.doi.org/10.1037/0022-0663 .95.2.211

MacGinitie, W. H., MacGinitie, R. K., Maria, K., Dreyer, L. G., & Hughes, K. E. (2000). *Gates-MacGinitie Reading Tests* (4th ed.). Itasca, IL: Riverside.

Miciak, J., Roberts, G., Taylor, W. P., Solis, M., Ahmed Y., Vaughn, S., & Fletcher, J. M. (2017). The effects of one versus two years of intensive reading intervention implemented with late elementary struggling readers. *Learning Disabilities Research & Practice, 33*(1), 24–36.

Perfetti, C. A. (2011). Phonology is critical in reading: But a phonological deficit is not the only source of low reading skill. In S. A. Brady, D. Braze, & C. A. Fowler (Eds.), *Explaining individual differences in reading* (pp. 153–171). New York, NY: Routledge.

Ritchey, K. D., Silverman, R. D., Montanaro, E. A., Speece, D. L., & Schatschneider, C. (2012). Effects of a Tier 2 supplemental reading intervention for at-risk fourth grade students. *Exceptional Children, 78*(3), 318–334.

Roberts, G. J., Capin, M. A., Roberts, G., Miciak, J., Quinn, J. M., & Vaughn, S. (2018). Examining the effects of afterschool reading interventions for upper elementary struggling readers. *Remedial and Special Education.* (Advance online publication.) http://doi:10.1177/0741932517750818

Roberts, G., Vaughn, S., Fletcher, J., Stuebing, K., & Barth, A. (2013). Effects of a response-based, tiered framework for intervening with struggling readers in middle school. *Reading Research Quarterly, 48*(3), 237–254. http://doi:10.1002/rrq.47

Scammacca, N. K., Roberts, G. J., Cho, E., Williams, K. J., Roberts, G., Vaughn, S. R., & Carroll, M. (2016). A century of progress: Reading interventions for students in Grades 4–12, 1914–2014. *Review of Educational Research, 86*(3), 756–800. http://dx.doi .org/10.3102/0034654316652942

Toste, J. R., Capin, P., Vaughn, S., Roberts, G. J., & Kearns, D. M. (2016). Multisyllabic word-reading instruction with and without motivational beliefs training for struggling readers in the upper elementary grades. *The Elementary School Journal, 117*(4), 593–615.

Toste, J. R., Capin, P., Williams, K. J., Cho, E., & Vaughn, S. (2017). Replication of an experimental study investigating the efficacy of a multisyllabic word reading intervention with and without motivational beliefs training for struggling readers. *Journal of Learning Disabilities.* (Advance online publication.) http://dx.doi.org/10.1177/0022219418775114

Vaughn Gross Center for Reading and Language Arts (VGCRLA). (2010). *Steps for explicit vocabulary instruction.* Austin, TX: Author.

Vaughn Gross Center for Reading and Language Arts (VGCRLA). (2013). *Vocabulary and oral language development.* Austin, TX: Author.

Vaughn, S., Cirino, P. T., Wanzek, J., Wexler, J., Fletcher, J. M., & Denton, C. D. (2010). Response to intervention for middle school students with reading difficulties: Effects of a primary and secondary intervention. *School Psychology Review, 39*(1), 3–21.

Vaughn, S., Roberts, G. J., Miciak, J., Taylor, P., & Fletcher, J. M. (2018). Efficacy of a word- and text-based intervention for students with significant reading difficulties. *Journal of Learning Disabilities.* (Advance online publication.) http://dx.doi.org /10.1177/0022219418775113

Vaughn, S., Solis, M., Miciak, J., Taylor, W. P., & Fletcher, J. M. (2016). Effects from a randomized control trial comparing researcher and school-implemented treatments with fourth graders with significant reading difficulties. *Journal of Research on Educational Effectiveness, 9*(Suppl. 1), 23–44.

Vaughn, S., Wexler, J., Leroux, A., Roberts, G., Denton, C., Barth, A., & Fletcher, J. (2012). Effects of intensive reading intervention for eighth-grade students with persistently inadequate response to intervention. *Journal of Learning Disabilities, 45*(6), 515–525.

Vaughn, S., Wexler, J., Roberts, G., Barth, A. A., Cirino, P. T., Romain, M. A., . . . Denton, C. A. (2011). Effects of individualized and standardized interventions on middle school students with reading disabilities. *Exceptional Children, 77*(4), 391–407.

Wanzek, J., Petscher, Y., Al Otaiba, S., Kent, S. C., Schatschneider, C., Haynes, M., . . . Jones, F. G. (2016). Examining the average and local effects of a standardized treatment for fourth graders with reading difficulties. *Journal of Research on Educational Effectiveness, 9*(Suppl. 1), 45–66.

Wanzek, J., & Roberts, G. (2012). Reading interventions with varying instructional emphases for fourth graders with reading difficulties. *Learning Disability Quarterly, 35*(2), 90-101.

Wanzek, J., Stevens, E. A., Williams, K. J., Scammacca, N., Vaughn, S., & Sargent, K. (2018). Current evidence on the effects of intensive early reading interventions. *Journal of Learning Disabilities.* (Advance online publication.) http://dx.doi.org/10.1177/00222219418775110

Wanzek, J., Vaughn, S., Scammacca, N., Gatlin, B., Walker, M. A., & Capin, P. (2016). Meta-analyses of the effects of Tier 2 type reading interventions in Grades K–3. *Educational Psychology Review, 28,* 551–576.

Wanzek, J., Vaughn, S., Scammacca, N. K., Metz, K., Murray, C. S., Roberts, G., & Danielson, L. (2013). Extensive reading interventions for students with reading difficulties after grade 3. *Review of Educational Research, 83*(2), 163–195. http://dx.doi.org/10.3102/0034654313477212

Wanzek, J., Wexler, J., Vaughn, S., & Ciullo, S. (2010). Reading interventions for struggling readers in the upper elementary grades: A synthesis of 20 years of research. *Reading & Writing, 23,* 889–912.

CHAPTER 13

Interventions to Improve the Literacy Skills of Children at Risk of Dyslexia

Robert Savage, George Georgiou, Rauno Parrila, Marie-France Côté, Kristina Maiorino, and Kristy Dunn

SUMMARY

Researchers and educators should continually search for optimal early interventions for struggling readers. To this end, we report two studies. In Study 1, we taught all Grade 1 at-risk poor word readers phonic rules (e.g., to blend sounds associated with letters *c, a,* and *t* to pronounce "cat"). In an experimental condition, we closely linked taught phonic rules to shared reading of books richly exemplifying such phonic units and also taught children strategies to help them think flexibly to link the strings of spoken sounds produced by phonic decoding (e.g., the sounds produced by decoding the letters *c – a – t*) to known words (e.g., *cat*). In Study 2, we taught all Grade 2 children the meanings and spellings of words. In our experimental condition, we also taught the pronunciation of the most commonly occurring complex letter clusters, such as *er, wh, igh,* and *ed* within these words. Results from both studies showed advantages for the experimental programs on literacy outcomes compared to control groups. These results suggested potentially important avenues for effective intervention for at-risk readers, including dual language learners, and also suggested ways to progress toward new optimal interventions.

INTRODUCTION

In this chapter, we present two studies of theory-driven interventions. In both, results showed advantages on literacy outcomes for the experimental programs compared to controls, suggesting potentially important avenues for effective intervention for at-risk readers. We discuss their promise for developing and improving intervention practices in schools and potential implications for policy, as well as some directions for future research.

STUDY 1: DIRECT MAPPING AND SET-FOR-VARIABILITY IN GRADE 1

Study 1 considered the impact of two distinct theory-driven components of reading intervention in English. The impacts of intervention on reading acquisition in a second language (French) are also considered.

Direct Mapping

We know a reasonable amount about effective early reading programs. For poor readers, there is good evidence that both systematic phonics teaching and shared book reading are important. These two practices thus commonly co-occur in reading intervention studies (Hatcher, Hulme, & Ellis, 1994; McArthur et al., 2012). A new idea developed in Study 1 is that for each grapheme–phoneme correspondence (GPC) taught in phonics programs, children should immediately read *on that day* text richly embodying the specific GPC units to consolidate grapheme-to-phoneme skill development (Chen & Savage, 2014). We refer to this practice as Direct Mapping of GPCs. This idea is not wholly new—the phonological linkage hypothesis (Hatcher et al., 1994; see also Foorman, Francis, Davidson, Harm, & Griffin, 2004) suggested that children must link graphemes to phonemes and then to text reading to become fluent readers. Hatcher and colleagues (1944) reported data consistent with this view, with an advantage for children taught phonics combined with book reading compared to three other conditions in which either phonics alone, book reading alone, or neither phonics nor book reading were provided. In the study by Hatcher and colleagues, children were not explicitly encouraged to link specific GPCs taught to authentic texts read in a lesson delivered *on that day*, so it does not speak to Direct Mapping as we construe it. Another study using Direct Mapping (Shapiro & Solity, 2008) does not speak directly to the needs of at-risk students because their sample consisted of typically developing readers.

Chen and Savage (2014) ran an intervention with Grade 2 struggling readers in which they first taught GPCs and then children undertook shared reading of texts with a high density of taught GPCs. The control group of similarly poor readers was taught "word usage," which was a vocabulary intervention. Results showed advantages for the intervention condition over the control group on word reading and spelling and on a specific aspect of motivation—children's perception of task difficulty.

Given the existing studies, we do not yet know if Direct Mapping improves reading compared to control interventions in which children are taught GPCs and then read texts without being shown explicit systematic linkage between the two activities. To address these gaps in current knowledge, we compared the effects of interventions in which the same GPCs taught *on that day* are explicitly and repeatedly reinforced in "real books" (popular published children's literature) with a second intervention in which teaching of the GPCs and real book reading co-occur but the linkage is not explicitly emphasized. We recruited a large group of at-risk readers from multiple schools in two sites across Canada. We report this study below, but first we outline two other aspects of the study.

Set-for-Variability

The second issue we address concerns some frequently unacknowledged challenges in using phonics to read words. In best practice synthetic phonics programs, children learn to blend speech sounds (phonemes) associated with letter(s) (graphemes)—for example, the sounds associated with *c – a – t* to read "cat" and those associated with *c – a – tch* to read "catch." It has become increasingly clear to researchers that there are a number of unacknowledged complexities in such procedures. Complexities frequently emerge from the fact that a string of phonemes, such as /k- æ -t/, produced during phonic assembly is distinct from stored words, such as "cat." The former is distinguished by linearity of phonemes, whereas in the latter each phoneme is co-articulated. In addition, children must deal with distinct speech features in phoneme strings and spoken words, such as schwas and glottal stops. The schwa (/ə/) is a mid-central, neutral vowel sound. In phonic blending, schwas occur as vowel attachments that unavoidably exist in articulated phoneme strings (e.g., /k/-/æ/ -/t/ is pronounced more like /kə - æ - tə/). Glottal stops produce truncations of phonemes in spoken words and can affect stress patterns (e.g., in *kitten* and *umpteen* in many dialects of English). Finally, any given phoneme is subtly influenced by the phonological context in which it occurs (Kearns, Rogers, Koriakin, & Al Ghanem, 2016) and is not universal. Consider, for example, variants of /t/ in *cat* and *stop*.

According to theorizing based on such analyses, it is possible to break phonemic decoding skill into component subskills. Tunmer and Chapman (2012) outlined a two-step model of word decoding that posits the existence of a second step in decoding—the linking of a spelling pronunciation to a word representation undertaken after children have created phoneme strings. This second step requires children to have a flexible mental set-for-variability (SfV) to match pronunciations derived from GPCs to entries in the mental lexicon (Elbro, de Jong, Houter, & Nielsen, 2012; Tunmer & Chapman, 2012).

Like the work on Direct Mapping, these ideas are also not wholly new. Gibson (1965) termed this flexibility "set for diversity." Later, Venezky (1999) referred to the need for additional processing to navigate spelling–sound inconsistencies as "set for variability." Both Gibson's and Venezky's accounts explicitly link SfV with the resolution of variable pronunciations of common vowels in English. In this sense, SfV has also been incorporated into some established intervention programs (Lovett, Lacerenza, & Borden, 2000). Steacy, Elleman, Lovett, and Compton (2016) provided evidence that explicitly teaching children about variable vowels improved reading of experimental items with variant vowels (e.g., *chosen*) at posttest compared to a phonics control group that learned about GPCs but did not learn about processing variable vowels. Steacy and colleagues (2018), in turn, provided evidence that performance on SfV tasks predicted use of less frequent vowel pronunciations of pseudowords in typically developing children in Grades 2–5.

Other researchers have construed SfV as a strategy for correcting the pronunciations of erroneously regularized exception words (e.g., *stomach*; see Dyson, Best, Solity, & Hulme, 2017). Consistent with this view, Dyson and colleagues (2017) conducted a brief experimental intervention with typically developing readers and reported that training in self-correction of exception words, a process they term "mispronunciation correction," tied with instruction in word meanings, facilitated transfer to children's self-correction of untaught experimental exception words. Dyson and colleagues interpreted these results as reflecting the combined influence of orthographic, phonological, and semantic processes within a triangle model of reading development (Plaut, McClelland, Seidenberg, & Patterson, 1996).

A third view of SfV construes it to be a process that applies to all words (Elbro & de Jong, 2017; Elbro et al., 2012; Kearns et al., 2016). This broader conception of SfV is consistent with the previous overview that all pronunciations derived from the application of spelling rules are distinct from conventional word pronunciations. Consistent with this broader view of SfV, correlational and longitudinal studies suggested that synthetic phonic blending skills and SfV explain unique variance in both regular and exception word reading (Elbro et al., 2012; Tunmer & Chapman, 2012).

In sum, a number of theoretical models incorporate SfV. Evidence from short-term interventions and longitudinal and correlational studies suggested that SfV affects literacy. The literature could thus benefit from a sustained intervention to show that the teaching of SfV along with foundational phonics affects word reading at immediate and delayed posttests among poor readers. From a purely practical perspective, SfV may hold value in improving the literacy of children who are at risk of reading difficulties.

Cross-Linguistic Transfer

A further aim of Study 1 was to explore cross-linguistic transfer. Part of the present study was undertaken in Quebec, Canada, where many children from English language backgrounds receive a significant amount of instruction in French (French immersion). This context is thus a fertile one for testing theories of cross-linguistic transfer. Much research shows a close association between word-reading ability in children's first and second languages (Chung, Chen, & Geva, 2018). Most models of biliteracy development are based on such correlations, and even the most contemporary accounts interpret this pattern as transfer (see, e.g., the Interactive Framework by Chung et al., 2018). Interventions in dual language contexts provide opportunities to test stronger and potentially causal claims about the influence of one language on the progress shown in another (Wawire & Kim, 2018). To date, however, no studies have unambiguously demonstrated that growth in word reading as a result of intervention in one language is then reflected in growth in word reading in an additional language (Côté, Savage, & Petscher, 2019). Thus, we explore this issue here.

The intervention study we undertook (see Savage, Georgiou, Parrila, & Maiorino, 2018, for comprehensive details) involved two sites in Canada (Quebec and Alberta). We followed a group of Grade 1 children from a first pretest (September), to a second pretest (December), to posttest (May), and to a delayed posttest administered in the fall of Grade 2. We initially recruited 497 children from 42 classrooms nested within 21 schools in five school boards in our two sites. All schools taught the curriculum through French immersion. We randomly allocated schools to Direct Mapping and SfV intervention (DMSfV) and to Current or Best Practices for Word Study (CBP) conditions.

In December of Grade 1, we undertook universal screening with standard measures of word reading and pseudoword decoding. We judged all children who performed below the 30th percentile on the Wide Range Achievement Test–Fourth Edition (WRAT) Word-Reading measure (Wilkinson & Robertson, 2006) at pretest (December of Grade 1) to be at risk of low literacy and placed them in the intervention group at their school; we identified 201 at-risk participants (119 in the DMSfV schools and 82 in the CBP schools). We then ran small-group interventions in the winter semester. Interventions typically consisted of groups of three to four children outside of the classroom for 30 minutes, three times per week. Children received an average of 11–12 hours of small-group intervention overall in each of the two conditions over 10 school weeks, delivered by well-trained research assistants.

In the DMSfV program, children received intense systematic focus on GPCs and variable vowel pronunciations within a synthetic phonics model that systematically taught them to blend these phonemes to pronounce words. Each lesson provided very close linkage between the taught GPCs and real books containing a high density of exemplars of what was taught on that day. For example, when children learned the *ou* – /ou/ GPC as pronounced in the word *mouse*, they then read a text that contained many words with that GPC. Once children were competent decoders of taught GPCs, they learned SfV to help them map phoneme strings to their pronunciations of stored words. We sometimes modeled SfV by asking children to play Simon Says (e.g., "Simon says . . . touch your /ar/ – /m/ or /k/ – /n/ – /ee/"). At other times, we used games with numbers or animals as familiar semantic categories. We significantly differentiated this curriculum to the needs of children, and we delivered it with a sense of fun and playfulness.

Children in the CBP program also received intense systematic training on blending within a synthetic phonics model. They also received daily instruction on common sight word pronunciations and shared book reading, but they received no close linkage between GPCs and shared reading of real books and no teaching of SfV. All other aspects of intervention delivery, such as differentiation and a sense of playfulness, were comparable to the DMSfV intervention. The close comparability of CBP intervention allows an evaluation of the unique features of DMSfV.

Preliminary analyses confirmed that there were no effects of potentially confounding variables of age, mother's education, home language, parent-reported language or literacy difficulties, or pretest attainment differences across the two intervention conditions. Observation of regular teaching practices suggested students were well matched on this. Together, this matching of intervention and control groups on wider extraneous variables suggests our results cannot be due to any of these wider factors. Our main focus was on the impact of different teaching conditions. The results showed that there were statistically significant advantages at posttest for the DMSfV program over CBP on measures of word reading and spelling. Advantages favoring the DMSfV group remained on word reading and sentence comprehension at delayed posttest at the beginning of Grade 2, 5 months after the intervention had finished. An additional question concerned the possible transfer of patterns after intervention from English to French in one site (Quebec). Results showed that children in the DMSfV condition, but not in the CBP condition, showed significant improvement in French pseudoword, regular word, and exception word-reading measures at posttest, even though the reading intervention was conducted solely in English. This result suggests that growth in reading in English may cause growth in French reading and that the SfV intervention facilitates this cross-linguistic causal transfer.

Our intervention and outcome measures in English involved regular and exception words. Given the robust effects, our preferred interpretation of these results is that SfV is a universal feature of the processing of all words in attempts to link spelling pronunciations to conventional pronunciations while learning to read (Elbro & de Jong, 2017). The French data described also fit this view of the role of SfV in reading. However, more nuanced data is needed to definitively pinpoint the role of SfV. Finally, it is important to note that these children remained relatively weak readers on sentence comprehension measures after interventions. While effective, DMSfV was no "inoculation" for these children's reading comprehension difficulties.

STUDY 2: THE SIMPLICITY PRINCIPLE IN GRADE 2

As noted previously, we know with some confidence that phonics instruction is effective in the early years (*Eunice Kennedy Shriver* National Institute of Child Health and Human Development, 2000). There has, however, been relatively little focus on the content of phonics programs to inform understanding of the optimal GPCs taught and, more broadly, on the principles that might drive generative approaches to intervention that potentially lead to more typical development (Compton, Miller, Elleman, & Steacy, 2014). Study 2 thus asked, "What is the optimal type and number of GPCs that should be explicitly taught to below–grade-level readers in Grade 2?"

A modest number of studies have sought to understand the nature and number of GPCs that should be taught to young children. Vousden and colleagues (2011) developed a database comprising all words found in 685 popular contemporary children's books read by children age 5–7 years in the United Kingdom. They extracted all of the GPCs within these words from texts and coded them by frequency of occurrence. Vousden and colleagues used this frequency-coded GPC list to model the percentage of all words in children's texts they rendered readable. This modeling suggested that teaching children the 60–70 most commonly occurring GPCs in children's books would allow them to read progressively larger numbers of words, but teaching additional GPCs after this, however, would show diminishing returns. This optimality of type and number of GPC units leading to greatest generalization in reading words in children's books is known as the Simplicity Principle for reading.

Beyond this pure computational modeling approach, Chen and Savage (2014) explored the effects of teaching the most frequently occurring complex GPCs derived from Vousden and colleagues (2011) on reading and reading motivation of at-risk readers. The sample included 38 Grade 1 and two children from two classes in one school. The children scored more than 2 standard deviations below average on a standardized reading test and were thus an at-risk group. In the simplicity program, children were taught complex GPCs (vowel digraphs and common units such as *a_e*, *pp*, *tch*, *igh*, and *ed*) ordered by their frequency of occurrence in children's texts. Children read texts that richly embodied the GPCs taught in that session as Direct Mapping. In a vocabulary control program, children learned about target word spellings and meanings, but their attention was not drawn to GPCs in words. After 30 supplemental small-group 20-minute sessions over 9 weeks, the simplicity group performed significantly better than the vocabulary group on measures of spelling, word recognition, and reading motivation.

Although encouraging, the findings of Chen and Savage (2014) are limited by the modest and potentially unrepresentative sample. Furthermore, given strong evidence that decoding is based on the dual foundation of phoneme awareness and GPC knowledge (*Eunice Kennedy Shriver* National Institute of Child Health and Human Development, 2000), it could be further predicted that teaching Simplicity Principle–derived GPCs will be most effective for children with average and above-average phonological awareness skills. In Study 2 (Savage, Georgiou, Parrila, Maiorino, Dunn, & Burgos, 2019), we replicated the study by Chen and Savage at a larger scale across multiple school sites in two distinct locations in Canada (Quebec and Alberta). We assessed phonological awareness with a widely used standardized measure (discussed next), and we explored the moderating effects of phonological awareness on students' response to intervention. We hypothesized that participants learning Simplicity Principle–derived GPCs would improve more on reading and spelling than the participants in a control group exposed to exactly the same letters and words but not taught the GPCs, and that the improvements would be strongest among children with average to above-average phonological awareness ability.

The design of the study was similar to that of Study 1. Sampling resulted in the initial recruitment of 510 children from 44 classrooms

nested within 21 schools in five school boards. Universal screening identified 149 at-risk participants (79 in the simplicity group and 70 in the
vocabulary intervention). In Study 2, we judged all children performing
below the 40th percentile on the WRAT Word Reading measure at pretest
(December/January of Grade 2) to be at risk. The 40th percentile has routinely been used to measure reading at grade level in the United States
and in response to intervention initiatives and in using related tools, such
as DIBELS (Mellard & Johnson, 2008). We wanted to work with all at-risk
children in Study 2 because we anticipated that the simplicity intervention
might help them. We did not categorize children on the basis of phonological awareness but instead treated performance on the Blending Words task
from the Comprehensive Test of Phonological Processing–Second Edition
(CTOPP–2; Wagner, Torgesen, Rashotte, & Pearson, 2013) as a continuous
moderator variable in predicted interactions with the effect of intervention.
Children received an average of 12–15 hours of small-group intervention
in each of the two conditions over 12 school weeks.

      We used Canadian data to construct a database of complex GPCs. We
obtained electronic records of the most frequently issued children's books
from the Toronto District Metropolitan Library system, a database of is-
suing patterns of some 100 libraries in the Toronto area. Using this database, we obtained 363 of 500 books and entered all main text into a word
database. This database contained 8,636 word types and 179,678 word to-
kens. Dr. Jonathon Solity's team in the United Kingdom used this database
to create a Canadian-text–based, Simplicity Principle–derived GPC list. We
used isolated GPCs with two exceptions: we kept *qu* on frequency of co-
occurrence, and we retained *-ing* because this unit also appears frequently
as the gerund form.

      Teaching in the simplicity condition involved 1) introduction, defini-
tion, and spelling of a new word of the day; 2) searching for that word
in authentic children's books selected to densely represent these words;
3) shared reading of researcher-written texts wherein children and the
RA co-read the text, with children reading the word of the day; and
4) introduction of the sound of the day—a GPC within the word of the day,
explicitly articulated by the RA. Children said and wrote the grapheme,
then identified this grapheme in texts that were typically researcher written, embodying a high density of the taught GPCs. Children also wrote
a sentence using the grapheme in their notebook, with emphasis on the
sound of this GPC.

      For weaker readers, if the GPC of the day was *sh* – /sh/, we asked the
child to read the target word *she* (i.e., we only asked weaker students to
read the sound of the day or words with that GPC). We asked stronger students to read more complex words with the taught GPC, such as *seashell*,
and encouraged them to read whole sentences or pages of the book or
short story. We also encouraged the stronger students to write more complex sentences (sometimes with two words containing the GPC) compared

to a single word for weaker readers. The control intervention program essentially mirrored the simplicity intervention in all respects, with the exception that rather than being introduced to the sound of the day children were introduced to the special spelling of the day and the RA did not call specific attention to the sound that the grapheme made; children simply identified it by sight and wrote it down.

As in Study 1, students were matched on a full range of relevant extraneous variables. The main results showed a significant intervention by phonological awareness interaction effect for measures of word and pseudoword reading at posttest. In each case, improvements were greater for the simplicity over the vocabulary condition at posttest, but only for the children with higher phonological awareness ability. Other effects did not reach significance. Improvements were evident for the simplicity over the vocabulary condition for children with higher phonological ability immediately at posttest compared to December pretest.

Overall, these results replicate and extend those of Chen and Savage (2014). Our results show for the first time that phoneme awareness moderates the impact of teaching using the Simplicity Principle. This study suggests that teaching one of the components of phonics is useful in Grade 2, albeit with complex GPCs, and for children with stronger phonological blending skill. Our approach has been described as one of optimizing the learner's statistical learning environment and thereby increasing the chance of item-level learning (Steacy, Elleman, & Compton, 2017). GPCs were taught daily in conjunction with the reading and spelling of words and with shared passage reading where taught GPCs were frequently represented—a Direct Mapping approach. Together, such approaches might also be generative of the rich orthographic knowledge beyond specific GPCs and may lead to more typical development (Compton et al., 2014; Steacy et al., 2018).

The simplicity intervention in Grade 2, like DMSfV in Grade 1, was no magic bullet. Many children did not improve in word reading and spelling ability in Study 2. Stanine scores on the sentence comprehension task remained well below average at posttest for nearly all children, even in the simplicity intervention. We need to develop improved Simplicity Principle–inspired interventions for those with poor phonological awareness abilities and distinct interventions to support text comprehension.

CONCLUSION

We have reported the results of two theory-driven interventions. The results show some promise in developing and improving intervention practice in schools and have potential implications for policy. There is, however, much scientific research still to do before we can undertake such work with confidence. A first step must be the replication of these findings. As a number of speakers at The Dyslexia Foundation conference (held in June 2018) noted, further experimental work to establish the precise nature of SfV is needed. At this meeting, Kate Nation noted that if children are taking advantage of SfV, then they are more likely to read pseudowords as real words in this condition, a claim that can be tested empirically in future studies. Study 2 was the first large-scale study to show effects of using a Simplicity Principle to derive optimal intervention content in terms of both type and progression of complex GPCs delivered. Results suggested that using a computational approach to selecting optimal GPC content based on authentic children's books can be efficacious in improving reading, though effects of a Simplicity Principle–based intervention are moderated by phonological awareness skills. Future programmatic intervention work should explore whether combining phonological awareness training with Simplicity Principle–derived GPC progression aids children with low phonological awareness or whether these children benefit more from interventions focusing on larger structural units, such as morphemes.

REFERENCES

Chen, V., & Savage, R. S. (2014). Evidence for a Simplicity Principle: Teaching common complex grapheme-phonemes improves reading and motivation in at-risk readers. *Journal of Research in Reading, 37,* 196–214. http://dx.doi.org/10.1111/1467-9817.12022.

Chung, S. C., Chen, X., & Geva, E. (2018). Deconstructing and reconstructing cross-language transfer in bilingual reading development: An interactive framework. *Journal of Neurolinguistics.* http://dx.doi.org/10.1016/j.neuoling.2018.01.003

Compton, D. L., Miller, A. C., Elleman, A. M., & Steacy, L. M. (2014). Have we forsaken reading theory in the name of "quick fix" interventions for children with reading disability? *Scientific Studies of Reading, 18,* 55–73. http://dx.doi.org/10.1080/10888438.2013.836200

Côté, M.-F., Savage, R. S., & Petscher, Y. (2019, *revised and resubmitted*). Cross-linguistic transfer of literacy skills between English and French among Grade 1 elementary school students attending French immersion programs.

Dyson, H., Best, W., Solity, J., & Hulme, C. (2017). Training mispronunciation correction and word meanings improves children's ability to learn to read words. *Scientific Studies of Reading, 21,* 392–407. http://dx.doi.org/10.1080/10888438.2017.1315424

Elbro, C., & de Jong, P. F. (2017). Orthographic learning is verbal learning. The role of spelling pronunciations. In K. Cain, D. Compton, & R. Parrila (Eds.), *Theories of reading development* (pp. 169–190). Amsterdam, The Netherlands: John Benjamins.

Elbro, C., de Jong, P., Houter, D., & Nielsen, A.-M. (2012). From spelling pronunciation to lexical access: A second step in word decoding. *Scientific Studies of Reading, 16,* 341–359. http://dx.doi.org/10.1080/10888438.2013.8119356

Eunice Kennedy Shriver National Institute of Child Health and Human Development, National Institutes of Health, Department of Health and Human Services. (2000). *Report of the National Reading Panel: Teaching children to read: Reports of the subgroups* (00-4754). Washington, DC: U.S. Government Printing Office. Retrieved from https://www1.nichd.nih.gov/publications/pubs/nrp/Pages/report.aspx

Foorman, B. R., Francis, D. J., Davidson, K. C., Harm, M. W., & Griffin, J. (2004). Variability in text features in six Grade 1 basal reading programs. *Scientific Studies of Reading, 8,* 167–197.

Gibson, E. J. (1965). Learning to read: Experimental psychologists examine the process by which a fundamental intellectual skill is acquired. *Science, 148,* 1066–1072. http://dx.doi.org/10.1126/science.148.3673.1066

Hatcher, P. J., Hulme, C., & Ellis, A. W. (1994). Ameliorating early reading failure by integrating the teaching of reading and phonological skills: The phonological linkage hypothesis. *Child Development, 65,* 41–57.

Kearns, D., Rogers, H. J., Koriakin, T., & Al Ghanem, R. (2016). Semantic and phonological ability to adjust decoding: A unique correlate of word reading skill? *Scientific Studies of Reading, 20*, 455–470. http://dx.doi.org/10.1080/10888438.2016.1217865

Lovett, M. W., Lacerenza, L., & Borden, S. L. (2000). Putting struggling readers on the PHAST track: A program to integrate phonological and strategy-based remedial reading instruction and maximise outcomes. *Journal of Learning Disabilities, 33*, 458–467.

McArthur, G., Castles, A., Kohnen, S., Larsen, L., Jones, K., Anandakumar, T., & Banales, E. (2012). *Phonics training for English-speaking poor readers.* The Cochrane Library. http://dx.doi.org/10.1002/14651858.CD009115.pub2

Mellard, D. F., & Johnson, E. (2008). *RTI: A practitioner's guide to implementing response to intervention.* Thousand Oaks, CA: Corwin Press.

Plaut, D. C., McClelland, J. L., Seidenberg, M. S., & Patterson, K. (1996). Understanding normal and impaired word reading; Computational principles in quasi-regular domains. *Psychological Review, 103*, 56–115. http://dx.doi.org/10.1037/0033-295X.103.1.56

Savage, R. S., Georgiou, G., Parrila, R., & Maiorino, K. (2018). Preventative reading interventions teaching direct mapping of graphemes in texts and set-for-variability aid at-risk learners. *Scientific Studies of Reading, 22*(3), 225–247. http://dx.doi.org/10.1080/10888438.2018.1427753

Savage, R. S., Georgiou, G., Parrila, R., Maiorino, K., Dunn, K., & Burgos, G. (2019). The effects of teaching complex grapheme-phoneme correspondences: Evidence from a dual site cluster trial with at-risk grade 2 students. *Scientific Studies of Reading* (revised and resubmitted).

Shapiro, L. R., & Solity, J. (2008). Delivering phonological and phonics training within whole-class teaching. *British Journal of Educational Psychology, 78*, 597–620. http://dx.doi.org/1.348/00070998x293850.

Steacy, L. M., Compton, D. L., Petscher, Y., Elliott, J. D., Elleman, A. M., Smith, K., & Rueckl, J. G. (2018). Development and prediction of context-sensitive vowel pronunciation in elementary readers. *Scientific Studies of Reading.* http://dx.doi.org/0.1080/108884 38.2018.1466303

Steacy, L. M., Elleman, A. M., & Compton, D. (2017). Opening the "black box" of learning to read: Inductive mechanisms supporting word acquisition development with a focus on children who struggle to read. In K. Cain, D. Compton, & R. Parrila (Eds.), *Theories of reading development* (pp. 99–124). Amsterdam, The Netherlands: John Benjamins.

Steacy, L. M., Elleman, A. M., Lovett, M. W., & Compton, D. L. (2016). Exploring differential effects across two decoding treatments on item-level transfer in children with significant word reading difficulties: A new approach for testing intervention elements. *Scientific Studies of Reading, 20*, 283–295. http://doi:10.1080/10888438.2016.1178267

Tunmer, W. E., & Chapman, J. W. (2012). Does set for variability mediate the influence of vocabulary knowledge on the development of word recognition skills? *Scientific Studies of Reading, 16*, 122–140. http://dx.doi.org/10.1080/10888438.2010.542527

Venezky, R. L. (1999). *The American way of spelling: The structure and origins of American English orthography.* New York, NY: Guilford Press.

Vousden, J. I., Ellefson, M. R., Solity, J., & Chater, N. (2011). Simplifying reading: Applying the Simplicity Principle to reading. *Cognitive Science, 35*, 34–78. http://dx.doi.org/10.1111/j.1551-6709.2010.01134.x

Wagner, R. K., Torgesen, J. K., Rashotte, C. A., & Pearson, N. A. (2013). *Comprehensive Test of Phonological Processing–Second Edition* (CTOPP-2). Austin, TX: PRO-ED.

Wawire, B. A., & Kim, Y.-S. (2018). Cross-language transfer of phonological awareness and letter knowledge: Causal evidence and nature of transfer. *Scientific Studies of Reading.* http://dx.doi.org/10.1080/10888438.2018.1474882

Wilkinson, G. S., & Robertson, G. J. (2006). *Wide Range Achievement Test–Fourth Edition.* Lutz, FL: Psychological Assessment Resources.

CHAPTER 14

Dyslexia, Reading Fluency, and Intervention

Ludo Verhoeven and Eliane Segers

SUMMARY

Neurocognitive research has identified major dysfunctions in the reading network. However, it is still unclear how these dysfunctions affect reading fluency development. Significant progress has been made with treatment of dyslexia, but the effects mainly address reading accuracy, not fluency. Learning to read in a transparent orthography such as Dutch is relatively easy for most children. Dutch children have been found to be highly accurate in their decoding from first grade on, and the further development of this skill is largely a matter of increasing speed (i.e., automatization of word decoding). The basic task confronting children in becoming fluent readers of Dutch is thus to progress from slow, sequential, grapheme-to-phoneme word decoding to fast, parallel, phonology-based orthographic word decoding. For children with dyslexia, accurate decoding turns out to be quite a challenge, particularly for longer or unfamiliar Dutch words. Even more problems present themselves when the reading process must be speeded up, as attested by the incremental backlogs that manifest themselves in the decoding efficiency of children with developmental dyslexia throughout the elementary school years. An important question is how reading fluency can be enhanced. This chapter focuses on the development and remediation of reading fluency in Dutch children. Reading problems in a transparent orthography such as Dutch are primarily a matter of speed, and early computer-supported intervention may help children with dyslexia to speed up their reading.

INTRODUCTION

Reading fluency is the hallmark of successful reading acquisition and has become a crucial marker of academic achievement (Verhoeven & Perfetti, 2017). Dyslexia can be considered a neurobiologically grounded developmental reading disorder characterized by severe dysfluency of reading. Neurocognitive research has identified major dysfunctions in the reading network. However, it is still unclear how these dysfunctions affect reading fluency development. Significant progress has been made with treatment of dyslexia, but the effects mainly address reading accuracy, not fluency. A major problem is that most of the relevant research is based on results for children learning to read in English, which has an opaque orthography and is one of the hardest orthographies to alphabetize (Share, 2008). An urgent need thus exists for research on learning to read in a language with a more transparent orthography than English. Only then can researchers better understand the exact nature of the phonological deficit underlying developmental dyslexia. Therefore, this chapter aims to uncover the foundation of a reading fluency deficit and identify success factors in reading fluency intervention in Dutch as a transparent orthography.

Prior to literacy, children acquire knowledge of the sound structure of spoken words as part of spoken-word recognition, and this information subsequently provides a foundation for the development of orthographic coding (Pugh & Verhoeven, 2018; Verhoeven, van Leeuwe, & Vermeer, 2011). Phonological awareness, serial rapid picture naming, and phonological working memory have thus been found to be important precursors to the emergence of the ability to phonologically recode orthographic representations (Goswami, 2000; Verhoeven, van Leeuwe, Irausquin, & Segers, 2016). According to Share (2004), phonological recoding gives children a self-teaching device for the incremental building of the orthographic representations associated with specific words. For successful phonological recoding, children must discover the shared units within the orthography and phonology of their language and, to do this, develop sublexical strategies to handle different sizes of information, ranging, for example, from graphemes, rimes, and syllables to morphemes (see Duncan & Seymour, 2003; Verhoeven & Perfetti, 2003). Once children can successfully recode an entire written word, they can form orthographic representations and directly address them in subsequent word reading.

Several studies have shown that a few exposures to a word are often sufficient for the detection and storage of word-specific orthographic information (e.g., Ziegler, Perry, & Zorzi, 2014). With additional exposure, this information will then provide an alternative lexical/orthographic source of knowledge for future word reading (Stanovich, 2000). Neurocognitive research has indeed evidenced that words can be read via two neural pathways working in close collaboration with each other (see Das, Padakannaya, Pugh, & Singh, 2011).

When it comes to reading problems and developmental dyslexia, the so-called phonological deficit hypothesis (Pugh et al., 2013; Ramus, 2004; Snowling, 2000) provides a broad theoretical framework. Considering the deficit from a dual-route perspective, the deficit can be hypothesized to arise in the *sublexical* processes associated with phonological recoding or the *lexical* processes associated with addressing orthographic representations stored in memory (Ziegler et al., 2008). Problems with the sublexical route are indicated by inaccurate word reading whereas problems with the lexical route are indicated by accurate but slow word reading (Castles, 2006). In general, the decoding performance of children with dyslexia is much more sensitive to word length than that of other children. Research has shown this length effect to hold mainly for accuracy of word reading of beginning readers and for efficiency of word reading as reading experience increases (Juphard, Carbonnel, & Valdois, 2004).

READING FLUENCY IN DUTCH CHILDREN WITH DYSLEXIA

Learning to read in a transparent orthography such as Dutch is relatively easy for most children. Dutch children have been found to be highly accurate in their decoding from first grade on, and the further development of this skill is largely a matter of increasing speed (i.e., automatization of word decoding). The basic task confronting children in becoming fluent readers of Dutch is thus to progress from slow, sequential, grapheme-to-phoneme word decoding to fast, parallel, phonology-based orthographic word decoding. For children with dyslexia, accurate decoding turns out to be quite a challenge, particularly when it comes to longer or unfamiliar Dutch words. Even more problems present themselves when the reading process must be speeded up, as attested by the incremental arrears that manifest themselves in the decoding efficiency of children with developmental dyslexia throughout the elementary school years (see Verhoeven & Keuning, 2018).

The basic task for children learning to read Dutch is thus to progress from the sequential grapheme-to-phoneme decoding of words to the automatic activation of the phonological pronunciation based on orthography (see Verhoeven & van Leeuwe, 2009). Initial reading instruction in the Netherlands already involves a large amount of phonics instruction with a focus on the decoding of regular consonant-vowel-consonant (CVC) word patterns. In a period of about 4 months, children learn all of the regular grapheme–phoneme correspondences within the contexts of words and small bits of text. In the subsequent months, the instruction is extended to include the reading of monosyllabic words with consonant clusters and bisyllabic words. By the end of first grade, Dutch children are expected to be able to decode simple and regularly written Dutch words. In second grade, the length of the words is increased, and irregularities or specific context-sensitive conversion rules for sounds to letters and letters to sounds are introduced. In subsequent years, the automatization of word decoding is further enhanced via a variety of book-reading routines.

To uncover the development of reading fluency in a transparent orthography, we elaborated on a study on the acquisition of word decoding in Dutch (Verhoeven & Keuning, 2018). In this study, we assessed the decoding abilities of 2,760 typically developing children as well as 397 peers with dyslexia for four types of words that varied in a principled manner with regard to orthographic transparency (see Nunn, 1998): 1) regular CVC words (e.g., *boek*, "book," *haar*, "hair"), 2) complex monosyllabic words with consonant clusters in prevocalic positions (e.g., *kleur*, "color") and postvocalic positions (e.g., *last*, "load"), 3) bisyllabic words, and 4) polysyllabic words with various orthographic inconsistencies and complexities. For each of these word classes, we administered a word-reading efficiency measure that took both accuracy and speed into account on two occasions in every grade. We developed a card containing 150 word patterns printed in rows for each type of word. To ensure the words would be meaningful for the

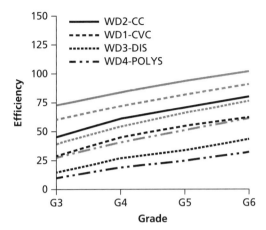

Figure 14.1. Performances on word decoding (WD) efficiency for children without dyslexia (gray) versus children with dyslexia (black) according to elementary grade. (*Key:* CC, consonant cluster; CVC, consonant-vowel-consonant; DIS, disyllabic word; POLYS, polysyllabic word.)

children, we selected only frequently used content words for these tests. For each card, we asked the child to read the words as accurately and rapidly as possible. There was a time limit of 1 minute for each list to be read aloud. For each child, we registered the total number of words read aloud and the number of errors for the four cards. Next, we calculated the number of words correctly read aloud per minute on each card as a general index of word decoding abilities for each of the four word types.

Figure 14.1 presents the development of the means for the four tests as a function of grade level (Grades 3–6). Analysis of variance with repeated measures showed significant effects for grade level, for test, and for the interaction between grade level and test. It is clear that the growth of word decoding is rapid during the first 30 months of instruction and tapers off thereafter. Although the interaction between moment of measurement and test proved significant, showing a greater divergence of scores with progression of time, the patterns of development for the different tests over time were quite similar.

READING FLUENCY AS A FUNCTION OF REPEATED EXPOSURE

An important question is how reading fluency emerges as a result of repeated exposure to words. We investigated the neural underpinnings of word decoding as a function of repeated exposure (Takashima et al., 2014). We trained Dutch participants repeatedly over the course of a month to articulate a set of novel disyllabic input strings written in Greek script to avoid the use of familiar orthographic representations. The syllables in the input were phonotactically legal combinations but nonexistent in the Dutch language, allowing us to assess their role in novel word decoding.

We tested not only trained disyllabic pseudowords but also pseudowords with recombined patterns of syllables to uncover the emergence of syllabic representations. We showed that with extensive training, articulation became faster and more accurate for the trained pseudowords. On the neural level, the initial stage of decoding was reflected by increased activity in visual attention areas of occipitotemporal and occipitoparietal cortices, and in motor coordination areas of the precentral gyrus and the inferior frontal gyrus. After 1 month of training, memory representations for holistic information (whole word unit) were established in areas encompassing the angular gyrus, the precuneus, and the middle temporal gyrus. Syllabic representations also emerged through repeated training of disyllabic pseudowords such that reading recombined syllables of the trained pseudowords showed similar brain activation to trained pseudowords and were articulated faster than novel combinations of letter strings used in the trained pseudowords.

Studies with adult readers have shown that interventions that require memory retrieval strongly improve long-term retention in comparison to continued studying. For example, once learners know the translation of a word, *restudy practice*, during which they see the word and its translation again, is less effective than *testing practice*, during which they see only the word and retrieve the translation from memory. We investigated the neurocognitive mechanisms underlying the benefits of retrieval in word learning, the so-called *testing effect* (van den Broek, Takashima, Segers, Fernandez, & Verhoeven, 2013). Twenty-six young adults without prior knowledge of Swahili learned the translation of 100 Swahili words and then further practiced the words in a functional magnetic resonance imaging (fMRI) scanner by restudying or by testing. Recall of the translations on a final memory test after 1 week was significantly better and faster for tested words than for restudied words. Brain regions that were more active during testing than during restudying included the left inferior frontal gyrus, ventral striatum, and midbrain areas. Increased activity in the left inferior parietal and left middle temporal areas during testing, but not during restudying, predicted better recall on the final memory test. Together, results suggested that testing may be more beneficial than restudying due to processes related to targeted semantic elaboration and selective strengthening of associations between retrieval cues and relevant responses, and it may involve increased effortful cognitive control and modulations of memory through striatal motivation and reward circuits.

READING FLUENCY INTERVENTION

A training study by Van Gorp, Segers, and Verhoeven (2014) examined the direct, retention, and transfer effects of a repeated reading intervention study of single CVC (consonant in the onset and a vowel and consonant in the rime) words in kindergarten students with partial letter knowledge. A total of 26 second-year kindergarten students participated in this study. Participants were divided over two feedback conditions: one group received feedback on the whole word, and the other group received feedback on the segmented sounds of the word plus the whole word. The intervention lasted 10 sessions, each of which consisted of reading the same 25 CVC words and 25 CVC pseudowords. Prior to and after the intervention, researchers administered a transfer task containing 50 other CVC words and pseudowords. Two weeks after training, they tested retention of the trained items. Results showed an increase in reading speed and accuracy after the 10 sessions, with no differences between the two feedback conditions. Also, researchers found strong transfer and retention effects. The results of this study indicated that a repeated reading intervention in kindergarten, in which prereaders are brought into a full alphabetic stage, is an effective method to improve reading speed and reading accuracy on trained and untrained words.

Van Gorp, Segers, and Verhoeven (2017b) investigated the effect of word repetition in Dutch first-grade students. They studied the direct, retention, and transfer effects of repeated word and pseudoword reading in a pretest, training, posttest, retention design. First-grade students (48 good readers, 47 poor readers) read 25 CVC words and 25 CVC pseudowords in 10 repeated word-reading sessions, preceded and followed by a transfer task with a different set of items. Two weeks after training, researchers assessed trained items again in a retention test. Participants received 1) phonics feedback, in which each word was spelled out and repeated; 2) word feedback, in which each word was repeated; or 3) no feedback. During the training, both good and poor readers improved in accuracy and speed. The increase in speed was stronger for poor readers than for good readers. The good readers demonstrated a stronger increase for pseudowords than for words. This increase in speed was most prominent in the first four sessions.

Two weeks after training, the levels of accuracy and speed were retained. Furthermore, transfer effects on speed were found for pseudowords in both groups of readers. Good readers performed most accurately during the training when they received no feedback whereas poor readers performed most accurately during the training with the help of phonics feedback. However, feedback did not differentiate for reading speed or for effects after the training. The effects of repeated word reading were found to be stronger for poor readers than for good readers. Moreover, these effects were found to be stronger for pseudowords than for words. This indicates that repeated word reading can be seen as an important trigger for the improvement of decoding skills.

In another training study, Van Gorp, Segers, and Verhoeven (2017a) tested the use of a word identification game to enhance the word-decoding efficiency of second-grade students with poor reading skills. The game included elements to enhance engagement and supported word identification (i.e., word reading) with word repetition, corrective feedback, and semantic retrieval. After the brief 5-hour tablet intervention across a period of 5 weeks, they found significant increases for decoding efficiency. They also found transfer effects to numerous untrained items. They tested the effects of a word identification game aimed at enhancing decoding efficiency in poor readers. Following a pretest, posttest, retention design with a waiting control group, 62 Dutch second-grade students who were poor readers received a 5-hour tablet intervention across a period of 5 weeks. During the intervention, participants practiced reading words and pseudowords while doing semantic categorization and lexical decision exercises in a gaming context. Prior to, directly after, and 5 weeks following the intervention, researchers assessed word decoding efficiency using a standardized read-aloud test consisting of six lists of untrained words and pseudowords with three levels of difficulty: CVC items, consonant cluster items, and disyllabic items. They found significant increases as a result of the brief gaming intervention for decoding efficiency on all six word lists. The game, which included repetition, immediate corrective feedback, and a semantics task, elicited transfer and retention effects.

CONCLUSION

Dutch word decoding development is largely a matter of growing speed. In the course of the primary grades, children make progress in their reading fluency. Children with dyslexia show a more or less constant gap in reading fluency when compared to their typically developing peers. Furthermore, two studies showed that repetition of word reading enhances children's reading fluency. On the basis of this finding, we built a reading intervention for poor readers to enhance their reading fluency through a game based on motivation and on repeated word identification via sematic categorization. The implementation of such a game in Grade 2 can prevent reading fluency problems in children at risk for dyslexia.

REFERENCES

Castles, A. (2006). The dual route model and the developmental dyslexias. *London Review of Education, 4,* 49–61.

Das, T., Padakannaya, P., Pugh, K. R., & Singh, N. C. (2011). Neuroimaging reveals dual routes to reading in simultaneous proficient readers of two orthographies. *NeuroImage, 54,* 1476–1487.

Duncan, L. G., & Seymour, P. H. K. (2003). How do children read multisyllabic words? Some preliminary observations. Journal of Research in Reading, 26, 101–120.

Goswami, U. (2000). Phonological and lexical processes. In M. L. Kamil, P. B. Rosenthal, P. D. Pearson, & R. Barr (Eds.), *Handbook of reading research* (Vol. 3, pp. 251–268). Mahwah, NJ: Lawrence Erlbaum Associates.

Juphard, A., Carbonnel, S., & Valdois, S. (2004). Length effect in reading and lexical decision: Evidence from skilled readers and a developmental dyslexic participant. *Brain and Cognition, 55,* 332–340.

Nunn, A. (1998). *Dutch orthography.* Utrecht, The Netherlands: Center for Language Studies.

Pugh, K. R., Landi, N., Preston, J. L., Mencl, E. W., Austin, A. C., Sibley, D., . . . Frost, S. J. (2013). The relationship between phonological and auditory processing and brain organization in beginning readers. *Brain and Language, 125,* 173–183.

Pugh, K., & Verhoeven, L. (2018). Dyslexia across languages and writing systems. *Scientific Studies of Reading, 22*, 1–6.

Ramus, F. (2004). Neurobiology of dyslexia: A reinterpretation of the data. *Trends in Neurosciences, 27*, 720–726.

Share, D. L. (2004). Orthographic learning at a glance: On the time course and developmental onset of reading. *Journal of Experimental Child Psychology, 87*, 267–298.

Share, D. (2008). On the Anglocentricities of current reading research and practice: The perils of overreliance on an "outlier" orthography. *Psychological Bulletin, 134*, 584–615.

Snowling, M. J. (2000). Language and literacy skills: Who is at risk and why? In D. V. M. Bishop & L. B. Leonard (Eds.), *Speech and language impairment in children: Causes, characteristics, interventions and outcome* (pp. 245–260). Hove, United Kingdom: Psychology Press.

Stanovich, K. E. (2000). *Progress in understanding reading: Scientific foundations and new frontiers*. New York, NY: Guilford Press.

Takashima, A., Wagensveld, B., Van Turennout, M., Zwitserlood, P., Hagoort, P., & Verhoeven, L. (2014). Training-induced neural plasticity in visual-word decoding and the role of syllables. *Neuropsychologia, 61*, 299–314.

van den Broek, G. S. E., Takashima, A., Segers, P. C. J., Fernandez, G. S. E., & Verhoeven, L. T. W. (2013). Neural correlates of testing effects in vocabulary learning. *NeuroImage, 78*, 94–102.

Van Gorp, K., Segers, E., & Verhoeven, L. (2014). Repeated reading intervention effects in kindergartners with partial letter knowledge. *International Journal of Disability, Development and Education, 61*, 225–239.

Van Gorp, K., Segers, P. C. J., & Verhoeven, L. T. W. (2017a). Enhancing decoding efficiency in poor readers via a word identification game. *Reading Research Quarterly, 52*(1), 105–123.

Van Gorp, K., Segers, P. C. J., & Verhoeven, L. T. W. (2017b). The role of feedback and differences between good and poor decoders in a repeated word reading paradigm in first grade. *Annals of Dyslexia, 67*(1), 1–25.

Verhoeven, L., & Keuning, J. (2018). The nature of developmental dyslexia in a transparent orthography. *Scientific Studies of Reading, 22*, 7–23.

Verhoeven, L., & Perfetti, C.A. (2003). The role of morphology in learning to read. *Scientific Studies of Reading, 7*, 209–217.

Verhoeven, L., & Perfetti, C. (2017). *Learning to read across languages and writing systems*. Cambridge, United Kingdom: Cambridge University Press.

Verhoeven, L., & van Leeuwe, J. (2009). Modeling the growth of word decoding skills: Evidence from Dutch. *Scientific Studies of Reading, 13*, 205–223.

Verhoeven, L., van Leeuwe, J., Irausquin, R., & Segers, E. (2016). The unique role of lexical accessibility in predicting kindergarten emergent literacy. *Reading and Writing, 29*, 591–608.

Verhoeven, L., van Leeuwe, J., & Vermeer, A. (2011). Vocabulary growth and reading development across the elementary school years. *Scientific Studies of Reading, 15*, 8–25.

Ziegler, J. C., Castel, C., Pech-Georgel, C., George, F., Alario, F. X., & Perry, C. (2008) Developmental dyslexia and the dual route model of reading: Simulating individual differences and subtypes. *Cognition, 107*, 151–178.

Ziegler, J. C., Perry, C., & Zorzi, M. (2014). Modelling reading development through phonological decoding and self-teaching: Implications for dyslexia. *Philosophical Transactions of the Royal Society, B: Biological Sciences, 369*, 20120397.

On the Value of Theory-Driven Research on Dyslexia

Devin M. Kearns

The four chapters in this section, "Identification and Treatment," address how to provide instruction for students with dyslexia. There are three important themes. First, the authors all use theoretical models of the cognitive processing that happens during reading and demonstrate how theory can lead to new ideas about identification and treatment of dyslexia. Second, the researchers appear to show that educators should consider integrating instruction on words' meanings within word-reading instruction. Third, the researchers' findings all support the idea that students need more individualized instruction to make the greatest improvement in their reading. The four chapters describe ambitious, theory-driven, data-based efforts to increase the reading success of individuals with dyslexia. The four research groups clearly take seriously the finding that semantic instruction is important within a word recognition context. However, at some point, research teams should consider how to address the role of the instructor in identifying and treating dyslexia. The vast complexity of this terrain will require more complex theoretical models: Teachers differ in content and pedagogical knowledge, the ability to support positive behavior, self-efficacy, and affect—all with consequences for student learning. However, the ultimate test of the effectiveness of identification and treatment approaches is whether they work in classrooms. What is needed is continued innovation of the kind Compton, Miller, Elleman, and Steacy (2014) recommended and avoiding the unintended mistakes made in earlier intervention research. The remarkable effects and findings of these four research teams are an important testament to the possible results of dispassionate science, where the goal is to understand and treat dyslexia, not to reify researchers' own perspectives.

INTRODUCTION

Compton and colleagues wrote that they "question the effectiveness of current intervention approaches designed to ameliorate word identification and reading comprehension deficits in children with RD [reading disabilities]" (2014, p. 68). Their argument was that research on and development of reading interventions had possibly stagnated such that many "new" interventions involved repackaging similar instructional elements in different ways. They suggested that intervention developers should consider how theoretical models of reading could be used to design new interventions with a greater chance of increasing student success. The authors of the chapters in this section, Identification and Treatment, are doing the kind of work I think exemplifies the suggestion of Compton and colleagues (2014)—that is, all of them link theoretical models of reading to instructional planning and design.

INNOVATION GUIDED BY DATA FROM COGNITIVE SCIENCE

Although cognitive models of learning have not typically been well regarded within the field of special education, they have potential value for developing interventions for individuals with dyslexia, as described in the four chapters in this section.

History of Distrust of Brain-Based Instruction

The field of special education—where many (though not all) reading interventions were developed—has a long history of distrust for cognitive models of learning. Cognitive models are often linked with the "brain-based" approaches to instruction that emerged in the 1960s and 1970s to treat learning disabilities. A prominent example is the Doman-Delacato treatment of children with neurological disabilities (Doman, Spitz, Zucman, Delacato, & Doman, 1960). This intervention involved activities such as crawling, breathing into a mask to increase cerebral blood flow, swinging from ladders, doing somersaults, and hanging upside down. However unusual, Doman and colleagues argued that their treatment could reverse learning difficulties, including reading disabilities. Randomized controlled trials of the intensive treatment showed no effects on language development (Sparrow & Zigler, 1978) or reading (Robbins, 1967), leading the American Academy of Pediatrics to suggest that "the demands placed on families are so great that in some cases there may be some harm in its use" (1982, p. 811).

There are less sensational examples, but the general point is that few brain-based approaches to learning have demonstrated positive effects on student achievement (see Burns et al., 2016, and Kearns & Fuchs, 2013, for reviews of these data). As a consequence, the field of special education seems to question whether interventions based on theories of cognition represent a swing back to the bad old days. Moreover, many in the field remain behavioral (in the Skinnerian sense) in their ideas about learning and may have an epistemological opposition to cognitive models. However, the chapters illustrate the potential folly of eschewing data built on theories of cognition.

Value of Cognitive Models in These Chapters

The four chapters use data from cognitive science, and their findings represent extensions of carefully and incrementally tested cognitive models. Chapter 11, by Castles and Kohnen, is one such illustration. They describe the well-known heterogeneity in the characteristics of individuals with dyslexia and suggest that the variability may indicate impairments related to different parts of the dual-route cascaded model of reading (Coltheart, Rastle, Perry, Landgon, & Ziegler, 2001). Their explanation of surface dyslexia (in which individuals have relatively strong decoding skills and comparatively weaker sight recognition) is a good example of how they apply the dual-route model to empirical data. They note that individuals with surface dyslexia show difficulty with tasks requiring highly specified orthographic representations—separating *salmon* from **sammon*, for example. In the dual-route model, this pattern describes difficulty in the lexical route: The connections between a word's orthography and its phonological and semantic constituents are weak.

A further extension relates to the orthographic input to the system, a component that researchers have only recently started to consider. As the authors point out, most models of word recognition operate on the assumption that the reader has identified and placed in order the letters in a word, but the authors and their colleagues have started to question that assumption (e.g., Kohnen, Nickels, Castles, Friedmann, & McArthur, 2012). As they note, some researchers had already questioned this assumption in their models of word recognition (e.g., Davis & Bowers, 2006), and data on transposed letter effects had also revealed this problem (e.g., Perea & Lupker, 2003, 2004). What is exciting—and makes an important case for using cognitive models—is that the authors subjected an untested part of the model to empirical scrutiny and identified a potentially new profile of reading difficulty, letter position dyslexia, in which readers have difficulty representing letters in the correct order.

Verhoeven and Segers (see Chapter 14) also framed their work within the dual-route model and considered the processes involved in reading fluency in Dutch. The authors note that fluency develops within the lexical pathway—mostly after words have been committed to sight word memory, as in the self-teaching account (Share, 1995). The model provides some insight about the reason that difficulties may reside in the lexical route. One possibility is that readers could have problems retrieving the semantic and phonological identity of a written word—even one they already know (Ramus & Szenkovits, 2008). Imprecise lexical representations, resulting from failure to amalgamate the orthographic, phonological, and semantic forms of the word (see Ehri, 1995), likely make it difficult to retrieve the word fluently.

Verhoeven and Segers and their colleagues (van den Broek, Takashima, Segers, Fernandez, & Verhoeven, 2013) addressed the importance of retrieval by teaching Dutch participants Swahili words. One group learned via restudying—regularly reviewing the translation of the word—and the other via repeated testing without feedback. The fascinating finding was that the adults remembered the translations better after a week in a condition in which they practiced without feedback. In the dual-route context, practice without feedback may lead to more elaborated semantic representations linked to the orthography than do repeated reminders of the definition.

Their colleagues Van Gorp, Segers, and Verhoeven (2017) then applied those findings by comparing restudying and testing in a reading intervention. Children with reading difficulty improved more in accuracy via restudying, but there was no condition effect on fluency. This might illustrate the potential tradeoff between direct instruction and extensive practice. Direct instruction on word reading might improve the strength of the decoding (nonlexical) pathway in the dual-route model, but extensive practice without feedback may permit more opportunies to amalgamate the representations of individual words via the lexical pathway.

In Chapter 13, Savage and colleagues present data from an intervention that relies on a similar premise to the studies described by Verhoeven and Segers: Practice is essential to word recognition development. In one part of their study, they focused on direct mapping, the idea that students benefit most when they receive sound-spelling instruction followed immediately by practice reading texts containing many examples of the sound-spellings taught. This aligns perfectly with the model of Castles and colleagues: Repeated practice with a given sound-spelling reinforces the representation of the unit and thus improves nonlexical skills; at the same time, extensive practice decoding words provides more opportunities to consolidate representations of words acquired via decoding. Their intervention produced positive effects in children with reading difficulty, lending credence to the theory-driven approach to instructional design.

Williams, Capin, Stevens, and Vaughn (see Chapter 12) describe a series of theory-based studies of reading comprehension interventions for adolescents with reading difficulty. The simple view of reading (Hoover & Gough, 1990) grounded the focus of the reported studies on word recognition and linguistic comprehension process. Within the linguistic comprehension component, the construction integration model supported the development of the strategies designed for reading comprehension. Particularly noteworthy are the differences in the intervention designs for the studies reported. The intervention that achieved the best results—with effect sizes of 0.56 and 1.20 for reading comprehension in middle school students—was highly targeted and individualized (Vaughn et al., 2012). In terms of the simple view, the authors were able to weight the emphasis of the intervention on word recognition or linguistic comprehension precisely in response to student need—and, of course, the best effects were achieved with the most targeted intervention.

In summary, the authors of these four chapters all reported on cognitive models to implement interventions in ways that showed strong effects—or design assessment that could inform the development of interventions. These are far different from the brain-based approaches of yesteryear. Not only did the authors begin with cognitive models, but they also tested the models in studies to evaluate whether the theory would lead to better instruction and assessment. All of the authors describe the thread of their work, showing how the results of each study led to further development of their theory-driven approaches.

INTEGRATION OF SEMANTICS
IN WORD RECOGNITION INSTRUCTION

Research on intervention for children with dyslexia has long focused on the connections between orthography and phonology—for obvious reasons: The orthography is a cipher for the phonology. However, most theoretical accounts of word recognition include a semantic component, and simulation studies have indicated that the quality of the lexicon improves as connections between orthography and semantics develop (Harm & Seidenberg, 2004). There is now an emerging consensus that semantic knowledge has an important effect on word recognition (see Steacy & Compton, 2019; Taylor, Duff, Woollams, Monaghan, & Ricketts, 2015). Several correlational studies have now shown that readers' semantic knowledge affects their ability to read words—even in isolation (Kearns & Al Ghanem, 2019; Ricketts, Davies, Masterson, Stuart, & Duff, 2016; Ricketts, Nation, & Bishop, 2007). Studies of orthographic learning even support the specific claim that readers develop stronger orthographic representations for words in the phonological lexicon (e.g., Ouellette & Fraser, 2009; Wang, Nickels, Nation, & Castles, 2013).

These four chapters continue to press this point. Castles and Kohnen (see Chapter 11) explored surface dyslexia with a clear interest in understanding what might cause the problems in the lexical system. They presented data from Friedmann and Lukov (2008) showing that orthographic choice tests and picture naming tests could test the strength of the orthographic and phonological lexicon. Friedmann and Lukov showed that individuals with surface dyslexia tended to have poor performance on these tasks.

Savage and colleagues (see Chapter 13) have also investigated ways to support semantic processing in word recognition. They drew on prior data concerning the importance of set-for-variability (SfV) on word reading. This "set" refers to the ability to turn an incorrect recoding (e.g., *spy-nitch*) into a known lexical entry (e.g., *spinach*). Recent data (Elbro, de Jong, Houter, & Neilsen, 2012; Kearns, Rogers, Al Ghanem, & Koriakin, 2016; Steacy et al., 2018; Tunmer & Chapman, 2012) suggested that this is a separable construct that correlates with word-reading skill. Savage and colleagues, along with Dyson, Best, Solity, and Hulme (2017), were some of the first to use these findings to design instruction. Savage and colleagues (like Dyson et al.) have done so in the studies reported here, with evident success.

Verhoeven and Segers (see Chapter 14) reported interventions for reading fluency to increase the use of the lexical pathway (Van Gorp et al., 2017). They wanted to maintain a focus on extensive practice but also to

increase semantic representations directly. The challenge is that a semantic focus in word recognition instruction often conflicts with the emphasis on practice. Van Gorp and colleagues (2017) avoided this problem by
including very simple semantic tasks, semantic categorization and lexical decision, in a tablet-based reading intervention. The intervention also
included explicit sound-spelling instruction—extensive practice with immediate feedback. Particularly thoughtful is that the authors found a way
to focus on semantics without sacrificing the apparent benefits of extensive
practice. The results, as the reader will see, were very good.

The studies reported by Williams and colleagues (see Chapter 12) focused on reading comprehension, so the focus on semantics is obvious,
but it is noteworthy that they included semantics also in their materials
focused on word recognition. Their emphasis was on locating and using
morphemes to read individual words. The data on the importance of morphological knowledge in word recognition are strong, so this emphasis
seems especially valuable. Moreover, morphemes have the distinction of
supporting both word recognition as orthographic units and an understanding of the syntactic or semantic function of a given word—what
Levesque, Kieffer, and Deacon (2017) called morphological decoding and
morphological analysis, respectively.

In short, these four research groups are taking seriously the finding
that semantic instruction is important within a word recognition context.
In some of the studies, there are also suggestions how this might be accomplished. The challenge will always be to integrate semantics without
sacrificing practice time, and we see some suggestions of that here.

HETEROGENEITY IN DYSLEXIA AND
PERSONALIZED INSTRUCTION BASED ON DATA

The sources of difficulty vary across individuals with dyslexia. Even
though the focus on word reading provides the historical foundation for
the construct (e.g., Hinshelwood, 1900), the definition has shifted to include other concerns such as reading comprehension. Most definitions describe reading comprehension difficulty as the result of word recognition
problems, but others consider comprehension problems part of the deficit
(see Kearns & Al Ghanem [2019], Table 1, for a list of various organizations'
definitions). Even if the deficit is clearly in word recognition, Castles and
Kohnen (see Chapter 11) describe three different causes of this difficulty.
What they recommend is to match instruction to their profile revealed by
assessment.

Their general point carries across all of the chapters: Individualize
instruction. Williams and colleagues (see Chapter 12) reported on remarkable effects—over 1 *SD* for middle school students within a single
year—for the version of the intervention in which Vaughn and colleagues
(2012) most carefully tailored instruction. They used an approach similar

to data-based individualization (see Kearns, Pollack, & Whaley, 2018, for examples) to adapt their instruction in response to student performance. Their results illustrate how powerful such an intervention can be.

Savage and colleagues (see Chapter 13) and Verhoeven and Segers (see Chapter 14) both presented data showing differences in the patterns of performance for good and poor readers. Savage and colleagues investigated the instructional value of the Simplicity Principle based on the idea that teaching the most useful grapheme–phoneme correspondences (i.e., those that occur in the most words) may provide advantages over less systematic approaches and those that involve larger units that occur less frequently (e.g., body-rime units). The proposed advantage is simple: There are fewer units to remember. This idea was put forward by Vousden, Ellefson, Solity, and Chater (2011) based on a corpus analysis comparing the value of grapheme–phoneme correspondences to body-rime units. Savage and colleagues found that instruction based on the Simplicity Principle was beneficial relative to an approach focused on lexical-level word reading, but readers with better phonological awareness appeared to benefit more. It is possible that poor readers—often limited by a deficit linking letter and sound information—perform better when they have larger units to read, regardless of whether they are maximally efficient. Verhoeven and Segers showed a difference in word-reading accuracy based on whether first-grade students received feedback or not—poor readers had higher accuracy with feedback. This also suggests the importance of individual differences and instruction aligned with specific student needs.

The direct mapping component of the Savage and colleagues' intervention also speaks to the importance of personalizing instructional materials. Adaptive online interventions certainly are designed to personalize materials in this way, but educators should have tools for doing this offline, too. For example, data on the characteristics of tradebooks collected by publishers could be used to match the text and instructional content. An automated system could make recommendations to educators about tradebooks that would best support direct mapping of sound-spellings.

This idea is at the heart of the work by Castles and Kohnen (see Chapter 11). What is exciting about their work is that they have gone beyond testing their models. They have created standardized assessments and made them available to educators to allow them to better identify the type of problems students are having; the MOTIf system has great potential as a diagnostic tool, and the field is fortunate that these researchers have linked research directly to practice.

CONCLUSION: WHAT IS NEXT?

These four chapters provide excellent examples of the value of cognitive models, the importance of semantic knowledge in word recognition, and the need to provide tailored support to individuals with dyslexia.

These researchers are no doubt already thinking ahead to their next studies, and I hope they will continue to press forward in these areas. What is mostly absent from these chapters is a description of the pedagogical approach to instruction. This is certainly not a criticism of the work: These chapters just represent a different phase of the research and development process. At some point, research teams should consider how to address the role of the instructor. The vast complexity of this terrain requires much larger and more complex theoretical models. Teachers differ in content and pedagogical knowledge, self-efficacy, ability to support positive behavior, and affect—with major consequences for achievement. It is clearly important, and I think the authors understand this. The ultimate test of the effectiveness of these strategies is whether they work in classrooms.

What should happen next is continued innovation of the kind Compton and colleagues (2014) recommended and avoiding the unintended mistakes made in earlier intervention research. The remarkable effects and findings of these four research teams are an important testament to the possible results of dispassionate science, where the goal is to understand and treat dyslexia, not to reify one's own perspectives.

REFERENCES

American Academy of Pediatrics. (1982). The Doman-Delacato treatment of neurologically handicapped children. *Pediatrics, 70,* 810–812.
Burns, M. K., Petersen-Brown, S., Haegele, K., Rodriguez, M., Schmitt, B., Cooper, M., . . . VanDerHeyden, A. M. (2016). Meta-analysis of academic interventions derived from neuropsychological data. *School Psychology Quarterly, 31,* 28–42. http://dx.doi.org/10.1037/spq0000117
Coltheart, M., Rastle, K., Perry, C., Langdon, R., & Ziegler, J. (2001). DRC: A dual route cascaded model of visual word recognition and reading aloud. *Psychological Review, 108,* 204–256. http://dx.doi.org/10.1037/0033-295X.108.1.204
Compton, D. L., Miller, A. C., Elleman, A. M., & Steacy, L. M. (2014). Have we forsaken reading theory in the name of "quick fix" interventions for children with reading disability? *Scientific Studies of Reading, 18,* 55–73. http://dx.doi.org/10.1080/10888438.2013.836200
Davis, C. J., & Bowers, J. S. (2006). Contrasting five different theories of letter position coding: Evidence from orthographic similarity effects. *Journal of Experimental Psychology: Human Perception and Performance, 32,* 535–557. http://dx.doi.org/10.1037/0096-1523.32.3.535
Doman, R. J., Spitz, E. B., Zucman, E., Delacato, C. H., & Doman, G. (1960). Children with severe brain injuries. Neurological organization in terms of mobility. *JAMA, 174,* 257–262. http://dx.doi.org/10.1001/jama.1960.03030030037007
Dyson, H., Best, W., Solity, J., & Hulme, C. (2017). Training mispronunciation correction and word meanings improves children's ability to learn to read words. *Scientific Studies of Reading, 21,* 392–407. http://dx.doi.org/10.1080/10888438.2017.1315424
Ehri, L. C. (1995). Phases of development in learning to read words by sight. *Journal of Research in Reading, 18,* 116–125. http://dx.doi.org/10.1111/j.1467-9817.1995.tb00077.x
Elbro, C., de Jong, P. F., Houter, D., & Nielsen, A. M. (2012). From spelling pronunciation to lexical access: A second step in word decoding? *Scientific Studies of Reading, 16,* 341–359.
Friedmann, N., & Lukov, L. (2008). Developmental surface dyslexias. *Cortex, 44,* 1146–1160.

Harm, M. W., & Seidenberg, M. S. (2004). Computing the meanings of words in reading: Cooperative division of labor between visual and phonological processes. *Psychological Review, 111,* 662–720. http://doi.org:10.1037/0033-295X.111.3.662

Hinshelwood, J. (1900). Congenital word-blindness. *The Lancet, 155,* 1506–1508. http://dx.doi.org/10.1016/S0140-6736(01)99645-X

Hoover, W., & Gough, P. (1990). The simple view of reading. *Reading and Writing: An Interdisciplinary Journal, 2,* 127–160.

Kearns, D. M., & Al Ghanem, R. (2019, January 14). Orthographic, phonological, and semantic information in polysyllabic word reading: The effects of item-specific and general child knowledge. *Journal of Educational Psychology.* https://dx.doi.org/10.1037/edu0000316

Kearns, D. M., & Fuchs, D. (2013). Does cognitively focused instruction improve the academic performance of low-achieving students? *Exceptional Children, 79,* 263–290.

Kearns, D. M., Pollack, M. S., & Whaley, V. M. (2018). Systematic implementation of intensive intervention: A high-leverage practice for improving academic outcomes in students with disabilities. In J. McLeskey, L. Maheady, B. Billingsley, M. T. Brownell, & T. J. Lewis (Eds.), *High leverage practices for inclusive classrooms.* New York, NY: Routledge.

Kearns, D. M., Rogers, H. J., Al Ghanem, R., & Koriakin, T. (2016). Semantic and phonological ability to adjust recoding: A unique correlate of word reading skill? *Scientific Studies of Reading.* http://doi.org:10.1080/10888438.2016.1217865

Kohnen, S., Nickels, L, Castles, A., Friedmann, N., & McArthur, G. (2012). When "slime" becomes "smile": Developmental letter position dyslexia in English. *Neuropsychologia, 50,* 3681–3692.

Levesque, K. C., Kieffer, M. J., & Deacon, S. H. (2017). Morphological awareness and reading comprehension: Examining mediating factors. *Journal of Experimental Child Psychology, 160,* 1–20. http://dx.doi.org/10.1016/j.jecp.2017.02.015

Ouellette, G., & Fraser, J. R. (2009). What exactly is a yait anyway: The role of semantics in orthographic learning. *Journal of Experimental Child Psychology, 104,* 239–251. http://dx.doi.org/10.1016/j.jecp.2009.05.001

Perea, M., & Lupker, S. J. (2003). Transposed-letter confusability effects in masked form priming. In S. Kinoshita & S. J. Lupker (Eds.), *Masked priming: The state of the art* (pp. 97–120). New York, NY: Psychology Press.

Perea, M., & Lupker, S. J. (2004). Can CANISO activate CASINO? Transposed-letter similarity effects with nonadjacent letter positions. *Journal of Memory and Language, 51,* 231–46.

Ramus, F., & Szenkovits, G. (2008). What phonological deficit? *The Quarterly Journal of Experimental Psychology, 61,* 129–141. http://dx.doi.org/10.1080/17470210701508822

Ricketts, J., Davies, R., Masterson, J., Stuart, M., & Duff, F. J. (2016). Evidence for semantic involvement in regular and exception word reading in emergent readers of English. *Journal of Experimental Child Psychology, 150,* 330–345.

Ricketts, J., Nation, K., & Bishop, D. V. M. (2007). Vocabulary is important for some, but not all reading skills. *Scientific Studies of Reading, 11,* 235–257. http://dx.doi.org/10.1080/10888430701344306

Robbins, M. P. (1967). Test of the Doman-Delacato rationale with retarded readers. *JAMA, 202,* 389–393. http://dx.doi.org/10.1001/jama.1967.03130180055008

Share, D. L. (1995). Phonological recoding and self-teaching: Sine qua non of reading acquisition. *Cognition, 55,* 151–218. http://dx.doi.org/10.1016/0010-0277(94)00645-2

Sparrow, S., & Zigler, E. (1978). Evaluation of a patterning treatment for retarded children. *Pediatrics, 62,* 137–150.

Steacy, L. M., & Compton, D. L. (2019). Examining the role of imageability and regularity in word reading accuracy and learning efficiency among first and second graders at-risk for reading disabilities. *Journal of Experimental and Child Psychology, 178,* 226–250.

Steacy, L. M., Compton, D. L., Petscher, Y., Elliott, J. D., Smith, K., Rueckl, J. G., . . . Pugh, K. R. (2018). Development and prediction of context-dependent vowel pronunciation in elementary readers. *Scientific Studies of Reading, 23,* 49–63. http://dx.doi.org/10.1080/10888438.2018.1466303

Taylor, J. S. H., Duff, F. J., Woollams, A. M., Monaghan, P., & Ricketts, J. (2015). How word meaning influences word reading. *Current Directions in Psychological Science, 24,* 322–328. http://dx.doi.org/10.1177/0963721415574980

Tunmer, W. E., & Chapman, J. W. (2012). Does set for variability mediate the influence of vocabulary knowledge on the development of word recognition skills? *Scientific Studies of Reading, 16,* 122–140. http://dx.doi.org/10.1080/10888438.2010.542527

van den Broek, G. S., Takashima, A., Segers, E., Fernández, G., & Verhoeven, L. (2013). Neural correlates of testing effects in vocabulary learning. *NeuroImage, 78,* 94–102.

van Gorp, K., Segers, E., & Verhoeven, L. (2017). The role of feedback and differences between good and poor decoders in a repeated word reading paradigm in first grade. *Annals of Dyslexia, 67,* 1–25.

Vaughn, S., Wexler, J., Leroux, A., Roberts, G., Denton, C., Barth, A., & Fletcher, J. (2012). Effects of intensive reading intervention for eighth-grade students with persistently inadequate response to intervention. *Journal of Learning Disabilities, 45,* 515–525. http://dx.doi.org/10.1177/0022219411402692

Vousden, J. I., Ellefson, M. R., Solity, J., & Chater, N. (2011). Simplifying reading: Applying the simplicity principle to reading. *Cognitive Science, 35,* 34–78. http://dx.doi.org/j.15516709.2010.01134.x

Wang, H. C., Nickels, L., Nation, K., & Castles, A. (2013). Predictors of orthographic learning of regular and irregular words. *Scientific Studies of Reading, 17,* 369–384.

Research and Practice
Outreach, Scale-Up, and Policy

CHAPTER 15

Screening for Dyslexia in Low-Resource and Multilingual Contexts

Jennae Bulat, Anne M. Hayes, Eileen Dombrowski, Margaret M. Dubeck, and Carmen Strigel

SUMMARY

Effectively screening for dyslexia is a challenge in low- and middle-income countries (LMICs), in large part due to a lack of locally appropriate screening tools and trained professionals and a poor understanding of what dyslexia is. Furthermore, support for students identified with dyslexia in these contexts is largely inadequate. RTI International introduced a phased approach to dyslexia screening, which encourages education systems to meet the needs of students with dyslexia and other learning challenges—including instituting basic screenings for all students—while developing the tools, expertise, and systems needed to expand to more specific and comprehensive dyslexia evaluations. Innovations in low-cost, easily administered vision and hearing screening, and in specific screening for reading challenges, offer options for education systems as they take stock of current inclusive education practices and plan for the future.

INTRODUCTION

Of the 1 billion people with disabilities globally, 80% live in LMICs. An estimated 150 million are children (14 years of age and younger), of which 93 million are estimated to have a moderate or severe disability (World Health Organization, 2011). Most live in Africa (United Nations Educational, Scientific and Cultural Organization [UNESCO], 2005). The majority of countries across the globe (177 as of July 2018) have ratified the *United Nations Convention on the Rights of Persons with Disabilities,* which mandates that all children with disabilities have the right to a quality education to reach their full potential (United Nations, 2018). However, the best ways to achieve this goal are less clear. This is particularly true in LMICs, which tend to lack the resources and supports needed to support students with additional learning needs. It is even more challenging in multilingual contexts.

The international education field lacks rigorous, scientifically based shared knowledge about indicators of dyslexia and ways to remediate it

---

Definition of dyslexia

Dyslexia is one of the more common forms of learning disability and is caused by differences in brain structure that are usually present at birth and are often hereditary (Pullen, Lane, Ashworth, & Lovelace, 2017). It is a language-based learning disability that affects a person's ability to read, spell, decode, and comprehend text (Mercer, Mercer, & Pullen, 2011) and is found across alphabetic languages and in nonalphabetic languages, such as Chinese and Japanese (Hoeft, McCardle, & Pugh, 2015).

---

in local languages in low-income countries. Research suggests, for example, that problems associated with phonological deficits, visual memory, short-term verbal memory, and syntax manifest in dyslexia across different types of languages (Landerl et al., 2018; Vellutino, Fletcher, Snowling, & Scanlon, 2004) but do so depending on the nature of the language (e.g., orthographically transparent vs. opaque languages, alphabetic vs. nonalphabetic systems; Frost, 2012; Rueckl et al., 2015; Ziegler & Goswami, 2005). However, very few studies exist on dyslexia specific to languages local to LMICs, and knowledge about the interaction between language and reading disabilities is not used as part of screening in LMICs.

Although it is likely that dyslexia rates in orthographically transparent local languages are similar to those of orthographically transparent international languages, little research in this area exists. (An orthographically transparent language is one that has consistent symbol-to-phoneme relationships.) An overall lack of prevalence data in LMICs also inhibits progress in the field of international education. This lack of data is, in large part, due to the challenges of screening and testing for dyslexia in contexts that are bi- and trilingual, where the expertise needed to conduct screening and more in-depth evaluation is limited, where it is difficult to assess the quality of the reading instruction that is available, and where a lack of support for children identified with dyslexia introduces ethical considerations related to screening and identifying children as having this type of disability.

In part due to deepened interest on the part of international development funding agencies—such as the U.S. Agency for International Development (USAID), the U.K. Department for International Development, and the World Bank—in improving the quality of education for children with disabilities, this research base continues to grow and to inform intervention practices. One of the first steps already taken by LMIC education systems is giving teachers strategies for differentiated instruction that can help all struggling readers in the classroom, including those who may have dyslexia. These strategies include using screening tools that are appropriate for LMIC contexts to rule out other obstacles to reading and to identify students who may struggle to learn to read even with appropriate instruction.

LITERACY IN LOW- AND MIDDLE-INCOME COUNTRIES

The underlying process by which children develop literacy is similar across languages (Bulat et al., 2017; Frost, 2012). However, characteristics of individual languages either ease or impede this development (Rueckl et al., 2015; Seymour, Aro, & Erskine, 2003), and each child's experiences and early exposure to language and literacy activities play a critical role in his or her rate and degree of literacy acquisition. Research documents that early access to literacy-rich experiences is critical to the development of literacy skills (Bruck, Genesee, & Caravolas, 1997; Whitehurst & Lonigan, 1998). Furthermore, learning to read early in a child's formal education is key to subsequent academic success. Evidence shows, for example, that students who struggle to learn how to read in first grade must achieve twice the reading fluency gains in second grade to catch up with those students who are not struggling (Good, Simmons, & Smith, 1998).

Children in LMICs often lack the early quality language and literacy exposure and educational opportunities that are needed for effective literacy development. Commitments by world governments over the past decades to make primary education free have resulted in increased net enrollment rates for primary schools in LMICs. In 2015, primary school enrollment in LMICs was estimated at 91% (RTI International, 2015). Although this unprecedented level of access to school is a critical step in raising global literacy rates, it is not sufficient and, in some ways, has diminished education quality. Dramatic increases in student enrollment have crippled already weak education systems, exacerbating large class sizes. Already insufficient materials are being spread even more thinly across students, and teacher professional development has failed to keep pace with the new classroom demands (Riddell, 2003). It is not surprising, then, that student dropout rates in LMICs are high: only 64% of students in LMICs complete primary school, and in south and west Asia, up to 13% of students drop out of school in the first grade (Gove & Cvelich, 2011). Furthermore, the average student in LMICs performs worse than 95% of students in Organisation for Economic Co-operation and Development (OECD) classrooms. In fact, in many LMICs, at the end of Grade 2 the majority of students are unable to read a single word (Gove & Cvelich, 2011).

This critical state of learning among the youngest and most impoverished children in the world is even more dire for those who have a disability. Although education is a global human right for all children, most children with disabilities in LMICs have no access to any form of education. The World Bank estimates that nearly one third of children with disabilities have never been in school, and the primary school completion rate for children with disabilities in 19 low-income countries is just 48% (Male & Wodon, 2017). The World Federation of the Deaf (2018) suggests that as many as 80% of worldwide school-age students who are deaf or hard of hearing are out of school. Barriers to education include inaccessible infrastructure and transportation, harmful misperceptions,

> **Global prevalence of dyslexia**
>
> Conservative estimates suggest that approximately 4%–8% of students globally have dyslexia (Swanson, 2011). However, the actual percentage may be as high as 15% or more (Cortiella & Horowitz, 2014) because many children continue to not be identified, even in high-income countries.

discriminatory views, and stigma (United Nations Children's Fund, 2013). Moreover, girls with disabilities are less likely to attend school than boys with disabilities, which means they face multiple levels of discrimination based on both their disability and gender.

Likewise, most LMICs continue to maintain two parallel education systems: one system for students without disabilities and another segregated or "special" system for students with identified disabilities. This secondary system for students with disabilities is typically understaffed and underfunded, with substantial financial and operational support often being provided by local and international nongovernmental organizations rather than the country's ministry of education. In many countries, these schools do not follow the national curriculum and often do not require the teacher training standards and qualifications that are maintained within the general education system. Indeed, only recently have many LMICs begun to think about making the transition to an inclusive education system and how to best educate children with a diverse range of disabilities in an inclusive setting.

SCREENING FOR AND IDENTIFYING DYSLEXIA IN LOW- AND MIDDLE-INCOME COUNTRIES

A number of challenges exist when trying to screen for and ultimately diagnose dyslexia in many LMICs. One core obstacle is that many LMICs do not officially recognize learning disabilities; many African countries have not established formal local definitions of learning disabilities, and students with learning disabilities are typically not recognized as needing specialized support in the classroom. Even in LMICs that do recognize dyslexia, students with learning disabilities, including dyslexia, are physically and often behaviorally difficult to distinguish from students without disabilities, particularly outside of school settings (Friend & Bursuck, 2011), and without physical characteristics, identification can be challenging in contexts that lack identification protocols and tools. Other disabilities, such as low vision or hearing difficulties, can also mask dyslexia. In addition, environmental factors, such as poor nutrition or lack of adequate formal education, are common and may either cause learning challenges or may interfere with a diagnosis of dyslexia.

Even more challenging is recognizing dyslexia in students who are second language learners because it is hard for teachers to distinguish if a student is struggling to read due to dyslexia or learning a new language. In LMICs, it is common for children to use one language at home and learn one or more languages at school that are a mix of the local language, regional lingua francas, and international languages. Therefore, when screening students for dyslexia in multilingual environments, it is most effective to assess a child's literacy skills in both his or her native language and in the language of instruction (August & Shanahan, 2006). However, valid screening tools in local languages are limited (Abedi, 2002; August & Shanahan, 2006). As a result, screenings are often delayed until students reach a level of language proficiency that justifies using the international language assessment, resulting in students dropping farther behind in literacy development. Another layer of complication in situations where nonnative speakers are assessed with an international language assessment is that results are often compared to normed groups that may or may not include learners from their language background; false profiles of children's literacy abilities are thus likely to emerge.

A consistent lack of trained professionals in LMICs further impedes screening. Many children with learning disabilities are initially identified by a parent or classroom teacher as they see the child struggle to learn (Hayes, Dombrowski, Shefcyk, & Bulat, 2018). However, in many LMICs, teachers are not trained to identify challenges that may be indicative of a learning disability, nor do they know how to rule out extenuating issues that may present as a potential disability. Moreover, many classrooms are overcrowded, leading to environments in which teachers are unable to give individualized attention, so teachers often miss the signs of a potential learning disability. Finally, locally adapted literacy measures that can distinguish between reading problems that stem from language deficits and those associated with reading difficulties, such as dyslexia, are largely absent.

PHASED APPROACH TO SCREENING FOR DYSLEXIA

To support LMICs that are beginning to identify students as having a disability but lack the tools, training, and other resources to do so accurately, RTI International proposed a three-phased approach to identification (see Figure 15.1) in its *Learning Disabilities Screening and Evaluation Guide for Low- and Middle-Income Countries*. This approach encourages stakeholders to gradually adapt to the complexities of identification while responsibly developing the appropriate tools that reflect the culture and language of the environment and providing immediate support to students who are struggling to acquire literacy (Hayes et al., 2018). In this iterative process, students receive increasingly targeted support as education systems build increasingly comprehensive tools, expertise, and systems.

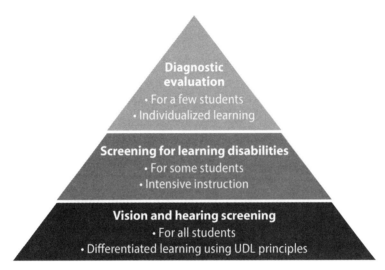

Figure 15.1. Dyslexia Screening and Evaluation Phases. (*Key,* UDL, universal design for learning.) (*Source:* Hayes, Dombrowski, Shefcyk, & Bulat, 2018.)

Phase 1: Nascent Screening and Differentiated Instruction

In Phase 1, stakeholders are encouraged to provide universal hearing and vision screening to all students in the classroom using inexpensive and adaptable tools. This is important because many LMICs do not have systems in place to provide widespread vision and hearing screening or medical treatment to students. In carrying out this screening, the teacher is trained to determine if reading difficulties are caused by environmental factors, such as class sizes and seating arrangements that prevent students from seeing and hearing the teacher, before administrating additional screening techniques. In this phase, teachers are also encouraged to introduce the concepts of universal design for learning (UDL) into their instruction and to differentiate learning. Stakeholders can also begin to build the standards, tools, and systems needed to screen students while educating parents on learning disabilities and the benefits of inclusive education.

Phase 2: Emerging Screening and Individualized Instruction

Once the foundations of Phase 1 are established, Phase 2 introduces more targeted screening procedures to assess if children who struggle to learn would benefit from additional educational supports and services. This includes developing locally relevant screening tools and establishing in-country experts who can serve as part of multidisciplinary assessment teams. In addition, stakeholders are encouraged to institute policies and protocols on how these tools should be used in the classroom. Teachers must be thoroughly trained on how to provide accommodations to students who have additional learning needs, how to individualize instruction, and how to implement the individualized education program. Finally, families and individuals need to be educated on their role in the screening and evaluation processes and in advocating for education rights.

Phase 3: Established Systems and Supports

Once Phase 1 and 2 systems and structures are in place, more comprehensive evaluations for disabilities can be conducted, as needed, under Phase 3. This phase should be used to assess each student's unique learning needs as they relate to a specific disability, including dyslexia. These assessments should only take place after vision and hearing tests (Phase 1) and initial screenings (Phase 1 and 2) have occurred. In this phase, evaluations should be conducted over a period of time, using a range of tools and sources of information, and should take place in different environments within the school. Trained individuals, including a multidisciplinary teacher, should conduct the evaluation while actively engaging and partnering with families throughout the process. One effective tool for evaluation in LMICs is an ecological assessment, which observes children across different school-related settings. The assessment compares students to their natural environment, as well as to other students in the same school environment (Elder, 2015). The goal of an evaluation is not to label a student or remove him or her from the general education classroom but rather to assess specific learning challenges and design interventions and supports that can best support learning.

INNOVATIVE SCREENING APPROACHES

At the core of effectively implementing a phased approach to screening for dyslexia is beginning to screen for disabilities early in a child's life and continuing to screen throughout his or her school years. Regular screening for possible disabilities, such as vision or hearing loss or delays in acquiring grade-level literacy skills, will help determine in a timely way if a student is struggling to learn to read, why, and how to meet her or his learning needs. To help fill the dearth of locally appropriate screening tools for LMICs, RTI International is collaborating with other researchers to explore options for low-cost, easily implemented vision, hearing, and dyslexia screening.

Using Technology to Support Students
With Low Vision and/or Hearing Impairment

Paper-based assessments and observational screening methods by trained professionals have dominated the approaches used to identify learning disabilities, even in high-income contexts (see International Dyslexia Association, 2017), although in countries where Internet access is prevalent, commercial vendors or nonprofit organizations can offer computerized, online dyslexia screening programs. The increased availability and affordability of offline mobile technologies across the globe, however, offer promise for potentially even more accessible, and accurate, screening approaches. Smartphone technology, for example, has proven effective in a recent pilot of commercially available, clinically validated screening tools for vision and hearing challenges in Ethiopia. This study successfully screened children for previously unidentified hearing and vision challenges and identified important contextual variables determining the feasibility for using such tools in LMIC contexts (RTI International, 2019).

In Ethiopia, the USAID-funded Reading for Ethiopia's Achievement Developed Technical Assistance (READ TA) project piloted an assistive technology initiative that included vision and hearing screening in 63 schools across five regions. The project team screened more than 3,700 Grade 2 students in 109 selected classrooms for their vision and hearing levels, using smartphone-based, clinically validated tools. Among the students assessed, 150 (4%) were identified with some form of a hearing-related disability, and 211 (5.6%) had some form of a vision-related disability. These numbers are in stark contrast to teacher surveys, in which teachers originally estimated that no more than 2% of their students had a disability.

Teachers who participated in the pilot study for READ TA received headphones, smartphones loaded with the screening tools, an inclusive multimedia lesson plan, and training on the use of all materials. The inclusive multimedia lesson plans build on principles of UDL and include target audio supports for phonemic awareness activities and stories. After 3 months of implementation, teachers' attitudes toward and self-efficacy for inclusive education improved significantly, as did teacher adoption of foundational inclusive practices in the classroom. At the student level, although the study found measurable differences in reading between these groups at baseline, students identified for a potential vision or hearing disability in intervention classrooms demonstrated similar learning progress compared to peers who could see and hear.

This technology is currently being piloted as well in the Philippines. As new technologies and technology features emerge and become available, there is optimism for innovative screening approaches that may provide

---

Use of technology: One teacher's response

Ms. Agere Melaku of the rural Zenzelima School in Amhara Region, Ethiopia, enthusiastically incorporates the new smartphone-based technology into her teaching practices. She notes, "Although I often had intentions to support needy children in my class, my conviction has amplified after the training I received with this pilot. I am now a step ahead of other teachers; I am using technology in addition to the chalk and board."

The double-deficit theory and African languages

The double-deficit theory of developmental dyslexia asserts that children facing deficits in both phonological awareness (PA) and random automatic naming (RAN) will have more difficulty learning how to read than children with a deficit in only one skill or in neither skill. This has been widely researched in opaque and transparent orthographies (see, e.g., Babayigit & Stainthorp, 2010; de Jong & van der Leij, 1999; Wolf & Bowers, 1999), but it has yet to be explored in local African languages, such as the Bantu language of Chichewa. Chichewa is the lingua franca and the language of instruction in lower primary government schools in Malawi. It is a transparent orthography with a dominance of open syllables (Mchombo, 2004).

---

stakeholders in LMICs a more practical and reliable way to screen children for both sensory disabilities and learning disabilities. Appropriate research will be critical to help identify the important factors underpinning the successful implementation of these screening approaches in diverse settings and across languages and scripts.

Double-Deficit Screening for Dyslexia

Researchers and educators are also exploring low-technology and low-cost innovations for dyslexia-specific screening in LMICs. For example, a study in Malawi demonstrated the utility of simple early reading tasks to screen for students who have a double deficit in reading acquisition—a deficit in both phonological awareness (PA) and rapid automatic naming (RAN)—and who will likely struggle to acquire literacy even with adequate instruction.

We followed the descriptions of the subtypes of phonological deficit described in detail by Morris and colleagues (1998) and informed by detailed summaries by Elliott and Grigorenko (2014) of construct descriptions. We did not take a position about whether serial rapid naming is distinct from phonology. Instead, in a context where few are learning to read, we explored whether two distinct measures for screening could distinguish those who might struggle with reading acquisition, regardless of instruction (Dubeck, Kaunda, Slade, & Stern, 2017). To answer this question, we developed a simple assessment consisting of a RAN measure of common objects and a PA measure using illustrations specifically for the Malawian context. We designed this assessment to be administered by school or district personnel with relatively minimal training and to take approximately 5 minutes to administer to a student, which is appropriate

---

The double-deficit theory and Bantu African languages

The *double-deficit* theory of dyslexia has been shown in opaque and transparent orthographies (e.g., de Jong & van der Leij, 1999; Furnes & Samuelsson, 2011) but it had yet to be explored in Chichewa or other Bantu African languages.

Table 15.1. No deficit, single, and double deficit word reading over time

Grade 3 oral reading fluency	Time 1	Time 2	Time 3	Time 4
No deficit	16.4	28.2	36.7	43.8
PA or RAN deficit	8	22.3	21.6	35.2
Double deficit	7.1	10	15.3	16.3

Key: PA, phonological awareness; RAN, rapid automatic naming.

for screening large numbers of students quickly. Because this assessment uses illustrations of common objects, it can also be readily adapted to any language or context.

We tested cohorts of Grade 1, 2, and 3 students ($n = 3{,}901$ from 33 schools) in RAN and PA at four times over the course of one school year. We classified students who scored poorly on either RAN or PA at baseline, as compared to their grade-level peers (i.e., below the grade-level average), as having one deficit; we classified students who scored poorly on both RAN and PA at baseline as compared to their peers as having double deficits. It is compelling to note that students with only one deficit performed similarly to those with double deficits at the beginning of the year on a measure of oral reading fluency; both groups underperformed their peers with no noted deficit and by the same amount. However, by year end, the single deficit group more than doubled the average score of their double-deficit counterparts (see Table 15.1). Although the single deficit group did not reach the level of performance as students with no noted deficit, they did make more gains than students with deficits in both skills, who showed no growth over the course of the year in oral reading fluency. This pattern was seen in all grade levels.

These results are not longitudinal and are preliminary; additional research into the use of this type of screening model in local languages in LMICs is needed. That said, this screening approach does show promise in identifying students who may struggle with literacy acquisition, even in the presence of adequate instruction, in classrooms where teachers and school staff may not be trained to effectively administer more comprehensive batteries of screening tools.

CONCLUSION

Students with disabilities have the moral and legal right to receive quality education. In many LMICs, however, education systems do not have the core capabilities to provide these students access to this education. This holds true for students with or at risk of having dyslexia. Stakeholders across the globe are exploring ways to meet the specific learning needs of students with dyslexia, including making effective screening available.

RTI International is one such stakeholder and has proposed a phased approach to dyslexia screening and evaluation—an approach that relies heavily on the use of contextually and linguistically appropriate screening tools. RTI International and others are piloting innovative tools to screen for vision and hearing loss in the school, as well as to examine indications of reading challenges, tools that show great progress in helping education systems meet the needs of these vulnerable students, including in LMICs.

REFERENCES

Abedi, J. (2002). Assessment and accommodations of English language learners: Issues, concerns, and recommendations. *Journal of School Improvement, 3*(1), 83–89.

August, D., & Shanahan, T. (Eds.). (2006). *Developing literacy in second-language learners: Report of the National Literacy Panel on Language-Minority Children and Youth.* Mahwah, NJ: Lawrence Erlbaum Associates.

Babayigit, S., & Stainthorp, R. (2010). Component processes of early reading, spelling, and narrative writing skills in Turkish: A longitudinal study. *Reading and Writing, 23*(5), 539–568. https://doi.org/10.1007/s11145-009-9173-y

Bruck, M., Genesee, F., & Caravolas, M. (1997). A cross-linguistic study of early literacy acquisition. In B. Blachman (Ed.), *Foundations of reading acquisition and dyslexia: Implications for early intervention.* New York, NY: Routledge.

Bulat, J., Dubeck, M., Green, P., Harden, K., Henny, C., Mattos, M., . . . Sitabkhan, Y. (2017, February). *What we have learned in the past decade: RTI's approach to early grade literacy instruction* (RTI Press Publication No. OP-0039-1702). Research Triangle Park, NC: RTI Press. https://doi.org/10.3768/rtipress.2017.op.0039.1702

Cortiella, C., & Horowitz, S. H. (2014). *The state of learning disabilities: Facts, trends and emerging issues.* New York, NY: National Center for Learning Disabilities.

de Jong, P. F., & van der Leij, D. A. V. (1999). Specific contributions of phonological abilities to early reading acquisition: Results from a Dutch latent variable longitudinal study. *Journal of Educational Psychology, 91,* 450–476.

Dubeck, M. M., Kaunda, Z. H. W., Slade, T. S., & Stern, J. M. B. (2017, July). *Chichewa rapid automatic naming (RAN) and phonological awareness: Exploring the double-deficit in Malawi.* Poster session presented at the Society for the Scientific Study of Reading, Halifax, Nova Scotia, Canada

Elder, B. (2015). Right to inclusive education for students with disabilities in Kenya. *Journal of International Special Needs Education, 18*(1), 18–28.

Elliott, J. G., & Grigorenko, E. L. (2014). *The dyslexia debate* (No. 14). Cambridge, United Kingdom: Cambridge University Press.

Friend, M., & Bursuck, W. D. (2011). *Including students with special needs: A practical guide for classroom teachers* (6th ed.). Boston, MA: Pearson Education.

Frost, R. (2012). Towards a universal model of reading. *Behavioral and Brain Sciences, 35*(5), 263–279. https://doi.org/10.1017/S0140525X11001841

Furnes, B., & Samuelsson, S. (2011). Phonological awareness and rapid automatized naming predicting early development in reading and spelling: Results from a cross-linguistic longitudinal study. *Learning and Individual Differences, 21*(1), 85–95.

Good, R. H., III, Simmons, D. C., & Smith, S. B. (1998). Effective academic interventions in the United States: Evaluating and enhancing the acquisition of early reading skills. *School Psychology Review, 27*(1), 45–56.

Gove, A., & Cvelich, P. (2011). *Early reading: Igniting education for all. A report by the Early Grade Learning Community of Practice* (Rev. ed.). Research Triangle Park, NC: Research Triangle Institute. Retrieved from https://shared.rti.org/content/early-reading-igniting-education-all-report-early-grade-learning-community-practice

Hayes, A. M., Dombrowski, E., Shefcyk, A. H., & Bulat, J. (2018). *Learning disabilities screening and evaluation guide for low- and middle- income countries* (RTI Press Publication No. OP-0052-Bulat). Research Triangle Park, NC: RTI Press. https://doi.org/10.3768/rtipress.2018.op.0052.1804

Hoeft, F., McCardle, P., & Pugh, K. (2015). *The myths and truths of dyslexia in different writing systems*. Retrieved from https://dyslexiaida.org/the-myths-and-truths-of-dyslexia/

International Dyslexia Association. (2017). *Dyslexia assessment: What is it and how can it help?* Retrieved from https://dyslexiaida.org/dyslexia-assessment-what-is-it-and-how -can-it-help/

Landerl, K., Freudenthaler, H. H., Heene, M., de Jong, P. F., Desrochers, A., Manolitsis, G., . . . Georgiou, G. K. (2018). Phonological awareness and rapid automatized naming as longitudinal predictors of reading in five alphabetic orthographies with varying degrees of consistency. *Scientific Studies of Reading*, 1–15. https://doi.org/10.1080/10888438.2018.1510936

Male, C., & Wodon, Q. (2017). Disability gaps in educational attainment and literacy. The price of exclusion. Disability and Education Notes Series. Washington, DC: The World Bank.

Mchombo, S. (2004). *The syntax of Chichewa*. Cambridge, United Kingdom: Cambridge University Press. https://doi.org/10.1017/CBO9780511486302

Mercer, C. D., Mercer., A. R., & Pullen, P. C. (2011) *Teaching students with learning problems* (8th ed.). Upper Saddle River, NJ: Pearson.

Morris, R. D., Stuebing, K. K., Fletcher, J. M., Shaywitz, S. E., Lyon, G. R., Shankweiler, D. P., . . . Shaywitz, B. A. (1998). Subtypes of reading disability: Variability around a phonological core. *Journal of Educational Psychology*, *90*(3), 347–373. https://doi.org/10.1037/0022-0663.90.3.347

Pullen, P. C., Lane, H. B., Ashworth, K. E., & Lovelace, S. P. (2017). Specific learning disabilities. In J. M. Kauffman, D. P. Hallahan, & P. C. Pullen (Eds.). *Handbook of special education* (2nd ed., pp. 286–299). New York, NY: Routledge, Taylor & Francis Group.

Riddell, A. (2003). The introduction of free primary education in sub-Saharan Africa. *EFA Global Monitoring Report 2003/4: The leap to equality*. Retrieved from http://unesdoc. unesco.org/images/0014/001469/146914e.pdf

RTI International. (2015). *Early Grade Reading Assessment (EGRA) Toolkit* (2nd ed.). Washington, DC: U.S. Agency for International Development.

RTI International. (2019). *Vision and hearing screening tools pilot activity in the Philippines— Final report*. Washington, DC: U.S. Agency for International Development. Retrieved from https://shared.rti.org/content/vision-and-hearing-screening-tools-pilot-activity -philippines

Rueckl, J. G., Paz-Alonso, P. M., Molfese, P. J., Kuo, W. -J., Bick, A., Frost, S. J., . . . Frost, R. (2015). Universal brain signature of proficient reading: Evidence from four contrasting languages. *Proceedings of the National Academy of Sciences*, *112*(50), 15510–15515. https:// doi.org/10.1073/pnas.1509321112

Seymour, P. H. K., Aro, M., & Erskine, J. M. (2003). Foundation literacy acquisition in European orthographies. *British Journal of Psychology*, *94*, 143–174.

Swanson, H. L. (2011). Learning disabilities: Assessment, identification, and treatment. In M. A. Bray & T. J. Kehle (Eds.), *The Oxford handbook of school psychology* (pp. 334–350). New York, NY: Oxford University Press.

United Nations. (2018). *Convention on the rights of persons with disabilities (CRPD)*. Retrieved from https://www.un.org/development/desa/disabilities/convention-on-the-rights-of -persons-with-disabilities.html

United Nations Children's Fund. (2013). *Children and young people with disabilities: Fact sheet*. Retrieved from https://www.unicef.org/disabilities/files/Factsheet_A5__Web_ REVISED.pdf

United Nations Educational, Scientific, and Cultural Organization (UNESCO). (2005). *Guidelines for inclusion: Ensuring access to education for all*. Retrieved from http://www. ibe.unesco.org/sites/default/files/Guidelines_for_Inclusion_UNESCO_2006.pdf

Vellutino, F. R., Fletcher, J. M., Snowling, M. J., & Scanlon, D. M. (2004). Specific reading disability (dyslexia): What have we learned in the past four decades? *Journal of Child Psychology and Psychiatry*, *45*(1), 2–40.

Whitehurst, G. J., & Lonigan, C. J. (1998). Child development and emergent literacy. *Child Development*, *69*(3), 848–872.

Wolf, M., & Bowers, P. G. (1999). The double-deficit hypothesis for the developmental dyslexias. *Journal of Educational Psychology*, *91*(3), 415–438. https://doi.org/10.1037/0022 -0663.91.3.415

World Federation of the Deaf. (2018). *Advancing human rights and sign language worldwide.*
    Retrieved from https://wfdeaf.org/our-work/human-rights-of-the-deaf/
World Health Organization. (2011). *World report on disability.* Retrieved from http://www.
    who.int/disabilities/world_report/2011/report.pdf
Ziegler, J. C., & Goswami, U. (2005). Reading acquisition, developmental dyslexia, and
    skilled reading across languages: A psycholinguistic grain size theory. *Psychological
    Bulletin, 131*(1), 3–29. https://doi.org/10.1037/0033-2909.131.1.3

CHAPTER 16

The Emperor's New Clothes in the Preparation of Reading Teachers

R. Malatesha Joshi and Emily Binks-Cantrell

SUMMARY

Several reports in the United States have shown that many students, especially inner-city and minority children, are not reading at grade level. This poor academic performance has been attributed to various reasons, such as home literacy environment and oral language development, or the fact that evidence-based instruction is not provided in schools due to poor teacher knowledge of this type of instruction. We explored the reasons for the teachers' lack of knowledge of evidence-based instruction, based on our hypotheses that teachers are not provided with such information at their universities and that textbooks used in teacher preparation classes in the universities might not be providing the necessary information relating to scientifically based reading instructional programs. This chapter presents the results of this investigation, which in our opinion indicate that when it comes to university preparation of reading teachers, the emperor has no clothes.

INTRODUCTION

Literacy skills—the ability to read and write—are basic for survival. Failure to acquire these skills has grave consequences for the individual and for society. For instance, about 75% of students who drop out of high schools have reading problems, and about 85% of individuals in the juvenile court system are functionally illiterate (Lyon, 2001). The advantages of being literate are demonstrated by the fact that when literacy help is provided for the individuals in the juvenile system, there is a 16% chance that these individuals will return to the prison system; however, when literacy help is not provided, there is about a 70% chance that they might return to prison (Begin to Read, n.d.), which costs taxpayers and the government a huge amount of money. In addition, more than 50% of the individuals in the welfare system and with substance abuse problems have reading problems (Lyon, 2001). Even though there may not be a cause and effect relationship between illiteracy and the problems mentioned, these alarming statistics led the National Institutes of Health (NIH) to declare illiteracy a "national public health issue" (Lyon, 2001; McCardle & Chhabra, 2004).

According to the most recent Nation's Report Card (National Assessment of Educational Progress [NAEP], 2017), one third of fourth-grade students in the United States are not comprehending grade-level materials, and among minority and inner-city children, this percentage may be as high as 66%. This high percentage is unfortunate, especially considering that evidence-based instructional programs are available to help these students. As mentioned previously, there are various reasons for not being able to master literacy skills, but the most important reason might be poor instruction in schools, especially at the early grade levels. For instance, Juel (1988) followed a group of children from Grade 1 to Grade 4 and found that those children who knew the names of letters and their common sounds at the end of Grade 1 were reading better at the end of Grade 4, whereas those students who did not know the names of letters at the end of Grade 1 had reading difficulties at the end of Grade 4. The effect of poor early reading skills shows even at the eighth-grade level (Landerl & Wimmer, 2008). Likewise, 74% of students with reading difficulties in Grade 3 also show problems in literacy skills in Grade 9 (Lyon & Weiser, 2009). Furthermore, if children are identified as having reading problems in early grades, it takes about 20 minutes of extra instruction for 4 days per week for 12 weeks to remedy the reading problems; however, when students are identified at later grades, remediation may be more difficult, and it is likely to take a longer time to bring the students to grade level (Torgesen, 2008). According to Snow, Burns, and Griffin, "Quality classroom instruction in kindergarten and the primary grades is the single best weapon against reading failure" (1998, p. 343), and according to Denton, Foorman, and Mathes (2003), effective instruction can "beat the odds."

ROLE OF TEACHER PREPARATION

The National Reading Panel (NRP; *Eunice Kennedy Shriver* National Institute of Child Health and Human Development [NICHD], 2000), based on experimental evidence, has identified five important components of reading: phonological awareness (including phonemic awareness), phonics, fluency, vocabulary, and text comprehension. Furthermore, the NRP also identified explicit ways of teaching these components. The International Literacy Association (ILA), formerly known as the International Reading Association, similarly has recommended that the critical features of effective teacher preparation programs in reading must include a balance of oral language, phonemic awareness, phonics, word identification, fluency, vocabulary, and comprehension across grade levels (International Reading Association, 2003). Many successful reading programs are based on linguistic features such as phonological awareness, phonics, morphological awareness, and orthographic awareness as outlined by the NRP and the ILA.

Teacher Knowledge of Basic Language Constructs

Beginning with the seminal work of Moats (1994), researchers have consistently shown that many classroom teachers are not familiar with the linguistic concepts related to teaching literacy skills, such as inflection and derivation morphemes, phonics and phonological awareness, letter sounds, and phonemes (Binks-Cantrell, Washburn, Joshi, & Hougan, 2012; Bos, Mather, Dickson, Podhajski, & Chard, 2001; Fielding-Barnsley & Purdie, 2005; Mather, Bos, & Babur, 2001; Washburn, Binks-Cantrell, & Joshi, 2013; Washburn, Joshi, & Binks-Cantrell, 2011a, 2011b), and in-service and preservice teachers often overestimate their knowledge of such important constructs (Cunningham, Perry, Stanovich, & Stanovich, 2004). Despite the strong correlations that have been demonstrated between teacher knowledge, classroom instruction, and student achievement (McCutchen, Abbott, et al., 2002; Piasta, McDonald, Fishman, & Morrison, 2009; Spear-Swerling & Brucker, 2004), there has been little to no improvement since 1993 in teacher knowledge and preparation of reading teachers. We should, however, add that teachers did spend more time on teaching the five components of reading recommended by the NRP (Gamse, Jacob, Horst, Boulay, & Unlu, 2008).

Reasons for Poor Teacher Preparation

Given that teacher knowledge is a necessary condition for improving reading skills in elementary school children, why do teachers lack the required knowledge? Our hypothesis was that one reason may be that preservice teachers are not receiving adequate information relating to evidence-based procedures to teach literacy skills at the university level—and that this in turn might be due to a lack of knowledge among those who prepare the teachers themselves (i.e., the university instructors). Furthermore, textbooks used in teacher preparation programs may not be providing information on explicit instruction based on scientific evidence. We thus expanded the study of teacher knowledge of basic language constructs to a new population of teachers—university instructors.

We created a 60-item survey based on the work of Moats, McCutchen, and Cunningham to assess both perception and actual knowledge of basic language constructs fundamental to evidence-based reading instruction. Questions such as "How well do you think you are prepared to teach . . . [typically developing readers, struggling readers, phonological awareness, decoding, etc.]" assessed perceptions, whereas items to assess knowledge asked questions related to definition of terms (e.g., "phoneme/morpheme refers to . . ."), explanation (e.g., number of speech sounds in *box, moon*; number of morphemes in *observer, heaven*), vocabulary instruction (e.g., vocabulary webs), and comprehension (e.g., summarizing, reciprocal teaching). The survey had a reliability of 0.92 (Cronbach's alpha) and was further validated through confirmatory and exploratory factor analyses (Binks-Cantrell, Joshi, & Washburn, 2012).

Ninety-eight university instructors of reading education courses completed the survey, ninety of whom had a doctorate and eight of whom were working on their doctorates. All participants had taught in elementary schools and were currently teaching two to four courses in reading education. Furthermore, all indicated they were well prepared to teach reading. The analyses of the completed surveys showed that the university instructors performed fairly well on items relating to syllables, with more than 90% of the participating instructors identifying the number of syllables in a word. However, only about 60% could identify types of syllables, such as open or closed syllables. The worst performance was on items relating to instruction, such as when does the letter c make the /k/ or /s/ sound, and on identifying the number of morphemes in words such as *frogs, teacher,* and *observer.* In addition, only 15% of the college instructors could name the components of good reading as outlined by the NRP. We next asked the preservice teachers being instructed by these university instructors to complete the same survey. The analyses of the survey items showed that preservice instructors performed very similarly to their university instructors; there were no statistically significant differences between the performance of these two groups, with the exception of syllable counting. In a nutshell, both demonstrated a lack of understanding of these important concepts (Washburn et al., 2011a).

The researchers expanded the Peter Effect (Applegate & Applegate, 2004), which states that a person cannot give what he or she does not possess, to reading education. We further followed a group of university instructors who had participated for at least 2 years in a bi-yearly professional development program that consisted of explicit training in scientifically based reading research (SBRR) and how to incorporate it into their teaching of university classes. In addition, collaboration among instructors was enhanced through the implementation of an online community, assistance with model lessons, preparation of syllabi, assistance with course content alignment, and assistance in making presentations for students and faculty at their respective institutions. Not only was the performance of the university instructors who had participated in the professional development significantly higher on the knowledge survey than performance of those who had not, but the knowledge of their students (the preservice teachers) was significantly higher as well (Binks-Cantrell, Washburn, et al., 2012). This demonstrates that university instructors' knowledge and understanding of how to teach reading most effectively can be heightened to a proficient level when relatively simple efforts are made to stay abreast of current research and practices in the field—and, most important, that this knowledge will carry over to their students, the preservice teachers.

We wanted to explore whether poor teacher knowledge is specific to the United States or whether poor teacher preparation also occurs in other countries. We first explored this in English-speaking countries by administering the teacher knowledge survey to the undergraduate students in the teacher preparation programs in Canada, the United Kingdom, Australia, and New Zealand. The number of participants in different countries was as follows: Canada (*n* = 80), England (*n* = 55), New Zealand (*n* = 26), and the United States (*n* = 118). Preservice teachers performed poorly on the survey despite differences among different countries on certain aspects. For instance, compared to the United States, preservice teachers in the United Kingdom performed worse on items relating to phonological awareness and phonemic awareness but better on items relating to phonics and morphological awareness. The performance differences might be partly attributed to the emphasis placed on teacher preparation in the respective countries. For instance, the NRP report (NICHD, 2000) has placed a strong emphasis on the importance of phonological awareness and phonemic awareness in the United States, and the Rose (2009) report in the United Kingdom has placed a heavy emphasis on the importance of phonics instruction; this might be the reason for the differences in performance between the U.K. and U.S. preservice teachers (Washburn, Binks-Cantrell, Joshi, Martin-Chang, & Arrow, 2016). Findings of poor teacher knowledge of linguistic concepts were also observed in other languages, such as Spanish in Spain and Peru (Soriano-Ferrer, Echegaray-Bengoa, & Joshi, 2016) and more surprisingly in Finnish (because Finland has consistently been placing high in reading achievement in international rankings, as in the Programme for International Student Assessment [PISA]; Organisation for Economic Co-operation and Development [OECD], 2017).

English is considered an international language, and many countries begin teaching English at early grade levels. For instance, in Beijing, China, children are introduced to basics of spoken English in Grade 1 and in South Korea and Israel in Grade 3. We administered a modified survey based on Binks-Cantrell, Washburn, and colleagues (2012) to teachers of English as a second language (ESL) in China, South Korea, and Israel. Most ESL teachers also performed poorly on the survey. However, Korean ESL teachers had more positive self-perceptions than their counterparts and performed better on items relating to phonics than their Chinese counterparts (Bae, Yin, & Joshi, 2019).

Do Textbooks Provide the Needed Information?

We next explored whether the textbooks used in the teacher preparation classes at the universities help preservice teachers to learn about evidence-based reading methods. Walsh, Glaser, and Wilcox (2006) found that the vast majority of the most popularly used reading education textbooks neglected to provide information on all five essential components of effective reading instruction as identified by the NRP. We also wanted to consider whether, in addition to lacking the necessary quantity of information, the quality of information provided—such as definitions of phonemic awareness, phonics, and related terms and concepts—might be poor.

We contacted eight well-known textbook publishing companies and requested the titles and authors of the best-selling books in reading education from each. We received 17 titles and have included content examinations of these popular textbooks in this chapter.

Quantity   We first looked at whether all five components recommended by the NRP were included in the textbook and whether they were
clearly defined, especially the concepts of phonological and phonemic
awareness. We calculated the percentage of the book devoted to each of
the topics by counting the number of pages that discussed the topic, then
dividing by the total number of pages in the textbook. The percentage of
the book that covered the five components of reading ranged from 4% to
60%. We then examined the percentage of coverage the book devoted to
each of the five components individually and found that the majority of
the textbooks covered reading comprehension more than the foundational
skills of phonological awareness, phonemic awareness, and phonics. On
average, phonological awareness and phonics comprised less than 5% of
the textbooks, whereas comprehension comprised more than 13%. Out of
17 textbooks examined, 4 had not covered all the topics, and the common
topic not covered was phonemic awareness. This is rather unfortunate because the knowledge of phonemic awareness has been shown to be crucial
in learning to read and spell in alphabetic languages such as English and
Spanish (NICHD, 2000). Considering that these textbooks were used in the
preparation of elementary school teachers, those responsible for the aspects
of instruction relating to "learning to read," more information on teaching
the foundations of reading should have been provided (Joshi et al., 2009).

Quality   The next step in the analyses of textbooks was to examine
whether the concepts were clearly defined. Out of the 13 textbooks that
covered all five components, three textbooks had given the wrong definition and incorrect information about the concepts. For instance, two textbooks defined phonemic awareness as the knowledge of the relationship
between letters and sounds and indicated that phonemic awareness can be
improved by teaching letter–sound correspondences. Phonemic awareness
is actually the knowledge of the individual sounds in spoken language
and not the knowledge of letter–sound correspondences (NICHD, 2000).
Furthermore, even though phonemic awareness and letter–sound correspondences have reciprocal relationships, phonemic awareness should be
taught by drawing attention to the individual sounds in spoken language.

Another error was the definition of a grapheme. One of the textbooks
stated, "A grapheme is the smallest unit in a written language, a letter of
the alphabet in alphabetic languages" (Sadoski, 2012, pp. 61–62) and continued to provide wrong information about the teaching of phonics and
the number of graphemes in English orthography by stating the following:

> This system (phonics) is unfortunately not a matter of one-to-one cor-
> respondence, as can be readily inferred from the mismatch between 26
> graphemes and 44 phonemes. Phonics is a complex, imperfect system,
> and some of it is seldom if ever taught, but readers develop considerable
> phonics knowledge whether they are taught it or pick it up on their own.
> (pp. 61–62)

This textbook, which is used in many classes, is replete with incorrect information. First of all, the definition of a grapheme as the smallest unit of letter(s) to represent a sound is wrong; that is, a grapheme can have more than one letter, as in *sh* in *shirt*, and can have as many as four letters, as in *ough* in *through*. Hence, English does not have 26 graphemes but may have as many 200. About the statement "phonics is a complex, imperfect system, and some of it is seldom if ever taught," the NRP (NICHD, 2000) has recommended systematic explicit teaching of phonics as a foundation for developing good reading skills.

CONCLUSION

Literacy skills are basic for survival, and failure to acquire them has serious consequences at the individual, societal, and global levels. Even though various factors such as home literacy environment and oral language development may influence literacy acquisition, poor instruction has been identified as one of the major causes of failure to master literacy skills. Although one of the reasons for the high prevalence of reading problems may be poor instruction, many classroom teachers may not possess the required basic knowledge about constructs needed to teach reading. This lack of knowledge may be due to lack of preparation at the university level, where the instructors themselves may not have the knowledge. Furthermore, the textbooks used in reading methods classes do not provide the necessary information and sometimes even provide incorrect information. It is not possible to give what one does not have, a phenomenon referred to as the Peter Effect (Applegate & Applegate, 2004; Binks-Cantrell, Joshi, et al., 2012). When instructors were provided with the necessary knowledge through professional development and mentoring, both instructors and their students (preservice teachers) demonstrated a gain in knowledge. McCutchen, Harry, and colleagues (2002) provided professional development on systematic, explicit instruction to in-service teachers during summer months and observed that the students of these teachers performed better on reading measures than a comparative group of students taught by teachers who had not received the professional development. Poor knowledge of linguistic concepts related to literacy was observed in many countries and in different languages; there were some differences among different countries and languages, but all were weak on these concepts in general.

In some ways, teacher knowledge (and the important role teacher preparation programs play in improving teacher knowledge) is starting to receive the recognition it deserves. For instance, several professional organizations have adopted knowledge and practice standards for teachers of reading, such as the ILA and the Council for Exceptional Children (CEC). (See the ILA [2017] *Standards for the Preparation of Literacy Professionals*, available on the ILA web site, and the CEC [2014] *Standards for Evidence-Based Practices in Special Education*, available through the CEC web site.)

In 2009, the International Dyslexia Association (IDA) set forth its own list of standards to fill in gaps of specificity, clarity, and scientific grouping that the former sets of standards lacked (Moats, 2014). With recognition that these standards are only truly meaningful if they are put into practice, IDA has begun to look at the alignment of the standards with teacher preparation programs.

The study of teacher knowledge and preparation in SBRR is also expanding beyond the United States. In one of the first teacher knowledge studies outside of the United States, Fielding-Barnsley and Purdie (2005) found that in-service teachers in Queensland, Australia, often lacked the knowledge of basic language constructs and favored a whole-language approach to teaching reading. Washburn, Binks-Cantrell, and Joshi (2013) found that although there are some differences between American and British preservice teachers in the misconceptions of teaching reading and dyslexia, both populations are largely leaving their teacher preparation programs lacking the knowledge they need to teach reading effectively, especially to those at risk for reading difficulties. Most recently, two special forums have been held on teacher knowledge from an international perspective at the 2013 and 2014 annual conferences of the Society for the Scientific Study of Reading, highlighting patterns in knowledge among teacher educators, in-service teachers, and preservice teachers in New Zealand, Canada, China, Portugal, Israel, Finland, and Zambia.

As mentioned in the Peter Effect study (Binks-Cantrell, Joshi, et al., 2012), a professional development program for university instructors was established through a combination of state and university funds that resulted in significant outcomes for university instructors and preservice teachers alike.

The term *dysteachia* has on occasion been used to refer to the phenomenon of students who exhibit dyslexic-like tendencies, not because of a neurologically based reading disability but because of inadequate instruction. Studies have shown that despite good evidence-based instruction following response to intervention, a small percentage of children will not gain mastery of literacy skills (Gilbert et al., 2013). However, good evidence-based instruction can bring down the current incidence of high literacy problems of about 35% to perhaps 5% (Hall, 2018). The hope is that as teacher knowledge and teacher preparation (including the knowledge and professional development of teacher educators, as well as the textbooks used in teacher preparation courses) begin to receive more attention, the quality of instruction will increase and the rate of dysteachia will decrease. Although these initiatives demonstrate some positive directions, many of the current educational policies and funding priorities still target curriculum materials, school organization, and high-stakes testing results rather than the teacher and the teacher knowledge, teacher preparation, and teacher professional development that maximizes teacher quality (Moats, 2014).

Because quality classroom instruction is the best weapon against reading failure (Snow et al., 1998), educators must do a better job of preparing and maintaining teachers who have the knowledge and ability to deliver just that. Teacher education programs must ensure that their teachers are provided with up-to-date information about research-based reading instruction, both during their initial teacher preparation (e.g., in the colleges of education and alternative certification programs) and throughout their career (e.g., professional development opportunities). Moats (1999) likened the teaching of reading to rocket science. Spending millions of dollars on curriculum programs that are thrown out every few years is not the answer. Producing and maintaining a more knowledgeable and better prepared teaching force is the most important challenge for the education field to undertake. Students deserve no less. In addition, preservice teachers should be provided with evidence-based practices in university teacher preparation programs, and textbooks used in these programs should also provide such practices.

REFERENCES

Applegate, A. J., & Applegate, M. D. (2004). The Peter Effect: Reading habits and attitudes of teacher candidates. *The Reading Teacher, 57,* 554–563.

Bae, H. S., Yin, L., & Joshi, R. M. (2019). Teacher knowledge of EFL teachers in China and Korea: A cross cultural comparison. *Annals of Dyslexia, 69,* 136–152. doi.org/10.1007/s11881-018-00169-z

Begin to Read. (n.d.). *Literacy statistics* [web page]. Retrieved from https://www.begintoread.com/research/literacystatistics.html

Binks-Cantrell, E., Joshi, R. M., & Washburn, E. (2012). Validation of an instrument for assessing teacher knowledge of basic language constructs of literacy. *Annals of Dyslexia, 62,* 153–171.

Binks-Cantrell, E., Washburn, E., Joshi, R. M., & Hougen, M. (2012). Peter effect in the preparation of reading teachers. *Scientific Studies of Reading, 16,* 526–536. http://dx.doi.org/10.1080/10888438.2011.601434.

Bos, C., Mather, N., Dickson, S., Podhajski, B., & Chard, D. (2001). Perceptions and knowledge of pre-service and in-service educators about early reading instruction. *Annals of Dyslexia, 51,* 97–120.

Council for Exceptional Children. (2014). *Standards for evidence-based practices in special education.* Retrieved from https://www.cec.sped.org/~/media/Files/Standards/Evidence%20based%20Practices%20and%20Practice/EBP%20FINAL.pdf

Cunningham, A. E., Perry, K. E., Stanovich, K. E., & Stanovich, P. J. (2004). Disciplinary knowledge of K–3 teachers and their knowledge calibration in the domain of early literacy. *Annals of Dyslexia, 54,* 139–167.

Denton, C., Foorman, B. R., & Mathes, G. G. (2003). Schools that "beat the odds": Implications for reading instruction. *Remedial and Special Education, 24,* 258–261.

Eunice Kennedy Shriver National Institute of Child Health and Human Development (NICHD). (2000). *Report of the National Reading Panel: Teaching Children to Read: Reports of the Subgroups (00-4754).* Washington, DC: U.S. Government Printing Office.

Fielding-Barnsley, R., & Purdie, N. (2005). Teachers' attitude to and knowledge of metalinguistics in the process of learning to read. *Asia-Pacific Journal of Teacher Education, 33,* 65–75.

Gamse, B. C., Jacob, R. T., Horst, M., Boulay, B., & Unlu, F. (2008). *Reading First impact study. Final report* (NCEE 2009-4038). Washington, DC: U.S. Department of Education, National Center for Education Evaluation and Regional Assistance.

Gilbert, J. K., Compton, D. L., Fuchs, D., Fuchs, L. S., Bouton, B., Barquero, L. A., & Cho, E. (2013). Efficacy of a first-grade responsiveness-to-intervention prevention model for struggling readers. *Reading Research Quarterly, 48*, 135–154.

Hall, S. L. (2018). *10 success factors for literacy intervention: Getting results with MTSS in elementary schools*. Alexandria, VA: Association for Supervision and Curriculum Development.

International Literacy Association (ILA). (2017). Standards for the preparation of literacy professionals. Retrieved from https://www.literacyworldwide.org/get-resources/standards/standards-2017

International Reading Association. (2003). *Prepared to make a difference: An executive summary of the National Commission on Excellence in elementary teacher preparation for reading instruction*. Newark, DE: Author.

Joshi, R. M., Binks, E., Graham, L., Dean, E., Smith, D., & Boulware-Gooden, R. (2009). Do textbooks used in university reading education courses conform to the instructional recommendations of the National Reading Panel? *Journal of Learning Disabilities, 42*, 458–463.

Juel, C. (1988). Learning to read and write: A longitudinal study of 54 children from first through fourth grades. *Journal of Educational Psychology, 80*, 437–447.

Landerl, K., & Wimmer, H. (2008). Development of word reading fluency and spelling in a consistent orthography: An 8-year follow-up. *Journal of Educational Psychology, 100*, 150–161.

Lyon, G. R. (2001, March 8). *Measuring success: Using assessments and accountability to raise student achievement*. Hearing before the Subcommittee on Education Reform, Committee on Education and the Workforce, U.S. House of Representatives.

Lyon, R., & Weiser, B. (2009). Teacher knowledge, instructional expertise, and the development of reading proficiency. *Journal of Learning Disabilities, 42*, 475–480. http://dx.doi.org/10.1177/0022219409338741

Mather, N., Bos, C., & Babur, N. (2001). Perceptions and knowledge of preservice and inservice teachers about early literacy instruction. *Journal of Learning Disabilities, 4*, 471–482.

McCardle, P., & Chhabra, V. (Eds.). (2004). *The voice of evidence in reading research*. Baltimore, MD: Paul H. Brookes Publishing Co.

McCutchen, D., Abbott, R. D., Green, L. B., Beretvas, S. N., Cox, S., Potter, N. S., . . . Gray A. L. (2002). Beginning literacy: Links among teacher knowledge, teacher practice, and student learning. *Journal of Learning Disabilities, 35*, 69–86.

McCutchen, D., Harry, D. R., Cox, S., Sidman, S., Covill, A. E., & Cunningham, A. E. (2002). Reading teachers' knowledge of children's literature and English phonology. *Annals of Dyslexia, 52*, 205–228.

Moats, L. C. (1994). The missing foundation in teacher education: Knowledge of the structure of spoken and written language. *Annals of Dyslexia, 44*, 81–102.

Moats, L. C. (1999). *Teaching reading is rocket science*. Washington, DC: American Federation of Teachers.

Moats, L. C. (2014). What teachers don't know and why they aren't learning it: Addressing the need for content and pedagogy in teacher education. *Australian Journal of Learning Difficulties*. http://dx.doi.org/10.1080/19404158.2014.941093.

National Assessment of Educational Progress (NAEP). (2017). *The Nation's Report Card: Reading*. Washington, DC: National Center for Educational Statistics.

Organisation for Economic Co-operation and Development (OECD). (2017). *Reading performance (PISA)*. http://dx.doi.org/10.1787/79913c69-en

Piasta, S. B., McDonald, C., Fishman, B. J., & Morrison, F. J. (2009). Teachers' knowledge of literacy concepts, classroom practices, and student reading growth. *Scientific Studies of Reading, 13*, 224–248.

Rose, J. (2009). *Identifying and teaching children and young people with dyslexia and literacy difficulties*. Retrieved from https://www.education.gov.uk/publications/standard/publication detail/page1/DCSF-00659-2009

Sadoski, M. (2012). *Imagery and text*. Mahwah, NJ: Lawrence Erlbaum Associates.

Snow, C. E., Burns, M. S., & Griffin, P. (Eds.). (1998). *Preventing reading difficulties in young children*. Washington, DC: National Academies Press.

Soriano-Ferrer, M., Echegaray-Bengoa, J., & Joshi, R. M. (2016). Knowledge and beliefs about developmental dyslexia in pre-service and in-service Spanish speaking teachers. *Annals of Dyslexia, 66,* 91–110.

Spear-Swerling, L., & Brucker, P. O. (2004). Preparing novice teachers to develop basic reading and spelling skills in children. *Annals of Dyslexia, 54,* 332–364.

Torgesen, J. K. (2008). Recent discoveries from research on remedial interventions for children with dyslexia. In M. Snowling & C. Hulme (Eds.), *The science of reading* (pp. 521–537). Oxford, United Kingdom: Blackwell Publishers.

Walsh, K., Glaser, D., & Wilcox, D. D. (2006). *What education schools aren't teaching about reading and what elementary teachers aren't learning.* Washington, DC: National Council on Teacher Quality (NCTQ).

Washburn, E., Binks-Cantrell, E., & Joshi, R. M. (2013). What do pre-service teachers from the US and UK know about dyslexia? *Dyslexia, 20,* 1–18.

Washburn, E. K., Binks-Cantrell, E. S., Joshi, R. M. Martin-Chang, S., & Arrow, A. (2016). Preservice teacher knowledge of basic language constructs in Canada, England, New Zealand and the United States. *Annals of Dyslexia, 66,* 7–26. http://dx.doi.org/10.1007/s11881-015-0115-x

Washburn, E. K., Joshi, R. M., & Binks-Cantrell, E. S. (2011a). Are preservice teachers prepared to teach struggling readers? *Annals of Dyslexia, 61,* 21–43.

Washburn, E., Joshi, R. M., & Binks-Cantrell, E. (2011b). Teacher knowledge of basic language concepts and dyslexia. *Dyslexia, 17,* 165–183.

CHAPTER 17

Scaling Up Evidence-Based Interventions for Reading Disorders

Bringing Research-Based Interventions
to Community Practice in Diverse Settings

Maureen W. Lovett, Karen A. Steinbach, and Maria De Palma

SUMMARY

Great progress has been made in understanding how to help children and teens with reading disabilities and what to do in the very early grades to reduce the risk of reading acquisition failure in children who struggle with reading. Many children remain without access to these evidence-based programs, however, in part due to the difficulties in translating research programs and findings into classroom practices. In this chapter, we describe a 35-year journey spent developing and evaluating reading interventions for children and youth with severe reading disabilities, testing the efficacy of these programs in community schools, and finally scaling up to reach struggling readers and their teachers across Canada and in some remote and international settings. We consider what is required to scale up programs for community schools, to provide meaningful professional development and mentoring for teachers, and to build an infrastructure for long-term sustainability. Building capacity requires partnerships that are respectful, equitable, and aware of the different levels of the systems within which children are embedded at school and at home. Literacy initiatives also involve a commitment to active patience: Changing systems—and entrenched habits of learning and teaching—takes time and extensive practice. A long-term perspective, knowing that a framework for cumulative effects is being built, is essential in any educational scaling initiative.

Acknowledgments: The Empower Reading Programs described in this chapter are published and trademarked by The Hospital for Sick Children, Toronto, Canada. The Programs are run as a nonprofit entity from within the Hospital's Research Institute; all revenues from materials and training are reinvested to support operational costs and the continued development and support of the program. We thank Dr. Jan Frijters for data analyses and statistical expertise. We thank the school boards and partners who shared their data with us, particularly the Hamilton-Wentworth District School Board, Avon Maitland District School Board, Waterloo Region District School Board, the Cree School Board, the Dr. Anjali Morris Education and Health Foundation in Pune, India, and Dr. Jeff Gruen and the Lexinome Project at Yale University. The research providing the framework within which the programs were developed was supported by operating grants from the *Eunice Kennedy Shriver* National Institute of Child Health and Human Development (NICHD) and the Institute of Education Sciences (IES).

INTRODUCTION

In the past 35 years, substantial strides have been made in our understanding of how to effectively intervene with children and teens who struggle to acquire basic literacy skills. Tens of thousands of children have profited from this research and received much-needed evidence-based intervention, but many thousands more remain without access to effective remediation.

The process of determining the efficacy and effectiveness of an intervention is complex and lengthy. The difficult journey of taking the results of intervention research to widespread practice has many stages of investigation: from initial stages of determining whether any benefits accrue following an intervention (relative to appropriate comparison and control conditions), to assessing the feasibility of implementation in real-life settings, to evaluating whether an intervention can be scaled up and used widely with demonstrated benefits. There are many examples of well-researched interventions that do not achieve the impact expected when scaled up to hundreds of classrooms. A special journal issue (see Foorman, 2016) is devoted to consideration of the many challenges to implementing effective reading interventions within schools. The collectively weak results suggest a need to better understand implementation processes, scaling-up issues, and the contextual factors that underlie successful implementation.

What are the obstacles to scale-up within schools? Why do many well-designed research interventions yield effects in controlled efficacy studies but far more variable findings in classroom-level practice? LaRusso, Donovan, and Snow (2016) examined differences in implementation of the Word Generation (WG; Snow, Lawrence, & White, 2009) and of the Strategic Adolescent Reading Intervention (STARI; Kim, Boyle, Zuilkowski, & Nakamura, 2016) programs as part of larger randomized controlled trials (RCTs) being conducted to evaluate them. Implementation levels varied widely across teachers and schools and averaged only 40% program activity completion in Grades 4–5 and 31% in Grades 6–7 for WG and 47% completion for STARI in Grades 6–8. Interview data and coaches' reports identified a range of obstacles to implementation of the WG full-class program and successful completion. These included lack of time for WG activities, competition from other new programs in the school, and class time lost due to testing and test preparation. The nature of teachers' experiences provided insight into the systemic challenges that undermined full implementation and suggested the supportive infrastructure that could have made a difference.

At the minimum, protected access to sufficient instructional time is absolutely critical for interventions to have the intensity and duration needed to effect change (Foorman, Dombek, & Smith, 2016; Grover, 2016). This is particularly true for interventions targeting struggling learners, who frequently require more time and more intensive instruction than peers. The failure to ensure sufficient instructional time is a major institutional barrier to quality implementation.

Wanzek and Vaughn (2016) reported different levels of implementation fidelity and quality of implementation for different components of their Promoting Adolescents' Comprehension of Text (PACT) reading comprehension intervention (Vaughn et al., 2013). They found high fidelity among teachers for parts of the program that used more familiar practices (e.g., comprehension checks) in contrast to components using less familiar teaching practices (critical reading and knowledge application). These data suggest the need for professional development support to enable teachers to consolidate and use new practices comfortably.

Fidelity monitoring, crucial to intervention efficacy trials, is also important to implementation and scale-up research. Without fidelity measures, we cannot know whether interventions fail due to poor implementation, flaws in the theoretical framework or methods on which the intervention is based, or a combination of both (Allen, Linnan, & Emmons, 2012). Reardon and Stuart (2017) argued that we will never understand how interventions work until we understand how intervention effects vary across time, place, people, and outcome measures. They advocated building evidence on effect heterogeneity across sites and samples, noting that only by doing so will we be able to predict what works, under what conditions, for whom, and in what context.

The best evidence-based models of intervention will not work without an infrastructure to support and sustain quality implementation. That infrastructure includes teachers but also requires support for teachers from their school community. Factors of school culture are extremely important. Administrators' buy-in and enthusiasm, teachers' openness to change, organizational support for quality implementation, and long-term access to champions and supportive mentors all contribute to fidelity and quality of implementation (Allen et al., 2012) and will affect the level of change achievable with well-researched efficacious interventions.

A CANADIAN PROGRAM OF INTERVENTION RESEARCH AND OUTREACH

This chapter summarizes some of our own experiences in leading a long-term program of research examining the ingredients of effective reading intervention, and in developing and evaluating multiple-component intervention programs to address the learning difficulties of children, youth, and adults who struggle with reading. Over 35 years, we have worked to understand the core learning problems of children and youth with severe reading disabilities. We have developed a series of research-based reading interventions with evidence of efficacy demonstrated in both multisite RCTs and, when RCTs were not possible, in quasi-experimental designs. These investigations have been conducted in schools in Canada and the United States, and the results have been reported in several papers (e.g., Lovett, DePalma et al., 2008; Lovett et al., 2017; Lovett, Lacerenza, De Palma, & Frijters, 2012; Morris et al., 2012). We have evaluated these interventions both in laboratory classrooms with our research teachers delivering them and in schools (still within experimental designs) with community teachers trained and mentored by our research teams.

In early studies, we compared phonological skill-based and strategy-training approaches to the remediation of severe reading disabilities. Although both approaches yielded positive effects, faster learning and better reading outcomes were achieved when we adopted a multiple-component intervention approach—one combining direct and dialogue-based instruction, explicitly teaching children different levels of subsyllabic segmentation and directly training them in the acquisition, use, and monitoring of multiple decoding strategies (Lovett, Lacerenza, Borden, et al., 2000). The critical importance of decoding strategy instruction, attributional and motivational retraining, and promotion of a flexible approach to word identification and text reading appeared necessary for achieving generalization and maintenance of intervention gains. Transfer and application of new learning was a focus of our research. The results led to the development of PHAST (for Phonology and Strategy Training) Reading (Lovett, Lacerenza, & Borden, 2000), since revised and updated to become the Empower Reading Programs, as shown in Figure 17.1. These programs have been described in Lovett, Lacerenza, Steinbach, and De Palma (2014).

Our interventions are taught in small groups and typically involve 1 hour of intense instruction, 5 days per week. Psychosocial factors play an important role in intervention response and long-term outcomes; among the most critical are motivation and the individual's perception of his or her self-efficacy as a learner. Most struggling readers have complex personal

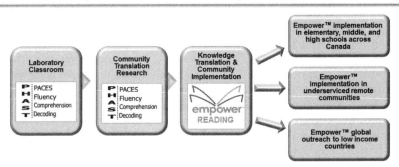

Evolution and Outreach of the Empower™ Reading Programs

PHAST Reading Programs are the research versions of Empower Reading

Figure 17.1. Knowledge translation and scaled implementation of our research-based reading intervention programs as Empower Reading.

histories that shape their experience of intervention and their trajectories of reading growth. We have found that interventions that target maladaptive attributions and motivational profiles during reading intervention result in improved reading outcomes and positive changes in motivation in adolescents with reading disabilities (Lovett, Frijters, Steinbach, Sevcik, & Morris, in preparation). In fact, the interweaving of motivational and attributional retraining, cognitive strategy instruction, and reading remediation characterizes our PHAST and our Empower Reading intervention programs at every developmental level, from the early grades (Lovett et al., 2017; Morris et al., 2012) through middle school (Frijters, Lovett, Sevcik, & Morris, 2013; Lovett, De Palma, et al., 2008), and into high school (Lovett et al., 2012).

With motivational issues in mind, our reading interventions are deliberately designed for small-group implementation. We have witnessed over decades the positive impact for struggling readers of dealing with literacy learning problems in the company of their similarly struggling peers. The impact of the instructional group can be substantial; yet, this is an aspect of findings that is not often interpreted in intervention research reports. Instructional group effects point to the need to study how group factors can mobilize or derail change for learners, and how teacher–student and student–student affiliation can contribute to intervention outcomes. Neglect of instructional group dynamics, teacher–student and student–student affiliation, and how group factors can mobilize change for struggling learners limits our understanding of the implementation contexts that facilitate the best outcomes for learners.

BEYOND THE LABORATORY CLASSROOM

Motivated by Canadian school board demand for the research-based interventions we had developed and reported beneficial for struggling readers, we undertook a limited outreach initiative in 2006 starting with five school board partners. We encouraged school boards to collect their own evaluation data, and we did no assessments ourselves. Sometimes school boards used their own accountability measures (e.g., Developmental Reading Assessment [DRA; Beaver, 2003], Running Records [Clay, 2000]), and sometimes they used standardized measures (e.g., Woodcock-Johnson subtests [Woodcock, McGrew, & Mather, 2001]) or asked us for the experimental measures used in our research. The school boards purchased the materials for the program and the teacher training and mentoring from The Hospital for Sick Children, our home institution that published and trademarked the intervention programs (originally known as PHAST Reading) under the name of Empower Reading. There are five Empower Reading Programs targeting different grade levels (Grades 2–5, 6–8, and High School)—some focusing on decoding and spelling, and some on vocabulary and comprehension. A more detailed history of the research and development of the Empower Reading Programs has been published (Lovett et al., 2014).

School boards are never given access to the materials without the teachers participating in the full professional development and extended mentoring programs attached to them. This includes professional development training days and a relationship with an Empower Reading mentor who visits teachers' classes. The professional development program consists of 4 full days of teacher training (two before teachers start teaching the program, and two throughout the school year) and onsite coaching by a mentor. The trainer/mentor visits the teacher's class and offers a range of services, providing supportive feedback, modeling parts of the lesson, observing teacher and students, and encouraging the teacher's progress. Between visits, the mentor is accessible by phone, e-mail, and text, and teachers are encouraged to communicate freely with them. The ideas underlying the professional development are described in Lovett, Lacerenza, De Palma, Steinbach, and Frijters (2008).

Training continues throughout the first year of implementation and into subsequent years. Every year, refresher training sessions are offered for teachers who have been trained in earlier years. Continued contact and communication with trainers and mentors is available as teachers become experienced in teaching Empower Reading over a period of years. Teachers' communication with the mentors and trainers is confidential, and school administrators are not provided feedback about how their teachers are doing.

As stated previously, school boards are encouraged to collect their own outcome data and monitor their children's progress in the programs. These findings are sometimes shared with us, and, with permission of the school boards involved, we include some examples here. School board results are described briefly to illustrate intervention efficacy as measured by staff in their own school settings. These accountability data do not provide an assessment of effectiveness equivalent to an RCT, but they do provide some indication of whether implementation in school board settings is associated with gains in student performance. Probably the best school board evidence provided thus far was collected by the Hamilton-Wentworth District School Board (HWDSB), located in Hamilton, an industrialized city located about 1 hour west of Toronto.

HWDSB was one of the five original Empower Reading partners; HWDSB was engaged with us first as a school board site for our research studies, and then in our very first outreach efforts in late 2006. HWDSB routinely administers to all children the DRA, a curriculum-based tool designed to assess annually or semi-annually a child's reading progress. HWDSB recently provided us with data from their ongoing assessments of 760 children who had received the Empower Reading: Decoding and Spelling intervention during their Grade 2 year. DRA results were available for several time points before, during, and after their Empower Reading participation. Figure 17.2a depicts the average changing trajectory of these 760 students during and following their participation in the Empower

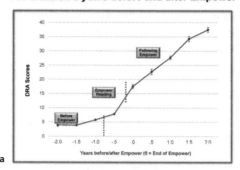

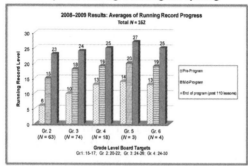

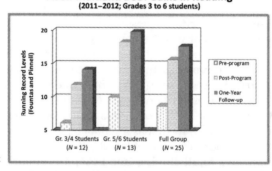

Figure 17.2. Accountability data collected by school boards as part of their implementation and evaluation of the Empower Reading Programs. a) Results from Hamilton Wentworth District School Board collected on 760 children. Outcomes used were Developmental Reading Assessment (DRA; Beaver, 2003) scores administered every 6 months for 2 years prior to Empower Reading participation and 2 years following program participation in Grade 2. b) Results from Waterloo Region District School Board. Outcomes used were Running Record (Clay, 2000) levels measured before, mid-way through, and following 110 lessons of Empower Reading: Decoding and Spelling Program. c) Results from Avon Maitland District School Board. Outcomes used were Running Record levels measured before, after, and 1 year following 110 lessons of Empower Reading: Decoding and Spelling Program.

Reading intervention. Although no control data exist, visible acceleration of the reading trajectories of these children is evidence of successful implementation by HWDSB. A significant change in trajectory was confirmed by growth curve modeling of these data. These data are reported in a manuscript in progress by White, Woerhle, and Frijters (Frijters, personal communication, August 24, 2018).

Other school boards also have shared their outcome data. We include two examples here. The Waterloo Region District School Board (WRDSB) used Running Records (Clay, 2000) as their outcome measure. Children referred for Empower Reading participation were tested before, midway through (approximately Lesson 55), and following their program (Lesson 110). The data are summarized in Figure 17.2b and are presented separately by grade. Most participants were drawn from Grades 2 and 3 although some struggling readers from Grades 4–6 were also offered the Empower Reading Program. Results demonstrated continued growth throughout the program for all grades but with seemingly steeper trajectories for children who received intervention in Grades 2 and 3. Another school board, Avon Maitland District School Board (AMDSB), also used Running Records as their reading measure but incorporated a 1-year follow-up testing point in addition to pre- and post-Empower Reading testing. These data, shown in Figure 17.2c, demonstrated solid average growth through the intervention year and maintenance of gains a year later; the growth rate was slower during the following year, however, than during the intervention year itself.

Scaling Up and Sustaining Evidenced-Based Practices in Schools

Scale-up of our research-based intervention programs has reached more than 2,500 teachers, whom we have trained to teach Empower Reading Programs to more than 55,000 children and teens across Canada. Although effectiveness evidence relies on descriptive rather than RCT-obtained results, average gains from our research studies using the precursor PHAST programs and average gains obtained in the Empower Reading outreach programs appear quite comparable. Figure 17.3a illustrates average pretest and posttest scores on standardized measures of decoding and word reading for second- and third-grade struggling readers who were taught either in the research PHAST classes or in the outreach Empower Reading classes. Figure 17.3b examines pretest and posttest outcomes on a sensitive outcome measure used in many of our intervention studies, the multisyllabic Challenge Words Test (Lovett et al., 1994). In this example, struggling readers were taught either in the research-run PHAST classes ($N = 112$) or in a range of different Empower Reading outreach settings. These included an early outreach implementation by a Canadian school board (HWDSB, $N = 227$), a partnership in Pune India (Anjali Morris Foundation, $N = 175$), a partnership with the Cree School Board in eight remote community sites ($N = 53$), and a research implementation of Empower Reading Programs

Comparing research and "real world" implementation gains

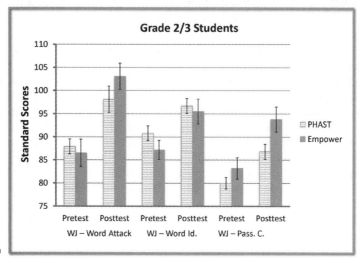

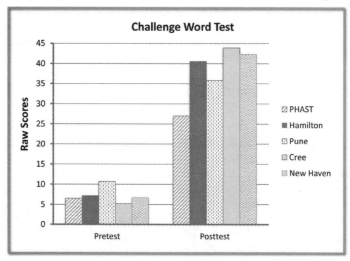

Comparing research and diverse site implementation gains

Figure 17.3.   Comparison of average gains following implementation of the PHAST (Phonology and Strategy Training) Reading research programs (Lovett, Lacerenza, & Borden, 2000) and following implementation of the Empower Reading Programs run in diverse community settings. a) Comparison of average pretest and posttest standard scores on Woodcock-Johnson (WJ; Woodcock, McGrew, & Mather, 2001) Word Attack, Word Identification (Word Id.), and Passage Comprehension (Pass. Cp.) subtests for second- and third-grade struggling readers taught either in the research PHAST classes or in the outreach Empower Reading classes. b) A comparison of average pretest and posttest scores on an experimental intervention measure, the Challenge Word Test (Lovett et al., 1994), which assesses reading aloud a set of uninstructed multisyllabic words specifically related to instructed content and strategies. Originally containing 110 items, it now consists of 55 items. Performance on the shorter version is presented in this figure.

as part of a longitudinal genetics research program being undertaken in New Haven Schools by Dr. Jeff Gruen at Yale University ($N = 38$). Across these diverse sites, intervention gains from very different groups of struggling readers appear to be on par with and in some cases exceeding those of children from the research classes.

There may be some differences in our approach to outreach that contrast with other approaches to scale-up in schools and that contribute to positive results to date. As one example, we invest considerable effort in initial communication before undertaking any outreach implementation. We build school and administrative support for new Empower Reading teachers and implementation sites so that a supportive infrastructure for quality implementation is in place for the teacher even before the first lessons occur. This is accomplished through presentations to superintendents, special education advisory groups, and principals about the program, the type of child for whom the program is intended, the importance of the duration and frequency of instruction, and the importance of increasing teacher experience with the instructional methods. An Empower Reading "community" is built across school districts, by connecting new boards/schools with existing boards/schools for advice. Excited and enthusiastic program teachers are the most effective advertisement for any new initiative. "Lunch and learn" sessions are available for other school staff, and we offer evening parent information sessions. All of our trainers and mentors are expected to approach new sites with a clear attitude of mutual respect and genuine regard for what teachers do and use already. Open dialogue and collaborative problem solving with all teachers being trained is essential, and trainers and mentors are themselves observed and monitored to ensure that the desired values are being represented in their training relationships.

Another consistent feature of our perspective on scale-up has been to start small, working from the ground up rather than imposing an initiative from the top. When new school board partners express a desire to place the program in every school in their system, we suggest starting with 5–10 schools and then building capacity gradually over a few years. By increasing capacity slowly, an opportunity is afforded to allow exemplary teachers to emerge and perhaps be identified and recruited into helping to support new teachers within following years.

There has been recent comment on the need for better-articulated and more productive research–practitioner partnerships in education (Grover, 2016; Snow, 2015). There has also been recognition of the fact that partnerships must be of mutual benefit to all participating parties, and characterized by genuine mutual respect, if they are to become sustainable (Foorman et al., 2016).

A synthesis of evidence on scaling up literacy education in low- and middle-income countries adds to the commentary on scaling-up issues generally. The *Landscape Report on Early Grade Literacy* includes this comment: "It is critical to build capacity, including among influential local champions who will support the program in the future. As capacity increases, the potential for significant local ownership increases as well" (Kim et al., 2016, p. 60).

Scholars of system change have concluded that there is no universal blueprint or validated formula for scaling up evidence-based practices. Coburn (2003) was an early contender, however, of the view that to be truly "at scale," ownership of the practice must shift. With this shift in ownership, she speculated that reforms, practices, and innovations became self-generative and more likely to be sustainable over time (Coburn, 2003; McLaughlin & Mitra, 2001).

Analysis of the body of evidence described in the *Landscape Report* is also relevant to another perspective on the challenges of scaling up. In their conclusions, Kim and colleagues (2016) made explicit the important observation that initiatives to improve children's literacy require systemic efforts and involve stakeholders at multiple levels. Children attending school are embedded in multiple systems—those of classroom, school, district, province, or state—but they are embedded also within the systems of family and community.

Reaching Vulnerable Communities of At-Risk Children: A Need to Understand the Contexts

Factors of family and community culture are also especially important to understand in establishing new partnerships, particularly in remote settings or in different countries. We have undertaken initiatives to reach vulnerable populations of at-risk children in remote communities. We established programs in eight remote regions within the Cree School Board serving the Cree Nation, an Indigenous people in northern Quebec. Indigenous people in Canada suffer a huge gap in literacy and education relative to their non-Indigenous neighbors. We worked with our Cree Board colleagues to honor the Cree traditions and language and to establish opportunities for English reading development for elementary children and high school youth functioning many grade levels below expectations.

Descriptive results from these sites are positive, as are family and teacher feedback. There are many contextual challenges, however. These include the complexity of the heterogeneous language and literacy environments within the children's families. Cree is the mother tongue, primarily spoken at home. English is the main second language, and for some, French is a third language. Parents vary in their own literacy skills. Most Cree teachers are assigned to teach Cree language and culture and general education; as a result, there are few Cree teachers teaching Empower Reading. A lack of culturally relevant text materials for intervention is also a continuing problem, as are absenteeism and unreliable Internet access in some communities.

Global and international literacy efforts are the ultimate test of developing interventions with and for partners and attempting scale-up together. We are also participating in a literacy partnership with the Dr. Anjali Morris Education and Health Foundation (AMF) in Pune, India. Together, we are using the Empower Reading Programs to facilitate the English reading acquisition of Indian children who attend English-medium schools and require reading intervention. Learning disabilities are not widely recognized in India, and teachers are not prepared to teach children who struggle with basic academic skills. The AMF offers assessment and intervention services in its center, and it also provides training and consultation to schools, offering professional development in recognizing and remediating learning disabilities.

The partnership initiative in India is exposing us to a new range of implementation challenges related to a lack of infrastructure in many local Pune schools for such an intensive program as Empower Reading and the reality that time during the school day is not allocated or available for remedial interventions to be offered. As in many global literacy contexts, multiple language backgrounds complicate reading instruction and reading remediation. In Pune, Marathi is the most common language, and children are expected to acquire competence with English, Hindi, and Marathi. Although the AMF teachers are well trained and well prepared to deal with children's learning challenges, many teachers in local English-medium schools lack English language proficiency and any knowledge of learning disabilities and remediation practices. Data from the first 175 children receiving Empower Reading (both at the AMF center and in the schools) are encouraging, however, and suggest that the intervention framework can be adapted and produce gains on standardized and experimental outcome measures. Support for the acquisition of oral proficiency in the language of literacy instruction will always be an important part of the adaptation process.

CONCLUSION

Scaling up is ultimately about building capacity for quality implementation of an intervention or practice. There is no point in attempting to address the complexities of scale-up unless there is a commitment to high-quality implementation across settings. Such an innovation must be evidence based; that is, it must have already been demonstrated to have robust and replicable efficacy in rigorously controlled evaluation research.

Capacity building requires partnerships that are respectful, equitable, and cognizant of the different levels of the systems within which children are embedded at school and at home. As articulated by Kim and colleagues (2016), improving children's literacy abilities requires systemic involvement and engagement and necessitates the commitment of stakeholders at multiple levels, including the classroom and school as well as the family and community. Literacy initiatives also involve a mindset of active patience: Changing systems, and entrenched habits of learning and teaching, take time and extensive practice. A cumulative effects perspective is essential in any educational scaling initiative (Kim et al., 2016). Stakeholders and local champions should be encouraged to look for progress milestones but realize that change on a larger scale will take years and decades rather than months. Literacy assumes a certain level of oral language proficiency because reading and writing are scaffolded on a framework of speech and language competence (Seidenberg, 2017). Becoming literate requires thousands of hours of practice, and acquiring oral language takes even longer.

In the realm of dyslexia and reading disabilities, we know that design, implementation, evaluation, tailoring, and building capacity are all key to facilitating good outcomes for affected children and teens. Sharing findings and procedures across silos of expertise can improve the quality of classroom literacy instruction and reduce the number of children requiring dyslexia interventions. Access to effective intervention for dyslexia and other reading problems was the starting point for this chapter, and we suggest that unequal access to intervention and inadequate teacher preparation are also issues requiring a systems perspective. Whether dealing with dyslexia intervention, classroom reading instruction, or global literacy initiatives, the challenges of bringing programs and practices to scale are common to everyone striving to allow all children access to a literate future and the abundant opportunities associated with a literate life.

REFERENCES

Allen, J. D., Linnan, L. A., & Emmons, K. M. (2012). Fidelity and its relationship to implementation effectiveness, adaptation, and dissemination. In R. C. Brownson, G. A. Colditz, & E. L. Proctor (Eds.), *Dissemination and implementation research in health: Translating science to practice* (pp. 281–304). New York, NY: Oxford University Press.

Beaver, J. (2003). *Developmental Reading Assessment*. Parsippany, NJ: Celebration Press.

Clay, M. (2000). *Running Records: For classroom teachers*. Northcote, Auckland: Pearson Education New Zealand.

Coburn, C. E. (2003). Rethinking scale: Moving beyond numbers to deep and lasting change. *Educational Researcher, 32*(6), 3–12.

Foorman, B. (2016). Challenges and solutions to implementing effective reading intervention in schools. *New Directions for Child and Adolescent Development, 154,* 7–10.

Foorman, B., Dombek, J., & Smith, K. (2016). Seven elements important to successful implementation of early literacy intervention. *New Directions for Child and Adolescent Development, 154,* 49–65.

Frijters, J. C., Lovett, M. W., Sevcik, R. A., & Morris, R. D. (2013). Four methods of identifying change in the context of a multiple component reading intervention for struggling middle school readers. *Reading and Writing: An Interdisciplinary Journal, 26*(4), 539–563.

Grover, V. (2016). Commentary: Implementing interventions: Building a shared understanding of why. *New Directions for Child and Adolescent Development, 154,* 109–112.

Kim, J. S., Hemphill, L., Troyer, M. T., Thomson, J. M., Jones, S. M., LaRusso, M., & Donovan, S. (2017). Engaging struggling adolescent readers to improve reading skills. *Reading Research Quarterly, 52*(3), 357–382.

Kim, Y.-S. G., Boyle, H. N., Zuilkowski, S. S., & Nakamura, P. (2016). *Landscape report on early grade literacy*. Washington, DC: USAID.

LaRusso, M. D., Donovan, S., & Snow, C. E. (2016). Implementation challenges for Tier One and Tier Two school-based programs for early adolescents. *New Directions for Child and Adolescent Development, 154,* 11–30.

Lovett, M. W., Borden, S. L., DeLuca, T., Lacerenza, L., Benson, N. J., & Brackstone, D. (1994). Treating the core deficits of developmental dyslexia: Evidence of transfer-of-learning following strategy- and phonologically-based reading training programs. *Developmental Psychology, 30*(6), 805–822.

Lovett, M. W., De Palma, M., Frijters, J. C., Steinbach, K. A., Temple, M., Benson, N. J., & Lacerenza, L. (2008). Interventions for reading difficulties: A comparison of response to intervention by ELL and EFL struggling readers. *Journal of Learning Disabilities, 41*(4), 333–352.

Lovett, M. W., Frijters, J. C., Steinbach, K. A., Sevcik, R. A., & Morris, R. D. (in prep.). *Motivational changes in adolescents with reading disabilities following reading intervention.* Manuscript in preparation.

Lovett, M. W., Frijters, J. C., Steinbach, K. A., Wolf, M., Sevcik, R. A., & Morris, R. D. (2017). Early intervention for children at risk for reading disability: The impact of grade at intervention and individual differences on intervention outcomes. *Journal of Educational Psychology, 109,* 889–914.

Lovett, M. W., Lacerenza, L., & Borden, S. B. (2000). Putting struggling readers on the PHAST track: A program to integrate phonological and strategy-based remedial reading instruction and maximize outcomes. *Journal of Learning Disabilities, 33*(5), 458–476.

Lovett, M. W., Lacerenza, L., Borden, S. L., Frijters, J. C., Steinbach, K. A., & De Palma, M. (2000). Components of effective remediation for developmental reading disability: Combining phonological and strategy-based instruction to improve outcomes. *Journal of Educational Psychology, 92,* 263–283.

Lovett, M. W., Lacerenza, L., De Palma, M., & Frijters, J. C. (2012). Evaluating the efficacy of remediation for struggling readers in high school. *Journal of Learning Disabilities, 45*(2), 151–169.

Lovett, M. W., Lacerenza, L., De Palma, M., Steinbach, K. A., & Frijters, J. C. (2008). Preparing teachers to remediate reading disabilities in high school: What is needed for effective professional development? *Teaching and Teacher Education, 24*(4), 1083–1097.

Lovett, M. W., Lacerenza, L., Steinbach, K. A., & De Palma, M. (2014). Empower Reading: Development and roll-out of a research-based intervention program for children with reading disabilities. *Perspectives on Language and Literacy, 40,* 21–31.

McLaughlin, M. W., & Mitra, D. (2001). Theory-based change and change-based theory: Going deeper and going broader. *Journal of Educational Change, 2*(4), 301–323.

Morris, R. D., Lovett, M. W., Wolf, M. Sevcik, R. A., Steinbach, K. A., Frijters, J. C., & Shapiro, M. (2012). Multiple-component remediation for developmental reading disabilities: IQ, socioeconomic status, and race as factors in remedial outcome. *Journal of Learning Disabilities, 45*(2), 99–127.

Reardon, S. F., & Stuart, E. A. (2017). Editors' introduction: Theme issue on variation in treatment effects. *Journal of Research on Educational Effectiveness, 10*(4), 671–674.

Seidenberg, M. S. (2017). *Language at the speed of sight: How we read, why so many can't, and what can be done about it.* New York, NY: Basic Books.

Snow, C. E. (2015). Rigor and realism: Doing educational science in the real world. *Educational Researcher, 44*(9), 460–466.

Snow, C. E., Lawrence, J. F., & White, C. (2009). Generating knowledge of academic language among urban middle school students. *Journal of Research on Educational Effectiveness, 2*(4), 325–344.

Vaughn, S., Swanson, E. A., Roberts, G., Wanzek, J., Stillman-Spisak, S. J., Solis, M., & Simmons, D. (2013). Improving reading comprehension and social studies knowledge in middle school. *Reading Research Quarterly, 48*(1), 77–93.

Wanzek, J., & Vaughn, S. (2016). Implementation of a text-based content intervention in secondary social studies classes. *New Directions for Child and Adolescent Development, 154,* 31–48.

Woodcock, R. W., McGrew, K. S., & Mather, N. (2001). *Woodcock-Johnson- III Tests of Achievement.* Itasca, IL: Riverside.

CHAPTER 18

Statistical Considerations for Creating, Evaluating, and Choosing Behavioral Screening Assessments
Yaacov Petscher, Christopher T. Stanley, Brian Gearin, and Hank Fien

SUMMARY

It is extremely important to detect struggling readers early, including those with dyslexia, so they may receive targeted instruction and intervention to remediate their reading difficulties. Understanding and choosing the assessments that measure literacy skills is an important part of a screening process because not all assessments are created equal. Although many reading assessments measure the accuracy or automaticity of letter knowledge, phonological awareness, and word reading, they often vary in their technical adequacy for the purpose of screening for dyslexia risk. In this chapter, we review some of the key considerations and best practices related to universal screening tools. One consideration is accuracy, the extent to which screeners will offer results that are able to capture a reader's true abilities. We cover related topics, including various forms of reliability, or how consistent measurement scores are. We also introduce validity, which is related to the degree to which a tool measures what it is supposed to measure. The chapter concludes with a summary of the factors that go into understanding, choosing, and using a screening tool for dyslexia risk. This decision-making process is summarized with reference to a list of 15 questions individuals may consider, which are intended to simplify understanding and discussion among and between parents, educators, and administrators. Although there are many considerations when it comes to literacy-related assessments, there are some essential considerations and best practices that shed light on screening tools and processes.

INTRODUCTION

There are converging and diverging viewpoints about what constitutes best practice in universal screening for dyslexia risk. Viewpoints tend to converge on the overarching approach schools should take when implementing universal screening. For instance, state laws generally favor the use of universal screening within a response to intervention (RTI) framework or a multi-tiered system of support (MTSS; Youman & Mather, 2015). Within such frameworks, all students are screened early and at multiple time points to assess risk for reading problems (e.g., benchmark assessments at fall, winter, and spring in Grades K–3, one or more times per year for dyslexia in Grades K–2). Scores that assess risk for poor reading or dyslexia are then used to make instructional decisions, such as group placement or the receipt of supplemental intervention. There is also widespread agreement that school systems should carefully attend to the foundational elements of universal screening, such as the technical adequacy and efficiency of screeners and the ways in which screening data will ultimately inform placement and instruction (e.g., Pentimonti, Walker, & Edmonds, 2017). Finally, there is basic agreement about core components to attend to when evaluating the technical adequacy of screeners, such as the reliability of scores and classification accuracy (Compton, Fuchs, Fuchs, & Bryant, 2006; Johnson, Jenkins, & Petscher, 2010).

Viewpoints tend to diverge when it comes to the specific decisions that schools must make when implementing universal screening in an RTI/MTSS framework, such as the selection of screeners and how to best use screening scores (e.g., VanDerHeyden & Burns, 2017). Several factors likely contribute to the diverging viewpoints. The first factor is the sheer number of decisions school systems must make when choosing and implementing universal screening. Effectively implementing universal screening is not a simple matter of selecting and administering a test. School systems have to consider when the screener will be administered, to whom, and how the scores will be used. Because each one of these decisions must be evaluated against the local context, and because school systems differ in terms of their student populations, financial resources, technical infrastructure, and schedules, what is best practice for one school might not be best practice for another.

A second factor complicating the identification of best practices is that screening for any condition usually involves tradeoffs in risks, costs, and benefits. For instance, one screener might be highly sensitive and occasionally indicate the presence of a condition in individuals who do not actually have it (i.e., a false positive), whereas another screener may be less sensitive and occasionally fail to indicate the presence of a condition when one is actually present (i.e., a false negative). Both scenarios have costs and benefits. The first scenario may lead to unnecessary treatment for the condition, whereas the latter scenario may lead to the lack of necessary treatment. Because screening involves a competition between values, it can be difficult to gain universal support for a particular practice. Much of the ongoing research on dyslexia screeners aims to elucidate how various aspects of screening (e.g., the number of measures, the level of cut scores, the administration protocol) can be adjusted to achieve a different balance between cost and benefits (e.g., Andrade, Andrade, & Capellini, 2015; Johnson, Jenkins, Petscher, & Catts, 2009).

CORE CONSIDERATIONS IN BEHAVIORAL SCREENING

Core concepts and statistical underpinnings of school-based screening have been covered extensively in educational and psychological literature (e.g., Glover & Albers, 2007). In many ways, these exemplar sources take advantage of, or presume, a reader's knowledge of more basic conceptual and statistical concepts that themselves undergird the screening process. An organizing heuristic to ground our discussion is that behavioral screening concepts may exist as a hierarchy. The base consideration of a screener is the population of interest (e.g., students with dyslexia, students with language disorders); followed by the scope of assessment (e.g., what type of risk is being screened, what kind of screener is being developed or used, what is its compatibility with needs); and then statistical considerations of reliability, validity, and classification accuracy to finally inform decision making.

Population of Interest

Although a seemingly intuitive component of behavioral screening, a well-operationalized population of interest informed by etiology and symptomatology is the critical foundation for evaluating, creating, or choosing a screener for direct services in a school setting. For example, if the intended population is children with dyslexia, there is a necessary but insufficient aspect to this brief descriptor. The developmental part of the population has been identified (i.e., children) as well an identified outcome (i.e., dyslexia) that separates the individuals from other identified outcomes (e.g., students with language disorders, students with psychological disabilities); however, it is lacking in specificity for the age range of the population and the expected symptomology associated with the identification outcome. A close correspondence between what is developmentally appropriate in content for measurement and the identified outcome safeguards against poor assessment decision making, such as screening for dyslexia risk in preschool-age children with a nonword fluency assessment or administering a letter-naming fluency task to fifth-grade students.

Because varying definitions of dyslexia are adopted by professional associations, states, and hospitals, clarity in definition is necessary to separate etiology (i.e., an array of causes of a particular condition) and symptomology (i.e., an array of observable symptoms characteristic of a particular condition). Moreover, definitional clarity can provide a strong thread among the population, a particular screener, and an operationalized outcome tied to the operationalized definition. For example, the definitions of dyslexia by the Mayo Clinic (2018) and by The International Dyslexia Association (2002) vary significantly in terms of specificity in etiology and symptomology. As a result, the definition of dyslexia adopted can significantly affect the development and use of dyslexia screeners. Furthermore, primary research findings can yield different conclusions and implications for definitions of dyslexia that may lead to different methods of screening for dyslexia risk (see differences in viewpoint on the inclusion of cognitive models in dyslexia between de Jong [see Chapter 4] and Castles and Kohnen [see Chapter 11]).

Scope of Assessment

The *scope of assessment* level of building or evaluating behavioral screeners is multidimensional with significant depth. Flowing from the population of interest are issues related to scope, such as: 1) the alignment between the operationalized outcome (e.g., what risk is being screened for; Keenan & Meenan, 2014) and the operationalized screener (e.g., what risk is being screened by; Glover & Albers, 2007), 2) whether the screener is speed based (e.g., time limited) or power based (e.g., fixed-item or computer adaptive accuracy measures), and 3) whether single or multiple assessments should be combined (e.g., Compton et al., 2010). Assessment scope issues such as compatibility with service delivery needs, localizing screeners, and frequency of administration have been covered by others (e.g., Glover & Albers, 2007).

Screener–Outcome Alignment   Alignment between how dyslexia risk is operationalized as an outcome for validated screener assessments (e.g., norm- or criterion-referenced word reading or poor reading comprehension) and what a screener measures in its content has important implications for the screening process because not all assessments are created equal. To illustrate, even though reading comprehension assessments, such as the Gray Oral Reading Test (GORT; Wiederholt & Bryant, 1992), Qualitative Reading Inventory–3 (QRI; Leslie & Caldwell, 2002), Woodcock-Johnson III Passage Comprehension (WJPC; Woodcock, McGrew, & Mather, 2001), and Peabody Individual Achievement Test (PIAT; Dunn & Markwardt, 1970), are viewed as standardized, norm-referenced tests of reading comprehension, the individuals they identify as having poor comprehension skills may vary. In a sample of 995 children, Keenan and Meenan (2014) found that for those students achieving at the lowest 10% of the distribution of each assessment, only 39%–56% of students were consistent across pairs of the assessment. That is, when categorizing students at or below the 10th percentile of the WJPC, only 39% of those students were found to be at or below the 10th percentile of the GORT. Not only can variability exist in who gets identified based on the operationalized outcome, but the interplay between outcome and screener can also matter. The way a stimulus is designed to measure reading skills in the screener and the outcome assessment is critical to understand when evaluating screening assessments because there are important implications for which students are identified with dyslexia based on the alignment between the screener and the outcome.

Speed- or Power-Based Assessments   The research on trade-offs between speed-based assessments, such as curriculum-based measurements (CBMs) that measure speed and accuracy, and power-based assessments, such as computer-adaptive assessments (CAAs), is in its infancy. CBMs in reading have long been used for universal screening due to the brevity in administration and psychometric properties of reliability and validity (Petscher, Cummings, Biancarosa, & Fien, 2013). CAAs have more recently permeated the screening landscape because they are more reliable than fixed-item assessments at the individual level (Wainer, Dorans, Flaugher, Green, & Mislevy, 2000) and leverage accuracy-based performance without regard to automaticity. An important consideration for CAAs is that they elevate the potential for estimating the true correlation between assessments. That is, a known psychometric property of reliability is that a correlation between two assessments cannot exceed the square root of the product of the reliability for measures (Nunnally & Bernstein, 1994). Suppose that a researcher has a screener with a reliability of .75 and an outcome with a reliability of .85; in this case, the maximum correlation that can be estimated is $\sqrt{.75(.85)} = .798$. As the reliability of either measure changes, so does the maximum correlation. An implication for screening is that an advantage of CAAs compared to CBMs lies in the ability of CAAs to maximize student-level reliability that may then yield larger possible correlations and classification accuracy.

Univariate or Multivariate Screening   The extent to which one or more screeners are necessary for dyslexia screening or broader reading risk is not a new discussion. A critical goal in the screening process is to ensure that false positives and false negatives are minimized so that more accurate screening results may be observed. Previous research noted that univariate screening produces too many false positives (e.g., Johnson et al., 2010; Johnson et al., 2009). Research into multiple-screener methods revealed that multivariate screening models, such as two-stage (Compton et al., 2006; Compton et al., 2010) and four-step screening (Gilbert, Compton, Fuchs, & Fuchs, 2012), and hybrid model approaches yield greater classification accuracy and longitudinal stability of classification by not only leveraging multiple screening assessments but also including measures of estimated growth on the screeners. In one of only a few existing screening studies for language impairment risk or dyslexia compared to typical word reading, Adlof, Scoggins, Brazendale, Babb, and Petscher (2017) found that a combined battery of word reading and listening comprehension was approximately equal in discriminatory power of identification (i.e., area under the curve; AUC = .79) over using only word reading (AUC = .78) in risk for language impairment. Moreover, risk of dyslexia was not improved by a combined battery (AUC = .85) compared to using only word reading (AUC = .86).

Another contextual consideration in multivariate screening is the extent to which multiple informants may improve screener decision. Despite calls from the field to include and evaluate how well teacher ratings may improve screening (e.g., Davis, Lindo, & Compton, 2007), few studies have done so. Compton and colleagues (2012) used a battery of universal screening measures, Tier 1 and Tier 2 progress monitoring data, teacher ratings of student attention and behavior, standardized tests of word reading and listening comprehension, and tutor ratings of attention and behavior of students in Tier 2 to evaluate how much data was necessary for screening for non-RTI across tiers. Results showed that adding both Tier 1 progress monitoring and teacher ratings improved AUC from .88 in a model with only screeners to .92 with added measurements. However, it is unclear the extent to which teacher ratings served as the active ingredient in moving the AUC compared to the progress monitoring data, especially in light of research that shows the unique value of slopes in predicting outcomes above benchmark status measures (e.g., Kim, Petscher, Schatschneider, & Foorman, 2010; Zumeta, Compton, & Fuchs, 2012).

When viewing the scope of assessments, the tension of univariate or multivariate screening is related to process rather than measure. That is, screeners are developed individually, are frequently administered as individual assessments, and have recommendations for screening at the individual assessment level. The decision as to whether univariate or multivariate scores should be used should be informed by how well those individual assessment scores may be combined in a meaningful way that collectively can improve screening beyond the utility of the individual measures. Furthermore, given the previous sections that have been outlined related to considerations for scope of assessment, it is important that continued research evaluates alignment issues of screeners to outcomes and the impact of reliability on dyslexia screening.

Statistical Considerations for Screeners

After reviewing the population of interest and the multidimensional components related to the scope of the assessment, three of the final four components in the screening hierarchy discussed at the outset of this chapter are statistical in nature (i.e., reliability, validity, and classification accuracy). Each of these features of screener psychometrics themselves are necessary but insufficient ingredients in creating, choosing, and using a behavioral screener. In the following subsections, we touch on each technical standard and raise key aspects one might be mindful of in evaluating tools.

Reliability   The most basic definition of reliability is the consistency of a set of scores for a measure; yet, this definition may be deceptively simplistic in the context of psychometrics due to the number of ways it can be estimated. Different forms of reliability include internal consistency, alternate form reliability, test–retest reliability, split-half reliability, and interrater reliability. Careful evaluation of the reliability of a screener is necessary because not all forms of reliability are created equal.

Internal Consistency   Internal consistency is how well a set of scores (e.g., item responses) from an assessment correlate with each other. The importance of reporting this form of reliability is that one is able to quickly gauge the coherence of items for a screener and then view its potential impact on correlation and classification accuracy (see the previous section on speed- and power-based assessments). A known limitation of internal consistency is that researchers frequently report it via Cronbach's alpha, a statistic that has received criticism due to its easy-to-meet methodological assumptions and the fact that it may be artificially inflated simply by adding items (McNeish, 2017). When reporting internal consistency via Cronbach's alpha or alternative statistics such as omega total, coefficient H, or the greatest lower bound, the ideal is for internal consistency to minimally exceed .80 for research purposes and .90 for clinical decision making (Nunnally & Bernstein, 1994).

Alternate Form Reliability

Screener technical reports frequently include alternate form reliability, also referred to as parallel form reliability, which is defined as the consistency of scores (i.e., the correlation) between two different versions of the same test. This form of reliability can be useful for characterizing the feasibility of using different forms across groups of individuals, or within a group across multiple waves of data collection. A strength in reporting alternate form reliability is that when its evidence is strong, the use of alternate forms allows practitioners to guard against practice or exposure effects (i.e., the likelihood for an individual to get an item right because of previous exposure to the same stimulus). A potential weakness is that the threshold for acceptable levels should be high to ensure that individual difference performances across forms are due to actual ability changes and not form effects. For example, an alternate form reliability of .70 might suggest a strong correlation, but it also suggests significant nonoverlap in measurement because a .70 estimate translates to only 49% shared variance in scores between two forms. Likewise, alternate form reliability of .90 points translates to very high overlap in the scores (i.e., 81%), but nearly 20% of the variance between the forms is unexplained. This finding does not by itself point to a fatality in form equivalence but speaks to a broader contextual issue that has emerged in the last decade of screening research related to if, when, and how to adjust for lack of equivalence across forms of assessments (Francis et al., 2008; Petscher & Kim, 2011).

Test–Retest Reliability

The longitudinal consistency of scores is frequently reported when the screener is given at two short-interval time points. Retest reliability can be useful in the very short time frame of administration (e.g., 1 week) to demonstrate that the relative rank ordering of scores does not change over time. Two limitations of this form of reliability are temporal and growth-expectation factors. The former refers to the amount of time between administrations for test–retest reliability; a review of many screeners that have been evaluated by the academic screening tool chart from the National Center on Intensive Intervention (2019) showed example retest spacing of 1 week, 2 week, and 4 week. The greater the amount of time between testing occasions, the more maturation effects influence the strength of the correlation. In a related manner, the theoretical expectation for growth is also critical for evaluating test–retest reliability. That is, beyond considering the retest spacing, does a researcher expect individuals in the sample to differentially change over the 1-week, 2-week, or 4-week period? To the extent that individual differences change over time, low retest reliability may reflect such an expectation.

Split-Half Reliability   Split-half reliability tests for how well one portion of the screener (e.g., odd items) correlates with another portion of the screener (e.g., even items). Although this form of reliability can provide a proxy for alternate form reliability, it is also limited due to the possibility of manipulating how the halves are constructed in order to achieve optimal estimates (Chakrabartty, 2013).

Interrater Reliability   A final form of reliability worth evaluating is interrater reliability, and it is the consistency of scores on a particular behavior between two or more raters. Interrater reliability is key when validating scores from observation tools such as teacher ratings of student behaviors (Anastopoulous et al., 2018). Even within the context of direct student assessment, interrater reliability can be useful in understanding the extent to which differences among students in screener scores are due to administration or scoring errors. Cummings, Biancarosa, Schaper, and Reed (2014) evaluated the relation between examiner errors in scoring oral reading fluency probes and found that 16% of the variance in scores was due to examiner differences. Such findings underscore the potential importance of calibrating administrations of screeners to reduce scoring errors and misidentification.

The interplay among reliability types in creating, choosing, and using screeners for dyslexia is balance and purpose for evaluating reported statistics based on the need for each type. If researchers were to take a set of indices (e.g., Social Security number, date of birth, and height), collected data would demonstrate excellent test–retest reliability but poor internal consistency (McCrae, Kurtz, Yamagata, & Terracciano, 2011). On the other hand, an assessment of stress might have good internal consistency and poor test–retest reliability. The choice of which forms of reliability are most important for a dyslexia screener is inextricably tied to the scope of the assessment. CBMs operate as speeded assessments and thus do not report information at the item level; thus, estimates of internal consistency are not provided. Instead, these types of assessments rely on alternate form and test–retest reliability. CAAs operate with inherent equivalence across forms (i.e., all items are calibrated to the same scale). Thus, CAA reliability tends to be reported via marginal reliability (akin to internal consistency) and test–retest reliability.

Validity   Just as reliability is multifaceted in nature, so is the concept of validity to the point that we may be able to provide an alphabetized and nonexhaustive sample of forms of validity that include etiological, conclusion, concurrent, construct, content, convergent, criterion, discriminant, ecological, external, face, factor, hypothesis, in situ, internal, nomological, predictive, translational, treatment, and washback. At its core, validity is simply concerned with the extent to which something measures what it purports to measure. A word-reading test should measure word reading and not receptive vocabulary. An historical perspective of validity was that three independent types of validity existed (i.e., content, criterion, and construct validity) and could be readily interchanged (Messick, 1995). Content validity is primarily established by the consistency of expert judgments that test content is related to its described use. A classical definition of criterion validity is the simple correlation between a test score and an outcome score, and construct validity is concerned with the interpretation and use of scores (Messick, 1995). Messick (1989) sought to reconceptualize all forms of validity as forming a cohesive, unified framework of construct validity. This framework includes the six areas that should be evaluated to measure construct validity of a test, including a screener.

Content Validity   Evidence for content validity includes characterizations of the relevance of the content, the overall representativeness of the content (e.g., test items or stimuli), and the quality of the test items or stimuli. This form of validity is especially important when one is building an assessment, such as a screener, and is relevant to the scope of the assessment previously described because it provides a foundation by which score interpretations can be defended. That is, a domain that has been evaluated for content validity via the definitions of the domain, item representation, and domain relevance allows for interpretations and score use to be parsimoniously developed and defended (Sireci, 1998).

Substantive Validity   A general perspective of substantive validity is that this form is established by describing the theoretical rationales that explain consistency in one's response to test items. Tasks such as rater judgment of items relative to an established taxonomy (Rovinelli & Hambleton, 1976), rater judgment of the extent to which a particular knowledge base or skill is essential to successful item completion (Lawshe, 1975), or calculating the proportion of raters who assign an item to its theorized content (Anderson & Gerbing, 1991) have all been used to provide evidence of substantive validity.

Structural Validity   Structural aspects of validity are concerned with how well the structure of the assessment aligns with the construct domain and can be tested via quantitative methods such as exploratory or confirmatory factor analysis.

Generalizability   The interpretation of scores and how well they generalize across tasks, samples, and time points reflects the generalizability aspect of validity. It may be ascertained by a description of what the defined population and boundaries for that population are; the sample representativeness in the conducted study to validate the assessment; the employed design, data collection measures, procedures, and analyses within the validation study; a review of potential biases (e.g., sample selection bias or information bias) and confounds; as well as studies of replication.

External Validity   External validity is concerned with quantitative evidence, including convergent, discriminant, and predictive forms of validity. Convergent validity measures the degree to which scores that should be related are in fact related to each other. For example, a measure of uppercase alphabet letter knowledge should be strongly correlated with a measure of lowercase alphabet letter knowledge, and a researcher-developed measure of receptive vocabulary should be moderately to strongly correlated with a standardized measure of receptive vocabulary such as the Peabody Picture Vocabulary Test (Dunn & Dunn, 1997). Discriminant validity is characterized by how unrelated scores from two domains should be when they are expected to be unrelated. For example, a measure of alphabet letter knowledge should not be correlated with intake of sugar-sweetened beverages. Predictive validity is the longitudinal association between a test score at one time point and another test score at a later time point.

Consequential Validity   One of the more hotly debated forms of validity is consequential validity (Cizek, Rosenberg, & Koons, 2008), and in the area of screening for dyslexia risk, it is unsurprising that this should be a hallmark of evaluating screeners. Due to the confluence of accountability testing, screening legislation, individualized education program (IEP) provision, and instructional and intervention supports for at-risk readers, there is a burden on screener developers and users to carefully take stock of implications of at-risk and not at-risk classifications on screeners specifically pertaining to what happens when correct decisions and decision errors occur. It is key that that score labels (e.g., high risk, moderate risk, low risk) are accurate and precise descriptors of what is being assessed (Messick, 1989) and that assessment developers and test users clearly describe, as well as possible, the potential and actual consequences of using a selected screener.

Classification Accuracy   The language around classification accuracy and the process by which students are correctly or incorrectly identified as at risk is diverse in the same ways as reliability and validity. Classification accuracy is a form of concurrent and predictive validity that looks at how a sample of individuals falls into two outcome groups (i.e., pass or fail on an outcome) based on two screener groups (i.e., at risk

Table 18.1.   Sample 2 × 2 contingency table

	Outcome	
Screen	Fail	Pass
At risk	A: True positive	B: False positive
Not at risk	C: False negative	D: True negative

or not at risk on the screen). When a sample of individuals is given a screener and a gold standard outcome measure, a 2 × 2 contingency matrix (see Table 18.1) can be created from which one is able to mathematically calculate important classification accuracy indexes.

Four cells characterize student performances on the screen and outcome measure: Cell A individuals are called true positives because these are individuals who were identified as at risk on a screener and failed the outcome. Cell B individuals are called false positives because they were classified as at risk on the screener but ultimately passed the outcome. Individuals in Cell C are false negatives because they were identified as not at risk on the screener and failed the outcome, and Cell D individuals are the true negative individuals who were not at risk on the screener and passed the outcome. Each cell by itself provides meaningful information about base classifications; however, there are ancillary computations that result in statistics that researchers and practitioners use to evaluate the screening efficiency at given screener-outcome cut-point selections and may be broadly classified as population-based indices, sample-based indices, and overall contextual indices.

Population-Based Indices   Three important population-based, or column-based, indices can be computed (Streiner, 2003). These indices have traditionally been considered to be sample invariant such that when a screener is used across similar types of samples the indices should not change; however, to the extent that the screener is used across different types of samples (e.g., varying levels of severity, comorbidity, base rates), population-based indices should be evaluated across the varying contexts. Sensitivity is the proportion of individuals who are correctly classified as having the problem and is computed as A/(A+C) from Table 18.1 (i.e., the proportion of all individuals who failed the outcome that were identified as at risk on the screener). Specificity is the proportion of individuals who are correctly classified as not having the problem and is calculated as D/(B+D) from Table 18.1 (i.e., the proportion of all individuals who passed the outcome that were identified as not at risk on the screener). Positive and negative likelihood ratios are the likelihoods of observing an outcome for an individual with or without the condition. Positive likelihood ratio is computed as Sensitivity/(1–Specificity) and describes the likelihood that a person who was at risk on the screener result has failed the outcome.

Negative likelihood ratio is computed as Specificity/(1–Sensitivity) and is the likelihood that a person who was not at risk on the screener result has passed the outcome.

Sample-Based Indices   Positive predictive power (PPP) and negative predictive power (NPP) are two of the more widely reported sample-based indices and are also referred to as row-based indices due to their computations deriving from the cell values in rows. PPP is the percent of at-risk students that the screener correctly identifies; that is, the percentage of students who failed the outcome of all the students identified as at risk on the screener. PPP is computed as A/(A+B). NPP is the percent of not at-risk students that the screener correctly identifies and is computed as D/(C+D). Unlike the population-based indices, PPP and NPP are known to fluctuate across samples due to their dependence on the calculated base rate [i.e., the percent of individuals in the sample who failed the outcome; (A+C)/(A+B+C+D); see Table 18. 1] of the condition being studied (Streiner, 2003).

Overall Contextual Indices   The overall correct classification (OCC) and Cohen's kappa are two of the more widely used statistics that capture agreement in correct decisions. The OCC is calculated as (A+D)/(A+B+C+D) and reflects the percent of correct classifications, positive and negative, in the sample. A frequent comment in the literature is that the OCC is limited in scope because it does not account for chance agreements (e.g., Streiner, 2003). One alternative to the OCC for screening purposes is the phi coefficient (φ), computed as $(AD–BC)/\sqrt{[(A+B)(C+D)(A+C)(B+C)]}$, in which higher values reflect stronger overall accuracy in correct identification in the sample.

DECISION MAKING

The plethora of considerations when creating, evaluating, choosing, or using a screener for dyslexia can be overwhelming. In this final section, we endeavor to provide guidance and questions to be thoughtful about screener assessments. To that end, we created a list of 15 questions related to the hierarchy of these core considerations of screeners when reviewing a screener technical report, tool chart, or assessment summary (Petscher, 2018; available at https://psyarxiv.com/vukt2). These are intended to help facilitate discussion among administrators, advocates, data teams, parents, and others invested in which screeners are used in schools for early screening.

CONCLUSION

There is little debate about whether early identification of students who are at risk for reading problems is useful so they can be routed to appropriate next steps, such as intensive interventions or more in-depth diagnostic testing for reading disabilities. This chapter highlights core considerations and questions to employ when choosing a screener for use in school settings. Our final recommendation is to underscore the importance of researcher–practitioner partnerships. As practitioners look to use screeners in their local contexts with students who present with varying characteristics, they may encounter challenges in how to choose a screener. Selecting a screener may seem daunting, considering the number of technical quality standards presented here. Researcher–practitioner partnerships can mitigate the complexities. Researchers can learn about the local context to then support the practitioner in weighing the trade-offs, such as 1) characteristics of students in the school compared to those in the screener validation study; 2) the scope of assessment related to content and the screening needs in the school; and 3) which forms of reliability, validity, and classification accuracy should be preferred and at what level of reporting. The intended fruit of such partnerships would be a smaller set of screening tools that demonstrate close correspondences between intent of the screener and appropriateness for the context. Ideally, this would also include a working collaborative between frontline workers in schools and researchers to continue to enhance screening practices.

REFERENCES

Adlof, S. M., Scoggins, J., Brazendale, A., Babb, S., & Petscher, Y. (2017). Identifying children at risk for language impairment or dyslexia with group-administered measures. *Journal of Speech, Language, and Hearing Research, 60*(12), 3507–3522.

Anastopoulos, A. D., Beal, K. K., Reid, R. J., Reid, R., Power, T. J., & DuPaul, G. J. (2018). Impact of child and informant gender on parent and teacher ratings of attention-deficit/hyperactivity disorder. *Psychological Assessment, 30*(10), 1390–1394.

Anderson, J. C., & Gerbing, D. W. (1991). Predicting the performance of measures in a confirmatory factor analysis with a pretest assessment of their substantive validities. *Journal of Applied Psychology, 76*(5), 732.

Andrade, O. V., Andrade, P. E., & Capellini, S. A. (2015). Collective screening tools for early identification of dyslexia. *Frontiers in Psychology, 5*, 1581.

Chakrabartty, S. N. (2013). Best split-half and maximum reliability. *IOSR Journal of Research & Method in Education, 3*(1), 1–8.

Cizek, G. J., Rosenberg, S. L., & Koons, H. H. (2008). Sources of validity evidence for educational and psychological tests. *Educational and Psychological Measurement, 68*(3), 397–412.

Compton, D. L., Fuchs, D., Fuchs, L. S., & Bryant, J. D. (2006). Selecting at-risk readers in first grade for early intervention: A two-year longitudinal study of decision rules and procedures. *Journal of Educational Psychology, 98*(2), 394.

Compton, D. L., Fuchs, D., Fuchs, L. S., Bouton, B., Gilbert, J. K., Barquero, L. A., . . . Crouch, R. C. (2010). Selecting at-risk first-grade readers for early intervention: Eliminating false positives and exploring the promise of a two-stage gated screening process. *Journal of Educational Psychology, 102*(2), 327.

Compton, D. L., Gilbert, J. K., Jenkins, J. R., Fuchs, D., Fuchs, L. S., Cho, E., . . . Bouton, B. (2012). Accelerating chronically unresponsive children to Tier 3 instruction: What level of data is necessary to ensure selection accuracy? *Journal of Learning Disabilities, 45*(3), 204–216.

Cummings, K. D., Biancarosa, G., Schaper, A., & Reed, D. K. (2014). Examiner error in curriculum-based measurement of oral reading. *Journal of School Psychology, 52*(4), 361–375.

Davis, G. N., Lindo, E. J., & Compton, D. L. (2007). Children at risk for reading failure; constructing an early screening measure. *Teaching Exceptional Children, 39*(5), 32–37.

Dunn, L. M., & Dunn, L. M. (1997). *PPVT-III: Peabody Picture Vocabulary Test.* Circle Pines, MN: American Guidance Service.

Dunn, L. M., & Markwardt, F. C. (1970). *Examiner's manual: Peabody Individual Achievement Test.* Circle Pines, MN: American Guidance Service.

Francis, D. J., Santi, K. L., Barr, C., Fletcher, J. M., Varisco, A., & Foorman, B. R. (2008). Form effects on the estimation of students' oral reading fluency using DIBELS. *Journal of School Psychology, 46*(3), 315–342.

Gilbert, J. K., Compton, D. L., Fuchs, D., & Fuchs, L. S. (2012). Early screening for risk of reading disabilities: Recommendations for a four-step screening system. *Assessment for Effective Intervention, 38*(1), 6–14.

Glover, T. A., & Albers, C. A. (2007). Considerations for evaluating universal screening assessments. *Journal of School Psychology, 45*(2), 117–135.

International Dyslexia Association. (2002). *Definition of dyslexia.* Retrieved from https://dyslexiaida.org/definition-of-dyslexia/

Johnson, E. S., Jenkins, J. R., & Petscher, Y. (2010). Improving the accuracy of a direct route screening process. *Assessment for Effective Intervention, 35*(3), 131–140.

Johnson, E. S., Jenkins, J. R., Petscher, Y., & Catts, H. W. (2009). How can we improve the accuracy of screening instruments? *Learning Disabilities Research & Practice, 24*(4), 174–185.

Keenan, J. M., & Meenan, C. E. (2014). Test differences in diagnosing reading comprehension deficits. *Journal of Learning Disabilities, 47*(2), 125–135.

Kim, Y. S., Petscher, Y., Schatschneider, C., & Foorman, B. (2010). Does growth rate in oral reading fluency matter in predicting reading comprehension achievement? *Journal of Educational Psychology, 102*(3), 652.

Lawshe, C. H. (1975). A quantitative approach to content validity. *Personnel Psychology, 28*(4), 563–575.

Leslie, L., & Caldwell, J. (2002). *Qualitative Reading Inventory (QRI-3).* New York, NY: Allyn & Bacon.

Mayo Clinic. (2018). *Dyslexia: Symptoms and causes.* Retrieved from https://www.mayoclinic.org/diseases-conditions/dyslexia/symptoms-causes/syc-20353552

McCrae, R. R., Kurtz, J. E., Yamagata, S., & Terracciano, A. (2011). Internal consistency, retest reliability, and their implications for personality scale validity. *Personality and Social Psychology Review, 15*(1), 28–50.

McNeish, D. (2017). Thanks coefficient alpha, we'll take it from here. *Psychological Methods, 23*(3), 412–433.

Messick, S. (1989). Validity. In R. L. Linn (Ed.), *Educational measurement* (3rd ed., pp. 13–103). New York, NY: Macmillan.

Messick, S. (1995). Validity of psychological assessment: Validation of inferences from persons' responses and performances as scientific inquiry into score meaning. *American Psychologist, 50*(9), 741.

National Center on Intensive Intervention at American Institutes for Research. (2019). Academic Screening Tools Chart. Retrieved from https://charts.intensiveintervention.org/chart/academic-screening

Nunnally, J. C., & Bernstein, I. H. (1994). *McGraw-Hill series in psychology: Vol. 3. Psychometric theory.* New York, NY: McGraw-Hill.

Pentimonti, J. M., Walker, M. A., & Edmonds, R. Z. (2017). The selection and use of screening and progress monitoring tools in data-based decision making within an MTSS framework. *Perspectives on Language and Literacy, 43*(3), 34–40.

Petscher, Y. (2018, October 27). *Guiding questions for evaluating a screener.* Retrieved from https://doi.org/10.31234/osf.io/vukt2

Petscher, Y., Cummings, K. D., Biancarosa, G., & Fien, H. (2013). Advanced (measurement) applications of curriculum-based measurement in reading. *Assessment for Effective Intervention, 38*(2), 71–75.

Petscher, Y., & Kim, Y. S. (2011). The utility and accuracy of oral reading fluency score types in predicting reading comprehension. *Journal of School Psychology, 49,* 107–129. http://dx.doi.org/10.1016/j.jsp.2010.09.004

Rovinelli, R. J., & Hambleton, R. K. (1976, April 19–23). *On the use of content specialists in the assessment of criterion-referenced test item validity.* Paper presented at the 60th Annual Meeting of the American Educational Research Association, San Francisco, California.

Sireci, S. G. (1998). The construct of content validity. *Social Indicators Research, 45*(1–3), 83–117.

Streiner, D. L. (2003). Diagnosing tests: Using and misusing diagnostic and screening tests. *Journal of Personality Assessment, 81*(3), 209–219.

VanDerHeyden, A. M., & Burns, M. K. (2017). Four dyslexia screening myths that cause more harm than good in preventing reading failure and what you can do instead. *Communique, 45*(7), 1.

Wainer, H., Dorans, N. J., Flaugher, R., Green, B. F., & Mislevy, R. J. (2000). *Computerized adaptive testing: A primer.* New York, NY: Routledge.

Wiederholt, J. L., & Bryant, B. R. (1992). *Gray Oral Reading Tests: GORT-3.* Austin, TX: PRO-ED.

Woodcock, R. W., McGrew, K. S., & Mather, N. (2001). *Woodcock-Johnson III Tests of Achievement.* Rolling Meadows, IL: Riverside.

Youman, M., & Mather, N. (2015). Dyslexia laws in the USA: An update. *Perspectives on Language and Literacy, 41*(4), 10.

Zumeta, R. O., Compton, D. L., & Fuchs, L. S. (2012). Using word identification fluency to monitor first-grade reading development. *Exceptional Children, 78*(2), 201–220.

CHAPTER 19

Dyslexia Trifecta
Research, Education Policy, and Practice

Joan Mele-McCarthy

SUMMARY

The inclusive discussion regarding research, policy, and practice has the potential to be a dyslexia trifecta; we have an opportunity to create an epic win for children who have dyslexia by describing and optimizing this relationship to serve children better. Education research, policy, and practice are pieces of a complex puzzle that intricately combine to educate all children effectively and to improve outcomes in academic achievement. Scientific knowledge (research) and education practice form an important reciprocal relationship and exist in the U.S. education system within a prevailing set of intricate education policies. In complex education systems of developed, industrialized nations and in more simplistic, localized education systems of developing nations, the practice of education depends largely on the education policies of the system, which are guided by the sociopolitical climate, governance, and economics of the system, entity, or country (Verger, Novelli, & Altinyelken, 2012). These policies drive legislation and regulation. There is an interdependent, causal, and even circular relationship intuitively among scientific research, education practice, and education policy. Does research drive practice and practice drive policy? Perhaps research drives policy, which in turn drives practice, or research drives both practice and policy. In reality, it is plausible and actual that education policy drives research (through funding initiatives and legislative requirements), which in turn drives the principles of practice. A fourth component that feeds into the research–policy–practice relationship is stakeholder needs and wants. Policies and legislation are often driven by what members of a society see as a need (Berry, 1999; Casey, 2011). Stakeholder advocacy is frequently the springboard from which research, policy, and/or practice arise. In fact, stakeholder will leads to advocacy, which can lead the charge for a true dyslexia trifecta.

INTRODUCTION

Cunningham noted that "Policy is like an elephant, you recognize it when you see it, but it is somewhat more difficult to define" (1963, p. 229). Does that mean that the pure definition of policy is in the eyes of the beholder? In reality, policy is not "pure"; it is advanced within a governance structure that is dependent on the sociopolitical climate and economic status of the organization or system or entity (Verger et al., 2012). It has been described as a sanctioned assertion of intent and goals, as a consistent norm of conduct (Guba, 1984), and as a sanctioned act by an institutional authority that provides a standard of some sort for measuring performance (Delaney, 2017).

Let's apply those policy concepts using U.S. special education legislation, the Individuals with Disabilities Education Improvement Act of 2004 (IDEA 2004; PL 108-446). The intent of IDEA 2004 was to ensure a free appropriate public education (FAPE), delivered in the least restrictive environment (LRE), for students with disabilities. The sanctioned behavior is the individual education program (IEP) process for identification and classification of students with disabilities, provision of services for students who are classified, and the legal due process available to families and schools when a student with disabilities allegedly does not receive a FAPE in the LRE because of violations of protections outlined by the legislation. There is consistency and regularity in the implementation of this federal legislation with respect to federal guidelines and regulations that must be met by the states, but the way in which states implement federal guidelines and regulations varies.

Delaney's (2017) policy components mirrored those offered by Guba (1984) but went a step further. Delaney indicated that education policy should include a standard way to measure performance or success of the actions required by the legislation that was generated by education policy. IDEA 2004 required the use of multiple points of data to engage in the identification process that classifies a student in need of special education services, as well as measurable educational goals and objectives to mark progress. Measurable performance is geared toward the individual student, not to overall progress of local or state systems. Overall progress at the school building, district, and state levels is dictated by the general education legislation, the Every Student Succeeds Act of 2015 (ESSA 2015; PL 114-95). This legislation provided federal standards for the education of all children, including students with disabilities and students who represent underserved populations, and ultimately held states accountable for all students' academic progress. These pieces of legislation should be used to ensure appropriate instruction for children who struggle with reading. Many times, legislation falls short of its intent for a variety of reasons.

STAKEHOLDERS, POLITICAL CLIMATE, CIVIL RIGHTS POLICY, AND LEGISLATION

Separating policy into simple component parts is easier said than done. The proposed dyslexia trifecta of research, policy, and practice is deficient because it is missing one important component, the stakeholder. Indeed, the policy–legislation partnership is frequently driven by stakeholder wants and needs in a democratic society (Berry, 1999). Stakeholder groups bring awareness of a shortcoming within a system and lobby for policy-driven legislation that would address the shortcoming. Such was the case for individuals with disabilities.

The exclusion of individuals with disabilities from many activities of daily life, employment, and educational opportunities was viewed as an urgent societal ill. The movement to integrate individuals with disabilities into all facets of society, promoted by individuals with disabilities and their families, fostered the need to recognize a universal human birthright for equality and equity of all citizens; promote compassion for all human conditions; and advocate for governmental policy, legislation, and regulation to ensure civil rights for all people.

In the United States, there has been a steady progression in disability rights that can be traced from the 1950s and 1960s. Starting in the 1950s, through U.S. education policy, legislation, and regulations, the country embarked on a journey to ensure equal education opportunities for all students. The 1954 Supreme Court ruling in *Brown v. Board of Education* resulted in the landmark civil rights decision debunking the "separate but equal" notion of public education. No longer was it legal to segregate students of color from their white peers in school settings. The civil rights movements for individuals of color outside of education were gaining momentum. Separate but equal facilities in U.S. society were no longer legal, nor was requiring individuals of color to sit at the back of the bus. The national conversation began to focus on equal opportunities for all people, without regard to race, gender, creed, or national origin.

The Civil Rights Movement that began in the 1950s addressed equalities for race and gender (Evans, 1979; Freeman, 1975; Taylor, 1989) and began to include individuals with disabilities in the 1960s. The Civil Rights Act of 1964 (PL 88-352) was a landmark civil rights and labor law that outlawed discrimination based on race, color, religion, sex, or national origin. As equality for all individuals with disabilities became a national conversation in policy, legislation, and regulation, increased access for all members of society became the norm. The provision of sign language interpreters in public forums, universities, church services, and doctor's offices as well as signage on buildings in braille have resulted from policies to ensure equal access to services and daily life activities. By creating access to employment, the need to increase access to places of employment resulted in requirements that buildings have ramps, escalators, and elevators. Curb cuts at crosswalks and access to public transportation were also an outgrowth of access to employment.

In federal employment at first and then in the private sector, the notion of reasonable accommodations became an expected practice in the workplace. Advances in technology, such as audio formats (text-to-speech) for printed material in textbooks, advanced new levels of literacy for individuals with vision impairments and individuals with reading disabilities, such as dyslexia. Old-fashioned tape recorders and CD players fell by the wayside with advances in the technology itself, its affordability, and the availability of portable and versatile electronic devices (phones, tablets, computers). Speech-to-text software further leveled the playing field for individuals who might have been blocked from employment because of weak writing skills. Legislation that requires payment for purchase of speech-generating devices by the Centers for Medicare & Medicaid Services (CMS) for individuals who qualify has created access for many individuals who had little hope of participating in mainstream society, let alone in employment opportunities. (See the Steve Gleason Enduring Voices Act of 2017.)

The Civil Rights Movement also prompted attention to public school equality for children. Although *Brown v. Board of Education* outlawed separate but equal education for children of color, it did not address quality of education for minority children. Research demonstrated that there was a significant achievement gap between children who were impoverished (many of whom were minorities) and those who came from middle- and upper-income households (Coleman, 1966). Beginning with Title IV of the Civil Rights Act of 1964, decisive legal protections in education for children of color were enacted (Losen & Welner, 2002). The Elementary and Secondary Education Act of 1965 (ESEA 1965; PL 89-10)—a forerunner to the current legislation, ESSA 2015—was enacted to address the inequities of educational opportunity for underprivileged children. The following year, in 1966, ESEA was amended (ESEA 1966 Amendment; PL 89-750) to establish a grant program to help states set up programs for the education of children with disabilities. Thus, the Civil Rights Movement set the stage for education reforms related to underserved populations, which came to include children with disabilities.

The 1970s provided more legal protections and supports for individuals with disabilities. The Rehabilitation Rights Act of 1973 (Rehabilitation Act 1973; PL 93-112) was enacted and authorized grants to states for vocational rehabilitation services, with an emphasis on individuals with the most severe disabilities. This legislation was especially significant for its inclusion of Section 504, which created and extended civil rights to individuals with disabilities, including children and adults with disabilities in education, employment, and other settings. The follow-up to Section 504, significant for children with dyslexia and other disabilities, was the enactment of the Education for All Handicapped Children Act of 1975 (PL 94-142). This legislation, currently superseded by IDEA 2004, was designed to ensure and entitle FAPE to students with disabilities by providing special education services to children who qualify through implementation of an IEP, guaranteeing that decisions would be fair and appropriate, establishing specific management and auditing requirements for special education, and providing federal funds to help states educate students with disabilities.

However, the provisions for equality in PL 94-142, which persisted through to IDEA 2004, fell short in a very important way. Title 1 of IDEA 2004, Section 1/A/602/30(A) defined specific learning disability as

> A disorder in one or more of the basic psychological processes involved in understanding or in using language, spoken or written, which disorder may manifest itself in the imperfect ability to listen, think, speak, read, write, spell, or do mathematical calculations.

Section 1/A/602/30(C) is a qualifier to that definition: "Disorders not included—Such term does not include a learning problem that is primarily the result of visual, hearing, or motor disabilities, of mental retardation, of emotional disturbance, or of environmental, cultural, or economic disadvantage." The last string of qualifiers, *environmental, cultural, or economic disadvantage,* is in fact racially and culturally unjust, and technically has the potential to keep children who come from diverse racial, economic, and linguistic backgrounds from identification and qualification for special education services. Dyslexia, a form of a specific learning disability as defined by statute (Section 1/A/602/30[B]), crosses socioeconomic status, racial, linguistic, and cultural lines. Excluding children, including children whose learning profile aligns with symptoms associated with dyslexia, from the rights and protections of IDEA because they are impoverished and/or racially, linguistically, and culturally diverse is unethical and illegal, and it violates the principle of FAPE. These underserved students are already at risk for low academic achievement, low education attainment, and underemployment (U.S. Commission on Civil Rights, 2018); denying them FAPE becomes a matter of equity as well.

FREE APPROPRIATE PUBLIC EDUCATION, EQUALITY, AND EQUITY

The Civil Rights Movement and subsequent shifts in policy, legislation, and practices such as FAPE were geared toward the precept of equality: equal access to employment, education, and public facilities. In fact, the concept of equality must be replaced by equity. The difference between the two concepts is significant. The concept of equal denotes "the same," whereas the concept of equality denotes "fair share." Blair Mann (2014) provided a clear example of the difference between equal and equity: "Should per student funding at every school be exactly the same? *That's a question of equality.* But should students who come from less get more in order to ensure that they can catch up? *That's a question of equity.*"

Today, the discussion surrounding access to educational opportunities for all students should be one of equity:

> The concept of equity goes beyond the notions of equality and appropriateness; it extends to the broader context of fairness, whereby individuals receive what they need to be successful in an environment (or society), even if what is needed by some students or groups of learners is more than what is needed for others. Access to services and accommodations through special education legislation should provide that equity for students with disabilities. Let's rebrand FAPE to include equity: a 'free appropriate *and equitable* public education,' since what is appropriate for one learner to be successful in school may not be appropriate for another. (Mele-McCarthy & Powers, 2020)

Equity certainly sits at the heart of ESSA Title 1 provisions, which are designed to "provide all children significant opportunity to receive a fair,

---

More about ESSA Title 1 provisions and equity

Each year, the U.S. government provides formula-based grants (currently up to approximately $15 billion in total) to state educational agencies. The grants, based on the number or percentage of students coming from low-income families, are then distributed to the school district level. For more information about legislative provisions for equity, see these resources:

- The ESSA Section 1001 Statement of Purpose at http://www.everystudentsucceedsact.org/title-1-
- The National Center for Education Statistics (NCES) Fast Facts page for Title 1 at https://nces.ed.gov/fastfacts/display.asp?id=158

---

equitable, and high-quality education, and to close educational achievement gaps" (ESSA 2015). Yet, the reading gap persists for students with disabilities and for children in underserved populations. Both IDEA 2004 and ESSA 2015 include the requirement for disaggregation of data to track the progress of underserved children, including students with disabilities. However, the data to date is not encouraging.

CURRENT READING STATISTICS IN THE UNITED STATES

The reading proficiency of all students has not markedly improved since national assessments were initiated in 1965 (Nation's Report Card, n.d.a), with only 37% of all fourth-grade students and 36% of all eighth-grade students reading at proficiency or better (Nation's Report Card, n.d.a, n.d.b). National Assessment of Education Progress (NAEP) reading proficiency data disaggregated according to the lowest performing subgroups of children are even more concerning (see Table 19.1).

Table 19.1. National Assessment of Education Progress reading proficiency data disaggregated by subgroups

Subgroup	Fourth grade	Eighth grade
African American	16th percentile	16th percentile
Hispanic	18th percentile	21st percentile
American Indian/Alaskan Native	18th percentile	20th percentile
School Lunch Eligibility Program[1]	18th percentile	20th percentile
Students with disabilities[2]	9th percentile	7th percentile
English language learners	8th percentile	5th percentile

[1]*Source:* https://www.federalregister.gov/documents/2018/05/08/2018-09679/child-nutrition-programs-income-eligibility-guidelines
[2]Excluding those students with 504 plans.

These disappointing data are evident despite federal monies allocated to reading research as well as research focused on dyslexia (e.g., Institute for Education Science; *Eunice Kennedy Shriver* National Institute of Child Health and Human Development). Legislative, policy, and research efforts to provide equity in education to underserved learners have not yet been fully realized in improvements in academic achievement.

The overall reading proficiency in the United States is problematic, but consider the state of reading relative to special education. NAEP 2017 data revealed that students with disabilities represent the second weakest group of readers in fourth and eighth grades. In 2015, there were approximately 51.5 million school-age children in total in the United States, and 13%, or 6.7 million, qualified for special education services. According to 2015 IDEA data, 34% of children (2,278,000 million) who qualified for special education services were classified as having a specific learning disability, and anywhere from 80% to 90% of students referred for special education services for specific learning disability exhibited difficulties with reading (Kavale & Reese, 1992; Lerner, 1989). According to the Dyslexia Center of Utah (n.d.), 85% of children in that 80% group have dyslexia. These data reflect that up to 4.5% of all school-age children in the United States potentially receive special education services for reading. Given that current research indicates the prevalence of dyslexia in children to be between 5% and 10% in the United States (Badian, 1999; Hanford, 2017; Peterson & Pennington, 2015; Shaywitz, Shaywitz, Fletcher, & Escobar, 1990), how are the remaining 6.5% of children accounted for and served?

DYSLEXIA AS A TYPE OF SPECIFIC LEARNING DISABILITY

Dyslexia research continues to provide sound information on which to base policy decisions and practice with respect to heredity, neurobiological origins and oral language roots, behavioral assessment, and intervention practices. Yet, state and local policies, and by default schools, continue to gatekeep identification and implementation of services for students who struggle with dyslexia.

Dyslexia is hereditary; yet, schools typically do not consider the presence of familial incidence of reading and learning difficulties. Parents reported they were told, "He's a boy, and boys develop reading skills later than girls," "He has a late birthday," or "We can't test for dyslexia until third grade." Dyslexia exists separate from intellect (Fletcher et al., 2002), yet many schools continue to rely on the discrepancy formula (a difference between IQ and reading scores) (Fuchs, Mock, Morgan, & Young, 2003; Siegel, 2006) for identification of a specific learning disability, despite language in IDEA 2004 that asserts multiple points of data may be used to determine the presence of a specific learning disability without relying on an IQ discrepancy model (ASHA, n.d.; Rosen, n.d.).

Science has demonstrated the linguistic underpinnings of dyslexia (Norton, Beach, & Gabrieli, 2014; Vellutino, Fletcher, Snowling, & Scanlon, 2004); yet, evaluations in school settings often do not include data relative to word retrieval, phonological awareness, vocabulary knowledge, global listening comprehension, or ability to process complex sentences and sophisticated inferences. There are a plethora of studies that attest to the importance of intervention that includes phonological awareness and systematic phonics instruction integrated with spelling instruction (Bryant & Goswami, 2016; *Eunice Kennedy Shriver* National Institute of Child Health and Human Development, 2000; Foorman, Breier, & Fletcher, 2003; Gerston et al., 2009; Lovett, 1999; Montgomery, 2006; Torgesen, 2005). Yet, many schools insist on implementing a "balanced approach to literacy," a philosophy of teaching reading that does not include the necessary core components of reading instruction (Joshi, Dahlgren, & Boulware-Gooden, 2002; Wren, 2002).

It appears that there is a breakdown in the trifecta of integrated research, policy, and practice. Policy-driven legislation—ESSA 2015 and IDEA 2004—requires research-based instruction and data-driven decision making. Stakeholders are calling for research-based interventions. Teachers want to be effective. They want to feel pride in their work. They want to help children. Families of children who struggle with dyslexia are becoming more and more active in advocating for improvements in the education of their children (Ward-Lonergan & Duthie, 2018).

PRACTICE BARRIERS IN THE RESEARCH–POLICY–PRACTICE COLLABORATIVE

The elements of this potential trifecta have moved forward to improve instruction for all children, as well as services to children with dyslexia, as evidenced by burgeoning dyslexia legislation in many states (Ward-Lonergan & Duthie, 2018), driven by stakeholders (parents of children with dyslexia). Yet, many barriers still exist that impede realization of this dyslexia trifecta. Although barriers within education policy and legislation exist, practice barriers are evident despite advances in dyslexia research and in policy initiatives that result in legislation to address dyslexia in federal (IDEA 2004, ESSA 2015) and state statutes; here I focus only on practice barriers. Practice is not restricted to teachers or educators. Rather, effects on practice can be deconstructed into five broad categories: funding, legislative and regulatory restrictions, teacher training, job satisfaction, and sociopolitical factors.

Funding Barriers

Funding is frequently an issue in education. The No Child Left Behind Act (NCLB 2001; PL 107-110), currently superseded by ESSA 2015, was criticized as underfunded legislation because of the cost of accountability testing. But funding goes beyond the cost of accountability testing. A report to Congress by the U.S. Commission on Civil Rights revealed that students who live in poverty lack access to high-quality schools; their schools have less experienced teachers, less rigorous course offerings, and outdated technology and instructional materials (U.S. Commission on Civil Rights, 2018). This report highlighted that funding inequities in U.S. schools render profoundly unequal education opportunities for many students, which is a practice issue that affects student achievement outcomes.

In addition to general education funding, special education funding is also a practice barrier for student progress. The funding goal for IDEA is 40% of the national average per pupil expenditure multiplied by the number of special education students in each state. However, in 2015–2016, IDEA funded only 15.3% of special education costs to states (Education Commission of the United States, 2018). States and local school districts are responsible for filling in the funding gaps. Some states and school districts have more available funds for education than others; the states and local school districts with less per capita income and resources cannot fund special education services to meet the demand. As a result, it is possible that either students who could qualify for special education services are not served, or worse, policies could be put in place to reduce eligibility criteria.

Funding translates into costs for personnel, teacher training, materials, administration, and physical plant, and when the availability of funds does not align with practice needs, it has a negative effect on instruction. Even before a law is approved and enacted, funding guides legislative parameters (Guterman, 2017). In the United States, whenever a law reaches the congressional floor, it must be "scored" by the Congressional Budget Office (Congressional Budget Office [CBO], n.d.). When the cost of the law outweighs the availability of funding of potential legislation, then the law either does not move forward, or it is edited to better align with anticipated budgetary constraints before being sent out to the floor for a vote.

Legislative and Regulatory Restrictions

Legislative and regulatory restrictions affect practice. For example, federal guidelines set eligibility criteria for IDEA 2004, which are further modified by states and local school districts. Likewise, states and local school districts also set dismissal criteria. There are many children who do not qualify for special education services because of cut-off criteria yet struggle academically in the classroom. Research has established that dyslexia and specific learning disabilities in general exist on a continuum (Fletcher, 2009); therefore, arbitrary cut-off scores restrict provision of appropriate instruction and FAPE to many children. IDEA 2004 introduced the practice of multi-tiered systems of supports (MTSS), also known as response to intervention (RTI), to provide children with instruction to meet their needs when they struggle to meet grade-level expectations but do not (yet) qualify for special education services. These prereferral supports were included in legislation to avoid the "wait to fail" model. ESSA 2015 defined a multi-tiered system of supports as "a comprehensive continuum of evidence-based, systemic practices to support a rapid response to students' needs, with regular observation to facilitate data-based instructional decision-making." In addition, IDEA 2004 includes a provision for early intervention services to support students who have learning needs to ameliorate the need for special education services. Despite these prereferral strategies in the years post IDEA 2004 enactment, reading achievement for all children has not improved (Balu et al., 2015; Knoff, Reeves, & Balow, 2018).

Teacher Training

The literature is replete with studies about the poor quality of teacher training for reading instruction (Joshi et al., 2009; Chapter 16, this volume), and there still exists a debate in higher education about how best to teach reading in general (Snow, Burns, & Griffin, 1998; Soler, 2016) and how to teach reading to students with dyslexia (Moats, 2007; Washburn, Joshi, & Binks-Cantrell, 2011), despite accepted neuroscientific evidence regarding how the brain is activated during reading in typically developing readers (Pugh et al., 2001) and in readers who have dyslexia (Pugh et al., 2001). Therefore, another practice barrier that impedes effective instruction is the information imparted to college students in preservice and graduate programs of education. In addition to the pedagogy of theoretical foundations in reading and reading instruction, current discussions in the field concern how teachers apply theoretical foundations and research-based instruction to the actual act of teaching (Darling-Hammond, 2006). Stakeholders and policy makers are calling for a more clinically based teacher training model whereby teachers have a full year of student teaching with the requirement to pass stringent practice competencies as well as qualifying exams. With respect to reading instruction, research shows that many teachers are not prepared to teach reading in general and are even less prepared to teach reading to struggling readers (Joshi et al, 2009; Moats, 2014; Salinger et al., 2010; Walsh, Glaser, & Wilcox, 2006). Given that only 4.5% of all children in the United States qualify for special education services as children with a specific learning disability, that a majority of these children are likely to have dyslexia (Dyslexia Center of Utah, n.d.), and that approximately 10% of children have dyslexia, these underserved students are underinstructed.

Job Satisfaction

Job satisfaction is another consideration to practice effectiveness. Nance and Calabrese (2009) cited numerous studies regarding teacher stress in the workplace. One significant stressor for both general education and special education teachers is learning how to perform their duties on the job. Nance and Calabrese reported that when teachers are stressed, they believe their working conditions are not ideal, which in turn leads to job dissatisfaction. Special education teachers are frustrated with the amount of paperwork they must complete for accountability purposes, whereby there is a mismatch between their expectations for time teaching versus actual time needed for paperwork completion (Carlson, Chen, Schroll, & Klein, 2002; Nance & Calabrese, 2009). Research shows that one third to one half of beginning special education teachers leave the profession during the first 5 years of employment, with many moving to general education (Billingsley, 2004; Menlove, Garnes, & Salzberg, 2004). A report from the National Center for Education Statistics (n.d.) indicated that in 2012–2013, about 10% of public school teachers left teaching voluntarily, and about 51% of those teachers reported that their workload was better in their nonteaching position. Fifty-three percent of teachers who left the profession said general work conditions were better in their nonteaching positions (Goldring, Taie, & Riddles, 2014).

Sociopolitical Factors

In the United States, teachers are often blamed for the ills of public school education, when in fact problems with its effectiveness and outcomes are multilayered and complex. They include policy initiatives and research funding and dissemination, as well as the sociopolitical context within which the education system exists. Fullan (2000) used the term *outside forces* for those factors outside of education that affect the education system. In today's world, examples would be political will; technology and social media; economics; stakeholder wants and demands; social, cultural, and linguistic biases; and generational mores. Full discussion of these examples extends beyond the scope of this chapter, but these issues are important to mention within the context of factors that have the potential to impede effective education practice.

CONCLUSION

The time for a dyslexia trifecta is overdue. Research has described and continues to describe the neurobiological, heritable, and behavioral characteristics of developmental dyslexia; early and school-age identification of dyslexia; and the efficacy of explicit, phonics-based interventions. Education policy and legislation are utilizing dyslexia research in federal (IDEA 2004, ESSA 2015) and state laws (Ward-Lonergan & Duthie, 2018). Yet, improvements in education practice for dyslexia lag behind. Change in instructional practices for reading in general and specifically for dyslexia is needed, but change is slow to get started and difficult to sustain. Fullan (2000) talked about change as a three-stage process: adoption, implementation, and strong institutionalization.

For large-scale, sustainable change to occur, strong institutionalization is key. There are some individual public schools and independent schools that specialize in teaching children with dyslexia and learning differences and that have adopted, implemented, and institutionalized change in their educational practice, but these instances are exceptions, not the rule in the public school systems across the nation. Sustained change is not possible without a strong interconnected, reciprocal, and circular relationship among research, policy, and practice.

Education practice, in partnership with research and policy, matters because it provides the foundation for the culture and productivity of members within a sociopolitical system. The product of education practices ultimately matters—academic achievement and independent critical thinking—because education facilitates knowledge, and knowledge is power. The concept of knowledge as power is attributed to Age of Enlightenment philosopher Francis Bacon. That power forms the basis for political development, democracy, and social justice (Schaeffer, 2012).

How can practice be strengthened so this dyslexia trifecta can be optimized and realized? It is likely through stakeholder will. The historic series of Supreme Court rulings and legislative actions in the Civil Rights and Disabilities Rights Movements were brought about by stakeholder dissatisfaction with the status quo and by the need to improve the quality of life and access to employment and equitable education for all individuals in the United States. Stakeholder activism brought about change in policy, legislation, and practice for individuals with disabilities from cradle to grave, and across the spectrum of life activities. Stakeholder will can make the difference in reading achievement and equity in education for all children, including children with dyslexia.

Who are the stakeholders? We are the stakeholders, and we can be the "dreamers of dreams . . . and the movers and shakers of the world" (O'Shaughnessy, 1873) through our work to promote access, equity, and effective science-based instruction within and across our education system for all children, including children who have dyslexia. Indeed, as a wise person once said, "Never doubt that a small group of thoughtful, committed citizens can change the world; indeed, it's the only thing that ever has."

REFERENCES

American Speech-Language-Hearing Association (ASHA). (n.d.). Specific learning disabilities: What IDEA says. *ASHA Issue Brief.* Retrieved from https://www.asha.org /advocacy/federal/idea/04-law-specific-ld/

Badian, N. A. (1999). Persistent arithmetic, reading, or arithmetic and reading disability. *Annals of Dyslexia, 49,* 43. https://doi.org/10.1007/s11881-999-0019-8

Balu, R., Zhu, P., Doolittle, F., Schiller, E., Jenkins, J., & Gersten, R. (2015). *Evaluation of response to intervention practices for elementary school reading* (NCEE 2016-4000). Washington, DC: National Center for Education Evaluation and Regional Assistance.

Berry, J. M. (1999). *The new liberalism: The rising power of public interest groups.* Washington, DC: Brookings Institution.

Billingsley, B. S. (2004). Special education teacher retention and attrition: A critical analysis of the research literature. *The Journal of Special Education, 38*(1), 39–55.

Brown v. Board of Education, 347 U.S. 483 (1954). Retrieved from https://www.ourdocuments .gov/doc.php?flash=false&doc=87

Bryant, P., & Goswami, U. (2016). *Phonological skills and learning to read.* New York, NY: Routledge.

Carlson, E., Chen, L., Schroll, K., & Klein, S. (2002). SPeNSE: Study of Personnel Needs in Special Education. Final report of the paperwork substudy. Retrieved from https://files .eric.ed.gov/fulltext/ED479674.pdf

Casey, J. (2011). *Understanding advocacy: A primer on the policy making role of nonprofit organizations.* New York, NY: Baruch College, City University of New York, Center for Nonprofit Strategy. Retrieved from https://goo.gl/oegXGG

Civil Rights Act of 1964, PL 88-352, 20 U.S.C. §§ 241 *et seq.*

Coleman, J. S. (1966). *Equality of educational opportunity.* Washington, DC: U.S. Dept. of Health, Education, and Welfare, Office of Education/National Center for Education Statistics.

Congressional Budget Office. (n.d.). *Processes.* Retrieved from https://www.cbo.gov/about /processes

Cunningham, C. (1963). Policy and practice. *Public Administration, 41*(3), 229–238. Retrieved from https://doi.org/10.1111/j.1467-9299.1963.tb01786.x

Darling-Hammond, L. (2006). Constructing 21st-century teacher education. *Journal of Teacher Education, 57*(3), 300–314.

Delaney, J. G. (2017). *Education policy: Bridging the divide between theory and practice.* Alberta, Canada: Brush Education.

Dyslexia Center of Utah. (n.d.). *5 steps for identifying dyslexia in your child.* Retrieved from https://www.dyslexiacenterofutah.org/Statistics

Education Commission of the United States. (2018). *Is the federal government shortchanging special education students?* Retrieved from https://www.ecs.org/is-the-federal -government-short-changing-special-education-students/

Education for All Handicapped Children Act of 1975, PL 94-142, 20 U.S.C. §§ 1400 *et seq.*

Elementary and Secondary Education Act Amendments of 1966, PL 89-750, 80 Stat. 1191, 20 U.S.C. §§ 873 *et seq.*

Elementary and Secondary Education Act of 1965, PL 89-10, 20 U.S.C. §§ 241 *et seq.*

Eunice Kennedy Shriver National Institute of Child Health and Human Development, National Institutes of Health, Department of Health and Human Services. (2000). *Report of the National Reading Panel: Teaching children to read: Reports of the subgroups* (00-4754). Washington, DC: U.S. Government Printing Office.

Evans, S. M. (1979). *Personal politics: The roots of women's liberation in the Civil Rights Movement and the New Left.* New York, NY: Vintage Books.

Every Student Succeeds Act of 2015, PL 114-95, 20 U.S.C §§ 6301 *et seq.* Retrieved from https://www.ed.gov/essa?src=rn

Fletcher, J. M. (2009). Dyslexia: The evolution of a scientific concept. *Journal of the International Neuropsychological Society, 15*(4), 501–508.

Fletcher, J. M., Foorman, B. R., Boudousquie, A., Barnes, M. A., Schatschneider, C., & Francis, D. J. (2002). Assessment of reading and learning disabilities a research-based intervention-oriented approach. *Journal of School Psychology, 40*(1), 27–63.

Foorman, B. R., Breier, J. I., & Fletcher, J. M. (2003). Interventions aimed at improving reading success: An evidence-based approach. *Developmental Neuropsychology, 24*(2-3), 613–639.

Freeman, J. (1975). *The politics of women's liberation.* New York, NY: David McKay.

Fuchs, D., Mock, D., Morgan, P. L., & Young, C. L. (2003). Responsiveness-to-intervention: Definitions, evidence, and implications for the learning disabilities construct. *Learning Disabilities Research and Practice, 18*(3), 157–171.

Fullan, M. (2000). The three stories of education reform. *Phi Delta Kappan, 81*(8), 581–584.

Gersten, R., Compton, D., Connor, C. M., Dimino, J., Santoro, L., Linan-Thompson, S., & Tilly, W. D. (2009). *Assisting students struggling with reading: Response to intervention and multi-tier intervention in the primary grades. A practice guide.* Washington, DC: U.S. Department of Education, National Center on Education and the Economy. Retrieved from http://ea.niusileadscape.org/docs/FINAL_PRODUCTS/LearningCarousel /AssistingStudentsStrugglingwithReading.pdf

Goldring, R., Taie, S., & Riddles, M. (2014). *Teacher attrition and mobility: Results from the 2012–13 teacher follow-up survey* (NCES 2014-077). Washington, DC: U.S. Department of Education, National Center for Education Statistics. Retrieved from http://nces.ed.gov/pubsearch

Guba, E. G. (1984). The effect of definitions of "policy" on the nature and outcomes of policy analysis. *Educational Leadership, 42*(2), 63–70.

Guterman, S. (2017). *On balance: What's the score? The Congressional Budget Office and its role in the policy process.* Retrieved from the Society for Benefit-Cost Analysis web site: https://benefitcostanalysis.org/balance-what%E2%80%99s-score-congressional-budget-office-and-its-role-policy-process

Hanford, E. (2017). *Hard to read: How American schools fail kids with dyslexia. Retrieved* from https://www.apmreports.org/story/2017/09/11/hard-to-read

Individuals with Disabilities Education Improvement Act (IDEA) of 2004, PL 108-446, 20 U.S.C. §§ 1400 *et seq.*

Joshi, R. M., Binks, E., Hougen, M., Dahlgren, M. E., Ocker-Dean, E., & Smith, D. L. (2009). Why elementary teachers might be inadequately prepared to teach reading. *Journal of Learning Disabilities, 42*(5), 392–402.

Joshi, R. M., Dahlgren, M., & Boulware-Gooden, R. (2002). Teaching reading in an inner city school through a multisensory teaching approach. *Annals of Dyslexia, 52*(1), 229–242.

Kavale, K. A., & Reese, J. H. (1992). The character of learning disabilities: An Iowa profile. *Learning Disability Quarterly, 15*, 74–94.

Knoff, M., Reeves, D., & Balow, C. (2018). *A multi-tiered service and support implementation blueprint for schools and districts: Revisiting the science to improve the practice.* Retrieved from https://www.illuminateed.com/blog/2018/05/essa-the-pathway-to-successful-implementation-of-multi-tiered-systems-of-support/

Lerner, J. (1989). Educational interventions in learning disabilities. *American Academy of Child and Adolescent Psychiatry, 28*(3), 326–331.

Losen, D. J., & Welner, K. G. (2002). Legal challenges to inappropriate and inadequate special education for minority children. In D. J. Losen & G. Orfield (Eds.), *Racial inequity in special education* (pp. 167–194). Boston, MA: Harvard Education Publishing Group.

Lovett, M. W. (1999). Defining and remediating the core deficits of developmental dyslexia. In R. M. Klein & P. McMullen (Eds.), *Converging methods for understanding reading and dyslexia* (p. 111). Cambridge, MA: The MIT Press.

Mann, B. (2014). *Equity and equality are not equal.* Retrieved from the Education Trust web site: https://edtrust.org/the-equity-line/equity-and-equality-are-not-equal/

Mele-McCarthy, J., & Powers, B. (2020). Great expectations: A current perspective on education, disability and society. In E. Grigorenko, Y. Shtyrov, & P. McCardle (Eds.), *All about language: Science, theory, and practice* (Неделя языка: наука, теория, практика). Baltimore, MD: Paul H. Brookes Publishing Co.

Menlove, R., Garnes, L., & Salzberg, C. (2004). Why special educators leave and where they go. *Teacher Education and Special Education, 27*(4), 373-383.

Moats, L. (2007). *Whole-language high jinks: How to tell when "scientifically-based reading instruction" isn't.* Washington, DC: Thomas B. Fordham Institute.

Moats, L. C. (2014). What teachers don't know and why they aren't learning it: Addressing the need for content and pedagogy in teacher education. *Australian Journal of Learning Difficulties, 19*(2) 75–91. http://dx.doi.org/10.1080/19404158.2014.941093

Montgomery, D. (2006). *Spelling, handwriting and dyslexia: Overcoming barriers to learning.* New York, NY: Routledge.

Nance, E., & Calabrese, R. L. (2009). Special education teacher retention and attrition: The impact of increased legal requirements. *International Journal of Educational Management, 23*(5), 431–440.

National Center for Education Statistics. (n.d.). *Fast facts: Title I.* Washington, DC: Author. Retrieved from https://nces.ed.gov/fastfacts/display.asp?id=158

Nation's Report Card. (n.d.a). *2017 NAEP mathematics and reading assessments.* Retrieved from https://www.nationsreportcard.gov/reading_math_2017_highlights/

Nation's Report Card. (n.d.b). *NAEP data explorer.* Retrieved from https://www.nationsreportcard.gov/ndecore/xplore/NDE

No Child Left Behind Act of 2001, PL 107-110, 115 Stat. 1425, 20 U.S.C. §§ 6301 *et seq.*

Norton, E. S., Beach, S. D., & Gabrieli, J. D. (2014). Neurobiology of dyslexia. *Current Opinion in Neurobiology, 30,* 73–78.

O'Shaughnessy, A. (1873). An ode. *Appleton's Journal.* New York, NY: D. Appleton & Co.

Peterson, R. L., & Pennington, B. F. (2015). Developmental dyslexia. *Annual Review of Clinical Psychology, 11,* 283–307.

Pugh, K. R., Mencl, W. E., Jenner, A. R., Katz, L., Frost, S. J., Lee, J. R., . . . Shaywitz, B. A. (2001). Neurobiological studies of reading and reading disability. *Journal of Communication Disorders, 34*(6), 479–492.

Rehabilitation Rights Act of 1973, PL 93-112, 87, Stat. 355. Retrieved from https://mn.gov /mnddc/parallels2/four/rehab_act/Rehab_Act.pdf

Rosen, P. (n.d.). *The Discrepancy Model: What you need to know.* Retrieved from https://www.understood.org/en/school-learning/evaluations/evaluation-basics/the-disc repancy-model-what-you-need-to-know

Salinger, T., Mueller, L., Song, M., Jin, Y., Zmach, C., Toplitz, M., . . . Bickford, A. (2010). *Study of teacher preparation in early reading instruction* (NCEE 2010-4036). Washington, DC: National Center for Education Evaluation and Regional Assistance.

Schaeffer, U. (2012). *Knowledge is power: Why education matters.* Retrieved from https://www.dw.com/en/knowledge-is-power-why-education-matters/a-15880356

Shaywitz, S. E., Shaywitz, B. A., Fletcher, J. M., & Escobar, M. D. (1990). Prevalence of reading disability in boys and girls. Results of the Connecticut Longitudinal Study. *Journal of the American Medical Association, 264*(8), 998–1002.

Siegel, L. S. (2006). Perspectives on dyslexia. *Paediatrics & Child Health, 11*(9), 581–587.

Snow, C. E., Burns, M. S., & Griffin, P. (Eds.). (1998). *Preventing reading difficulties in young children.* Washington, DC: National Academies Press.

Soler, J. (2016). The politics of the teaching of reading. *Prospects, 46*(3-4), 423–433. https://doi.org/10.1007/s11125-017-9415-8

Steve Gleason Enduring Voices Act of 2017 (PL 115-123). Retrieved from https://www.gpo .gov/fdsys/pkg/CRPT-115hrpt469/pdf/CRPT-115hrpt469-pt1.pdf

Taylor, V. (1989). Social movement continuity: The women's movement in abeyance. *American Sociological Review, 54,* 761–775.

Torgesen, J. K. (2005). Recent discoveries from research on remedial interventions for children with dyslexia. In M. J. Snowling & C. Hulme (Eds.), *Blackwell handbooks of developmental psychology. The science of reading: A handbook* (pp. 521–537). Malden, MA: Blackwell. http://dx.doi.org/10.1002/9780470757642.ch27

U.S. Commission on Civil Rights. (2018). *Public education funding inequity in an era of increasing concentration of poverty and resegregation.* Retrieved from https://www.usccr .gov/pubs/2018/2018-01-10-Education-Inequity.pdf

Vellutino, F. R., Fletcher, J. M., Snowling, M. J., & Scanlon, D. M. (2004). Specific reading disability (dyslexia): What have we learned in the past four decades? *Journal of Child Psychology and Psychiatry, 45*(1), 2–40.

Verger, A., Novelli, M., & Altinyelken, H. K. (2012). Global education policy and international development: An introductory framework. In A. Verger, M. Novelli, & H. K. Altinyelken (Eds.), *Global education policy and international development: New agendas, issues and policies* (pp. 3–32). London, United Kingdom: Bloomsbury Academic. Retrieved from http://dx.doi.org/10.5040/9781472544575.ch-001

Walsh, K., Glaser, D., & Wilcox, D. D. (2006). *What education schools aren't teaching about reading and what elementary teachers aren't learning.* Washington, DC: National Council on Teacher Quality.

Washburn, E. K., Joshi, R. M., & Binks-Cantrell, E. S. (2011). Teacher knowledge of basic language concepts and dyslexia. *Dyslexia, 17*(2), 165–183.

Ward-Lonergan, J. M., & Duthie, J. K. (2018). The state of dyslexia: Recent legislation and guidelines for serving school-age children and adolescents with dyslexia. *Language, Speech, and Hearing Services in Schools, 49*(4), 810–816.

Wren, S. (2002). *Ten myths of reading instruction.* Retrieved from the Southwest Educational Development Laboratory web site: http://www.sedl.org

Knowledge at the Intersection of Research and Practice

Nicole Patton Terry

The implementation of evidence-based practices to support achievement in school rests on many interrelated factors, including efficient mechanisms to allow for nimble adoption of new approaches and effective collaboration among leadership, teachers, and other key stakeholders across the system. Yet, a fundamental prerequisite for the long and arduous process toward implementation for improvement is knowledge. Researchers must produce knowledge of the skills, practices, instruments, and processes that allow for successful implementation. Meanwhile, teachers, leaders, and other stakeholders must be critical consumers of this knowledge, not only putting it into practice but also providing necessary supports for success. The authors in this section, "Research and Practice: Outreach, Scale-Up, and Policy," provide diverse perspectives on how they have taken on the research-to-practice gap to improve reading achievement. Together, these chapters make clear that knowledge matters and that it can be improved, impeded, and supported. Moreover, as the evidence-based movement in the field of education makes the transition to a focus on scaling up evidence-based practices, the critical role of knowledge must be considered in research, practice, and policy.

INTRODUCTION

Researchers and practitioners in almost every field lament the research-to-practice gap (Cook, Smith, & Tankersley, 2012; Fixsen, Naoom, Blase, Friedman, & Wallace, 2005; Foorman & Moats, 2004; Halle, Metz, & Martinez-Beck, 2013; Kelly & Perkins, 2012; Palinkas & Soydan, 2012; Rosenfield & Berninger, 2009). The issue is quite simple: In applied settings, practices that have not been validated empirically and may be ineffective at best and harmful at worst are commonly used despite the availability of alternative practices that have been proven effective by rigorous research. In other words, educators often do not do what they know works despite ample evidence to suggest that they will get the outcomes they want.

The evidence-based practice movement in the field of education is an ongoing example of the opportunities and challenges experienced by actors and activists on both sides of the bridge between research and practice. On one side, researchers continue to innovate and introduce new interventions, methodologies, and approaches to support student achievement and school success. On the other side, practitioners continue to execute and implement practices, programs, and policies to support student achievement and school success. The paradox is clear: both share a common goal that appears to be impossible to achieve together—support student achievement and school success, and more important, ensure it despite troubling, persistent, and complex societal issues that manifest in schools.

The authors in this section take on this issue, detailing how they have not only studied issues related to reading achievement but also attempted to bridge the research-to-practice gap. Their chapters make clear that the bridge to "knowing" and "doing" what works is not so easy to travel, in part because of where it starts: knowledge. In this commentary, I highlight four central themes that arise about knowledge from the chapters in this section: 1) it matters, 2) it can be improved, 3) it can be impeded, and 4) it can be supported. By focusing on the knowing, perhaps we can get closer to doing in a manner that achieves our shared goals.

KNOWLEDGE MATTERS

Arguments for the importance of knowledge to support reading achievement are not new and have been presented extensively (see, e.g., McCardle & Miller, 2009). Here, the authors continue to advocate for the importance of knowledge at various points along the bridge from research to practice. Both Joshi and Binks-Cantrell (see Chapter 16) and Lovett, Steinbach, and De Palma (see Chapter 17) stress the importance of knowledge about the science of teaching reading, both for preservice and in-service teachers and for teacher educators in colleges and universities, noting that teachers at all levels may lack the prerequisite knowledge to ensure reading success in schools. Petscher and colleagues (see Chapter 18) argue that this prerequisite extends beyond instructional methods and includes knowledge of assessments to guide and inform instruction. Contributions by the other authors make clear that this knowledge extends beyond classroom teachers; stakeholder knowledge across the system is required to ensure reading success. Mele-McCarthy (see Chapter 19) stresses the importance of informed policy and policy makers in the United States, whereas both Bulat and colleagues (see Chapter 15) and Joshi and Binks-Cantrell (Chapter 16) note its importance to supporting global literacy.

KNOWLEDGE CAN BE IMPROVED

Just as the literature is replete with arguments in support of increasing knowledge about the science of reading, so too is the evidence that this knowledge can be improved and that improving it results in positive changes in teacher instruction and student achievement (see, e.g., Foorman, Francis, Fletcher, Schatschneider, & Mehta, 1998; Snow, Griffin, & Burns, 2005). Both Bulat and colleagues (Chapter 15) and Lovett and colleagues (Chapter 17) observed similar findings in their work. Lovett and colleagues describe positive student outcomes for struggling readers

whose teachers provided PHAST and Empower Reading intervention programs; teachers were provided with extensive training on the program
before, during, and after implementation with their students. Bulat and
colleagues also report improved reading outcomes among students whose
teachers increased their awareness and use of screeners and evidence-
based lesson plans to support students with disabilities in their classrooms.
Teachers also reported improved attitudes and self-efficacy with inclusive
education; that is, improving their knowledge not only changed their instructional practices, but it also changed their beliefs about whether they
were capable of supporting students with significant learning needs effectively. It is worth noting that in both chapters, the authors report improved
outcomes for teachers and students in very challenging, under-resourced
contexts in the United States, Canada, India, and Ethiopia.

BARRIERS TO KNOWLEDGE

Now, more than 20 years into the evidence-based practice movement in
the field of education, it is sobering that reading achievement gaps have
remained relatively stable (National Center for Education Statistics, 2018).
Many children, in particular those from race-, ethnic-, and language-
minority groups and those growing up in poverty, continue to perform
well below grade-level expectations. Researchers, educators, policy makers, and other stakeholders are increasingly concerned with understanding why they can know so much about how to help these students and
yet seem unable to do so at scale. For many, the answers rest with their
relationships with the knowledge brokers.

Take, for example, the Regional Educational Laboratory (REL) Program
administered by the Institute of Education Sciences in the United States.
Established in 1965 and reauthorized in 2002, these labs were authorized
initially to conduct basic research and to develop and disseminate educational innovations. However, by 1985, the goals of the labs became much
more focused on improving schools and classrooms, especially for at-risk
students and low-performing schools. Aligned with the evidence-based
practice movement in education (or perhaps in response to it), by 2006,
the RELs transformed into research alliances comprised of researcher–
practitioner partnerships. Here, the theory of change is that barriers to
knowledge acquisition and use will be overcome by putting researchers
and practitioners at the same table to work collaboratively on designing
and implementing solutions to educational underachievement.

Like the RELs, the authors in these chapters grapple with the relationships between knowledge creators and knowledge users, each highlighting how knowledge brokers can be barriers to or promoters of reading
achievement. For example, Joshi and Binks-Cantrell (Chapter 16) focus
on two groups of knowledge brokers—postsecondary faculty and textbook
authors—calling for both groups to improve their own knowledge and their
dissemination of that knowledge to preservice and in-service teachers.

Meanwhile, Lovett and colleagues (see Chapter 17) focus on a different set of knowledge brokers: school boards and administrators. Recognizing that a supportive infrastructure for quality implementation is necessary to ensure positive outcomes, the researchers devote significant time to establishing a healthy partnership, communication, and commitment with the school board and administrative teams, all well before teachers begin professional development or instruction with students. Both Mele-McCarthy (see Chapter 19) and Bulat and colleagues (see Chapter 15) focus on knowledge brokers at an even higher level: departments and ministries of education. While championing efforts to improve literacy worldwide, Bulat and colleagues note that many low- and middle-income countries lack infrastructure and resources to support a literate society, let alone understand, identify, and treat learning difficulties such as dyslexia. Meanwhile, Mele-McCarthy highlights the complex historical relation between policy makers and stakeholders in the development and implementation of special education legislation in the United States, noting how funding, legislative, and regulatory restrictions can not only limit effective practice for children with reading difficulty but also create conditions that impede the deployment of a skilled and motivated teaching work force.

SUPPORT FOR KNOWLEDGE

Despite the enormous challenges encountered by each team, the authors also identify solutions to knowledge acquisition and use them to improve reading achievement at scale. Each approach reveals a balance between improvement and innovation; that is, although it appears that educators know so much about promoting reading achievement that they should just do better, these teams make clear that there is room for innovation to understand the conditions that will allow what educators know to work at scale. For example, Bulat and colleagues (Chapter 15) highlight promising advances in offline mobile technology to increase access to effective screening tools. Coupled with instructional materials and professional development, this technology supports improvements in teacher practice and student outcomes. Both Bulat and colleagues and Petscher and colleagues (Chapter 18) describe methodological advances that have allowed for better screeners to identify children with learning needs (see also information on a new preschool screener in Chapter 5 by Gaab, Turesky, & Sanfilippo); both also note that partnerships with researchers can help practitioners account for their local context to make screeners more useful.

These researchers also emphasize the importance of deliberate, phased, and collaborative approaches to scale-up that are informed by the local context. For example, recognizing that many low- and middle-income countries lack basic tools, training, staff, and other resources to promote effective literacy instruction, Bulat and colleagues (Chapter 15) developed a phased, multiyear approach to support the gradual adoption of effective practices, programs, and policies. Lovett and colleagues

(Chapter 17) describe a process akin to what Chorpita and Daleiden (2014) call collaborative design. Here, researchers and practitioners work together to adapt an evidence-based practice as it is being adopted in real-world conditions.

In both cases, the process was slow, and success was predicated by starting small—an approach that appears to be incongruent with going to scale because scale denotes big and fast. Yet, evidence from the field of implementation science makes clear that successful systems-level shifts require patience and time (Fixsen et al., 2005). As the evidence-based movement makes the transition from a focus on efficacy studies to effectiveness and dissemination studies, innovations in research, practice, and policy will be required to understand conditions that promote or prevent the effective use of practices in real-world settings at large scale and to create solutions to their successful adoption. The chapters in this section make one thing clear: Knowledge and all stakeholders' relationship to it will be central to this next step.

REFERENCES

Chorpita, B. F., & Daleiden, B. F. (2014). Structuring the collaboration of science and service in pursuit of a shared vision. *Journal of Clinical and Child & Adolescent Psychology, 43*(2), 323–338.

Cook, B. G., Smith, G. J., & Tankersley, M. (2012). Evidence-based practices in education. In K. R. Harris, S. Graham, & T. Urdan (Eds.), *APA educational psychology handbook* (Vol. 1, pp. 495–528). Washington, DC: American Psychological Association.

Fixsen, D. L., Naoom, S. F., Blase, K. A., Friedman, R. M. & Wallace, F. (2005). *Implementation research: A synthesis of the literature* (FMHI Publication #231). Tampa: University of South Florida, Louis de la Parte Florida Mental Health Institute, The National Implementation Research Network.

Foorman, B. R., Francis, D. J., Fletcher, J. M., Schatschneider, C., & Mehta, P. (1998). The role of instruction in learning to read: Preventing reading failure in at-risk children. *Journal of Educational Psychology, 90*, 37–55.

Foorman, B. R., & Moats, L. C. (2004). Conditions for sustaining research-based practices in early reading instruction. *Remedial and Special Education, 25*, 51–60.

Halle, T., Metz, A., & Martinez-Beck, I. (2013). *Applying implementation science in early childhood programs and systems*. Baltimore, MD: Paul H. Brookes Publishing Co.

Kelly, B., & Perkins, D. F. (2012). *Handbook of implementation science for psychology in education*. New York, NY: Cambridge University Press.

McCardle, P., & Miller, B. (2009). Why we need evidence-based practice in reading and where to find that evidence. In S. Rosenfield & V. Berninger (Eds.), *Implementing evidence-based academic interventions in school settings* (pp. 19–48). New York, NY: Oxford University Press.

National Center for Education Statistics. (2018). *NAEP Reading Report Card*. Washington, DC: U.S. Department of Education, Institute of Education Sciences. Retrieved from https://www.nationsreportcard.gov/reading_2017?grade=4

Palinkas, L. A., & Soydan, H. (2012). *Translation and implementation of evidence-based practice*. New York NY: Oxford University Press.

Rosenfield, S., & Berninger, V. (2009). *Implementing evidence-based academic interventions in school settings*. New York NY: Oxford University Press.

Snow, C. E., Griffin, P., & Burns M. S. (2005). *Knowledge to support the teaching of reading*. San Francisco, CA: John Wiley & Sons.

Finale

CHAPTER 20

Challenges and Future Directions
Donald L. Compton

SUMMARY

The 17th Extraordinary Brain Symposium held at Cathedral Peak Hotel in South Africa was titled "Dyslexia 101: Revisiting Etiology, Diagnosis, Treatment and Policy." The purpose of the meeting was to revisit the current foundational knowledge base about dyslexia, including its etiology, diagnosis, treatment, and public policy status. Although developing knowledge in areas such as genetics, brain imaging, cognitive psychology, and educational intervention has expanded the understanding of dyslexia considerably, disagreements continue regarding its definition, etiology, diagnosis, and treatment. In this summary chapter, I synthesize, across the presentations and discussion, important issues that highlight five existing challenges: 1) Dyslexia symptomatology is relatively transparent, whereas etiology is opaque; 2) identification is fairly straightforward once children have had the opportunity to learn to read, less so before reading instruction commences; 3) cognitive and computational models hold great promise for helping educators better understand and instruct children with dyslexia but have a way to go before they can bear considerable fruit; 4) treatments are evolving to include more efficacious components, but researchers are still struggling to identify what works, for whom, and under what conditions; and 5) the research community is woefully ill-equipped to disseminate knowledge to policy makers and those serving children with dyslexia, both in the United States and globally.

INTRODUCTION

Much of Africa's history has been passed on through the generations orally. A consequence of this is that traditional wisdom has been crystallized in the form of proverbs. The Zulu, the largest ethnic group in South Africa, have a rich tradition of proverbs. One such proverb goes something like this: *The bones must be thrown in three different places before the message can be accepted,* meaning you should consider a question multiple times in multiple ways before reaching a decision. This proverb provides some insight into our planning for the 17th Extraordinary Brain Symposium, *Dyslexia 101: Revisiting Etiology, Diagnosis, Treatment, and Policy.* The purpose of the meeting was to revisit our current foundational knowledge base about dyslexia. Disagreements continue regarding dyslexia's definition, etiology, diagnosis, and treatment despite developing knowledge in areas such as genetics, brain imaging, cognitive psychology, and educational intervention. Thus, it appeared to be a good time to throw the bones again, if you will, and take stock in recent advances in our understanding of dyslexia from some of the leading researchers and practitioners in the world. As stated in the introduction to this volume, we were particularly keen to explore basic learning mechanisms underlying dyslexia (using various methodologies) and how these interact with important sociodemographic variables such as language (or dialect) differences, poverty, or cultural differences. The absence of this information represents a critical omission in our work to develop a comprehensive understanding of dyslexia.

So, what did we glean from the "bones" this time around? To be sure, the meeting highlighted how the field of dyslexia continues to advance in meaningful and exciting ways, but a series of challenges still exist, including: 1) Dyslexia symptomatology is relatively transparent, whereas etiology is opaque; 2) identification is fairly straightforward once children have had the opportunity to learn to read, less so before reading instruction commences; 3) cognitive and computational models hold great promise for helping educators better understand and instruct children with dyslexia, but they have a way to go before they can bear considerable fruit; 4) treatments are evolving to include more efficacious components, but researchers are still struggling to identify what works, for whom, and under what conditions; and 5) the research community is ill-equipped to disseminate knowledge to policy makers and those serving children with dyslexia both in the United States and globally. In the sections that follow, I attempt to highlight the major findings from the symposium and how these findings lead to the five challenges I have identified for the field.

SYMPTOMATOLOGY VERSUS ETIOLOGY

A variety of definitions of dyslexia have been put forward by various organizations, but all have certain elements in common. The majority recognize dyslexia as neurobiological in origin, with difficulties in the development of accurate and/or fluent word recognition and spelling being the dominant characteristic. Furthermore, there is general agreement that difficulties typically result from a deficit in the phonological component of language that is often unexpected in relation to other cognitive abilities and the provision of effective classroom instruction. Clearly the primary symptomatology is the failure to develop adequate word recognition, decoding, and spelling skills despite sufficient ability and opportunity to learn. This set of symptoms has not changed significantly since the term *dyslexia* was first coined by Rudolf Berlin in 1887 at the University of Oxford. Although arguments persist regarding what *adequate* and *sufficient* mean in this content, the primary symptoms revolve around an inability to develop sensitivity to, knowledge of, and the ability to use the alphabetic underpinning of written language. These symptoms become observable as children experience early reading instruction, and the severity of symptoms is typically gauged using normative measures of word reading, decoding, and spelling.

Understanding of etiology, on the other hand, is still evolving. For instance, the International Dyslexia Association (IDA) definition focuses on a single deficit in the phonological component of language representing the dominant phonological-deficit hypothesis (see Stanovich, 1988). However, Pennington (2006) and others have advanced a multiple genetic and environmental risk factor model that operates probabilistically by allowing multiple risk factors to increase the liability to a disorder and multiple protective factors that decrease the liability. These etiological factors produce the behavioral symptoms of dyslexia by influencing the development of relevant neural systems and cognitive processes. There is no single etiological or cognitive factor that is sufficient to cause a disorder such as dyslexia. Instead, multiple cognitive deficits (each due to multiple etiological factors) need to be present to produce a disorder at the behavioral level. Such a model of developmental dyslexia requires understanding the phenomenon across multiple levels (i.e., convergence across multiple levels of analysis) that include

> Defining symptoms or behaviors; its neuropsychology (underlying cognitive, emotional, or other psychological processes that are not directly observable and not part of the disorder's definition); its pathophysiology (for cognitive disorders, changes in brain structure and function); its etiology, or distal causes, including genetic and environmental risk and protective factors; and its social context. (Petersen & Pennington, 2015, p. 284)

Across multiple chapters in this volume, the researchers grapple with the multiple-deficit hypothesis and how this affects both symptomatology and etiology. For instance, de Jong and Castles are at opposite ends concerning the role of cognitive factors in clarifying the diagnosis of dyslexia. De Jong (see Chapter 4) argues that there is not sufficient evidence to grant the diagnosis of dyslexia exclusively to individuals with specific underlying cognitive deficits; instead, diagnosis is warranted in cases of severe reading and/or spelling problems that are not caused by a lack of opportunity to learn to read and spell. Castles and Kohnen (see Chapter 11), on the other hand, argue that the application of cognitive models of reading is key to making sense of the heterogeneity in the population of children with dyslexia. They conclude that cognitive models can assist teachers and clinicians to have clearer expectations about the types of problems they might expect to see in a poor reader, thus guiding assessment protocols and ultimately improving treatment recommendations. The two groups unmistakably disagree on whether there is a role for etiology, above and beyond symptomatology, in the diagnosis of dyslexia. These debates seem critical as researchers move forward with updated definitions of dyslexia that move away from the IQ–achievement discrepancy framework.

The multiple-deficit hypothesis allows for varied pathways to common symptoms through interactions between distal and proximal factors. Per de Jong, proximal causes refer to components of the reading system (e.g., phonemic awareness skill), whereas distal causes are related to reading development but do not concern a component of the reading system (e.g., growing up in poverty). This etiological framework allows expanded opportunities to explore how interactions between social context, cognitive skill, and orthographic systems operate probabilistically to increase the liability to a disorder such as dyslexia. Several authors address these complexities in their chapters. For instance, Washington and Lee-James (Chapter 9) argue that diagnostic accuracy of dyslexia is significantly affected by, and confounded with, many sociodemographic variables that include race, socioeconomic status, and linguistic differences. Therefore, children who are impoverished, are minorities, and who speak dialects or languages that differ from mainstream American English are less likely to be diagnosed with dyslexia and receive the appropriate interventions needed to become proficient in reading and writing.

Saiegh-Haddad (see Chapter 8) explores the sociolinguistic context of diglossia, in which two language varieties are used within the same speech community. In Arabic, diglossia results in increasing the linguistic distance between the written and spoken language, increasing the orthographic depth of the writing system and adding another factor of complexity that potentially interferes with linguistic processing and reading in dialect-speaking Arab children. Our understanding of the interplay between social context, linguistic diversity, cognitive skill, and orthographic systems is still at its infancy, but clearly these factors interact in important ways to increase or decrease the probability that a child will develop dyslexia.

Nation and Mak (see Chapter 7) apply the multiple-deficit hypothesis to mechanisms underlying orthographic learning. Orthographic learning refers to the processes and knowledge that enable a person to make the transition from a novice to an expert reader of words. Furthermore, failures in orthographic learning have been linked to the development of dyslexia in children. In Chapter 7, Nation and Mak speculate that phonological deficits are unlikely to be the sole factor that leads to poor orthographic learning in dyslexia and examine the literature for other possible deficit loci. In particular, deficits in paired-associative and statistical learning were considered as independent contributors to orthographic learning problems. Although there is some evidence to support the independent roles of paired-associative and statistical learning, the authors caution that important theoretical and methodological issues still need to be addressed before strong conclusions can be made. The search for additional deficit areas is of critical importance in elaborating etiology and perhaps informing diagnosis and treatment.

Finally, effectively connecting etiology to symptomatology will require specification of the link between genes, brain function, and behavior (i.e., reading skill). This level-of-analysis work is in its early stages; however, it holds great promise for improving understanding of the multiple pathways associated with dyslexia. Landi and colleagues have begun to combine the use of neuroimaging and molecular genetics methods (i.e., neuroimaging genetics approaches) to identify which neural anomalies are associated with specific genes and to identify new potential risk loci from these neural profiles. Landi (see Chapter 3) calls for studies that extend imagining genetics approaches in the study of dyslexia by examining educational and other environmental factors. This work holds tremendous promise for improving understanding of complex probabilistic deficit models of dyslexia and associated treatments.

These chapters clearly illustrate the point that dyslexia symptomatology is relatively transparent whereas etiology is still quite opaque. We as researchers are still struggling to identify the social, linguistic, and cognitive factors that interact with the orthographic system to produce dyslexia and to further link these factors to the genetics and neurobiology of behavior that control the reading system. Multidisciplinary teams of scientists continue to tackle these issues, and I expect important advancements in understanding of etiology and mechanism in the near future.

CHALLENGES OF EARLY IDENTIFICATION

Advocates of multi-tiered systems of supports (MTSS) suggest the following advantages over traditional models of dyslexia identification: 1) earlier identification of dyslexia to avoid a wait-to-fail model, 2) a strong focus on providing effective instruction and improving student outcomes, and 3) a decision-making process supported by continuous progress monitoring of skills closely aligned with desired instructional outcomes. The success of MTSS, in terms of both prevention and identification, hinges on the accurate determination of a risk pool of children to enter the Tier 2 intervention. Early identification of a risk pool of kindergarten and first-grade students facilitates their participation in second-tier intervention before the onset of significant reading problems while increasing the possibility that they will establish and maintain normal levels of growth in critical early reading skills. Pushing early identification down to preschool children would be a major advance that would allow structured early intervention prior to the initiation of formal reading instruction. However, for MTSS to work effectively, procedures for determining reading risk must yield a high percentage of true positives while identifying a manageable risk pool by limiting false positives.

Gaab, Turesky, and Sanfilippo (see Chapter 5) present their ongoing work to develop a preschool screening system to identify and treat children at high risk for developing dyslexia. The screening system consists of 1) screening children prior to formal reading instruction and 2) providing access to an evidence-based response to screening protocol (EBRS) that is customized to the specific preliteracy deficits identified in the screening step. A series of longitudinal magnetic resonance imaging (MRI) measurements in children from infancy to school age are currently underway to evaluate just how early effective screening can be accomplished. This work is extremely challenging, with many technical challenges to be overcome, however the potential payoff is enormous.

Along these lines, Petscher, Stanley, Gearin, and Fien (see Chapter 18) provide a comprehensive review of the technical challenges associated with early screening for dyslexia. They provide a hierarchical set of considerations that can help guide screener selection: 1) population of interest (e.g., students with dyslexia, students with language disorders); 2) scope of assessment (e.g., what type of risk is being screened, what kind of screener is being developed or used, what is its compatibility with needs); and 3) statistical considerations of reliability, validity, and classification accuracy, to finally inform decision making. The hope is that as understanding of etiology increases our ability to effectively select children at risk for developing dyslexia will improve.

COGNITIVE AND COMPUTATIONAL MODELS

Decades of research on the mechanisms of reading have given rise to a number of sophisticated computational models (e.g., dual-route and connectionist models). These models are in general agreement that the reading system comprises two major processing pathways: 1) a phonological pathway by which the phonological representation of a printed word is computed using knowledge of the correspondences between sublexical orthographic and phonological units, and 2) a lexical/semantic pathway that allows for the "direct" access to a printed word's meaning without reference to phonology. Although there is widespread agreement about the general structure of the word reading system, the nature of the representations and processes that implement these pathways remains a matter of substantial debate. Cognitive and computational models have the potential to test developmental mechanisms of reading, inform basic etiology and symptomatology of dyslexia, and explain the complex relationships between experiential (exogenous) and child-specific (endogenous) factors that contribute to individual differences in reading development.

Rueckl, Zevin, and Wolf (see Chapter 6) describe one such model (the "triangle model") and provide a preliminary report of computational simulations related to developmental dyslexia. In general, two subtypes of dyslexia are identified: *phonological dyslexia,* characterized by difficulties in the system responsible for processing the spoken properties of words, and *surface dyslexia,* in which differences in the mechanisms that translate written words into their spoken forms are implicated. In theory, these subtypes have different neurological topologies of deficits and may require a different focus of word reading and decoding intervention. Castles and Kohnen (see Chapter 11) also argue that, to capture the heterogeneity of dyslexia, it is important that assessment and identification be carried out in the context of detailed cognitive models of reading (in this case, the dual-route model).

This allows for precise specification of the nature of the reading difficulty at the proximal level, which can then support more targeted treatment of the dyslexia as well as more directed investigations of its distal causes.

The long-term goals of these modeling approaches are to enrich understanding of the processes that influence individual differences in word reading development in typically developing children and children with dyslexia and to significantly inform issues of practice (e.g., curriculum, instruction, diagnosis, intervention). As modeling efforts continue to progress, researchers can expect greater specificity with regard to individual response to specific interventions and reading experiences.

THE EVOLUTION OF TREATMENT

Since the early 1990's intense research efforts have been aimed at developing and disseminating validated intervention programs designed to improve the long-term reading development of children with dyslexia. The motivation behind this effort arises from an understanding of the negative cognitive and social consequences associated with poor reading skills and the increased demands on literacy skill in our ever-evolving information-driven society. Although these efforts have been generally lauded as successful, there is awareness among researchers that word-reading interventions still lack the power needed to close the gap between typically developing readers and children with dyslexia. As an example, the most powerful researcher-delivered code-based interventions aimed at ameliorating early word-reading problems leave as much as 10%–15% of the population of children emerging from treatment with inadequate word-reading skills (see Torgesen, 2000). In addition, many individuals identified as poor readers in high school or as adults still have significant word-reading difficulties. These results have motivated researchers to identify new components or approaches to improve the efficacy of our validated intervention approaches.

Three chapters (Chapters 13, 12, and 10) outline new intervention approaches to improve the reading outcomes of children at risk of developing or being diagnosed with dyslexia. Savage and colleagues (see Chapter 13) examine the effects of Direct Mapping and Set-for-Variability on the development of at-risk children's word reading. Direct Mapping is an approach in which children immediately read *on that day* text richly embodying the specific grapheme–phoneme correspondence (GPC) units taught in phonics programs. Set-for-Variability instruction encourages children to be flexible in mapping the decoded form of the word to actual pronunciation. The combination of these two intervention components added to a generally effective phonics program produced significantly better word-reading outcomes in young readers. In a second study, the group examined the added benefits of applying the Simplicity Principle to teaching grapheme–phoneme correspondence relations. The Simplicity

Principle optimizes the type and number of GPC units taught to encourage generalization while reading. The idea is to link corpus statistics of GPC occurrences in children's books to the teaching of GPC during phonics instruction. Again, this approach led to significantly better outcomes in word reading for at-risk children. Overall results suggested that adding important components (e.g., Set-for-Variability), optimizing instruction around useable GPCs (e.g., Simplicity Principle), and linking GPC instruction to meaningful practice in book reading (e.g., Direct Mapping) have an added positive impact on validated interventions for early readers.

Williams, Capin, Stevens, and Vaughn (see Chapter 12), working with older students with dyslexia in Grades 4–8, examined the efficacy of providing a multiyear, multicomponent intervention aimed at improving reading comprehension by targeting word reading, background knowledge, vocabulary knowledge, and the integration of ideas across texts. A key component of the intervention is the reading of both stretch texts (i.e., texts on grade level) and fluency texts (i.e., texts on students' reading level). Stretch texts instruction used expository social studies text, and students stopped at predetermined points and explained what was happening in the text. Student were asked text-based questions that required them to use information from different parts of the text. Fluency texts were read repeatedly to build fluency and automaticity. Results indicated that most of the students showed gains in standard scores, although differential gains between treatment and comparison conditions did not reach significance. Overall, the results suggested that it is extremely difficult to improve scores on reading comprehension measures for older students with dyslexia. Furthermore, Williams and colleagues argue that students with dyslexia need continued access to intensive interventions over multiple years just to maintain current reading levels.

Finally, Connor, Kim, and Yang (see Chapter 10) present several studies using the Assessment-to-Instruction (A2i) algorithm, a teacher professional support technology that provides recommendations for individualized (or differentiated) literacy instruction using dynamic forecasting intervention (DFI) algorithms. The A2i DFI algorithms compute the recommended amounts of instruction for each student based on language and literacy assessment scores. Results across multiple studies demonstrate the power of A2i to provide teachers with meaningful information that allows them to differentiate instruction for children in the early grades. It is important to note that this system is intended to improve the overall efficacy of validated instructional programs by providing teachers with estimates of the proper mix of code-to-meaning instruction for children. As we can see in all three intervention chapters, there is a significant push by researchers to increase the overall effectiveness of and validate interventions for children with dyslexia. The question that is beginning to emerge is whether considering etiology can improve outcomes through individualized interventions.

DISSEMINATION OF KNOWLEDGE

There is no shortage of literature on the topic of translating educational research into the classroom. The issue, however, is not as simple as producing research results with the belief that they will be used in practice. Actively promoting the adoption of research-validated instructional procedures is typically an uncomfortable position for researchers; however, it is something that is becoming more important in an era of evidence-based decision making. Five chapters (Chapters 2, 15, 17, 16, and 19) address the issue of creation and dissemination of knowledge to various stakeholders, including parents, teachers, and policy makers. From a knowledge generation standpoint, Miller and Alvarez (see Chapter 2) outline the NIH investment supporting research and training initiatives designed to enhance understanding of the development of reading and writing skills throughout the life course. In particular, the *Eunice Kennedy Shriver* National Institute of Child Health and Human Development (NICHD) has invested in dyslexia and reading-related research for more than 50 years and initiated a center-based program more than 25 years ago. The NICHD investment emphasizes the development of prevention, remediation, and intervention approaches to improve literacy by utilizing a confluence of methodological approaches to understand the behavioral, genetic, and neurobiological foundations of literacy development and its manifestation over time. The portfolio has recently included a substantial emphasis on understudied populations and research topics. Much of the research presented at the conference was supported by NICHD funding. New knowledge regarding the identification and treatment of dyslexia is clearly being generated through federal grant funding. Other private agencies are also interested in supporting innovative work designed to improve the academic outcomes and lives of individuals with dyslexia.

Several authors outline systematic approaches to bringing research knowledge to important stakeholders. Bulat, Hayes, Dombrowski, Dubeck, and Strigel (see Chapter 15) present work at RTI International, designed to provide low-cost, easily administered vision, hearing, and reading screening to allow low-resource countries the ability to intervene early with children who are at risk for poor literacy outcomes. This work is logistically quite challenging but has tremendous potential to improve the educational outcomes for children living in extreme poverty.

Lovett, Steinbach, and De Palma (see Chapter 17) present their 35-year journey spent developing and evaluating reading interventions for children and youth with severe reading disabilities, testing the efficacy of these programs in community schools, and finally scaling up to reach struggling readers and their teachers across Canada and in some remote and international settings. Scale-up of their research-based intervention programs (Empower Reading) has now reached more than 2,500 teachers and more than 55,000 children and teens across Canada. What is even more remarkable is their outreach work to bring the intervention to partnerships in Pune, India (Anjali Morris Foundation), and the Cree School Board serving Indigenous peoples in northern Quebec. These efforts have shown great initial results and demonstrate the potential power of implementing carefully designed programs in remote areas and for children from disadvantaged backgrounds. However, as promising as these results are, one must not underestimate the painstaking work necessary to make these partnerships successful.

Joshi and Binks-Cantrell (see Chapter 16) take on teacher training programs by exploring reasons for teachers' lack of knowledge regarding evidence-based instruction, based on the hypothesis that teachers are not provided with such information at their universities or in their textbooks. Results of teacher surveys and textbook analysis suggest that evidence-based information regarding effective reading instruction is not filtering into many university teacher education classrooms or textbooks. This clearly represents a critical bottleneck in getting research-validated instructional procedures into schools.

Finally, Mele-McCarthy (see Chapter 19) outlines what she calls the "dyslexia trifecta," in which research, policy, and practice combine to support educating all children with dyslexia effectively and improving outcomes in academic achievement. She acknowledges that to accomplish this, stakeholders will need to make it a priority. This has already begun to happen as parents and advocates push dyslexia legislation in many states. However, a much more concentrated and organized effort is needed to reach Mele-McCarthy's goal of a dyslexia trifecta. This is certainly a goal of The Dyslexia Foundation, and perhaps this meeting will have served as the impetus to finally bring all three groups (research, policy, and practice) to the table.

CONCLUSION

The time many of us spent together in South Africa for the 17th Extraordinary Brain Symposium was truly magical. The level of dialogue between presenters and delegates was extraordinary, both in terms of depth and breadth. There is much work left to do; yet, as we boarded the buses to head back to Durbin for flights home, I felt there was a commitment by the participants to something akin to the dyslexia trifecta. In this volume, those symposium presenters and their colleagues convey for you the content and conclusions discussed at this important meeting. In the coming years, the five key challenges to the field will need to be addressed systematically by groups representing research, policy, and practice. In my opinion, the message from the bones looked pretty encouraging. I truly hope in the near future we can gather to toss the bones again and take stock of what we have accomplished.

REFERENCES

Berlin, R. (1887). *Eine besondere Art yon Wortblindheit (Dyslexie)*. Monograph. Wiesbaden, Germany: Verlag von J. F. Bergmann.

Pennington, B. F. (2006). From single to multiple deficit models of developmental disorders. *Cognition, 101,* 385–413.

Peterson, R. L., & Pennington, B. F. (2015). Developmental dyslexia. *Annual Review of Clinical Psychology, 11,* 283–307.

Stanovich, K. E. (1988). Explaining the differences between the dyslexic and the garden-variety poor reader: The phonological core variable difference model. *Journal of Learning Disabilities, 21,* 590–604.

Torgesen, J. K. (2000). Individual differences in response to early interventions in reading: The lingering problem of treatment resisters. *Learning Disabilities Research & Practice, 15*(1), 55–64.

Index

References to tables and figures are indicated with a *t* and *f*, respectively.